DESIRE AND ITS DISCONTENTS

Praise for the Book

'Too often, queer activists and scholars seeking emancipation through legal rights forget how much context matters, and how much law is committed to maintaining the very hierarchies that state power relies upon. Readers of this volume are unlikely to ever forget again. Contributors expose the exclusionary representations of queer legal subjects produced by recently celebrated judgements in the context of India, tracking myriad linkages to the right-wing, neoliberal, Hindutva agenda of the present government. Readers will emerge better equipped to continue the struggle for liberation wherever they are located.'

—*Dianne Otto, Professorial Fellow, Melbourne Law School, The University of Melbourne*

'This uniquely caring anthology edited by Dipika Jain and Oishik Sircar at long last inaugurates an Indian critical queer theory, which is not a replica of the Euromerican approaches. Even as we welcome the decriminalization of gayness, we are asked to rethink beyond legal emancipation towards social emancipation—where there are very few subjects desiring neoliberalism. The struggles for a quest for queer politics constitute a response against the "violence and exclusions" of the triple enslavement constantly generated by forms, and forces of "Hindutva, neoliberalism and brahminism". The "conditions of postmodernity" that further affect the "spectacles of emancipation" invite contemplation: how is an "embracing of the disruptive potential" of trans and gender non-binary identities, to create a "sustainable, radical politics, while simultaneously asserting the right to access state benefits?". This book summons new futures beginning with a trans-constitutional renaissance.'

—*Upendra Baxi, Emeritus Professor of Law, Universities of Warwick and Delhi*

'Dipika Jain and Oishik Sircar's much anticipated second volume of essays extends their path-breaking original insights into the intimate entanglements of queer politics and neoliberalism. This volume too is poised to become nothing short of a classic, in bringing together some of the best-known voices on the politics of gender and sexuality. Turning their critical gaze to India, after the abrogation of Section 377, the essays offer refreshingly counter-intuitive analyses of such queer success and freedoms. In the aftermath of the decriminalization of homosexuality, the underlying nexus between Hindu nationalism, neoliberalism, casteism and queer rights has come fully to the fore. The volume provokes new ways to think of homonationalism and homocapitalism from this vantage point. Yet it is much more. From the relationship of queer to gender, caste, feminism and majoritarianism, to the transnational travel of Indian queerness to queering as a method, these remarkable interventions will singularly and together redirect our analytical and methodological impulses as well as reaffirm our political commitments to feminist queer worldmaking.'

—*Srila Roy, Professor, Department of Sociology, University of the Witwatersrand*

Desire and Its Discontents

Queer Politics in Contemporary India

Editors
Dipika Jain
Oishik Sircar

zubaan

ZUBAAN
128 B Shahpur Jat, 1st Floor
New Delhi 110 04974 8
Email: contact@zubaanbooks.com
Website: www.zubaanbooks.com

First published by Zubaan Publishers Pvt. Ltd 2024

Given this volume's legal focus, it uses a citation system commonly used in legal studies - the Bluebook style.

10 9 8 7 6 5 4 3 2 1

ISBN: 978 81 94253 38 9 (paperback)
ISBN: 978 81 94253 33 4 (ebook)

Zubaan is an independent, feminist publishing house based in New Delhi with a strong academic and general list. It was set up as an imprint of India's first feminist publishing house, Kali for Women, and carries forward Kali's tradition of publishing world-quality books to high editorial and production standards. *Zubaan* means tongue, voice, language, speech in Hindustani. Zubaan publishes in the areas of the humanities and social sciences, as well as in fiction, general non-fiction and books for children and young adults under its Young Zubaan imprint.

Typeset in 11/13.75 Garamond.

Printed and bound at Repro Books Limited.

Contents

Introduction:
Counterintuitions: The Fraught After-Lives of Queer Freedom vii
Dipika Jain and *Oishik Sircar*

Chapter 1 1
Multi-tasking Queer: Reflections on the Possibilities of Homosexual Dissidence in Law
Ratna Kapur

Chapter 2 30
Disrupting the Dinner Table: Re-thinking the 'Queer Movement' in Contemporary India
Ashley Tellis

Chapter 3 49
Continental Drift: Queer, Feminism, Postcolonial
Brenda Cossman

Chapter 4 73
Section 377 and the Myth of Heterosexuality
Zaid Al Baset

Chapter 5 98
Claiming Citizenship, Contesting Civility: The Institutional LGBT Movement and the Regulation of Gender/Sexual Dissidence in West Bengal, India
Aniruddha Dutta

Chapter 6 142
Complicating Privacy Further in the *Naz* Aftermath: Homonormativity and Queer Politics in India
Pawan Singh

Chapter 7 176
You Can't Fix Us: Trans Citizenship and the Classificatory Anxieties of the State
Gee Imaan Semmalar

Chapter 8 207
Finding the 'Gay' in Ambedkar: Contesting and Breaking Lines Between Caste and Sexuality
Akhil Kang

Chapter 9 241
Law, Sexuality and Diaspora
Sonia K. Katyal

Chapter 10 271
The Promise of an Event: Sexuality's Historiography
Anjali Arondekar

Chapter 11 288
Afterword
Rahul Rao

Acknowledgements 301

Editors 303

Contributors 305

Introduction

Counterintuitions: The Fraught After-Lives of Queer Freedom

Dipika Jain and *Oishik Sircar*

In 2009, Section 377 of the Indian Penal Code was read down by the Delhi High Court in the *Naz Foundation* judgment to decriminalize private and consensual sex between adults. It was considered a time marked by the hope that India would recognize sexually marginalized people as full and equal citizens. That popular commitment to hope wavered in the intervening moment of defeat posed by the *Koushal* judgment of 2013. The *Koushal* judgment, for a period of five years, effectively recriminalized adult, consensual and private sex by ruling against the *Naz* decision, calling India's queer populations a "miniscule minority" and passing the buck of 'reform' to the legislature. With the Supreme Court of India's *Navtej Johar* judgment of 2018, the movement against Section 377 has emerged victorious, allowing hope to prevail once again.

There have been parallel moments of legal victories that have also been celebrated through this period, particularly the 2014 *NALSA* judgment that putatively recognized transgender persons' right to self-determination, and the 2018 *Puttaswamy* judgment that recognized the fundamental right to privacy, arguably paving the way for *Navtej Johar*. This is the common-sense trajectory of queer emancipation in India, seen through a judicial lens.

Desire and Its Discontents: Queer Politics in Contemporary India offers a counterintuitive reading of this narrative of triumph by paying attention to the myriad ideological networks of power that constitute it. The chapters in this book critically interrogate the common sense of queer emancipation through the decriminalization of Section 377. While remaining cognizant of the strategic maneuvers of the legal challenge to Section 377, *Desire and Its Discontents* argues that queer emancipation in India needs to be understood in the larger context of the rise of Hindutva, neoliberalism, and an ever growing anti-Bahujan savarna consolidation. The motivation for such a line of inquiry lies in the ways in which expressions of queer desires in the language of rights, state recognition, inclusion, progress, and tradition have been echoed by a Hindutva-neoliberalism-savarna complex.

What has led to queer persons, as a historically despised and disenfranchised community, finding both full-blown and conditional allies in processes and ideas that would rather maintain their marginalised status? What has neoliberalism done to queer rights claims in the wake of the liberalization of the Indian economy and the accompanying rise of the Hindu Right? Has the desire for queer emancipation been appropriated by the desire for capitalist development? Prior to the event of decriminalization, had the queer agenda become captive within a singular focus on Section 377 of the Indian Penal Code? Has the decriminalization of private sex between consensual adults privatized and depoliticized queer politics? Is the queer movement immune to racist, casteist, sexist, or religious prejudice? Can there be a right-wing queer? In the aftermath of both the failures and triumphs in legal challenges to Section 377, the authors in this volume engage in a contemplative interrogation of the prejudiced ledge that the queer movement in India might just be perched on, to see if queer politics is and can be practiced in new ways that can resist the movements' alignment with the violence and exclusions of Hindutva, neoliberalism and brahminism.

In this introduction we will discuss and illustrate some of the broad themes that the book engages with and offer brief summaries of its chapters.

PRIDES AND PREJUDICE

In the India of 2022, the legal recognition of queer identities and rights is most powerfully socially manifest in our cultural and reproductive economies. For instance, queer people have occupied central screen space in several popular cultural representations like *Dostana, Kapoor & Sons, Ek Ladki Ko Dekha Toh Aisa Laga, Shubh Mangal Zyada Saavdhan, Moonlight, Blue is the Warmest Colour, Orange is the New Black, Pose,* and *Queer Eye for the Straight Guy* (along with its 2018 reboot *Queer Eye*). Queers have become target constituencies for marketing campaigns that promote everything from queer-friendly clothing to real estate to tourist destinations to wedding planners to adoption agencies to surrogacy clinics and sperm banks. Queer subjects are now being transformed from "figures of death"[1]—as primary vectors of AIDS—to "figures of life and productivity"[2]—as "homonormative"[3] subjects who reproduce heteronormativity through demands for the legal recognition of gay marriage.[4] Homonormativity has been said to have transformed queers from their association with diseases like HIV/AIDS to full-fledged citizens with 'family values', aspiring towards same-sex marriage and possessing purchasing power, "integrating them into the biopolitical optimization of life".[5]

Over the past decade or so globally, the rights demands of queer people have been met by the enactment of laws and economic policies, and states, particularly non-Western states, seem to favourably consider their claims of living up to the civilizational marker of being an evolved and progressive polity. In effect, while the borders of citizenship are expanding to include queer subjects, the process of inclusion is also making them engage in an exercise of privatized self-governance—where the trade-off is between the recognition of sexual citizenship in the public sphere, in exchange for a promise to conform to heteronormative governance tactics in the private.[6] It is not surprising that major legal decisions decriminalizing anti-sodomy laws have used the 'privacy' argument to depoliticize the radical histories of queer organizing. On the other hand, the public visibility of queer collectivization, particularly Pride marches, is increasingly corporatized.

The current corporatization of Pride in India is accompanied by thinly veiled Islamophobia and strong homonationalistic views. This was illustrated in 2020, when 51 people were arrested and charged with sedition for raising slogans in support of Jawaharlal Nehru University student and activist Sharjeel Imam at the Mumbai Pride Solidarity Gathering, co-organized by Queer Azadi Mumbai (QAM) and the Humsafar Trust.[7] Imam was arrested a few days prior to this incident for making a speech in opposition to the *Citizenship (Amendment) Act, 2019* and participants of the Mumbai Pride Solidarity Gathering had raised slogans in support of him.[8]

Notably, after the arrests were made, QAM, upon being approached by the police, denied any role in raising slogans and went so far as to publicly denounce the same.[9] QAM issued a formal statement on social media condemning the "abrupt radical slogans", using words like "irresponsible and potentially detrimental" to describe the persons held responsible by the police and completely disassociating itself from them.[10] QAM had informed participants on Facebook, one day before the Pride Solidarity Gathering, that they had promised the authorities that participants would not use language, symbols or posters that could "offend or infuriate the emotions of any person or community" and would not engage in any "activism".[11] QAM's statement invited backlash from a number of other organizations, who called them out for playing a role in "building a narrative of communalism (read: Islamophobia)".[12] The Ambedkar University Delhi Queer Collective stated the following, referring to QAM's actions in particular:

> we are in complete disagreement with the QAM's stand on what they consider 'abrupt and radical slogans' that go 'against the integrity of India'. Legislations [and policies] such as the CAA-NRC-NPR [Citizenship Amendment Act-National Register of Citizens-National Population Register] are going to affect queer individuals as much as they will affect anybody else, if not more. Moreover, by calling the sloganeering in support of student Sharjeel Imam's immediate release as 'radical' and 'against the integrity of the country' shows very clearly that the organisers come from a place of extreme privilege while echoing and upholding the right rhetoric of communal politics.[13]

One of the organizers of the Mumbai Pride Solidarity Gathering, Ashok Row Kavi, founder of the Mumbai-based LGBT rights NGO Humsafar Trust, has been the subject of controversy for his Hindu right-wing political positions.[14] Row Kavi, who claims to have been the first person to come out as gay in India, is admittedly a right-wing upper-caste cis gay man, who has openly denounced activism by minority communities, including Muslim queer persons, and unapologetically roots his beliefs in his upper-caste Hindu male identity.[15] His imaginings of what Pride should 'look like' have been alleged to envision Pride as an "imagination of the cis-Hindu upper class, upper caste gay male, [wherein] all the other kinds of queer people don't exist."[16] Vikramaditya Sahai, who has been publicly and disdainfully named by Row Kavi as a "Delhi left-liberal", has responded thusly: "These other queer communities (Dalits, women, Muslims) are politicising your [Row Kavi's] pride by bringing their identities, while you get to be this pure, abstract figure because Modi is in power".[17]

Many scholars and activists have advanced critiques of Pride as largely a representation of Savarna (caste Hindu) voices. The blatant casteism in Pride itself has been called out, for instance most recently, when a "Tam-Brahm 'equal rights' activist" mocked three Dalit queer persons asserting their caste identities at the Delhi Queer Pride Parade in 2015.[18] The casteism in Pride is claimed to be indicative of Savarna men's domination of the Indian queer movement, through their "savarna social capital", including funding and resources from NGOs, and the shunning, ridiculing and erasure of Dalit-Bahujan experiences.[19] The 'queer movement' in India has been labelled "classist, casteist, sexist and complicit with power structures of the most oppressive kind", accused of participating in the "rules of exclusion and marginalisation of the less privileged".[20] In the context of queer movements and highly visibilized Pride marches, not only is there a push to project a social movement as homogenous, there is also a denial of caste privilege and a dismissal of Dalit-Bahujan communities' concerns.[21] The spaces for non-Savarna voices "are very surreptitiously usurped by subtle social, cultural, political, and economic ministrations" that strip away Dalit-Bahujan persons' agency to visibly express themselves. Similarly, Inshah Malik writes in the context of the nationalist dimensions of Hindu queerness: "postcolonial nationalisms seek to homogenise political bodily experience", an especially troubling agenda for queer Kashmiri Muslims who are navigating their identities in the "idiom of India's illegal and military rule in Kashmir".[22] This navigation has gained intense significance in the wake of the 2019 abrogation of Article 370 of the Constitution of India by the Bharatiya Janata Party government that lends India's military occupation of Kashmir constitutional imprimatur.

This trend was already emerging through Pride marches in India, even before the Mumbai incident referenced above. At the 2010 Delhi Pride march people cried 'Jai Hind', while the Mumbai Pride march that same year saw participants sing the national anthem. It is pertinent to ask, "What does nationalist sloganeering mean for minorities like the Muslim/Adivasi/Dalit queer?"[23] The 2014 Pride march in Delhi also saw participants holding placards with the words 'Ek Bharat' in shades of the rainbow, which Sircar argues signifies a "vision of sexual unity conditional on secular (read: Hindu) assimilation, or secular assimilation conditional on sexual unity."[24] In both instances, Savarna queers are the ones who set the dominant cultural trends, and other queer communities are expected to follow.[25] However, Dalit-Bahujans are reorganizing the spaces and challenging the caste biases of Savarna activists who portray themselves as leaders of the queer movement. In 2015, for example, the Chennai Pride Parade organizers invited Dalit feminists, scholars and activists to a seminar on queer and queerness and the Pride Walk expressly stated the queer movement's solidarity with anti-caste struggles.[26] Nevertheless, Pride in India continues to be an unequal space, where only the voices of "a certain kind of queer" are amplified.[27]

FROM REPRESSION TO EMANCIPATION?

Stories of queer liberation always seem to be framed within linear narratives, from repression to emancipation.[28] These narratives are closely aligned with our understanding of liberal rights, where the advent of democracy, constitutional legalism, and capitalism are considered co-terminus with the advent of modernity and civilization, and thus the acceptance of sexual outlaws within the fold of full and equal citizenship.

This linear progressive trajectory of history was also used as the justification for colonialism, and still holds tremendous purchase when it comes to claiming identity-based LGBTQIA+ rights using the language of the law. Drawing on the colonial legacy today comes the accusation of non-Western countries being backward and homophobic, and in need of both immediate law reform to decriminalize sodomy and legalize same-sex marriage, and a civilizational uplift of cultures by opening up to secular markets and human rights. Such an explanation erases alternative histories of sexual desire and resistance, and makes us conveniently forget the colonial acts that in fact legislated homophobia into the law and subsequently into the cultures of postcolonial states.[29] A linear narrative of history thus relies heavily on flashpoints to mark the civilizational break between Western progress and Eastern primitivity, where constitutional/legal protection of LGBTQIA+ rights serves as the marker of how evolved a postcolonial democracy is (if it qualifies as a democracy at all in the West's view).

It is here that postcolonial theory and Subaltern Studies make an entry with theoretical tools that disrupt this neat narrative of universality to offer a queer history of layered contradictions. The chapters by Brenda Cossman and Ratna Kapur are part of this tradition.

Feminism: A Strained Ally?

Cossman's and Kapur's arguments help us recognize another linear trajectory akin to the move from repression to emancipation. This one suggests that the beginnings of queer theory came out of feminist theory, and now they are part of the same family, sharing similar political visions and theoretical roots. And their intimacy is, "just as in most bookstores [...] found on shelves located side by side or back to back."[30] Yet, as the blurb on the edited collection *Feminism Meets Queer Theory* says: "they can also seem like strangers, needing mediation, translation, clarification."[31] As the linear story goes: first there was feminist theory, and then came queer theory, and that is why queer theory ought to be understood as a derivative of feminist theory. However, the common-sense of this relationship was questioned by Gayle Rubin in her 1984 essay 'Thinking Sex', in which she challenged "the assumption that feminism is or should be the privileged site of a theory of sexuality."[32] A few standard contentions that queer theory has with feminist theory are the latter's difficulty with breaking out of the male/female binary, the mounting of an analysis that is uneasy with discussing sexuality outside of its critique of reproduction, domination and violence, resolving whether feminism "carries a brief"[33] for an unambiguous and essentialized subject called 'the woman', and an invariable comprehension of gender-subjugation as men dominating women.

Unhappy with feminism's continued discomfiture with and marginalization of queer sexuality, and drawing on queer theory's commitment to an anti-identitarian politics, in 2008 Janet Halley made a charmingly provocative argument about "how and why we should take a break from feminism" in her book *Split Decisions*.[34]

Cossman's and Kapur's essays engage with this suggestion of a 'break' to understand what the consequences of such a manoeuvre might be when queer theory moves to the postcolony. Does it recreate another binary, of theory being Western and experience being Southern?[35] Or does queer theory undergo a transformation through what Cossman calls in her chapter its "continental drifts"? Does theorizing become the queer academic's privilege where identity politics remain the drudgery of the materially discriminated homosexual? While Cossman and Kapur do not suggest a complete break from feminism (and acknowledge its contribution to their own political positioning as queer feminists), they do offer insights into the disruptive acts that queer theory can perform to push feminism's boundaries to imagine a "radical alterity" that makes space for solidarity building and "homosexual dissidence in law".

The strained relationship between feminism and queer sexuality has been more than apparent in India (and South Asia) as well, especially with the difficulty that the women's movement and feminist scholarship have had in speaking about lesbians and transwomen, let alone in considering queer-identifying women and sex workers as part of the movement.[36] On many occasions, queer sexuality has been considered a bourgeois issue that concerns only upper-class/caste women. In India, after a long history of silence on the question of sexuality within the women's movement, one of the first spaces where lesbians found articulation beyond the context of violence was at the 1994 edition of the National Conference of Autonomous Women's Movements held at Tirupati. As Nivedita Menon notes:

> [T]he initial response of the established leadership of the women's movement was entirely homophobic and even today the alliance is not an unproblematic one. [... At the Tirupati Conference] an open and often acrimonious discussion on lesbianism took place, with the greatest hostility coming from leftist groups, decrying lesbianism as an elitist deviation from *real* political issues.[37]

The Indian feminist movement needed to be careful not to 'taint' feminism with Western bourgeois lesbianism and distanced itself from lesbian politics "to defend a hard-won image of being in step with national concerns".[38] As a result, lesbians began organizing themselves in the 1980s under the categories of "single women" or as "women who love women".[39] Even within queer organizing in India, there was a clear gender disparity. For example, when *Bombay Dost*, a gay magazine, was founded by Row Kavi in 1990, it catered almost exclusively to gay men and had no content for lesbian women.[40] Further, given the politics of NGO funding related to HIV/AIDS prevention efforts, lesbian women were globally considered a no-risk demographic and could not tap into this stream of funds and concerted activism.[41]

While lesbians attempted to claim space in feminist and queer movements, trans and gender-diverse persons also found themselves excluded from cisgender activist-led organizing, including lesbian organizing.[42] Feminist and LGB liberation movements have historically been—and continue to be—divided on including trans persons and trans issues in the movement.[43] Feminist objections to trans inclusion were largely based on the rationalization that transwomen were raised as boys and hence had male privilege. Looking at US feminist organizing in the 1970s, Susan Stryker notes that most feminists were critical of practices such as cross-dressing, taking hormones, and having gender affirmative surgery.[44] Cisgender gay men, too, were often uncomfortable with the inclusion of transwomen in LGB spaces. In an interview, Marsha P. Johnson attested to "the virulent everyday misogyny of gay men" who she recalled as not being friendly towards transwomen, because transwomen remind gay men of women and they don't want to get too close to them.[45]

Much has been written about transphobia within various strands of feminist movements in the 1970s and onwards in the US. In 1979, Janice Raymond's influential work *The Transsexual Empire: The Making of the She-Male* gave voice to a decade of vocal opposition to trans inclusion in the movement.[46] Raymond argued that transgender persons, especially transwomen, lacked "a feminist consciousness of patriarchal gender roles and [were] suffering from a patriarchal, medically invented, psychological illness".[47] She contended that trans people reinforced the gender binary by transitioning and that the medical community supported this through surgeries and hormone therapies.[48] She further argued that a "feminist consciousness" inhibits the existence of transmen; female-bodied feminists, by virtue of being feminists, would not identify as transmen. Those who do, she theorized, desire to escape the oppression they face as women.[49] While Raymond's work was widely criticized, including by queer theorists such as Judith Butler,[50] its legacy lived on. In 1991, the Michigan Womyn's Music Festival removed a transwoman from its campground, stating that the festival was open only to "womyn-born-womyn", that is, cisgender women.[51] This policy continued until 2015, when the last festival was held.[52] Tension between cisgender feminists and activists (queer or otherwise) and trans persons has remained to date, especially in fiercely polarized debates around the work and ideas of those referred to as TERFs or Trans-Exclusionary Radical Feminists like Germaine Greer and Sheila Jeffreys,[53] even as the work of Andrea Long Chu has compellingly queered the pitch of this antagonistic relationship between radical feminism and trans identities.[54]

QUEERING DALIT AND TRANS CITIZENSHIP

Akhil Kang's and Gee Semmalar's contributions to this volume draw attention to the relationships between caste oppression, queerness, and citizenship in a bid to explore their historical contexts as well as current manifestations through the lived experiences and struggles of Dalit queer individuals and trans individuals with none of the privileges exercised by their cis gay male counterparts with caste privilege. Their respective chapters underscore the ongoing erasure of and disregard for Dalit and trans experiences in mainstream LGBQI discourse due to various factors, including but not limited to the systematic oppression experienced by these individuals at the hands of the state, which in the name of protecting rights has created a "classificatory regime" that seems to be aimed at engaging in regulation rather than in advancing emancipation. Both Kang and Semmalar seek to distance themselves from existing frameworks and limiting narratives, whether they be theoretical, judicial, linguistic or political in nature, to identify and critically engage with oppression, baggage and the policing of such identities, and to reimagine and re-explore the very scope of queer Dalit and trans identities under conditions of postcolonial modernity.

Semmalar explores the deep distrust for judicial processes held by trans people across castes, who know the oppressive nature of state institutions, and the contrastingly unrestrained faith in and reliance on judicial processes amongst cis, dominant-caste LGB sections. He highlights the state emphasis on assigning transgender persons their "proper place" in the classificatory system of citizenship and touches upon the history of state anxiety around the opacity of gender deviance in the Indian subcontinent and the many classificatory regimes imposed to make trans persons legible for administrative control and disciplining practices. Hierarchies of civility and respectability among various social groups have contributed to identity divisions between different categories such as gay, Hijra, trans, non-binary, and MSM (men who have sex with men), as well as between 'respectable' and 'unruly' Hijra and trans individuals. Despite the fact that many individuals within these communities occupy multiple and overlapping identities, these divisions persist.[55] These intra-community conflicts and definitional anxieties have been exacerbated by questions of who an 'authentic' trans person is and who can claim and receive benefits from the state post the 2014 *NALSA* judgment and the passage of the *Transgender Persons (Protection of Rights) Act, 2019*. Semmalar admits that transgender movements have to simplify and flatten their gender incongruity and diversities, and self-discipline the erotic while participating in legal discourse and struggles in order to demand equality under the frame of constitutional rights. In opposition, he calls for an embracing of the "disruptive potential" of trans and gender non-binary identities, while simultaneously asserting the right to access state benefits, to create a "sustainable, radical politics".

Grace Banu, a Dalit trans activist, has written about the invisibility of the Dalit transgender community, whose stories "when written by oppressor castes ... reinforce phobias and stigmas against us".[56] As Semmalar has argued elsewhere, the oppression of transgender persons varies according to their class, caste, gender, race and geographical location.[57] Dalit artist and trans activist Living Smile Vidya also speaks of transphobia as a type of Brahmanism,[58] with transphobia turning the hijra into an "untouchable subject",[59] akin to the caste system, which gives Dalit persons the 'dirty' jobs and then calls them 'dirty'.[60] In a 2013 interview, Vidya states that although caste is not as obvious in the hijra community due to everyone's name change after the process of transition is complete, many dominant caste trans persons still proudly assert their caste. Vidya also highlighted the problems with representational politics, noting that Savarna transgender persons who get NGO funding get to unfairly represent the community and claim all benefits.[61]

One of the most prominent transgender activists in India, Laxmi Narayan Tripathi, has claimed that there is no caste or religion in the hijra community.[62] Laxmi grew up in a Brahmin household and heads the Kinnar Akhara, an organization that has faced strong condemnation from many trans-led groups and individuals for its support of the construction of the Ram Temple in Ayodhya, a political project that is at the heart of the agenda of India's Hindu right-wing ruling establishment and a definitive step towards turning India into a Hindu Rashtra or nation.[63] Contrary to her claims, religious festivals and holidays are celebrated by *gharanas*, although many hijras practice a form of syncretism, drawing from multiple religions. Moreover, caste-based hierarchies exist within hijra communities. Dalit hijras have attested to facing discrimination based on their caste, such as not being allowed by their gurus to accompany others to collect ritual blessings.[64] NGOs too often employ transwomen from caste marginalised backgrounds in low-paid positions while upper-caste persons retain the high-level salaried posts.[65] Thus, the lived experiences of Dalit trans individuals are significantly different from those of their Savarna counterparts.

Kang's chapter tries to make sense of one's relationship to oppression as both a Dalit and a queer individual. They explore how the framework of intersectionality in India is essentially mediated through caste, and therefore distances himself from using said framework, instead opting to address "the caste of intersectionality". Kang emphasizes the value of reading queerness into caste to disrupt the gender dynamic in fundamental ways and to offer an alternative imagination of the identities of Dalit men and women. For Kang, "queering Dalit" is not just an exercise in amalgamating different identities, but being conscious of the different ways in which such identities thrive across caste and class locations. They also offer "queering Dalit" as a way of understanding the simultaneous practices of holding on to and letting go of identities, while critically perusing the "oppressive baggage" of both caste and queerness.

LAW AS SPECTACLE

Queer struggles in most parts of the world work towards demanding the repeal of anti-sodomy laws, and seek the legal recognition of same-sex marriage and trans and intersex rights, and anti-discrimination laws. We do not need to over-emphasize how important these efforts are. What the authors in this volume remain concerned about is the way in which the law is projected as the singular point where queer oppression and emancipation meet: one that is at the root of homo/trans/queerphobia, and one that is the most potent response to it. The cruelty of this experience is aptly captured in the term "Pharmakon". Derrida's reading of this expression,[66] first introduced by Plato, interprets it as a medicine that is a cure and a poison at the same time. Escaping this double bind of the law's promise of justice and the reality of violence becomes a formidable task for queer struggles, where the victory of rights recognition is accompanied by new forms of disciplinary regulation. Law's "spectacles of emancipation" work in such a way that legal achievements tend to anaesthetize our collective ability to gauge its consequences.[67] Can the decriminalization of sodomy be universally emancipatory? Can it not, in fact, be a more insidious mode of surveillance and regulation? Does the recognition of same sex-marriage reproduce hetero-patriarchy? Can the trope of the right to privacy, used on most occasions to legally challenge anti-sodomy laws, become a marker of class privilege? Can the claim to privacy be a depoliticizing move that domesticates sexuality? Does legal emancipation ossify sexual identities into something fixed and unchangeable? Is the almost universal demand for decriminalization part of any larger politics connected to agendas of global governance and aid? Do decriminalization and same-sex marriage rights operate as civilizational markers of progress?

The 2009 *Naz Foundation* and the 2018 *Navtej Johar* judgments reading down Section 377, as many would argue, are an outcome of the cultural acceptance of diverse sexualities that has taken place as a result of liberalization and globalization. This is evident from both judgments' constant allusions to international human rights law and precedents. These references make apparent the cultural logic behind the court's reasoning: India needs to live up to the progressive developments in other parts of the (Western) world by decriminalizing sodomy. As Anjali Gopalan, founder of the petitioner organization *Naz Foundation*, said after the judgment was delivered, "Oh my God, we've finally stepped into the 21st century!"[68] The excitement of the moment notwithstanding, this spectacular declaration is indeed a moment where the ostensibly progressive present contributes to the making of queer emancipation at the cost of obscuring us to a historicized understanding of the cruelly liberal genealogy of this very moment.[69]

The *Suresh Kumar Koushal* judgment that overruled the *Naz Foundation* judgment recriminalized private consensual same-sex sexual acts in 2013.[70] Responses to the judgment, whether in social media or in activist spaces, clearly characterized the judgment and the discourse of the Supreme Court as "backward", with the *Naz Foundation* judgment being clearly characterized as progressive.[71]

The Supreme Court's "medieval mindset" was called out, with activists accusing the Court of "putting the clock back" through this judgment, which "takes us back to a position of barbarism".[72] Even though the responses spoke up against Section 377's colonial origins and its inheritance by independent India, the comments also served to express "anguish" about how the judgment contradicted their idea of a progressive, modern India, symbolically altering India's 'image' internationally.[73] Such linear characterization of queer victories and defeats comes from the appropriation of queer rights articulations by Hindutva and neoliberal narratives, and blurs the lines between 'progressive' and 'regressive'.[74] The unlikely unification of right-wing religious groups from Hindu, Muslim, and Christian communities in opposing the *Naz Foundation* judgment in the Supreme Court was founded in the common belief that the decriminalization of Section 377 would cause a "degeneration of Indian culture".[75]

The legal grounds elucidated in the 2014 *NALSA* judgment, that recognized a third gender category (beyond the male-female binary) entitled to equal rights under the Constitution of India, marked a clear departure from the Supreme Court's narrow reasoning in *Suresh Kumar Koushal*.[76] Activists across the globe hailed the judgment as a "significant step forward" for the transgender community's rights in the country.[77]

However, amidst such a discourse of progress, the Court's judgment has also been characterized as "under-inclusive", as it does not explicitly recognize gender-variant people and communities who are not hijras, or persons assigned male at birth but belonging to the third gender category.[78] Further, the highly derogatory term "eunuch" is mentioned over 20 times in the judgment by the Court, furthering a colonial taxonomy.[79] The Court has explicitly recognized transgender individuals' right to self-identification as male, female or third gender, which marks an over-representation of hijra individuals, at the expense of other gender-variant peoples.[80] The judgment relies heavily on Hindu mythological texts such as the Ramayana and Mahabharata, making only cursory references to the Mughal period in India's history.[81] There are communal undertones evident in the judgment, which attempt to ignore "the Islamic cultural context that provided fertile ground for hijra communities to flourish" and instead focuses on Hindu-izing and homogenizing the transgender community.[82] The reliance on Hindu mythology, as Semmalar has written, was also brought in through the arguments made by the lawyers and articles written by Savarna commentators.[83] In making the claim that transgender persons are not "Western imports", these arguments present "a golden Hindu period where there was no discrimination" thus ignoring not only the significance of Islam within the community, but also caste- and class-based structures of oppression. The Court further displayed a lack of understanding of the intersectionality between caste, gender and sexuality, as well as the distinction between gender identity, sex and sexual orientation.

The *NALSA* judgment may be a watershed moment for the rights of gender minorities, but it cannot be denied that individuals possessing non-traditional trans identities are adversely implicated. The judgment overemphasizes a homogenous hijra identity, erroneously and repeatedly conflates hijra with transgender and, on a practical level, effectively erases the experiences of gender-variant persons with non-traditional identities.[84] This ambiguity, coupled with the broad discretion given to central and state governments and the prejudicial bureaucratic policing of gender, has undeniably adverse effects on the actual implementation of the "celebratory declarations" made in *NALSA*.[85] Therefore, simply labelling such spectacles of law as victories or progress erases the deeper question: can judicial thinking, even as it speaks the language of rights, recognize the pluralities of gender identities and the lived experiences of gender non-conforming people? Or does rights recognition result in the gatekeeping of identity categories by the state? Judicial failure to fully consider a litigant's lived experiences results in epistemic and systemic injustice.[86] Cisgender narratives dominate judicial discourse and "the state's manufactured language controls litigant identity in court", thus limiting litigants' rights demands and their presentation of selfhood.[87] The judiciary is only able to digest normative statements that position gender-diverse individuals as the 'other' through a foil-or-freak argument.[88] Since the judiciary retains the ability to define sex and gender, a legible gender-diverse citizenship is not possible without a confrontation of this logic. Moreover, the fact that all litigants are not equal at any given time—particularly on account of their caste, class, religion, indigenous identity and other factors—is crucial. The litigants who do make it to court are typically not representative of their communities.[89]

The 2018 *Navtej Johar* judgment that finally decriminalized consensual same-sex acts was widely hailed as a victory, a "verdict for all times".[90] As Akhil Kang has written, the fight for love "is as much as about caste, class, and religion as it is about gender, sexuality".[91] For Saptarshi Mandal, the judgment privileges a certain narrative that has shaped popular discourse around Section 377.[92] This narrative identifies the legal provision as criminalizing queer persons, but ignores the fact that certain groups of people, such as working-class trans persons, have been more vulnerable to its use by the police. While many elite queer individuals celebrated the decision, those from marginalized communities understood it as a symbolic victory that would not protect them from daily violence and police harassment.[93] The limitations of the judgment are also reflected in the litigation strategy, where the main petitioner was Navtej Singh Johar, a renowned Bharatanatyam dancer and choreographer. Other petitioners included restaurateur Ritu Dalmia, hoteliers Aman Nath and Keshav Suri, business executive Ayesha Kapur, and Johar's partner, journalist Sunil Mehra. In addition to these celebrity-professionals, the petition was supported by a group of "elite engineers" associated with the Indian Institutes of Technology.[94] Thus, upper-caste and upper-class queers became the "symbol of injustice" while Dalit-Bahujan queers found themselves excluded from community consultations, discussions among activists and lawyers on how to take the case forward, and from the halls of the Supreme Court itself.[95]

The *Johar* judgment was also celebrated as a decolonizing move, correcting the wrong that Thomas Macaulay had put in place in the form of Section 377 of the Indian Penal Code. One would have to be circumspect about the language of decolonization in Hindutva's times because decolonization is part of the Sangh Parivar's revisionist project of establishing a Hindu nation. As Nishant Upadhyay has noted:

> these revisionist narratives reduce homophobia to colonial legacies. Strategically, on the one hand, it may be important for the queer rights movement to reclaim Hinduism in its quest for justice; on the other hand, for some on the Hindu Right, who were blatantly homophobic until recently, this has become a key strategy to claim homophobia as a colonial inheritance and establish dominance of Hindu ideologies over their *Others*.[96]

Bringing our discussion back to the *Naz Foundation* decision: it cannot be denied that the judgment was progressive and historic. Upendra Baxi's celebratory declaration was that it marked an "'exceptional' adjudicative moment."[97] However, what Baxi missed was how this exceptionalism worked as a blinding spectacle that sought to recognize only the rights of those who have the privilege of access to private space. The primacy put on private sex was clearly an elitist qualifier to read down the law, because it excludes from its purview a whole range of non-elite and indigenous sexually marginalized people who do not enjoy the privilege of private space.[98] The privacy standard is a myth, because those who do have access to private space were already outside of the reach of the law. As Ashley Tellis had asked, "What is the point of allowing consensual sex between private adults of the same sex when most violations are of us in the public realm: in institutions, on the streets, in parks, toilets and wherever else?"[99] Jason Fernandes argued that the judgment prioritizes the interests of urban, English-speaking, middle-class leaders of the queer rights movement in India by overshadowing the very sexually marginalized communities (hijras, kothis, panthis)[100] they claim to represent.[101] The reading down of the law ostensibly allowed for same-sex acts within private spaces, yet it ironically offered no protection for same-sex practices outside the normative parameters of home and domesticity.[102]

Pawan Singh's chapter refers to the ideas of privacy developed through *Naz Foundation* (2009), *Suresh Koushal* (2013), *Puttaswamy* (2017) and *Navtej Singh Johar* (2018) to argue that the Supreme Court's construction of privacy as the basis for the legitimacy of queer identities and freedoms represents the grievances of queer persons with class and financial privilege that would "afford" them "an uncloseted visibility". He critiques the *Naz* judgment for the visible incongruity between the right to privacy and the public nature of violations, the invisibility of certain "risky subjects", hyper-visibility of gender non-normative bodies, and the safe, normative visibility of the persons who have been at the forefront of the movement to decriminalize homosexuality. A discussion of *Suresh Koushal* brought about a realization of how the idea of privacy itself is mired in social inequalities that are reflected in the presences and absences in the Indian LGBT movement, where the Supreme Court proceedings evidenced the conspicuous absence of physically injured non-normative bodies and the presence of those claiming symbolic injury. Within this complex field of visibility, *Naz's* privacy as decisional autonomy clearly privileged a homonormative minority that could invoke the lofty discourse of moral citizenship, claim pride, and stage dissent and political interventions.

Singh highlights the "paradoxical juncture of empowered visibility with potential vulnerability" in the lives of the Indian queer, pointing out that in postcolonial India, the moral policing of queer visibility may be combated by privacy-based justice, but at the expense of greater visibility and public exposure. Through an exploration of the 2010 case of Dr Siras, the late Aligarh Muslim University professor filmed in his bedroom with a male partner by his university colleagues without his consent, as well as the 2011 Hyderabad sting operation carried out by TV9 to expose "Gay Culture Rampant in Hyderabad", Singh explores the existence of violated subjects whose public visibility (post *Naz* privacy) remains in legal archives, media reports and a film (in Dr Siras' case), and whose 'successes' envision visibility and exposure. Singh states that the 'logic' of privacy as silence and invisibility has indeed been cast in homonormative terms of repression and erasure, as a form of tacit violence by Indian LGBT activists, and to be visible, demanding justice and an identity-based affirmation is reinforced as the linear logic of rights-based homonormativity equating visible public presence with the teleological outcome of progress.

Singh's argument speaks to the US's decriminalization of sodomy on the grounds of privacy, on which Wendy Brown has commented: "depending on the function of privacy in the powers that make the subject, and depending on the marked identity that is at issue, privacy will be seen variously to advance or deter emancipation, to cloak inequality or procure equality."[103] The lesson, then, is to not treat the liberal virtues of privacy as a universal emancipatory idea but, rather, as one that also has the ability to disenfranchise.

Zaid Al Baset's chapter also provides a critique of the 'right to privacy' in the *Naz Foundation* judgment. Baset speaks of privacy being deployed as a spatial metaphor as well as a metaphor for personal autonomy in international law. As a spatial metaphor, he describes how 'privacy' is aligned with the family or home so that privacy connotes a physical space—involving the already heterosexual and "unconscious" conflation of the private with the home and family, and space with marriage and the family. Baset moves to state that the heteronormativity of the Indian family can force queer Indians inside the closet even within the private sphere. The notion of privacy as personal autonomy in a social context of heterosexism results in the exclusion of the homosexual from the "moral public", rendering personal autonomy itself largely meaningless. The space then provided to "homosexuals" in India is in effect a non-space, or simply an erased space insofar as it threatens to erase the queer subject from the public, thereby re-producing the closet. The metaphor of the closet is used to denote a space (or the lack of one) which functions to cohere heterosexuality and produce the 'homosexual' as its inevitable and often invisible other.

Baset critically reads *Naz* to attempt to understand how the text of the judgment constructs the myth of heterosexuality, which de-naturalizes the 'homosexual' subject as a naturally occurring 'unnatural' phenomenon. The judgment, which condenses 'queerness' into 'gay' or 'homosexual' (which are accordingly made to connote the entire spectrum of sexual and gender difference), carries with it the charge of concealing a variegated experience, 'erasing' other gender identities. Baset explores how the text of the judgment undermines the historicity of terms like 'gay' and 'homosexual', uprooting them from their context of deployment, ignoring historical intersections of class, gender, region, and race loaded within the terms, and emptying out their cultural content.

FRACTURES AND FAULTLINES

Most scholarly and activist writings on law, sexuality, and culture in India that have used the 'queer' tag in the naming and framing of their work do so within an identity politics framework where *queering* as a method of critique is given short shrift.[104] The chapters in this volume engage *queering* as a method of "reading for difference rather than dominance",[105] where queer is understood as a form of scholarly and political conduct that does not remain captive within its home base of sexuality alone.

Anjali Arondekar's chapter demonstrates a particular instance of such scholarly conduct from the vantage of the discipline of history. Arondekar pays attention to the process of how scholars derive meaning from archives and the way they perceive the past. She acknowledges the predominant archival economies of devaluation within India, through state-sponsored campaigns to purify India of "cultural pollution" under a Hindutva-based ideology, and opines that the reading of sexuality's past(s) has now clearly become a complicated affair, a balancing act between an embrace of sexuality's munificent incommensurability (as divergent temporalities are fodder for theories of queer difference) and a capture of its genealogical sameness (as the past surrenders lineages of our queer presents).

Arondekar describes her inquiry into the history of sexuality in India through an "archival trace", addressing "misalignments" along the way. She uncovers how historiographies, through different accounts of the "evil ladies of Girgaum" as "objects of sexuality" at various times, function as a fetishistic screen whereby we return over and over again to the vice of sexuality as the familiar place of historical redress and reform. Her piece ultimately imagines bringing sexuality within public discourses of culture and capital, uncoupling it from its "evil", and discussing it from within a feminist discourse.

Ashley Tellis challenges the appropriation of the term 'queer' by the (upper-caste and upper-class) proponents of the 'queer movement' in India for whom *queering* does not include a critique of the "normalizing impulses of the law and the state".[106] The term 'queer' travelled to India from the US, where it emerged in the context of radical AIDS activism and became a liberating term for queers of colour and other disenfranchised persons not acknowledged by the mainstream gay movement.[107] Now, 'queer' has simply been transmutated into elite spaces, and its use by mainstream activists is a symbolic representation of the elite and exclusionary nature of the movement.[108] Queer in India remains limited to identity, as stated in the QAM blog: "Queer stands for all LGBTIQ+ (Lesbian, Gay, Bisexual, Transgender, Intersex & Queer) Individuals."[109]

This identity-based way of thinking adds more letters to an alphabet soup to produce an illusion of inclusion, but what it omits foregrounding are the visible caste, religion and class-based tensions and fractures that mark the lives of non-binary, alternative and marginalized genders and sexualities both in neoliberal India,[110] as well as in Indian diasporic communities in North America. This dimension of the transnational travels of Indian queerness is explored in the chapter by Sonia A. Katyal, which highlights the importance of using the category of the 'diaspora' to theoretically interpret the intersection of law, sexuality and citizenship. She argues that diasporic individuals live in the in-between, the liminal, "caught in the discontinuous time of translation and negotiation", while also acknowledging the inherent "contradiction in terms" of a diaspora itself, which "relies on a fixed conception of the nation-state for its very identity between home and homeland, even as it challenges the concept of the nation state altogether. Somewhat similarly for the individual, the concept of belonging to a diaspora can be a positive or a negative experience," and Katyal speaks of the importance of "queering the diaspora", as well as "diasporizing the queer" to unpack the complications and complementarities that emerge. She claims that although it seems difficult to apply the idea of a "diaspora" to an LGBT identity, particularly given the diversity and variance that each identity comprises, she notes the inherent "contradiction in terms" of the diaspora itself, and states that the concept of a diaspora can operate both as a site of legal regulation but also as a site of theoretical resistance to and contestation of a unitary LGBT identity. The notion of a queer diaspora is seen to capture an oppositional set of themes stemming from the intersection of transnationality and sexuality, one involving homogenization and the another involving differentiation.

Katyal explores the notion of sexuality through the lens of diaspora, expounding the belief that by emphasizing a "particularized, singular idea of lesbian and gay identity", Western activists have actually overlooked certain complicated identities within "same-sex sexualities". She uses the *Naz Foundation* judgment, which draws significantly on Western jurisprudence, to underscore a manifestation of "constitutional hybridity", arguing that the judgment could be read as a "uniquely powerful example of cosmopolitan constitutional borrowing, balanced with a deep attention to Indian originalism". She argues that both types of diaspora, of persons and constitutional principles, are "movements that rewrite the meaning of the nation state and citizenship" and notes that queer diaspora creates a multiplicity of collective spaces in the face of state regulations that are always mobile, contingent, and dynamically formed in relation to the nation. She cites the transnational potential of *Naz* as paving the imagination towards a more regional and inclusive approach to comparative constitutional interpretation.

Aniruddha Dutta's chapter argues that as the "LGBT community" or their constituent identities are "constructed as intelligible and legitimate citizen-subjects deserving equal rights" a range of practices at the intersections of class, caste and gender—particularly the public assertion of gender identity and expression—are sought to be excluded from this construction.[111] For Dutta, institutionalized LGBT activism in India condemns certain forms of queer dissidence for their "social indecency" while celebrating respectable modes of queer resistance. The "hierarchies of civility and respectability fuel identitarian splits" between gay persons, MSM, transgender persons and even create the categories of 'good transgender' and 'badly-behaved transgender'.[112] In another article, Dutta and Roy have described the emergence of 'transgender' as a prominent category in the LGBT movement in the late 2000s, linking it to shifts in patterns of funding to community-based organizations.[113] In 2008, the United Nations Development Programme consultations to assess gaps in the HIV/AIDS infrastructure arrived at a common definition for the term which included identities such as hijra and kothi. This articulation, however, completely excluded trans-masculine identities and subsumed 'local' or regional terminology in a transnational and cross-cultural signifier.[114]

The relationship between queer identity, caste and Brahminical patriarchy is made evident in the increased visibilization of the hijra community, which was at the forefront of the *NALSA* litigation before the Supreme Court. The hijra community, in their social prominence, has become almost synonymous with the transgender community, at the expense of other gender-variant identities—and in recent years, members of the community have moved towards 'inclusion' in various aspects of mainstream societal structures, through government employment, activism and politics.[115] The movement has also witnessed a saffronization of sorts, with certain right-wing ideals indicated through efforts by activists like Laxmi Narayan Tripathi to reclaim transgender persons' "lost position in the [Hindu] religion".[116] Tripathi, a dominant-caste Brahmin transwoman leading the Kinnar Akhara, has made demands for transgender persons' participation in the Kumbh Mela on the basis that this is their right as Hindus,[117] and as previously mentioned, has made a definitive statement on behalf of the Akhara, calling for the construction of a Ram temple at the site where the Babri Masjid was demolished by Hindu right-wing militants in Ayodhya. The narrative Tripathi uses to claim rights hinges on an oft-used argument that transgender persons have been a part of Hindu epics and myths, proving that gender variance existed before colonial occupation, and that queerness and variant gender identities were not 'Western imports'.[118] For Semmalar, this argument where Hindu myths and legends are relied on to legitimize gender-variant identities can be dangerous, leading to a "regressive kind of trans identity politics that does not take into account the brutality of the caste system that finds its origin and sanction in the same Hindu religion."[119]

Tripathi's Hindutva-aligned stance on the building of the Ram Temple was met with outrage by other gender-variant communities, with "Indian Trans, Intersex and Gender Nonconforming (T/IS/GNC) individuals [and] groups" taking to social media and issuing a formal statement expressing their "deepest sense of anguish, concern and condemnation at this call", which they characterized as one "bound to fuel communal hatred and violence".[120] At the time of its release, 183 trans, intersex and gender non-conforming individuals, 20 LGBTQIA+ groups, 8 ally organizations and 146 individual allies had endorsed the statement, condemning the Kinnar Akhara's statement as well as specifically condemning Tripathi for playing "gross competitive politics" by seeking "legitimization of the third gender along religious lines".[121] The signatories pointed out the reality of many trans persons experiencing marginalization due to "a religiously rooted third-gender identity in state policy", which erases various gender identities, and stated that the same "communal politics" were also evident in the *Transgender Persons (Protection of Rights) Bill, 2016*,[122] which criminalized the hijra community's traditional begging system.[123] The *Transgender Persons (Protection of Rights) Bill, 2016* was declared a "move in the spirit of [...] Manuvadi patriarchy" and the signatories stated that along with the Kinnar

Akhara's statement, they would "deepen divisions and increase oppression for most transgender persons while also damaging the secular fabric of Hijra and transgender communities."[124] Activists have called for gender justice movements to be vocally anti-caste, considering the different ways in which the violence faced by trans communities is rooted in the caste system.[125]

INTERROGATING DESIRE

As discussed in this introduction, the chapters in *Desire and Its Discontents* offer a critical interrogation of the common-sense of queer emancipation through the reading down of Section 377 of the Indian Penal Code, arguing for a greater, contextual understanding of queer emancipation in India that takes into account the rise of Hindutva, Brahminism and neoliberalism. In present-day India, the legal recognition of queer identities and rights is socially manifest in our cultural and reproductive economies, and homonormativity has been said to have transformed queers from being associated with diseases like HIV/AIDS to full-fledged citizens with 'family values', aspiring towards same-sex marriage and 'integration'.[126]

Further, over the past decade, the response of non-Western states to rights demands by queer people reflects their desire to live up to the civilizational marker of being an evolved and progressive polity. Even though states, through the enactment of laws and economic policies, have been seen to 'expand' citizenship to include queer subjects, the subjects in question experience a trade-off between the public recognition of sexual citizenship and having to conform to heteronormative governance tactics in private.[127] The reliance of judicial decisions on 'right to privacy' arguments when decriminalizing anti-sodomy laws to depoliticize the radical histories of queer organizing is unsurprising in this context, and is covered in some of the chapters in this volume. The primacy put on 'private sex' in the *Naz Foundation* and *Navtej Singh Johar* judgments was clearly an elitist qualifier to read down the law, because it has been seen to exclude from its purview a whole range of non-elite and indigenous, sexually marginalized people who do not enjoy the privilege of private space.[128] The *Naz Foundation* judgment has been called out for offering no protection whatsoever for same-sex practices outside the normative parameters of 'home' and 'domesticity'.[129]

The chapters in this book recognize that stories of queer liberation always seem to be framed within linear narratives from repression to emancipation.[130] A linear narrative of history relies heavily on flashpoints to mark the civilizational break between Western progress and Eastern primitivity, where the constitutional/legal protection of LGBTI rights serves as the marker of how evolved a postcolonial democracy (if it is even recognized as such by the West) is considered. It is here that two of the chapters bring in postcolonial theory and subaltern studies with theoretical tools that disrupt this neat narrative of universality to offer insights into disruptive acts that queer theory can perform to push feminism's boundaries.

There is also a focus on the relationships between caste oppression, queerness and citizenship in a bid to explore their historical contexts, as well as manifestations through lived experiences and the struggles of Dalit queer individuals and trans individuals with none of the privileges exercised by their cis gay male counterparts. The chapters distance themselves from existing frameworks and limiting narratives, to identify and critically engage with oppression, trauma and the policing of such identities, and to reimagine and re-explore the very scope of queer Dalit and trans identities under conditions of postcolonial modernity. An attempt is made to understand one's relationship to oppression as both a Dalit and a queer individual, by "queering Dalit" (reading queerness into caste) in order to complicate the category of Dalit. The chapter brings queerness into Dalit identities to disrupt the gender dynamic in fundamental ways and to understand simultaneous practices of holding on to and letting go of identities, while critically perusing the "oppressive baggage" of both caste and queerness.

When looking at queer struggles in many parts of the world which demand legal and policy changes such as the legal recognition of trans and intersex rights, the enactment of anti-discrimination laws and the legal recognition of same-sex marriage, the authors of this volume express concern for the 'Pharmakon' of legal victories, where queer struggles often find that their victories of rights recognition turn out to be accompanied by new forms of disciplinary regulation. The law's "spectacles of emancipation" work in such a way that legal achievements tend to anaesthetize our collective ability to gauge its consequences,[131] illustrated in watershed moments like the 2014 *NALSA* judgment that erroneously overemphasizes a homogenous hijra identity and repeatedly conflates hijra with transgender, effectively erasing the experiences of gender-variant persons with non-traditional identities.[132] The ambiguity of judicial language, the lack of nuance when engaging with questions of reservation and caste, as well as the broad discretion given to central and state governments had undeniably adverse effects on the actual implementation of the platitudes of *NALSA*. The outcomes of *NALSA* for non-traditional queer identities can be read alongside the elitist 'privacy' arguments that marked *Naz Foundation* and *Navtej Singh Johar* to see that the 'queer movement' is prioritizing the interests of the urban, middle/upper-class leaders of the rights movement, by overshadowing those very communities (hijras, kothis, panthis) they claim to represent.

The chapters in this volume point to the complicated relationship between law and sex, where law is at the root of gender and sexuality-based marginalization but is also the most potent response to it, being a major tool in sexual struggles across the world. The struggles against the State for legal recognition and reform become the most attractive movements, with 'spectacles' allowing the State to carry on with its violent tactics of governance under the garb of promised law reform, and the outward (Westward) impression that is given is of 'social progress'. Furthermore, with the backdrop of such movements for legal recognition, the corporate market has been allowed to ply queer subjects with products and accessories specifically aimed at a class of consumers who could aspire to an elite lifestyle. Neoliberalism and Hindutva ideologies have culminated in Brahminizing India's sexual past through the creation of the evil and homophobic Muslim outsider, as the chapters in this book argue and substantiate. With these views on the 'outcomes' of the legal victories that were so hard-fought, the question remains as to what must now be done with these legal consequences, and how law, queer movements, and the intersection of caste, class, queerness and citizenship can be engaged, taking into account prevailing local, national and transnational contexts.

NOTES

1. Jasbir Puar, Terrorist Assemblages: Homonationalism in Queer Times xx (2007).
2. *Id.*
3. Lisa Duggan, The Twilight of Equality?: Neoliberalism, Cultural Politics, and the Attack on Democracy (2003).
4. Puar, *supra* note 1, at 28.
5. *See* Nikita Dhawan, *Homonationalism and State-Phobia: The Postcolonial Predicament of Queering Modernities', in* Queering Paradigms V: Queering Narratives of Modernity 52 (M. Viteri & M.L. Picq eds., 2016).
6. Brenda Cossman, Sexual Citizens: The Legal and Cultural Regulation of Sex and Belonging (2007).
7. The Wire Staff, *Mumbai Pride: Over 50 People Charged with Sedition for Slogans Supporting Sharjeel Imam,* The Wire (Feb. 04, 2020), https://thewire.in/law/mumbai-sedition-sharjeel-imam.
8. *Id.*
9. Scroll Staff, *Mumbai: 51 Booked for Sedition for Pro-Sharjeel Imam Slogans at Queer Pride March,* Scroll (Feb. 04, 2020, 11:48 AM), https://scroll.in/latest/952092/mumbai-51-booked-for-sedition-for-pro-sharjeel-imam-slogans-at-queer-pride-march.
10. *Id.*
11. *Id.*
12. The Feminist Collective, *#standwithkris Sign the Petition,* Facebook (Feb. 06, 2020, 2:14 AM), https://www.facebook.com/tfc.ashoka/posts/1429428037235396.
13. *Id.*
14. Nandita Singh & Nikhil Rampal, *India's First and Oldest Gay Rights Activist Is Also on the Extreme Right of RSS,* The Print (July 21, 2018, 10:02 AM), https://theprint.in/politics/indias-first-and-oldest-gay-activist-uses-a-brand-of-hindutva-to-fight-377/85919/.
15. *Id.*

16. *Id.*
17. *Id.*
18. Moulee, *Dear Savarna Queer Men, Let's Talk About Casteism Within Our Movement,* The News Minute (June 16, 2016, 1:24 PM), https://www.thenewsminute.com/article/dear-savarna-queer-men-lets-talk-about-casteism-within-our-movement-44951.
19. *Id.*
20. Ashley J. Tellis, *Disrupting the Dinner Table Re-thinking the 'Queer Movement' in Contemporary India*, 4 Jindal Global Law Review 142 (2012).
21. Maithili Patil & Kshiti Vikas, *Disqualified/Dalit Queerness,* 9 Eidos 86, 86-90 (2020).
22. Inshah Malik, *Kashmiri Desire and Digital Space: Queering National Identity and the Indian Citizen, in* Queering Digital India: Activisms, Identities, Subjectivities 191 (R.K. Dasgupta ed. 2018).
23. Oishik Sircar, *New Queer Politics in the New India: Notes on Failure and Stuckness in a Negative Moment*, 11 UNBOUND 1, 22 (2017).
24. *Id.* at 23.
25. Patil & Vikas, *supra* note 21, at 88.
26. Dhrubo Jyoti, *Being A Queer Dalit and the Assertion of Dalit Identities in Pride Marches*, Feminism in India (June 22, 2017), https://feminisminindia.com/2017/06/22/queer-dalit-assertion-pride-marches/.
27. Nadia Nooreyezdan, *How Indian Pride Festivals Have Become Political Battlegrounds*, Vice (Mar. 09, 2020), https://www.vice.com/en_in/article/5dmjjd/lgbtq-pride-festivals-india-political.
28. *See generally* Martha Nussbaum, From Disgust to Humanity: Sexual Orientation and Constitutional Law (2010). Nussbaum's work is a case in point of this repression to emancipation narrative.
29. *See generally* Human Rights Watch, *This Alien Legacy: The Origins of "Sodomy" Laws in British Colonialism* (Dec. 17, 2008), https://www.hrw.org/report/2008/12/17/alien-legacy/origins-sodomy-laws-british-colonialism; Suparna Bhaskaran, *The Politics of Penetration: Section 377 of the Indian Penal Code, in* Queering India: Same-Sex Love and Eroticism in Indian Culture and Society 15-29 (R. Vanita ed., 2001).
30. Feminism Meets Queer Theory vi (Elizabeth Weed & Naomi Schor eds., 1997).
31. *Id.*
32. Gayle S. Rubin, *Thinking Sex: Notes for a Radical Theory of the Politics of Sexuality, in* Culture, Society and Sexuality: A Reader 169 (R.G. Parker & P. Aggleton eds., 1999).
33. Janet Halley, Split Decisions: How and Why to Take a Break From Feminism (2008).
34. *Id.*
35. Gopal Guru & Sundar Sarukkai, Cracked Mirror: An Indian Debate on Experience and Theory (2012).

36. *See generally* Embodied Violence: Communalizing Women's Sexuality in South Asia (Kumari Jayawardena & Malathi de Alwis eds., 1996); A Question of Silence? The Sexual Economies of Modern India (Mary E. John & Janaki Nair eds., 1998); The Violence of Normal Times: Essays on Women's Lived Realities (Kalpana Kannabiran ed., 2005). Barring marginal references, all these works focus primarily on violence and a critique of reproductive heterosexuality.
37. Sexualities 23 (Nivedita Menon ed., 2007) [emphasis added].
38. Naisargi N. Dave, Queer Activism in India: A Story in the Anthropology of Ethics 37 (Duke University Press, 2012).
39. *Id.*
40. *Id.* at 39.
41. *Id.* at 37.
42. Gee Imaan Semmalar, *Unpacking Solidarities of the Oppressed: Notes on Trans Struggles in India*, 42 WSQ 286, 290 (2014).
43. Eli R. Green, *Debating Trans Inclusion in the Feminist Movement*, 10 J. Lesbian Stud. 231, 232 (2006).
44. Emma Heaney, *Women-Identified Women: Trans Women in 1970s Lesbian Feminist Organizing*, 3 TSQ 137, 138 (2016).
45. *Id.* at 140.
46. Green, *supra* note 43, at 234.
47. *Id.* at 235.
48. *Id.* at 236.
49. *Id.* at 238.
50. *Id.*
51. Emi Koyama, *Whose Feminism Is It Anyway? The Unspoken Racism of the Trans Inclusion Debate, in* The Transgender Studies Reader 699 (S. Stryker & S. Whittle eds., 2006).
52. Dominic Holden, *Michigan Music Festival That Excluded Transgender People To Shut Down*, Buzzfeed News (Apr. 22, 2015, 1:37 PM), https://www.buzzfeednews.com/article/dominicholden/michigan-music-festival-that-excluded-transgender-people-to.
53. Camilla Turner, *Bristol University Students Seek to Ban 'Terf' Speakers Who Question Transgender. Status of Women,* The Telegraph (Mar. 01, 2018, 9:00 PM), https://www.telegraph.co.uk/education/2018/03/01/bristol-university-students-seek-ban-terf-speakers-question/; Michelle Goldberg, *What is a Woman? The Dispute Between Radical Feminism and Transgenderism,* The New Yorker (July 28, 2014), https://www.newyorker.com/magazine/2014/08/04/woman-2.
54. Andrea Long Chu, *On Liking Women,* 30 N+1, https://nplusonemag.com/issue-30/essays/on-liking-women/.
55. Aniruddha Dutta, *Claiming Citizenship, Contesting Civility: The Institutional LGBT Movement and the Regulation of Gender/ Sexual Dissidence in West Bengal, India*, 4 Jindal Global Law Review 110 (2012).

56. Grace Banu, *Where Are the Archives of Our Dalit Trans Foremothers and Forefathers?*, The Print (Apr. 29, 2018, 10:51 AM), https://theprint.in/opinion/dalit-history-month/dalit-trans-resilience-is-a-fight-against-caste-and-patriarchy-though-we-are-missing-from-written-archives/53509/.
57. Semmalar, *supra* note 42, at 286.
58. Living Smile Vidya, *(Trans)gender and caste lived experience–Transphobia as a form of Brahminism: An Interview of Living Smile Vidya*, Sanhati (Jan. 26, 2013), http://sanhati.com/excerpted/6051/.
59. Semmalar, *supra* note 42, at 287.
60. *Id.*
61. Round Table India, *(Trans)gender and Caste Lived Experience - Transphobia as a Form of Brahminism: An Interview of Living Smile Vidya* (Mar. 02, 2013), https://www.roundtableindia.co.in/transgender-and-caste-lived-experience-transphobia-as-a-form-of-brahminism-an-interview-of-living-smile-vidya/.
62. Ina Goel, *Caste and Religion Create Barriers Within the Hijra Community*, The Wire (May 18, 2018), https://thewire.in/lgbtqia/caste-religion-hijra-community.
63. Sampoorna Network, *Trans, Gender Nonconforming & Intersex Collectives Strongly Condemn Kinnar Akhara's Support for Ram Temple at Ayodhya, India,* Sampoorna (Nov. 24, 2018), https://sampoornaindiablog.wordpress.com/2018/11/24/trans-gender-nonconforming-intersex-collectives-strongly-condemn-kinnar-akharas-support-for-ram-temple-at-ayodhya-india/.
64. Goel, *supra* note 62.
65. Gee Imaan Semmalar, *Why Trans Movements in India Must Be Anti-Caste*, Feminism in India (Dec. 26, 2017), https://feminisminindia.com/2017/12/28/trans-movements-india-caste/.
66. Jacques Derrida, Dissemination 61-172 (Barbara Johnson trans., 1981).
67. Oishik Sircar, *Spectacles of Emancipation: Reading Rights Differently in India's Legal Discourse*, 49 Osgoode Hall L.J. 527 (2012).
68. Elizabeth Flock, *The Law Breaker*, Forbes India (Dec. 26, 2009, 8:50 AM) https://www.forbesindia.com/article/person-of-the-year-09/the-law-breaker/8082/1.
69. These arguments have been drawn from Sircar, *supra* note 67.
70. One of the primary grounds of the Court's decision was that "lesbians, gays, bisexuals [and] transgenders" are a "miniscule fraction of the country's population". This implied that Section 377 of the Indian Penal Code could not be considered 'adequately discriminatory' as the LGBT community does not constitute a reasonably classifiable group of people, thus there was nothing to warrant the law being declared unconstitutional.
71. Sircar, *supra* note 23, at 15.
72. *Id.*
73. *Id.*
74. *Id.* at 16.
75. *Id.* at 14.

76. Dipika Jain, *Shifting Subjects of State Legibility: Gender Minorities and the Law in India*, 32 Berkeley J. Gender, L. & Just. 39, 48 (2017).
77. *Id.* at 57.
78. *See* Aniruddha Dutta & Raina Roy, *Decolonizing Transgender in India: Some Reflections*, 1 TSQ 320, 328 (2014), which notes the exclusion of trans-masculine identities and other local gender-variant people through the use of 'transgender' as a transnational umbrella term.
79. Jain, *supra* note 76, at 58.
80. *Id.* at 71.
81. *Id.* at 63.
82. *Id.* at 64.
83. Gee Imaan Semmalar, *Gender Outlawed: The Supreme Court Judgment on Third Gender and its Implications*, Round Table India (Apr. 19, 2014), https://www.roundtableindia.co.in/because-we-have-a-voice-too-the-supreme-court-judgment-on-third-gender-and-its-implications/.
84. *Id.*
85. *Id.*
86. Dipika Jain & Kimberly M. Rhoten, *Epistemic Injustice and Judicial Discourse on Transgender Rights in India: Uncovering Temporal Pluralism*, 26 Journal of Human Values 30 (2020).
87. *Id.* at 33.
88. *Id.* "The rights to be won from foil (i.e., stand in contrast to the binary) or freak (i.e., stand outside entirely of the binary) arguments are limited, as carving a positive from a negative so often is."
89. *Id.* at 44.
90. Michael Kirby & Ramesh Thakur, *Navtej Johar, A Verdict For All Times*, The Hindu (Dec. 31, 2018, 0:15 AM), https://www.thehindu.com/opinion/op-ed/navtej-johar-a-verdict-for-all-times/article25866598.ece; Priyanka Mittal & Neetu C. Sharma, *This is the Beginning of the End of Prejudice: Supreme Court*, LiveMint (Sep. 7, 2018, 1:56 PM), https://www.livemint.com/Politics/bRkgeh7EdUK5aeBHUb7YAM/Section-377-verdict-Supreme-Court-decriminalises-homosexual.html; Abhishyant Kidangoor, *India's Supreme Court Decriminalizes Homosexuality in a Historic Ruling for the LGBTQ Community*, Time (Sep. 6, 2018. 2:41 AM), https://time.com/5388231/india-decriminalizes-homosexuality-section-377/.
91. Akhil Kang, *SC Verdict on Section 377 Won't End Fight Against Inequality; Love Is As Much About Caste, Class and Religious Struggle*, Firstpost (Sep. 7, 2018, 11:39 AM), https://www.firstpost.com/india/sc-verdict-on-section-377-wont-end-fight-against-inequality-love-is-as-much-about-caste-class-and-religious-struggle-5126261.html.
92. Saptarshi Mandal, *Section 377: Whose Concerns Does The Judgment Address?*, EPW Engage (Sep. 15, 2018), https://www.epw.in/engage/article/section-377-whose-concerns-does-judgment.

93. Shreya I. Anasuya, *Beyond Section 377: What About Inequalities Within LGBTQ+ Groups?*, The Quint (Sep. 7, 2018. 1:20 PM), https://www.thequint.com/voices/opinion/section-377-supreme-court-verdict-queer-trans-community-rights.
94. Sai Sachin Ravikumar & Tanvi Mehta, *The Elite Engineers Leading a Challenge to India's Homosexuality Ban*, Reuters (July 18, 2018, 3:26 PM), https://www.reuters.com/article/us-india-lgbt-iit/the-elite-engineers-leading-a-challenge-to-indias-homosexuality-ban-idUSKBN1K812R.
95. Kang, *supra* note 91.
96. Nishant Upadhyay, *Hindu Nation and its Queers: Caste, Islamophobia, and De/coloniality in India*, 22 Interventions 464, 465-466 (2020).
97. Upendra Baxi, *Dignity in and with Naz, in* Law Like Love: Queer Perspectives on Law 246 (A. Narrain & A. Gupta eds., 2011).
98. Oishik Sircar, *Questions of Visibility*, 2 In Plainspeak 10 (2008).
99. Ashley Tellis, *Nothing to Celebrate About 377*, DNA (June 27, 2010, 12:57 AM), http://www.dnaindia.com/lifestyle/comment_nothing-to-celebrate-aboutsection-377_1401765.
100. These are identity categories that non-elite sexually marginalized persons use in India, instead of using the category 'gay'. Culturally, the performance of these identities is also very different from being just gay or homosexual.
101. Jason Fernandes, *The Dilemma After the Decision: Strays Thoughts After Gay Liberation*, DervishNotes (Aug. 18, 2009), http://dervishnotes.blogspot.com/2009/08/dilemma-after-decision-strays-thoughts.html.
102. Anjali Arondekar, *Time's Corpus: On Sexuality, Historiography and the Indian Penal Code, in* Comparatively Queer: Interrogating Identities Across Time and Culture 124 (Hayes et al. eds., 2010).
103. Wendy Brown, *Suffering the Paradoxes of Rights, in* Left Legalism/Left Critique 428 (W. Brown & J. Halley eds., 2002).
104. *See generally* Queering India: Same-Sex Love and Eroticism in Indian Culture and Society (Ruth Vanita ed., 2002); Because I Have a Voice: Queer Politics in India (Arvind Narrain & Gautam Bhan eds., 2005); Law Like Love: Queer Perspectives on Law (Arvind Narrain & Alok Gupta eds., 2011). An edited volume that attempted to move away from discussing sexualities from only an identitarian lens, but couldn't ultimately escape fixed notions of queer identities, is The Phobic and the Erotic: The Politics of Sexualities in Contemporary India (Brinda Bose & Subhabrata Bhattacharya eds., 2007). An edited volume that attains some success by not letting identity politics overshadow the engagement with critique is Menon, *supra* note 37 (though it does not offer a specific queer critique of sexualities).
105. J.K. Gibson-Graham, A Postcapitalist Politics xxxi-xxxii (2006).
106. Ashley Tellis, *Disrupting the Dinner Table: Re-thinking the 'Queer Movement' in Contemporary India*, 4 Jindal Global Law Review 142, 149 (2012).
107. *Id.* at 148.

108. *Id.* at 150.
109. Dutta, *supra* note 55, at 118.
110. *See* Svati P. Shah, *Queering Critiques of Neoliberalism in India: Urbanism and Inequality in the Era of Transnational "LGBTQ" Rights,* 47 ANTIPODE 635, 636 (2014).
111. Dutta, *supra* note 55, at 112.
112. *Id.* at 113.
113. Dutta & Roy, supra note 78, at 326.
114. *Id.* at 328.
115. Annie Gowen, *Transgender Activists in India Fight for Inclusion at Key Hindu Festival,* The Washington Post (Apr. 22, 2016), https://www.washingtonpost.com/world/asia_pacific/transgender-indians-see-key-hindu-festival-a-next-step-toward-inclusion/2016/04/22/7c76e258-0715-11e6-bfed-ef65dff5970d_story.html.
116. *Id.*
117. *Id.*
118. Semmalar, *supra* note 65.
119. *Id.*
120. *Trans, Gender Nonconforming & Intersex Collectives Strongly Condemn Kinnar Akhara's Support for Ram Temple at Ayodhya, India*, Orinam (Nov. 24, 2018), http://orinam.net/content/wp-content/uploads/2018/11/Trans-GNC-Intersex_Statement_Kinnar-Akhara_Ram-Temple.pdf.
121. *Id.*
122. The Bill has since come into force as law, and stands as the *Transgender Persons (Protection of Rights) Act, 2019.* It still provides reduced punishment for the rape and assault of transgender persons, lower than that given for cisgender women under the Indian Penal Code.
123. T/IS/GNC Statement, *supra* note 120, at 2.
124. *Id.*
125. Semmalar, *supra* note 65.
126. *See* Nikita Dhawan, *Homonationalism and State-Phobia: The Postcolonial Predicament of Queering Modernities', in* Queering Paradigms V: Queering Narratives of Modernity 52 (M. Viteri & M.L. Picq eds., 2016).
127. Brenda Cossman, Sexual Citizens: The Legal and Cultural Regulation of Sex and Belonging (2007).
128. Sircar, *supra* note 67.
129. Anjali Arondekar, *Time's Corpus: On Sexuality, Historiography and the Indian Penal Code, in* Comparatively Queer: Interrogating Identities Across Time and Culture 124 (Jarrod Hayes et al. eds., 2010).
130. *See generally* Nussbaum, *supra* note 28.
131. Sircar, *supra* note 67.
132. Semmalar, *supra* note 83.

CHAPTER 1

Multi-tasking Queer

Reflections on the Possibilities of Homosexual Dissidence in Law

Ratna Kapur

When I first began to write about sexuality in the context of violence against women and subsequently in the context of sex work and sex talk, my primary focus was to trace the critical genealogies that informed understandings of sexuality in the postcolonial world.[1] While my work was initially greatly influenced by the position of dominance feminism, in particular Catharine MacKinnon's scholarship, I began to question a position that focused almost exclusively on gender as the primary tool for feminist engagements with law.[2] The subsequent critiques of her work, especially by black feminists as well as those working on issues of sexuality, reinforced my concerns.[3]

Sexual violence was the primary focus of feminist engagements with law in the 1980s. In the 1990s, 'sexual subalterns', including gays and lesbians as well as sex workers, drew attention to the emergence of a diverse array of sexual subjects in India. The increased visibility of sexual subalterns challenged feminists on two fronts. The first was the equation of gender almost exclusively with the category of woman. Secondly, feminist scholars who addressed the issue of gender and sexuality in a more complicated way continued to do so within a heteronormative framework.[4] The failure to address the question of lesbianism or homosexuality was often met with an apology, thus staving off any critique of neglect or privilege.[5] The issue of sexuality has continued to trouble feminists, especially when it is addressed outside of the rather airtight compartments of gender categories and through the lens of violence, victimization and sexual negativity. The challenges posed by the increased visibility and advocacy of diverse sexual subjects has forced a deeper interrogation of the ways in which both sexuality and gender have operated within a matrix of power arrangements that also implicates the positions of progressive scholars and advocates. It was in this moment that I began a mapping of the critical genealogies that informed the legal regulation of sexuality as well as gender.[6]

Such a move enabled me to excavate how issues of sexuality were taken up within postcolonial contexts. The literature reveals how issues of law reform and violence against women were integral to the colonial encounter in the late nineteenth century and the national struggle for freedom. Historians have examined how issues of widow remarriage, rape, and the age of consent to marry were all taken up and understood within the context of the broader struggle for and assertion of the autonomy of the subjugated native, and efforts by the colonial power to extend its tentacles of power into the private domain in pursuit of its civilizing mission.[7] Locating issues of sexuality within these broader debates on tradition, nationalism, culture and the struggle for power provides the postcolonial scaffolding that frames these concerns.

It is against this historical backdrop and for these reasons that issues of rape, sexual assault, sexual harassment and sexual exploitation in the postcolonial present cannot be fully understood or explained within the terms of dominance feminism. Dominance feminism as articulated by Catharine MacKinnon posits that sexuality is constructed along the lines of female subordination and male domination.[8] As MacKinnon states: "what [women] have in common is not that our conditions have particularity in ways that matter. But we are all measured by a male standard for women, a standard that is not ours."[9] In her analysis, sexuality and sexual relations remain central to women's oppression: "If sexuality is central to women's definition and forced sex is central to sexuality, rape is indigenous, not exceptional, to women's social condition."[10] In her view, all women experience oppression at the hands of patriarchal power and she argues that power is invariably male.[11] In law, it is expressed through 'male laws' and 'male' systems of justice. Rape, sexual harassment, and other forms of sexual violence are used to generate gender and position men as superior and women as subordinate or inferior.[12] And heterosexuality has institutionalized the construction of male sexual dominance and female sexual submission. Thus, sexuality becomes the lynchpin of gender inequality.

MacKinnon's work has had an unparalleled influence on the feminist agenda in the international legal arena as well as on domestic feminist (and non-feminist) agendas that focus on violence against women. In contemporary India, feminist engagements with law have focused on sexual violence as a condition of female subordination and male domination.[13] While this is not to say that feminists have not been aware of the historical legacy that has framed understandings of sexual violence, in the arena of law particularly, sexuality continues to be framed within binary terms, where women are victims of male power. While such a position has been used to lobby for legal reform, it has aligned feminism with the regulatory state apparatus, primarily in the reform of criminal law. These interventions have resulted in a reinforcement of women as victims incapable of exercising sexual agency.[14] They have also left unproblematized normative understandings of female and male sexuality against which access to rights are determined. Juridical entitlements are contingent on conformity with sexual norms. This approach to sexual issues not only produces a perpetually traumatized sexual subject, it also renders other feminist positions almost inaudible. The critical genealogies within which the feminist project needs to be understood are totally marginalized.

While there is no question that women have struggled as victims to subvert power, this power has not emanated from a single source (men). The almost universal voice with which MacKinnon has cast the feminist position has also found many critics, including postcolonial feminist scholars. While these critiques are well-rehearsed in the literature, I elaborate briefly on the central concerns they raise.

Resistance to the colonial encounter was central to the experience of the subordination of women in the Asian subcontinent. This history cannot be understood simply in terms of the history of gender subordination or sexual violence perpetrated by men against women. It was also about broader economic and political subordination and the expropriation of other nations' labour, resources, land, raw materials and markets, and the exclusion of the native—both men and women—from sovereignty and legal entitlements. Resistance therefore had to be understood in terms of resistance to the imperial project and the processes of Empire, and not just as opposition to men.

At the same time, some postcolonial feminist scholars have complicated notions of agency as resistance, arguing that it remains primarily located within a logic that frames freedom within the liberal imaginary. They argue against the presumption that a universal desire for freedom and autonomy as prescribed by liberalism exists among women. They counter the idea that the end goal of resistance is confined to the toppling of the patriarchal order. Agency needs to be complicated, traced, unpacked, and understood in contexts that seem to be antithetical to the goals of feminism. For example, Saba Mahmood unpacks understandings of freedom and resistance within the context of Islamic women who practice veiling in the mosque movement in Egypt. Her discussion indicates how feminism has remained blind to articulations of agency that may seek liberation through practices that are neither comprehensible nor envisaged by liberal understandings of freedom, nor purely subversive or resistive.[15] Similarly, Gayatri Spivak calls for a feminism that does not seek to usurp the voice of the subaltern or demand that the subaltern speak in the voice of Western feminism. She uses the example of *sati,* not only to illustrate how colonialism was partly a mission by "white men to save brown women from brown men", but also to indicate the complicity of the white, Western woman in this endeavour. The move by feminists served to consolidate the sovereign notion of self within the liberal tradition. It constructed the sovereign subject it wanted, and its interventions as that of a benevolent saviour failed to attend to the claim of nativists that the women who commit the act of sati actually want to die.[16] These critiques caution against articulations of agency that merely reproduce the atomized liberal subject as the antidote to a victim-centred politics.

While postcolonial feminist scholars have problematized a politics of gender and sexuality based on the victim subject, other scholars have called for a 'break from feminism' in order to explore issues of sexuality through different analytical lenses. Janet Halley is the primary exponent of this position.[17] She sets out the central ingredients of what she identifies as the dominant strain of feminism, that is, 'governance feminism'. Halley describes governance feminism in the context of international criminal law addressing sexual violence as "a new feminist organizational style". Governance feminism is described as "muscular" and results in the "installation of feminists and feminist ideas in actual legal-institutional power."[18] It seeks to move feminist justice projects off the streets and into the state, and to harness institutional power. It seeks change from within mainstream institutions. The theoretical position of governance feminism is informed by dominance feminism. It operates against fixed anatomical categories of gender, a clear distinction between males and females, where female/feminine invariably exists in a situation of coercive domination by male/masculine in the area of sexuality. And it carries a brief for feminism. This brand of feminism has operated to marginalize other insights into the mechanics and operations of sexuality. While it may not be necessary to stage a break with feminism, Halley argues that it may be more productive to de-link from this particular strain of feminism that has become so prominent.[19]

In my own work, I have pursued a postcolonial feminist analysis of sexuality in and through the analytical category of sexual subalterns.[20] I argue in favour of critical genealogies which are historical and materially based, as well as discursively specific. The sexual subaltern traces sexual identities, practices, counter-normative discourses and histories that are hidden at the margins, partly because of the ways in which heteronormativity was produced in and through the colonial encounter. The sexual subaltern challenges some of the binary categories—male/female, victim/agent, heterosexual/homosexual—that characterize the field of sexuality as well as feminist studies.[21] While the category of the sexual subaltern includes all those practices and identities excluded or marginalized by sexual normativity, it is also an analytical device intended to unearth, expose, and challenge these very norms.

Amongst those who have been at the forefront of producing such challenges in India is the sex workers movement. The sex worker has instantiated herself into the debates on sexuality, trying to disinvest sexuality from its moral attachments, relational structures and gender binaries to produce a social space for sexual alterity and sexual pleasure. While the movement is dispersed and heterogeneous, one position has challenged the very terms of sexual normativity as a central obstacle to the full legibility of the sexual subject in the course of sex workers' agitation for sexual rights.[22] Framed within a postcolonial trajectory, this position also foregrounds the tensions between sexuality and culture, and how sex workers have challenged this opposition by complicating the relationship between sexuality and culture while also deconstructing the terms in which each is grounded. The sex workers operate as sexual subalterns to produce counter-narratives about sexuality that are obscured by both a dominance feminist lens as well as fossilized understandings of "Indian culture".[23]

Gays and lesbians have also been providing a challenge to the ways in which sexuality is understood within the public space, as well as complicating the terms of gender. The challenges by gays and lesbians mark a further stage in the production of multiple discourses on sexuality. Much like feminism, there have been colliding positions on how LGBT politics should be articulated in law. The term 'queer' has emerged as highly contested, with various constituents attributing different meanings and capacities to it. In the remainder of this paper, I unpack how the term 'queer' has come to be used in relation to law. I discuss whether the term performs the same work as sexual subaltern or if queer has become aligned with a more sanitized LGBT politics, based on a grid of fixed identities and positionalities. While the term queer seems to expand and contract depending on its time and location, I discuss how the elasticity of queer becomes cabined and somewhat confined when it arrives in the courtroom. In the last section, I provide a reading of the *Naz* decision and how the voice of the sexual subject emerges as somewhat muted when compared to the broader cultural and public spaces within which queer agitation has occurred.[24] What are the limits and possibilities of 'queer' in law? Can law be queered? And what exactly does queering law mean: inclusion, dissidence, subversion, or normalization?

EXHUMATION, RECOVERY AND RADICAL ALTERITY

Like the term 'sexual subaltern', the critical genealogies of the term 'queer' are important to understand in order to comprehend the work that queer does, or is capable of doing. The term queer has its origins primarily in Western scholarship,[25] and is, at times, used in a number of problematic ways.[26] The critical capacities of queer nevertheless have relevance within a postcolonial context as its critical guise is closely aligned with postcolonial theory.

While there has been a good deal of writing on homosexuality in the 1980s and 90s in India, most of it was in the form of anthologies, memoirs, and fiction.[27] The primary impulse of this writing was to validate the existence of lesbians and gays in Indian history and Indian culture.[28] The desire to ensure that homosexuality emerged as legitimate, familiar and respectable required excavation work and a tracing of this subject in some long-lost ancient Indian cultural past.

The term queer was rarely used, and most writing tended to focus on lesbian and gay identities. The work of Ruth Vanita and Saleem Kidwai was foremost in locating lesbian and gay identities within the historical context of India, drawing on what they describe as a 2000-year-old tradition of homosexuality. The text provides details of homoerotic love in the historical traditions of India. The authors attribute the erasure or marginalization of such literature and expressions of love primarily to the imposition of the British anti-sodomy law in India, which imported a Victorian morality. The book served, in part, to counter the frequently alleged homophobic myth that homosexuality was an import and not a part of Indian cultural values.

In the introduction to the text, Kidwai and Vanita state their conscious decision not to use the term queer in their work. They understand the term as encompassing "unconventional" or "strange" sexual behaviour and argue that in the texts they deal with, the behaviours and people are "not only not represented as strange or deviant, but are upheld by the texts as admirable."[29] Somewhat contradictorily, they go on to state that the term queer is "too wide" for their purposes as it includes all sorts of behaviour, "from fetishism to exhibitionism", not included in their study. While the authors acknowledge that some of the work included in their book that refers to sex change could be read as being about transgender, transsexual or intersex subjects, they insist that their focus is on the "homoerotic" dimensions of sexuality. There is a clear desire to distance their work from what they regard as more edgy practices associated with the term 'queer'. Same-sex love is confined primarily to viewing gender in binary terms, and homoeroticism is equated with gay and lesbian sexual practices. It exhumes the homosexual body and seeks to place same-sex practices on equal terms with heterosexual love and thus continues to operate along a hetero/homo binary. Kidwai and Vanita's work is indicative of the reluctance to use the term queer, partly out of a concern that its ostensible association with more extreme and deviant sexuality as well as its confusion of gender identities will deflect attention from the more well-defined categories of same-sex relationships.

During the course of the past decade, the term 'queer' has acquired considerable prominence in a number of postcolonial scholarly and theoretical texts. It has become the new buzzword of most academics and activists working in the field of sexuality and sexuality studies. And the meaning ascribed to queer has multiplied and taken on a number of hues. Arvind Narrain and Alok Gupta develop an argument in favour of a queer perspective on law where queer is intended to engage in multitasking.[30] They present an argument for recovering queer voices from a putatively more tolerant pre-colonial era when they were ostensibly not subject to official disciplinary regulation. They argue in favour of performing queer intersections where queer aligns with other excluded subaltern voices. In both instances, the authors are in search of a subject who can speak, without contemplating the impossibility of such a position.[31]

Sometimes they simply use the term as a substitute for LGBT. For example, the authors state that the *Naz* decision marked the beginning of the process by which "queer people" became the subjects of rights.[32] The term 'queer people' is repeatedly used as an identity category. It is a somewhat nostalgic turn where queer remains structured along fixed notions of identity and operates as an umbrella term that embraces diversity. At other moments, the authors clearly intend the term 'queer' to also perform a more critical function.

Queer politics does not speak only of the issues of these communities (lesbian, gay, bisexual, transgender) as 'minority issues', but instead speaks of larger understandings of gender and sexuality in our society that affect us all, regardless of our sexual orientation. It speaks of sexuality as intrinsically and inevitably connected with the politics of class, gender, caste, religion and so on, thereby acknowledging other movements and also demanding inclusion within them.[33]

In its critical guise, queer emerges as a normatively disruptive concept. The authors argue that the challenge to Section 377 not only generated concerns over the legitimizing of non-procreative sex, but also about "forms of intimacy which the social order finds disturbing."[34] Such transgressions are regarded as having a relational affinity to other forms of transgression. The authors thus locate the queer struggle within larger struggles against social subordination. As the authors argue, "what links queer people to couples who love across caste and community lines is the fact that both are exercising their right to love at enormous personal risk and in the process, disrupting existing lines of social authority."[35]

While there are constant slippages back into aligning queer with an identity category, which renders its usage confused and awkward at times,[36] it is queer's critical features that inscribe it with disruptive and transformative possibilities. It is in the recognition of the politics of love as transgressing social norms and dominant heteronormative practices where the analysis is strongest. The authors refer to the killings that take place to avenge "loss of honour" when lovers transgress the boundaries of caste, religion, as well as sexuality.[37] It is this defiance of norms and practices and the formation of radical alternative alliances that provides queer with a more robust, critical impulse in this text. Perhaps a central underlying tension that exists over the use of the term queer is the desire to disassociate or de-link homosexuality from its Western moorings and to situate it within the national and historical consciousness of postcolonial India.[38] Such a recovery of tradition has the potential to refute allegations that homosexuality is a Western contaminant and that the phobias associated with homosexuality are Western imports, introduced through legal codes and medical texts as well as a Victorian sensibility.[39] While securing legitimacy becomes an important political end goal, in the process sexuality becomes an important site for state regulation to protect national interests.[40] Such regulation includes enabling "good" homosexuals, who are regarded as respectable and encouraged to behave through state prescriptions of normality, and penalizing "bad" homosexuals, who continue to be cast as deviant.[41]

While there is an internal move to establish the legitimacy of same-sex desire, there is, at the same time, an equally intense desire to counter hegemonic Euro-American signifiers for same-sex love/ non-heterosexual desire, which are fast becoming the prescribed blueprint across the world.[42] The prescriptive gay subject is based on specific assumptions, including the idea that this subject exists in opposition to heterosexuality and that the fulfilment of same-sex desire and identity can be found through public visibility as well as a departure from heteronormative structures and the patriarchal institutions of the family. This powerful articulation of the end goals of same-sex desire marginalizes and de-legitimates other articulations and subjectivities in non-Euro-American contexts.[43] The ultimate performance of this identity rests in an "out of the closet" LGBT identity that is prescribed as the antidote for all Third World settings. A strategy based on the recovery of queer voices or same-sex desire is not up to the task of countering the newly emerging hegemonic, colonizing queer.

There is a proliferation of scholarship that rejects this mode of recovery as it does not engage the complexities of nationalist as well as neo-colonizing moves that enact the erasure of same-sex desire in the postcolonial context. Gayatri Gopinath dislodges fixed, prescriptive understandings of same-sex desire, using a "queer diaspora" framework, and her specific focus is on queer female diasporic subjectivity.[44] In order to understand the relationship between the diaspora, nationalism and the processes of transnational capitalism and globalization, Gopinath argues that it is critical to recognize how these linkages are mediated through powerfully gendered and sexualized discourses. Her understanding of queer examines recognizable cultural texts such as musical genres, films, novels and videos that are both transnational as well as rooted in the politics of the local.[45]

In her discussion of Hindi cinema, Gopinath illustrates how a genre that has functioned as a central way in which the homeland, nostalgically invoked in diasporic communities, also produces space for the production and representation of queer female desire.[46] Such readings are particularly evident in the song and dance sequences that constitute a central part of Hindi formula films which, given their detached existence from the exigencies of a coherent narrative, are amenable to dissemination independent of the film.[47] She examines how such readings are lost in translation and abruptly closed in the work of female South Asian diasporic filmmakers operating within the realist demands of Hollywood.[48] She traces this absence in the context of popular films such as Mira Nair's *Monsoon Wedding* (2001) or Gurinder Chadha's *Bend it Like Beckham* (2002), as well as Deepa Mehta's *Bollywood/Hollywood* (2001), illustrating how each film ends up being complicit with ideologically oppositional conservative agendas. The queer female subject is effaced or disavowed from any possibilities, often left out in the exchange between a feminist focus on gender transgression at the cost of transgressive sexuality. In all three films, queerness is displaced onto a male figure by these avowedly feminist South Asian filmmakers, in contrast to the female homoeroticism made possible in Hindi films.[49] The salience of Gopinath's focus on queer female subjectivities in popular culture is that not only does it disrupt the representations of nationalist, jingoistic, and anti-foreign narratives that are closely aligned with the Indian national identity,[50] it also disrupts the male-male relationship that finds its way into such narratives as a part and parcel of the patriarchal, national narrative.

Gopinath offers a postcolonial, queer reading that stands in sharp contrast to the ideological grain of progressive, liberal, feminist and First World signifiers of non-heterosexual sexualities. Tracing a "lesbian" in Hindi cinema would simply reproduce the logic of visibility dominant in Euro-American constructions of gay and lesbian identity.[51] Gopinath resists any effort to resurrect a Third World, authentic lesbian subject as a counter to the franchise of the 'gay international' emerging from within a Euro-American context, which is going viral as well as global. Queer is deployed by Gopinath to disrupt homonormative imaginings and prescriptions of same-sex desire or the 'Rainbow Flag' world view which erase such possibilities. Her position is not to eulogize the formation of a postcolonial, queer, female subject within Indian popular culture, but rather to illustrate how such formations are capable of both migrating to and pollinating other cultural spaces in ways that do not fit within a homosexual/heterosexual, male/female binary. Echoing the analyses Mahmood and Spivak offer, she clearly states that these translations are not always progressive or liberating.

Gopinath centres queer female sexual subjectivity, not through the excavation of some long-lost, submerged lesbian existence, but rather in spaces where the initial impression implies the near impossibility of the existence of such desire and subjectivity. She deploys what she describes as a "scavenger" methodology to unearth "evidence of queer diasporic lives and cultures, and the oppositional strategies they enact in the most unlikely places."[52]

Jasbir Puar's work has also complicated the deployment of queer, moving beyond the "recovery" mode of analysis and also the "gay international", both of which work with fixed categories. She deploys queer in relation to assemblages as opposed to binaries or excavations. Puar tracks how queer can be deployed in ways that are complicit with dominant formations of sexuality.[53] Queer assemblages consist of US sexual exceptionalism, which relates to the successful management of life with regard to people, something that is both heteronormative and homonormative. This exceptionalism operates to include some homosexuals, that is, those who conform or assimilate. Part of the assimilative project is the indoctrination of the sexual subject into a belief in the superiority and exceptionalism of the US as a nation and a culture.

In Puar's work, queer operates in relation to sexuality in the way gender has operated in relation to governance feminism. As Janet Halley has discussed in governance feminism, gender has aligned with the regulatory apparatus of the state and walks in the corridors of power. In a similar way, queer has become integral to the way in which imperial or US exceptionalism is constructed—as democratic, inclusive, liberal and exportable. It is implicated in dominant formations, and colludes with a nationalist narrative and representation of American exceptionalism that reinforces the US as a culturally and civilizationally superior state. Examining responses to the torture in Abu Ghraib prison, Puar illustrates how queer assemblages provide a way in which to understand what is excluded or marginalized in assessments based exclusively on homophobia. These include the racial and sexist dimensions that fall out of the narratives, as well as the uniformly unquestioned position that homophobia and sexual repression are the default position of the cultural other—that is, the Islamic.

Puar opens up the possibility of unpacking the ways in which postcolonial sexual subjectivities are constructed and deployed, and moves us away from a thesis based exclusively on sexual repression or sexual liberation. While sexual repression has been a primary mode of characterizing the native subject and has served as a justification for ostensibly liberating imperial interventions, the sexual liberation thesis based on a rights agenda does not examine how such moves reinforce the state's regulatory authority and freeze sexual subjectivities. The work of Gopinath and Puar are important interventions in how queer has been and can be deployed. These scholars trace the ways in which the techniques of gender and sexuality operate within a matrix of power arrangements, and use a queer lens to understand the work being done by these techniques.

Queering Naz

The *Naz* decision has attracted considerable scholarly and public attention. Within moments of the decision being pronounced by the Delhi High Court, there was euphoria in the courtroom, which was packed with advocates, community activists, and lawyers. Over the days that followed the court's pronouncement, gays, lesbians, transgender persons and others across the country embraced the decision. Couples declared that they now had the right to marry, and publicly exchanged garlands and oaths in a bid to provide an expansive meaning to the decision. While the actual decision limited the scope of the sodomy provision so that it applied only to non-consensual sexual contact, the meaning that the decision acquired in public discourse transcended this narrow position.

In revisiting the implications of *Naz*, some scholars have declared it an example of "queering the law", yet it is not at all clear what is meant by the phrase. Once the issue of same-sex desire and non-normative sexuality enters the courtroom, is it not the law that determines the level of complexity that will be permitted? In fact, the *Naz* decision only serves to read down Section 377 so as to decriminalize consensual sexual acts in private. It is not a wholesale endorsement of the homosexual person as a legible subject eligible for juridical entitlements. Does this mean that the best that can be hoped for is a form of strategic engagement with the law? But if strategic arguments produce nothing more than a de-sexualized, sanitized, liberal subject, what does such an outcome say about the impact of radical advocacy? Or is the law simply one of many arenas with which to engage? How is advocacy around same-sex desire complicit in reproducing the very homosexual/heterosexual binary its legal engagements set out to challenge?

Posing these questions is not to suggest that there is no queering that takes place in law. When the sexual subject comes to the law, her presence reveals not only the level of legal norms' dexterity, but also the elasticity of the legal subject. The sexual subject is not a fixed anatomical category. Her elasticity is revealed by the very fact that this subject has to be constantly reproduced and iterated in order to endure. At the same time, when she enters the court and the terrain of legal discourse, the extent of the queering is almost immediately limited. The conclusion is not then that the law cannot be queered, only that it is a more constrained, unreflective space.

Narrain locates the queering of law explicitly in terms of the idea of sex without conception, which had historically been viewed as a perversion or abhorrent crime. Yet he then lapses into talking about gays and lesbians as an identity category and does not develop the more provocative and challenging call to queer the law. In Narrain and Gupta's reading of the *Naz* decision, the victory is perceived purely in terms of formal rights and juridical entitlements rather than as a discursive space where the meanings associated with sexuality and sexual subjectivity are continuously contested and refashioned.[54] They declare that the *Naz* judgment heralds a shift from a discourse of criminality to a discourse of dignity, privacy and inclusiveness. While the decision rescues the sexual subject from the postcolonial closet, it also operates to subjugate the sexual subject to the regulatory apparatus of the state. The end result is not necessarily a liberated sexual subject, but one who is regulated and sequestered in and through the liberal discourse of tolerance.[55]

It is arguable that even an uncomplicated approach to sexual subjectivity, based on identity and framed within the heterosexual/homosexual binary, is to be welcomed given the prevailing hostility towards homosexuality and the carriers of virulent homophobia that continue to circulate. Such a strategy was invoked in the Supreme Court hearing on the challenge to the *Naz* decision. Orthodox and conservative religious groups rushed to the Supreme Court crying that religion and 'Indian cultural values' were in danger, and disavowed the existence of gays and lesbians in 'Indian culture'. During the course of the arguments in the Supreme Court, the judges expressed concern over, and sought evidence of, the extent to which homosexuality as well as non-procreative, non-normative sexual practices were validated in Indian culture and scriptures.

The Naz Foundation, as well as a host of interveners seeking the validation of the Delhi High Court decision, relied on fixed categories of homosexuality and heterosexuality to counter the narrow view of Indian culture put forward by the appellants. They argued that India's sexual past, cast primarily in Hindu terms, was open, inclusive, diverse and non-judgmental. The near glorification of India's sexual past was contrasted against the colonial imposition of Section 377 of the Indian Penal Code of 1860 that criminalized same-sex as well non-procreative sexual activities, and was driven by extremely conservative and puritanical Victorian cultural and sexual norms. The work of Vanita and Kidwai, as well as references to the *Manusmriti*, *Kama Sutra*, and *Arthashastra*, were all submitted to the Court in a bid primarily to validate the existence of homosexuality as an identitarian category in some long-lost, ancient Indian (read

Hindu) past.[56] While the full implications of such a strategy were seen only after the Court delivered its judgment, some of the interveners in the case, including gay and lesbian groups, argued that it was strategically essential to assert homosexuality as an identitarian category and prove its existence in India's cultural past to counter the disavowals and fiercely homophobic positions of orthodox groups. Confronted with a conservative judiciary and bench lacking a complicated understanding of sexuality, some intervenors argued that the aesthetic "politics of queering" would not be sufficient to counter deeply held beliefs based on a narrow and static understanding of 'Indian cultural values' and the rigid binaries of homosexuality and heterosexuality.

The fact that homosexuality is out of the postcolonial closet is to be celebrated, and the terms of its construction can now be debated. There still remains a need to interrogate whether the *Naz* decision incorporates the gay into a linear regulatory framework that cabins and confines, or operates to liberate and emancipate it. Is it better to breach the borders of heteronormativity or to remain content with a victory that produces tolerance of gay and lesbian sexual subjects, though not as rights-deserving citizens?[57]

It may be that, in the courtroom, there is a need to invoke 'strategic essentialism', as argued by Gayatri Spivak. It is necessary to reflect on which arguments have more subversive potential, as well as which arguments will resonate with the judges. Where there is space for creativity in legal arguments, it should be pursued in a manner that ensures that queer identity is somehow sustained and does not disappear into the shadows of the law. Perhaps one place where these arguments can be located is within the family. In response to the appeal against the *Naz* decision, parents of gays and lesbians requested the Supreme Court to direct the state to stop criminalizing their children. The move reaffirms family values, that is, the love of one's children, while at the same time subverting the notion of family as confined to a heteronormative, procreative order. In some ways, the move may be totally assimilating, as the arguments presented remain within, albeit on the peripheries of, familial norms.

After all, it is not as if gays and lesbians are asking to have kids. At the same time, such an argument may constitute precisely the kind of epistemological breach that creates possibilities for more radical arguments to be made and heard.

Once the case moves out of the courtroom, the entire issue morphs into a project that is much bigger and more spectacular. In the public space, homosexuals continue to claim space and are visible in ways that transgress the borders of heteronormativity in academic scholarship and debate,[58] in theatre and cinema,[59] and on the streets.

HOMOSEXUAL DISSIDENCE

This discussion brings us back to Puar's analysis. Are gays and lesbians being included in the fabric of a nation-state on terms that reinforce its regulatory authority? The High Court decision rejects exclusion from the state, but directs inclusion on terms that are consistent with the nationalist agenda of the Indian state, as well as with sexual normativity. It is precisely these moments that remind us of Foucault's interrogation of the revolutionary potential of homosexual sex. The law may not be a site where a breach in what is imaginable or possible can be inaugurated. It can, however, serve as a site where a queer politics can be partly forged, and radical kinships formed.[60]

The move towards radical kinship requires a move away from normative relationships such as marriage, monogamy, or homosexual exceptionalism.[61] According to Foucault, what is required is a "queering" of community, kinship, and sociality.[62] This queering can be produced by imagining homosexuality as a third position that takes us away from the binary categories of man/woman, male/female and masculine/feminine which sustain the heteronormative paradigm. This call holds within it the possibility of an open coalition with a range of fugitives, "an open assemblage that permits [...] multiple convergences and divergences."[63] It is this opposition to binary thought that needs to be foregrounded, rather than a focus on sexual acts and identities which, given its concern with the criminalization of a sexual act (sodomy), is what the *Naz* decision does.

Leela Gandhi provides an innovative argument on how rupture can be produced, as well as how affective communities can emerge. Drawing on the historical context of Empire, which introduced a virulent strain of homosexual anxiety or homophobia within the domestic space as well as within the colonies, Gandhi reveals how such moves simultaneously produced dissidence and introduced the possibility for wide-ranging political and epistemological transformation.[64] Her discussion builds on the work of Monique Wittig, who argues that heteronormativity is a closed, masculine economy where the feminine is banished, repressed or effaced from the modes of production and signification.[65] Wittig posits homosexuality as a third position operating outside of the binary of sex and securing a utopian space for the activity of homosexual identification.[66] Gandhi brings this analysis to the postcolonial context, arguing that Empire and the anti-colonial nation were both profoundly heteronormative projects. While the Empire privileged masculinity, it simultaneously cast the native as 'effeminate'. The native struggled to recuperate his lost masculinity, heralding the onset of "postcolonial heteronormativity" and simultaneously producing an aggressive and internalized homophobia.[67] Gandhi makes the case that a homosexual dissidence emerged as a utopian space that refused the polarities of gender and withheld its consent from both the nationalist and imperial social contract.

This moment of dissidence is reflected in the career of Edward Carpenter, a nineteenth century social reformer in Britain. Gandhi maps the way in which his political and ethical stands against imperial exploitation and Empire, amongst many other issues, were informed by his homosexuality. She traces Carpenter's call for the ruin of "fatuous Empires" as emerging from his homosexual location and accompanying sympathies with the repressed. His place on the margins produced an affinity for the fugitive or outcast. Gandhi posits the idea that homosexuality operated within anti-colonial thought;

that it was constitutively anti-colonial. The alliance of this outside position with fugitives and estranged sections of societies revealed a range of affectional possibilities.

Being excluded from the space of civilized community and a privileged circle of certain kinds of human beings and human alliances, the homosexual is denied inclusion and legitimacy. This subject belongs to a crowd of outcasts, which includes the colonial subject. This location compels the homosexual to reject the elite and exclusive space of civilized community and argue for radical, alternative kinship and alliances. Gandhi's arguments present homosexual politics as based not on sex acts or sexuality, but a critique of Empire.[68] While it may be argued that such a position represents a form of sexual evasiveness, Gandhi is not simply providing a justification for Carpenter's sexual equivocation. While homosexual sex acts may demand visibility and an aggressive strategy of "show and tell" in a homophobic world, such a focus obscures that which is queer about Gandhi's work—the productive possibilities of homosexuality in relation to anti-colonial nationalism.[69]

Gandhi's focus on Carpenter's anti-colonial stand reads queer not in terms of a sex act, nor sex as the repository of sexual insurrection. Queer politics are to be located in the unconventional alliances or radical relationships that may be regarded as intolerable or not normalizing. Gandhi's position provides a serious challenge to the "sex *qua* sex (or homosexuality-only-for-the-sake-of-homosexual-sex) as a viable or effective form of autonomy or resistance."[70] Sex no longer becomes the basis of a claim; rather, we are encouraged to seek out homosexual exceptionalism that transforms not only the conditions under which sex takes place, but also all the attending relationships and alliances implicated in the process of normalization.

The significance of Gandhi's work for queer politics or queering the law lies in not restricting it to a particular sexual organ with a special status. Foucault argues that such an argument enables the state to legislate particular parts of the body that are marked as sexual, such as the vagina or penis, differentiating them from the hand, hair or eyes.[71] In the process, the regulatory power of the state is brought into direct contact with the sexual organ, imbuing it with a specific meaning. In Foucauldian terms, sex is not simply something one has or a "static description of what one is".[72] It is the effect of the regulatory norm. And in terms of legal engagements, those who are not produced as fully formed subjects, those who are abject beings, inhabit a zone outside of the circumscribed domain of the legitimate or legible subject.[73] The legitimate subject comes into being partly through the repudiation of the abject subject. Queering lies in this repudiation and the subsequent emergence of the abject subject. The alliance between these abject subjects, the very possibilities of affectional kinship that Narrain and Gupta touch upon but do not fully develop, become the recipe for a queer politics that is no longer limited by the physical, the form, or the sex act.

CONCLUSION

The postcolonial theoretical arguments presented by Puar, Gopinath and Gandhi draw on the anti-resistant position of Foucault, who refuses to credit power as an agency of sexual repression or refusal. The modern state has witnessed a discursive explosion of sexualities rather than sexual prohibitions and increased sexual repression.[74] The emergence of Victorian prudery was an incitement to speak about sex in explicit detail and write about it voluminously.[75] Foucault challenges the idea that the proliferation of sexuality is always resistive or antagonistic to power. Instead, it is a complex relationship in which sexuality is invariably implicated in the production of power. The proliferation of sexualities cannot be declared revolutionary or autonomous. Rather, sexualities are constituted by the very apparatus of power that they seek to counter. Homosexuality itself has claimed legitimacy on the basis of the very natural disposition used to excoriate it. Similarly, as Gandhi argues, the anti-colonial nation-state could be regarded as being implicated in the "very imperial state from which it originally coveted its autonomy."[76]

The *Naz* decision, with its specific focus on the sex act of sodomy, becomes implicated in the production of power through its aggressive visibility and vocalization, and ultimately collaborates with the very power it sets out to challenge. It is not a viable form of resistance, but a means for assimilation and co-optation. Elsewhere, I have written about how the proliferation of sex speech and sex acts has come to be implicated in the neoliberal market and aligned with the regulatory power of the state, rather than producing an emancipated sexual subject.[77]

The idea of homosexuality as a third position has many possible trajectories. It can be a utopian space that challenges the sex binary on which sexual relationships are conducted. To withdraw from this binary opens up possibilities of developing radical alternative associations and a convergence of those who are divergent.[78]

If homosexual dissidence is not about sex, then what is its potential? It opens up the possibility of a queering not confined to equating men with being gay and women with being lesbian. The homosexual disconnects from the male/female, masculine/feminine binary logic and holds out political possibilities not confined to the specifics of a sex act. The homosexual demonstrates a gender ambiguity. The space produced includes the *Ardhnarishvara*, the one who is two-sexed, or the possibility of asceticism as well as the spiritual as manifested in the music and poetry of the Sufi tradition, and even the renunciate, who is celibate. Linking homosexuality to a tradition historically projected as backward and uncivilized brings it into a close alliance with that which is different and indeterminate, while also rejecting heteronormative masculinity. In the process, family, marriage, procreation, and monogamy are all challenged.

The third space may become the space for fomenting a queer politics that does not become just another letter at the end of the LGBT acronym, but where radical alterity becomes possible through alliances not trapped within paralyzing and essentializing binaries. It offers a trajectory for queering that enables many more spaces for fugitives to flourish, while also remaining attentive to the operations of power in which this occurs. When the post-colony finds freedom, the alliance is ruptured, revealing its temporariness and the strategic value that lies at its core. Similarly, radical kinships and the third space opened up by the homosexual disintegrate at the moment of their transition into full, legible subjectivity, where the skin of alterity has been shed. Whether this experience is carried into the space of legitimate subjectivity, thereby questioning the terms on which legitimacy is acquired, remains uncertain. In other words, whether queer loses its queerness is never fully certain. And hence the insurrectional possibilities of queerness remain.[79]

NOTES

1. Ratna Kapur, *A Love Song to Our Mongrel Selves: Hybridity, Sexuality and the Law,* 8 Soc. Legal Stud. 353 (1999); Ratna Kapur, *The Tragedy of Victimization Rhetoric: Resurrecting the "Native" Subject in International/Post-Colonial Feminist Legal Politics,* 15 Harv. Hum. Rts. J. 1 (2002); Ratna Kapur, *The Prurient Postcolonial: The Legal Regulation of Sexual Speech, in* The Phobic and the Erotic: The Politics of Sexualities in Contemporary India 235-54 (B. Bose & S. Bhattacharya eds., 2007).
2. Ratna Kapur, Erotic Justice: Law and the New Politics of Postcolonialism 95-136 (2005).
3. Angela Harris, *Race and Essentialism in Feminist Legal Theory,* 42 Stan. L. Rev. 581 (1991); Janet Halley, Split Decisions: How and Why to Take a Break from Feminism (2008).
4. *See* A Question of Silence: The Sexual Economies of Modern India (Mary John & Janaki Nair eds., 2000); Social Reform, Sexuality and the State (Patricia Uberoi ed., 1996); Geetanjali Gangoli, Indian Feminisms: Law, Patriarchies and Violence in India 57-78 (2007); Between Tradition, Counter Tradition and Heresy: Contributions in Honour of Vina Mazumdar (Latika Sarkar et al. eds., 2002); Kalpana Kannabiran & Vasantha Kannabiran, De-Eroticising Assault: Essays on Modesty, Honour and Power 68-104 (2005).
5. *See* John & Nair, *supra* note 4, at 36.
6. Kapur, *supra* note 2, at 13-50.
7. *See* Tanika Sarkar, Hindu Widow, Hindu Wife: Community, Religion, and Cultural Nationalism (2001); Mrinalini Sinha, The Manly Englishman and the Effeminate Bengali 138-180 (1995); Ania Loomba, *Dead Women Tell No Tales: Issues of Female Subjectivity, Subaltern Agency, and Tradition in Colonial and Postcolonial Writings of Widow Immolation in India,* 36 History Workshop J. 209, 212 (1993).

8. Catharine MacKinnon, *Feminism, Marxism, Method and the State: An Agenda for Theory*, 7 Signs 515 (1982).
9. Catharine MacKinnon, Feminism Unmodified: Discourses on Life and Law 76 (1987).
10. *Id.* at 172.
11. Catharine MacKinnon, *Rape, Genocide, and Women's Human Rights, in* Mass Rape: The War Against Women in Bosnia-Herzegovina 183-96 (A. Stiglmeyer ed., 1994); Catharine MacKinnon, *Crimes Of War, Crimes Of Peace, in* On Human Rights: The Oxford Amnesty Lectures 83-109 (S. Shute & S. Hurley eds., 1993); Catharine MacKinnon, *On Torture: A Feminist Perspective on Human Rights, in* Human Rights in the Twenty-First Century: A Global Challenge (K. Mahoney & P. Mahoney eds., 1992); *see also* Janet Halley, *Rape at Rome: Feminist Interventions in the Criminalization of Sex-Related Violence in Positive International Criminal Law,* 30 Mich. J. Int'l L. 1 (2009).
12. MacKinnon, *supra* note 8, at 515.
13. Ratna Kapur, *Slutwalk Couture and Pink Chaddis: The Postcolonial Politics pf Feminism Lite*, 20 Feminist Legal Stud. 1 (2012).
14. Third Wave Feminism: A Critical Exploration (Stacy Gillis et al. eds., 2007). Third Wave Feminism in Western scholarship has drawn specific attention to the issue of sexual agency and how female sexual pleasure found little to no space for articulation in a politics focused on sexual violence and victimization.
15. Saba Mahmood, The Politics of Piety: The Islamic Revival and the Feminist Subject 9 (2005). As Mahmood states, "Does the category of resistance impose a teleology of progressive politics on the analytics of power–a teleology that makes it hard for us to see and understand forms of being and action that are not necessarily encapsulated by the narrative of subversion and inscription of norms?"
16. Gayatri C. Spivak, *Can the Subaltern Speak?, in* Marxism and the Interpretation of Culture 308 (C. Nelson & L. Grossberg eds., 1988).
17. Halley, *supra* note 3; Halley, *supra* note 11; *see also* Janet Halley et al., *From the International to the Local in Feminist Legal Reponses to Rape, Prostitution/Sex Work, and Sex Trafficking: Four Studies in Contemporary Governance Feminism,* 29 HARV. J.L. & Gender 335 (2006).
18. Halley, supra note 11, at 3; Halley et al., supra note 17, at 340. While these muscular formations are generally in the form of non-governmental organizations, they are not exclusively so. *See also* Halley, *supra* note 3, at 20-22.
19 Judith Butler, Gender Trouble: Feminism and the Subversion of Identity (1990); Eve Sedgwick, Epistemology of the Closet (1990). Both scholars have developed analyses of both gender and sexuality which do not adhere to the strain of feminism critiqued by Halley.
20. Kapur, *supra* note 2, at 20-28.
21. Rosalind O'Hanlon, *Recovering the Subject: Subaltern Studies and Histories of Resistance in Colonial South Asia, in* Mapping Subaltern Studies and the

Postcolonial 72-115 (V. Chaturvedi ed., 2000); Dipesh Chakrabarty, *Radical Histories and Questions of Enlightenment Rationalism: Some Recent Critique of Subaltern Studies, in* Mapping Subaltern Studies and the Postcolonial 256-280 (V. Chaturvedi ed., 2000).

The subaltern studies project was initially focused on capturing the nuances of the agency of the colonized by foregrounding spaces of resistance in the discourse of anti-colonialism. The project was initially grounded in historical materialism and a search for an essential peasant consciousness. The project ultimately bifurcated, with the emergence of subaltern critiques that sought to challenge all traditions and disciplines defined within the logic or rationale of the Enlightenment project. It moved away from a preoccupation with the idea of a peasant as an autonomous political subject who writes her own history and an economic analysis as the primary zone of power, to unpack the multiple sites and locations of power through a discursive and textual analysis. The sexual subaltern emerges from this tradition, which regards subaltern as a critique rather than an identitarian category.

22. *See for example* the Durbar Mahila Samanwaya Committee's website: www.durbar.org. The Unstoppable Movement for Women's Equality is an initiative that emerged from the Sonagachi HIV/AIDS Intervention Project in Calcutta. It is a collective of men, women and transgender sex workers and demands the decriminalization of adult sex work, removal of stigma from non-normative sexual practices and performances, and the right to form a trade union. *See also* Kamala Kempadoo, Global Sex Workers: Rights, Resistance and Redefinition (1998); Jo Doezema, Sex Slaves and Discourse Masters (2010); Prabha Kotiswaran, Dangerous Sex, Invisible Labour: Sex Work and the Law in India (2011).
23. Kapur, *supra* note 2, at 132-34.
24. Naz Foundation v Govt. of NCT of Delhi, (2009) 160 DLT 277 (where the court read down the scope of Section 377 of the Indian Penal Code, 1860, which criminalizes sodomy, holding that it only applied to non-consensual sexual conduct).
25. Sedgwick, *supra* note 19; Butler, *supra* note 19; Gayle Rubin, *Thinking Sex: Notes for a Radical Theory of the Politics of Sexuality, in* The Lesbian & Gay Studies Reader 3 (H. Abelove et al. eds., 1993).
26. *See* Judith Butler, *Critically Queer*, 1 GLQ 17 (1993). For example, Judith Butler discusses how queer has historically been deployed as a homophobic expression for the purposes of shaming. She interrogates queer's capacity to be taken up and reclaimed, and critiques the ways in which the term ends up enforcing overlapping divisions between who is entitled to use the term and with what meaning.
27. Lotus of Another Colour: Unfolding of the South Asian Gay and Lesbian Experience (Rakesh Ratti ed., 1993); Nayan Shah, *Sexuality, Identity and the Uses of History, in* Social Perspectives in Lesbian and Gay Studies: A Reader 119 & 122-24 (P.M. Nardi & B.E. Schneider eds., 1998) (with the exception

of Nayan Shah's article, which challenges an excavation mode of engagement with the colonial archives as a way to legitimize the existence of homosexuality in India); Ruth Vanita & Saleem Kidwai, Same-Sex Love in India: Readings from Literature and History (2001). *See also* Ruth Vanita, *Introduction, in* Queering India: Same-Sex Love and Eroticism in Indian Culture and Society 1-14 (2002); Facing the Mirror: Lesbian Writing from India (Ashwini Sukthankar ed., 1999); Devdutt Pattanaik, The Man Who Was a Woman and Other Queer Tales of Hindu Lore (2002). *See for example* Queer Ink's website: www.queer-ink.com. Access to a good deal of this material has now become available on various websites.

28. *See for example* Giti Thadani, Sakhiyani (1996), which seeks to illustrate the abundance of Hindu iconography and depictions of same-sex sexual behaviours.
29. Ruth Vanita & Saleem Kidwai, Same-Sex Love in India: Readings From Literature and History xxi (2001).
30. Arvind Narrain & Alok Gupta, *Introduction, in* Law Like Love: Queer Perspectives on Law (eds., 2011).
31. Gayatri Spivak, *Can the Subaltern Speak?, in* The Post-Colonial Studies Reader 24-34 (Ashcroft et al. eds., 1995); Anjali Arondekar, For The Record: On Sexuality and The Colonial Archive in India (2009).

    In contrast to Narrain and Gupta, who attempt to excavate the voice of the sexual subject in the sodomy case of the Queen Empress v. Khairati, (1884) ILR 6 ALL 204 (India), Arondekar argues that such a retrieval is impossible. She proposes a reading of the archives that does not simply serve as a repository of missing voices, but also represents how the archive itself is an exercise of power/knowledge production, where the absence of the sexual subject itself is one of the effects. Arondekar warns against the possibility of recovering the lost or submerged contents of the colonial archive. It may be that there are only traces that remain, and hence only a fictionalized account of the subject can be produced. She argues in favour of a "thicker" reading of such traces, which is multilayered and interdisciplinary. For Arondekar, the queering process involves a need to move beyond the content of the exercise of fact-finding, to address the particular form and context of the material. *See also* Gayatri Spivak, *The Rani of Sirmur: An Essay in Reading the Archives,* 24 History & Theory 247 (1985).
32. Narrain & Gupta, *supra* note 30, at xii.
33. Because I Have a Voice: Queer Politics in India 3 (Gautam Bhan & Arvind Narrain eds., 2005).
34. Narrain & Gupta, *supra* note 30, at xiv. Section 377 of the Indian Penal Code, 1860 criminalizes carnal intercourse against the order of nature, and has been used to target men engaging in sodomy as well as to harass homosexuals.
35. *Id.*
36. Narrain & Gupta, *supra* note 30, at xxix & xxx. *See also* Arvind Narrain, *A New Language of Morality: From the Trial of Nowshirwan to the Judgment in Naz*

Foundation, in Law Like Love: Queer Perspectives on Law 253-77 (A. Narrain & A. Gupta eds., 2011), where the author uses the term LGBT persons throughout his discussion of the *Naz* decision and other cases, implying that the term queer and LGBT are interchangeable. In the same collection, Narrain develops queer through the notion of intersectionality as well as through a politics of radical kinship with other subordinated and marginalized groups, fugitives and outsiders. *See also,* Arvind Narrain, *Queering Democracy: The Politics of Erotic Love, in* Law Like Love: Queer Perspectives on Law 3-23 (A. Narrain & A. Gupta eds., 2011).

37. Narrain & Gupta, *supra* note 30, at xxxiv.
38. Jyoti Puri, Women, Body, Desire in Post-Colonial India: Narratives of Gender and Sexuality 176-83 (1999). Puri examines how queer narratives within postcolonial India have been imbricated in discourses of nationalism. She argues that gays and lesbians have often secured sexual rights claims in ways that also affirm their nationalist credentials. These include moves to appropriate the past as a means for establishing belonging and interiority.
39. *Id.* at 184.
40. Jyoti Puri, Encountering Nationalism 164 (2004).
41. *Id.* at 166.
42. Joseph Massad, *Re-orienting Desire: The Gay International in the Arab World,* 14 Pub. Culture 361 (2002). He refers to this move as the production of the "gay international".
43. Rahul Rao, *Queer in the Time of Terror, in* Law Like Love: Queer Perspectives on Law 43-66 (A. Narrain & A. Gupta eds., 2011).
44. Gayatri Gopinath, Impossible Desires: Queer Diasporas and South Asian Public Cultures 6-7 (2005).
45. *Id.* at 21.
46. Gopinath, *supra* note 44, at 94; *see also for example* Shohini Ghosh, Fire: A Queer Classic (2010), which discusses the implications of Deepa Mehta's film *Fire* as well as the debates on sexuality, representation and rights that were triggered by the film, both in India and globally.
47. Gopinath, *supra* note 44, at 100-101; *see for example* Monika Mehta, *What is Behind Film Censorship? The* Khalnayak *Debates,* 5 Jouvert (2001), https://legacy.chass.ncsu.edu/jouvert/v5i3/mehta.htm; Shohini Ghosh, *Queer Pleasures for Queer People: Film, Television, and Queer Sexuality in India, in* Queering India, Same-Sex Love and Eroticism in Indian Culture and Society 209-21 (R. Vanita ed., 2002).
48. Gopinath, *supra* note 44, at 120.
49. *Id.* at 125.
50. Sumita Chakravarty, National Identity and Indian Popular Cinema, 1947-1987 (1993).
51. *Id.* at 103.
52. *Id.* at 22.

53. Jasbir Puar, Terrorist Assemblages: Homonationalism in Queer Times 121-22 (2010).
54. Narrain & Gupta, *supra* note 30, at xxviii.
55. Ratna Kapur, *Out of the Postcolonial Closet and into the Liberal Box, in* Queer Theory: Law Culture and Empire 37 & 42-48 (K. Brooks & R. Leckey eds., 2010).
56. Patrick Olivelle, Manu's Code of Law: A Critical Edition and Translation of The Manava Dharmasastra (2005); R.P. Kangle, The Kautiliya Arthasastra (2010); Vatsayana, Kama Sutra (Richard Burton trans.), http://www.holybooks.com/the0kama-sutra-vatsyayana. (Examples of some of the works cited.)
57. Kapur, *supra* note 55.
58. Shakuntala Devi, The World of Homosexuals (1977); Vanita & Kidwai, *supra* note 29; Ruth Vanita, Love's Rite: Same-Sex Marriage in India and the West (2005); Vanita, *supra* note 27; Gopinath, *supra* note 44; Puar, *supra* note 53; Bhan & Narrain, *supra* note 33.
59. *See* Sonali Gulati, I Am (2011), https://www.sonalifilm.com/#/i-am/. In the documentary film *I Am,* gays and lesbians in India speak about their struggles for acceptance within the family, claiming their presence within the familial sphere in a very public way.
60. Leela Gandhi, Affective Communities: Anti-Colonial Thought and the Politics of Friendship (2006).
61. *Id.* at 50.
62. Michel Foucault, The History of Sexuality Vol. I: An Introduction 96 (R. Hurley trans., 1978).
63. Judith Butler, *Subjects of Sex/Gender/Desire, in* The Cultural Studies Reader 353 (S. During ed., 1993).
64. Leela Gandhi, *A Case of Radical Kinship: Edward Carpenter and the Politics of Anti-Colonial Sexual Dissidence, in* The Phobic and the Erotic: The Politics of Sexualities in Contemporary India 91-92 (B. Bose & S. Bhattacharyya eds., 2007).
65. Monique Wittig, The Straight Mind and Other Essays 6 (1992). Wittig argues that masculine should not be homologized with men.
66. Gandhi, *supra* note 64, at 92.
67. *Id.*
68. *Id.* Gandhi seeks to counter the perception of Carpenter's sexual evasiveness in light of arguments in favour of sexual specificity and identifying the corporeal practices of homosexuality as integral to developing the political dimension of erotic life.
69. Sedgwick, *supra* note 19. Questioning the position that regards the homosexual/heterosexual divide as relevant to only a small homosexual minority, as opposed to seeing it as an issue of importance in the lives of people across the spectrum of sexuality, Sedgwick argues that the binary of homo/heterosexual

overdetermines every aspect of life, even the least sexual aspects of personal existence.

70. Gandhi, *supra* note 64, at 101. Gandhi's work can be aligned with an emerging theoretical position that articulates failure as a political position which dismantles the logic of success and its obsessive focus on how to be in the world in a very specific way. The measures of success which have been brought into question in light of the collapse of the financial market, bad mortgages, and spiralling divorce rates compels a turn towards understanding the productive possibilities of failure; Judith Halberstam, The Queer Art of Failure (2011). Halberstam examines how failure is something that queers have done and do exceptionally well, and examines how this experience can be used to examine the gross inequalities of everyday life in the United States.
71. Michel Foucault, Politics, Philosophy, Culture: Interviews and Other Writings 1977-1984 200-202 (L.D. Kritzman trans., 1988).
72. Judith Butler, Bodies that Matter: On the Discursive Limit of Sex 2 (1993).
73. *Id.* at 3.
74. Foucault, *supra* note 62, at 49.
75. *Id.* at 18.
76. Gandhi, *supra* note 64, at 99.
77. Kapur, *supra* note 55, at 37-52.
78. Butler, *supra* note 19, at 19.
79. *Id.* at xxxvi. The more radical reading of queer is initiated through a discussion of a campaign by the "Consortium of Loose, Forward and Pub-Going Women", who countered protests by the Hindu Right on their celebration of Valentine's Day by sending pink underwear to the local head of the right-wing organization. *See also* Arvind Narrain, *Queering Democracy, supra* note 36, where Narrain develops this perspective with greater clarity.

CHAPTER 2

Disrupting the Dinner Table

Re-thinking the 'Queer Movement' in Contemporary India

Ashley Tellis

Like many countries in the Global South, India opened its gates to the free market and policies of liberalization/globalization/structural adjustment in the early 90s, after decades of being a protectionist state.[1] This has led to countries like India being introduced to what Josephine Ho, in the context of East Asia, calls 'global governance'[2] in the neoliberal moment. This governance, Ho writes, involves 'global civil society' holding out "further hope for democratic potentials that promote the spirit of responsible humanitarianism as well as respect for diversity while weakening state power and domination in certain national contexts."[3] Speaking of East Asia (and she could well be speaking of India), she continues,

> optimistic LGBT advocates and marginal groups look to changing, and seemingly liberalizing, political regimes and expanding civil society as sites for possible leverage or gains, while pride marches, lesbian and gay cultural events, and booming queer Internet communities corroborate the impression that queer Asia may be much more than a concept.[4]

All these phenomena mark the Indian postcolonial moment as well.

A recent High Court judgment read down the colonial Section 377 from the Indian Penal Code and now consensual gay sex between adults is allowed, pride marches abound, and so do lesbian and gay cultural events and booming queer Internet communities. But does this constitute a 'movement'? Before one addresses that question, it is important to follow the rest of Ho's argument. She speaks of the retrenchment of the deeply homophobic state as being a process simultaneous to the one on global governance; of how, using UN discourse, Christian fundamentalist NGOs are producing a new sense of civility inimical to queers, and how child protection is used to bash queers. While most NGOs in India are not overtly religious in any way, they are nationalist and deeply conservative on many issues, like those around child sexual abuse,[5] and certainly work to retrench nationalist and anti-sexual minority ideas—this is true even of figures and NGOs working ostensibly around issues of sexuality and HIV/AIDS.[6]

Further, the class formation of these NGOs and their 'activists' means that the very framing of the question of sexuality is deeply problematic. But let us stay with Ho for the moment. She proceeds to show how the UN, via NGOs, is producing new global principles and values. Then, she baldly states:

> There is, after all, nothing intrinsically progressive or democratic about international civil society. Internationally based NGOs have been known to set up branches in Third World nations not only as channels for needed funding and aid, but, more important, as a field where Western values and interests can exercise their influence and foster checks and balances to resist local state domination and control.[7]

Ho proceeds to show how building these universal international politics congeals around conservatism, especially with issues like "sex trafficking, child pornography, pedophiles and Internet content monitoring,"[8] all of which are issues in the contemporary moment in India.[9] She speaks of how nations are "strongly encouraged to bring their laws into alignment with UN decrees."[10]

The rest of Ho's essay deals with the specificities of various East Asian contexts but she ends on another important point. She refers to a protest at a WTO ministerial meeting in Hong Kong where "queer groups from quite a few East Asian states lined up with other social movement groups (labourers, farmers, women, and sex workers) in fierce protest against WTO policies."[11] It is difficult to think of one moment when the 'queer movement' in contemporary India has stood with labourers, farmers, women or sex workers or against WTO policies, though there are many struggles involving all of these groups and the definite presence of the WTO as well.[12]

While in East Asian contexts, the Christian Right has taken over the NGOs (though Ho does not specify the class formation of the Christian Right in these contexts), in India NGOization has largely been a voluntarist, bourgeois, entrepreneurial project. People who run and work in NGOs are largely middle and upper class and are unlikely to even talk to, let alone stand by, labourers, farmers and sex workers despite making many noises about such intersectionalities and alliances. What they are good at is creating newer identity categories to garner more and more funds, settle for piecemeal negotiations with the law by asking for a reading down of the section of the Indian Penal Code that criminalizes homosexuality so that it removes private, consensual sex from its purview (a blatantly classist and casteist demand), and courting the media to celebrate, in parties and marches, victories posing as 'Queer Liberation!'.

If one reads the text of the High Court judgment, one will see that all the precedents quoted in it are international, all the language is global and in perfect consonance with global governance.[13] While Ho does a good job of questioning global governance discourse and that of the NGOs, she leaves both the question of the politics of funding and the nature of the 'queer movement' in East Asia (the non-mainstream one which she invokes approvingly at the end of her piece) un-interrogated. In India, the politics of funding requires more investigation, something the 'queer movement' is unwilling to do. Another thing in dire need of interrogation, linked to the above, is how the term 'queer' circulates, both in India and in East Asia, and who exactly it is that mainly uses the term (and uses it to pose as a 'movement').

THE POLITICS OF FUNDING

If global governance refers to the discourse around or through which funding is granted, the specific discourse of global governance in what have come to be called sexuality NGOs, or NGOs that work with sexual minorities and around HIV/AIDS, is one of hegemonic global identity-speak,[14] once again from Euro-American contexts. If 'queer' is not quite funder-speak, it is certainly used by Indian activists and NGOs, alongside more 'indigenous' cultural categories, all of which seem to have emerged only in the last few decades.[15] That apart, the language of sexual minorities comes from international mainstream organizations (that groups like Queer Nation were marking themselves against) like Human Rights Watch, which has been readily adopted by Indian NGOs and 'queer' activists. How is it that the Indian 'queer', for all its radical claims, has not interrogated the hegemony of this language and its appropriateness for the sociological contexts of South Asia? How has it not questioned the institutional structures which produce this discourse and the power relations between them (the donors) and the receivers (NGOs)?

Perhaps it has to do with the sheer power of money. There has been a substantial body of work critiquing the non-profit complex, from the volume produced by Incite! Women of Color Against Violence entitled *The Revolution Will Not Be Funded* to James Petras' classic essay 'NGOs: In the Service of Imperialism?'[16] The Incite! anthology, apart from offering a detailed history of non-profit funding in the United States, brings together a range of voices from across the world to offer a very nuanced critique and appraisal of what it calls the non-profit industrial complex (NPIC). It raises several issues, from the similarities between the prison industrial complex

(PIC) and the NPIC in the context of the United States and how the latter forms a 'shadow state' that allows "government to make war, expand punishment, and proliferate market economies under the veil of partnership between the public and private sectors",[17] to the protecting of elitism in social justice movements facilitated by the logics of funding/funders rather than the constituents of the movements themselves; from the domestication of social justice to a career option to the creation of competition (around funding) between social movements; from the derailing of movements and the domestication of their radical potential to the exporting of conservatism to various less powerful contexts (for example, the squelching of revolutionary movements in Latin America by the United States).

Petras makes similar arguments in his essay and is critical even of so-called progressive NGOs because he feels that they prohibit structural change by favouring individual initiative (microcredit schemes), replace movement leadership with NGO leadership, take no risks, and are not accountable to the people with whom they claim to be working, among other things.

How is it that these critiques are never factored into the self-professed super-critical 'queer movement' in India? Perhaps this has to do with the fact that the three pioneering NGOs working on sexuality in India are organizations that were started on the basis of international grants originally given to the NGO founder as an individual, and not to an NGO? Perhaps this has to do with the fact that if one scratched the surface, one would find that HIV/AIDS is not a sexual minorities issue in India at all, and so the garnering of large amounts of funding and piggybacking on the HIV/AIDS pandemic are both rather dubious moves on the part of the 'queer movement'?

But even setting these unsavoury questions aside, what are some of the problems funding raises? First, given that funding agendas offer the language for and determine the discourse of sexuality, there is a resultant flattening of the sociological landscape into the paradigms of identity and rights that often actually inhibit the processes of change that are desirable, if not actually prohibit them. Second, given that most of this funding comes to urban NGOs, no real attention is paid to rural contexts where many people and groups have great difficulties articulating sexual self-constructions. Third, given that upper-class people run these NGOs and there is free interplay between NGOs and 'queer activists' (if not a set of networks that render them indistinguishable), it is these people's agendas that are in the foreground. At the same time minority formations, some of which have to be considered given the question of funding, are appropriated and othered as 'high risk populations' or similar epidemiological categories, and as indigenous cultural categories in need of modernization into twenty-first century 'queerness'—while others are ignored altogether. Which brings one to the use of the word 'queer' and why it is symbolically representative of the violences of the non-profit industrial complex and the logics of global governance.

'QUEER'? 'MOVEMENT'?

The word 'queer' emerged in the context of US gay movements in the 1990s. It emerged as an activist term used by groups like Queer Nation, a group of radical AIDS activists in New York. Queer Nation was a militant group with confrontational, situationist-style modes of intervention. The group members were activists from ACT UP and were tired of the continuing discrimination against people with HIV/AIDS by the neoliberal, Reaganite dispensation and sickened by the continuing heteronormativity of mainstream culture in the US. This term quickly became popular and was appropriated not just by the popular media but also by academia, spawning the subfield of Queer Studies in US academia. At the time in the US, this was a liberating term for LGBT folk of colour and many disenfranchised people along varying axes not acknowledged by the gay movement.[18]

How does queer travel from this specific context and reach the world over? How does the Indian 'queer movement' come into being? Is this use of queer not, as Neville Hoad points out, "innocent of its own colonizing fantasies?"[19] Michael Warner, whom Hoad was critiquing in the quote above (specifically for the book Warner edited, titled *Fear of a Queer Planet*), had himself written, "In the New World Order, we should be more than usually cautious about global utopianisms that require American slang."[20] Have the proponents of the 'queer movement' in India shown this caution? Not really.

Consider the various definitions and uses of queer in the introduction to *Because I Have a Voice: Queer Politics in India*, one of the first anthologies of the 'queer movement' in India. They remain ahistorical in their appropriation of the term and utopian in their impulse. "A multiplicity of desires and identities", "defiant political perspective", beyond "homosexual" and "heterosexual", "intrinsically and inevitably connected with the politics of class, gender, caste, religion and so on, thereby both acknowledging other movements and also demanding inclusion within them", and "questioning the fundamental assumptions of our society".[21] How any of this is actually actualized in reality is not the priority here as long as the correct laundry list of identities is read out.

What do these proponents see as the aims of this 'movement'? "To name, visibilize and counter the violence faced by queer people", "challenge the idea of a 'normal' and 'different' sexuality in itself", "object to all hierarchies and power structures", "intersections" with feminist and other "movements at the margins".[22] Once again, how exactly this is done, and any evidence of it being done, is conspicuous in its absence.

Among the listed modes of doing this are: challenging the law, protests and demonstrations, queering culture, and creating queer culture and queer lives as political projects. No critique of the normatizing impulses of the law and the state are offered, the AIDS Bhedbhav Virodhi Andolan is appropriated as 'queer', and Voices Against 377, a loose coalition of different groups against Section 377, and its presence at the World Social Forum in 2004 and the first Pride march are offered as evidence of the queer movement's activities.[23]

Some of the challenges facing the movement are: the tag of being Western, the fact that the movement is largely upper-class and urban-based, the absence of women, and the dangers of strict identity categories. Apart from the fact that none of these issues are really addressed, there are no critiques of the politics of funding, the NGOization of activist politics, or the structural contexts within which this 'queer movement' first emerged, all of which would generate an awareness of class, caste and other forms of elitism inherent in the 'movement.[24]

For the moment, it is important to point out that the word 'queer' - in its travel from the streets of New York to its appropriation and transmutation in the elite spaces of an upper-class and upper-caste set of people, many of whom run NGOs or are part of them and designate themselves as a 'movement'—needs to have its trajectory traced as the first step in the critical self-analysis needed to generate something like a critical movement.

While the editors of *Because I Have a Voice* do acknowledge in their introduction that the word 'queer' does not have much truck in India, it is not simply a question of the word's semantic viability. What is crucial to stress is that the use of 'queer' is a symbolic representation of the elite nature of this 'new' form of 'social movement' that the 'queer movement' represents in India. The proponents of this 'movement' have never been the kind of activists seen on the streets of New York in the ACT UP days. Yet to borrow that street cred and make large claims about their awareness of class, caste and other movements, to claim joint struggles with these movements, and to claim a radicality that is only at the level of words, while offering not one self-reflexive critique of their own location and imbrication in the New World Order, let alone, for example, joining tribals in Orissa protesting against the taking over of their lands, is audacious and makes one re-assert that this is not a 'movement' at all.

MODES/CHALLENGES

On the ground, what have been the self-proclaimed campaigns of and challenges to the 'queer movement' in relation to its self-proclaimed aims, and what do these campaigns say about said aims? To concentrate on one mode and one challenge and ask some questions of it in the hope of re-thinking the 'queer movement' in India, one must turn to the law which has been the major campaign in the 'queer movement' in India.

The High Court Judgment on Section 377

The 'queer movement's biggest campaign has been a legal one, involving the reading down of Section 377 of the Indian Penal Code. The first question to be asked here is why this privileging of the law? Why is the legal terrain the most important terrain for a movement which claims to concern itself with the most marginalized populations, with populations that defy all categories and identity formations? How can the self-professed radical 'queer movement' place, as its first struggle, recognition by the most conventional and normative institution, that of the law? How can it not be aware of the normatizing and surveilling manoeuvres of the law, and how 'queerness' as defined by the 'movement' will simply be illegible to that law or damaged irreparably by being domesticated by that law?

To be sure, this critique is not among those sexy post-colonialist ones that ask for a complete disregard of the law and no engagement with it.[25] But why is law the primary site of struggle? And if it has to be the primary struggle, why in the specific form it took?[26] It was the AIDS Bhedbhav Virodhi Andolan, an early HIV/AIDS advocacy group in Delhi, which first challenged Section 377 in court arguing that it prevented work with HIV-affected persons, but that petition was dismissed. The argument moved from repeal to reading down, proposed by an international NGO's Indian office and backed by the 'queer movement' and several other non-profits and groups. This move was, and is, inexplicable and, once again, only shows the lack of any real connection with the populations that are affected by Section 377 and the threat of HIV/AIDS, the main reason offered in the petition.

Elsewhere, I have argued against the elitist nature of this campaign and the judgment so widely celebrated by the media and 'the queer movement'.[27] To briefly reiterate some of the arguments relevant to this enquiry: how many marginalized groups were consulted when the decision to settle with the reading down of Section 377 was taken? How many such groups were active parts of the almost decade-long campaign? Why is it that the queer petitioners' long case in the text of the judgment only invokes international precedent, a consistent colonial rhetoric of India's need to modernize and catch up, the sparse, almost non-existent invocation of women, and the negligible and agency-less invocation of hijras? Why is it that the co-petitioners include state organizations but none of the key organizations involved in the struggles, not just the groups that come under the section but also marginalized groups that might be affected by similarly discriminatory sections?

Characteristically, the 'queer movement' has not addressed any of these questions. In a recent publication celebrating the judgment, the editors offer an inflated and contradictory account of the judgment's achievements and what it established, but no real engagement with any serious critique of it.[28] The editors claimed the judgment marked queers becoming subjects of rights and citizens, when nowhere does the section or judgment ever refer to the subjects they purportedly talk about. They argue that it proves that sexuality is integrally linked to identity, which completely contradicts their earlier anti-identitarian characterization of queerness in *Because I Have a Voice*. They argue that sexuality requires a partner, real or imagined, implicitly instituting monogamy as their model, and claim a broader acceptance of queerness in public culture (both an unverified and undesirable claim). The editors also offer the same old ahistorical and racist/communal history of homosexuality in the subcontinent (we were wonderfully pro-homosexual till the big, bad British came along), and make the usual claims about the holy trinity of caste, class and gender (only as a laundry list). They anachronistically call several earlier groups and moments 'queer' (ABVA, CALERI, PUCL_K), none of which were/are queer or queer-identified. They illustrate their investment in nationalism, claiming that queers are now part of the 'Indian nation', and offer uncritical and unexamined accounts of love and how queer love is like inter-caste love (with no specific analysis of either or the conjunction of both). And lastly, they assimilate irreconcilable contradictions under the umbrella of diversity, and announce that all of us are to partake in 'sexual freedom'.[29]

Class/Caste/Gender Formation

If the 'queer movement' has acknowledged, however implicitly, the classist (disguised as 'urban' in the introduction to *Because I Have a Voice*), casteist (though, tellingly, their articulation does not foreground caste at all, and caste is only invoked as the displaced/othered concern of 'other movements' with which the queer movement must connect or rather 'demand inclusion' from), and sexist nature (at least it openly acknowledges its marginalization of women, if not other disenfranchised and barely legible subjects of sexuality) of its own formation, what has it done about it?

Let us look at this through one of the documents of self-professed achievement in the definition of a 'queer' politics, the PUCL-K report along with queer activists and NGOs on the harassment of hijras in Bangalore.[30] Conducted firmly within the rubric of human rights, a framework the authors do not feel the need to question at all.[31] Hijras, they incredulously inform us, have been demanding to be part of the 'sexual minority movement' which is reflective of a global shift in the discourse of queer politics from issues of sexual orientation to issues of gender identity. Apart from the absurdity of hijras being up on queer politics as the engine behind some hijra organizing, the implicit acknowledgement that hijras have not been a part of the queer movement is important.

What follows are the usual unhistorical endorsements of 'queer' at the end of Chapter 1, and ahistorical accounts of the history of transgenderism in Chapter 2. Chapter 2 is entitled 'Social, Cultural and Political Context of Kothis and Hijras' and apart from absurd statements like "[t]he hijra community in India has existed with a recorded history of more than 4000 years"[32] and various accounts of their mythologies, no account is given of their castes, their religions, their beliefs, or their positions in the wider social context.

Despite speaking of the 'Intersection of Class, Gender and Sexuality' in a dedicated section (note the absence of caste), none of these intersections are even mentioned, let alone developed, apart from the idea that they "have a sort of sanctioned and visible place in Hindu society"[33] and that their marginalization is at the level of class. The narrative then moves onto their role as sex workers. None of the testimonies that follow locate these subjects in any of the dense networks and contexts of caste, class, region, religion, or language. We get no sense of the deep and abiding structures which allow for their violation but also the texture of their subjectivities. They are merely reproduced as hijras, and as unilateral victims. These victim narratives flatten the sociological complexity of these hijras and also strip them of all agency in the interest of portraying them as human rights victims.

Even when, in the next chapter, the authors claim to be dealing with 'Understanding the Institutional Basis for Violence', these institutions are just invoked as family, law, and so on, which leads to an account of laws and the media. Even the invocation of the Criminal Tribes Act does not lead them to ask how many of these hijras are adivasi how caste intersects with their marginalization. This radical othering and homogenizing of the hijra community not only shows the 'queer' activists, the NGOs, and the human rights community to be victims of their own class formations in their inability or unwillingness to read class, caste, religion, region, and language into the lives of hijras and the fabric of their violation, it also produces the community as homogenous in their or its, depending on your preference victimization and in need of help from outside.

The mobilization is mainly attributed to an NGO, and while mention is made of how the NGO had to realize "that organizing sexuality minorit[ies] for their rights could not be achieved without bringing in issues of gender, caste, class and language backgrounds and other internal differences among them",[34] nothing was said about how this translated into practice. What follows is a list of the strategies adopted in terms of crisis management, legality and media by the NGO. What is quite clear is that while lip service is paid to the complicated axes of marginalization that exist, none of these actually become part of the way in which cultures of resistance are built. Instead, the hegemonic narratives of law and media always come back in.

While there is no doubt that legal help has been important to Bangalore's hijras, how does it substantially change the realities of their lives? How will the structural and systematic ways in which they are kept where they are change by dealing only with their harassment by the police through the law?[35] The last section, which holds the 'future', is imagined only in terms of legality and defined as "mobilizing existing legal frameworks, challenging the existing legal frameworks and using progressive international legal developments".[36] Hijra voices die in this section. Do they not have a say in what their future holds? Why are there no testimonies in this section? The righteousness of the 'queer'/NGO and human rights activists appears to be completely successful in wiping out the hijras' agency and repeats the violent marginalization of them under the aegis of a benign intervention.

The fact is that the 'queer movement' has been, and is, a bit of a slick Boy's Club. Not old style and paternalistic, it is making all the right noises to be sure, but is also still participating in the Boy's Club rules of excluding and marginalizing the less privileged. What would a genuine interrogation, a 'queer' one, of this male, slick Boy's Club subject involve, and what kind of politics would it produce? Would it be able to resist the homogenization of subjectivity and politics that the global 'queer subject' produces? By shifting the onus onto this subject, one is not trying to argue that this class/caste/gender-based subject is the only source or hope of change in the field of sexuality (despite the disproportionately large amount of power in this subject's hands), nor that such self-reflexivity should not be the prime concern of this subject.

Rather, I want to make it clear that it is impossible for this subject to afford that self-reflexivity without a truly radical questioning of the many levels of structural oppressiveness in which he is implicated. Without an interrogation of the discourse of global governance, the global circulation of the term 'queer', the politics of international funding, the politics of NGOization, the power of colonialism, the poison of nationalism, the no-longer new economic order, the unquestioning faith in the law, the unstated inhabitation of Brahminism, the easy slide into patriarchalism, and the heady jolt of utopian rhetoric that enables one to simply vault over all of this to enter into a 'queer' paradise, there can be no 'queer movement' in India. And any such movement that claims to exist is not asking any of these questions.

CONCLUSION

The world of social movements must be one where the first thing to be interrogated is one's own formation and one's own limitations in terms of class, caste, gender, region, religion, and language. None of these conditions are static, yet they are not as easily surmounted/overcome/dismissed as we would like to think they are. Whether as individuals or collectives (and individuals are always collectives and vice versa), we need to be constantly vigilant of the axes of our own formation and the limits they impose on how we experience the world. Our strategies, campaigns and issues are as much in need of questioning as the questions we ask, the people we are willing to work with, the people we are likely to beseech. The resources we draw upon are also caught up in layers and layers of hierarchy and power, institutional and otherwise. Engagements with otherness, engagements outside our class, caste, gender, region, and language have to move out of the mode of patronizing help and move into a zone of creative dissonance. This process is not easy or sexy and can be deeply destabilizing, but it is almost always productive. Engaging with another's marginalization, seeing it in relation to one's own, indeed *as* one's own, is an educative experience. True education is never easy. If education does not disorient you and change the way you think, it is not education at all.

More importantly, a critique of the larger contexts within which the 'queer movement' unfolds in the contemporary moment in India is crucial. There has been a sophisticated critique of this for some time now in the US,[37] and more recently in Europe.[38] This is not a simple terrain in India and requires vigilance and rigorous and sustained critique if the sexual minority critique is to matter at all. We are situated lowest in the pecking order and have the least to lose. Instead of a place at the table, we need to pull the tablecloth to the floor and disrupt the bloody pleasures of the neoliberal dinner. We are best placed to do so even as the 'queer movement' seems the least inclined towards it.

NOTES

1. *See* Sugata Bose, Instruments and Idioms of Colonial and National Development: India's Historical Experience in Comparative Perspective *in* International Development and the Social Sciences: Essays on the History and Politics of Knowledge (F. Cooper & R. Packard eds., 1997).
2. Josephine Ho, *Is Global Governance Bad For East Asian Queers?*, 14 GLQ 457 (2008); *see also* Global Governance, Wikipedia: The Free Encyclopedia (Aug. 12 2023, 7:08 PM), https://en.wikipedia.org/wiki/Global_governance. Wikipedia has quite a detailed and referenced introduction to the term 'global governance,' the best definition of which is attributed to Thomas G. Weiss: "Global governance'—which can be good, bad, or indifferent—refers to concrete cooperative problem-solving arrangements, many of which increasingly involve not only the United Nations of states but also 'other UNs,' namely international secretariats and other non-state actors." It is important to

note that sexual governance, if it is mentioned at all, is not a prominent node in the analysis of the term.

3. Ho, *supra* note 2, at 457.
4. *Id.*
5. *See* Flavia Agnes, *Consent and Controversy*, The Indian Express (May 12, 2012, 3:16 AM), http://www.indianexpress.com/news/consent-and-controversy/948277/. Recently, a Bill (The Protection of Children from Sexual Offences) criminalizing sex between adolescents, drawn up in active conjunction with NGOS and educated experts, shows the increasingly US-centric understanding of sexual abuse that is permeating the Indian landscape. Fortunately, some subsequent judgments criticized this proposed Bill. *See also, HT Correspondent, Proposed Age of Consent for Sex Regressive, Hindustan Times* (May 13, 2012, 1:42 PM), https://www.hindustantimes.com/delhi/proposed-age-of-consent-for-sex-regressive/story-8dbh8hR9Z6QjbeJnjGTVOJ.html; *Express News Service, Raising Age Limit for Consensual Sex Will Be a Step Backward, Says Court, The Indian Express* (June 1, 2012, 1:46 AM), https://indianexpress.com/article/india/india-others/raising-age-limit-for-consensual-sex-will-be-a-step-backward-says-court/.
6. *See* Oishik Sircar, *Two Histories of Desire: Who Speaks for 'Indian' Sexualities?*, paper presented to the 13th National Conference of the Indian Association for Women's Studies, Wardha, January 2011. Sircar writes, A classic illustration of how nationalist pride can anesthetize the subversive potential of sexuality was a talk show on CNN-IBN discussing whether independent India is open to homosexuality, aired during the Independence Day week, just a few days after the Delhi High Court judgment in the Naz Foundation case in 2009. The 'experts' invited to speak were responding to a CNN-IBN and Hindustan Times survey in which almost 70 per cent of the respondents felt that homosexuality should be 'illegal'. The 'liberals' were represented by the likes of Shyam Benegal, Mukul Kesavan and Gautam Bhan. The 'conservative' was a young Hindu religious leader and sitting on the fence was Jaya Jaitley.

   The discussion sparked many a fire, but was hackneyed–the same arguments and the same defences that are not worth repeating here. Yet, the unprecedented 'openness' with which the audience was engaging with the issue of sexuality, and alternative sexuality, on prime time television was an encouraging sign. The findings of the survey (even if statistics are graver than damned lies) does throw light on the societal prejudice that 'queers' face in India, despite a progressive judgement like Naz. The sharp divide in beliefs and perspectives among the panelists on issues of sexual morality finally reached a climax through a moment of nationalism-induced catharsis. Sagarika Ghose, the anchor, abruptly ended the show by asking everyone to stand up to the national anthem. And as per her instructions everyone did–the conservatives, the liberals, the fence sitters, the homosexuals, the heterosexuals, the non-heterosexuals–everyone stood upright soaking in the buoyant verses of 'Jana

Gana Mana' and it seemed a perfect end to the crisis of India's morals, culture, sexuality and religion where national pride washed away all differences and made us realise that, after all, we are all 'Indians' first–like SRK's Chak De hockey team!

7. Ho, *supra* note 2, at 460.
8. *Id.* at 461.
9. *Devidutta Tripathy & Anurag Kotoky, Online Uproar as India Seeks Social Media Screening, Reuters* (Dec. 6, 2011, 1:31 PM), https://www.reuters.com/article/us-india-internet-idUSTRE7B50CV20111206. Recently, Minister Kapil Sibal sought to gag the internet in India, and faced severe criticism as a result.
10. Ho, *supra* note 2, at 462.
11. *Id.*
12. *See* Janet R. Jakobsen, Working Alliances and the Politics of Difference (1998). This text addresses the difficulties of alliance politics which concentrate on the women's movement in the United States, difficulties that persist despite the repeated refrain of queerness being about intersectionality and alliance politics. While the queer movement in India has sought the support of various other communities, like feminist groups, for its own cause (specifically the movement around the Naz judgment via Voices Against 377), it has seldom, if ever, come out with statements on all the important issues Ho raises, and around which several movements in India do exist. The author is involved in several campaigns, such as one addressing the figure of the imprisoned and tortured adivasi activist Soni Sori and national and Delhi-based rallies against sexual violence against women, and day labourers and informal labour and farmers in Maharashtra have never seen a single queer activist at any of these movements/campaigns/demonstrations or indeed any statement from queer NGOs or groups or individual activists on these issues. While there are doubtless exceptions (Sangama, for example, works with the female sex worker movement in Bangalore, and individual activists like Aryakrishnan Ramakrishnan do make connections in some writing), no argument can be made that there is a concerted public effort to establish 'queer' alliances with any of these movements.
13. *See* Ashley Tellis, *LGBT Politics in India: Problems and Possibilities, in* Class and Its Intersectionalities (M. Mohanty & G. Rodrigues eds., forthcoming). This article contains my extended critique of the judgment.
14. *See* Ashley Tellis, *Ethics, Human Rights and LGBT Discourse in India, in* Applied Ethics and Human Rights: Conceptual Analysis and Contextual Applications 151-70 (S. Motilal ed., 2010). What I mean by identity-speak is the language of identity politics used in North America and Western Europe. The above article provides a critique of this language.

15 Ashley Tellis, *Postcolonial Same-Sex Relations in India: A Theoretical Framework,* in Space, Sexuality and Postcolonial Cultures 221-231 (M. Ray ed., 2003). An example of this is the identity 'kothi'. This is a word (one of many) used to

refer to the passive role in anal sex. Suddenly in the late 90s and early 2000s this became an 'identity'.

16 The Revolution Will Not Be Funded: Beyond the Non-Profit Industrial Complex (Incite! Women of Color Against Violence ed., 2007); James Petras, *NGOs: In The Service of Imperialism,* 29 J. Contemp. Asia 429-440 (1999).

17. Incite! Women of Color Against Violence, *Introduction, in* The Revolution Will Not Be Funded 9 (2007).

18. This is not to suggest that an ACT UP-style politics is what the 'queer movement' in India might replicate here which would be more useful. The contexts are so different that this would be impossible. However, the political impulse, passion and anger behind that moment in the US would be good to emulate and is missing from the 'queer movement' in India altogether. How that might be articulated in the context of India is too heterogeneous and difficult (not to mention useless) to speculate about or draw a blueprint for, in this paper at any rate.

19. Neville Hoad, *Queer Theory Addiction, in* After Sex?: On Writing Since Queer Theory 35 (J. Halley & A. Parker eds., 2011. Hoad is citing his own pioneering essay on the racist and colonial genealogies of queer theory here. *See also*, Neville Hoad, *Arrested Development or the Queerness of Savages: The Imperial and Neo-Imperial Uses of Male Homosexuality,* 3 Postcolon. Stud. 133-58 (2000).

20. Michael Warner, *Something Queer about the Nation-State,* in After Political Correctness 361-371 (C. Newfield ed., 1995).

21. Arvind Narrain & Gautam Bhan, *Introduction,* in Because I Have a Voice: Queer Politics in India 1-29 (2005).

22. *Id.* at 6.

23. *Id.*

24. *Id.*

25. I have in mind the work of Nivedita Menon, Ashis Nandy and, implicitly, the work of Partha Chatterjee as examples.

26. *See* Ashley Tellis, *supra* note 13; *see also*, Ashley Tellis, *Why I Can't Join the Party,* July 12, 2009, *available at* http://blogs.thehindu.com/delhi/?p=25797.

27. *Id.*

28. Jason K. Fernandes, *The Dilemma after the Decision: Strays thoughts after Gay Liberation, Dervish Notes* (Aug. 18, 2009), http://dervishnotes.blogspot.com/2009/08/dilemma-after-decision-strays-thoughts.html. This article raises several issues including questioning the nationalism of the judgment and the PIL as a mode, and none of this is engaged with at all.

29. *See* Arvind Narrain & Alok Gupta, *Introduction,* in Law Like Love: Queer Perspectives on Law xi-lvi (2011).

30. People's Union for Civil Liberties, Karnataka (PUCL-K), *Human Rights Violations against the Transgender Community* (2003).

31. See Wendy Brown, "*The Most We Can Hope For...*" *Human Rights and the Politics of Fatalism,* 103 South Atl. Q. 459, 461 (2004). In her astute critique

of the paradigm of human rights, Brown writes: "rights are not simply attached to Kantian subjects, but rather produce and regulate the subjects to whom they are assigned." And again: "I have argued that we must take account of that which rights discourse does not avow about itself. It is a politics and it organizes political space, often with the aim of monopolizing it. It also stands as a critique of dissonant political projects, converges neatly with the requisites of liberal imperialism and global free trade, and legitimates both as well."

32. PUCL –K, *supra* note 30, at 17.
33. *Id.* at 21.
34. *Id.* at 60.
35. *See* Wendy Brown, *Suffering the Paradoxes of Rights*, in Left Legalism/Left Critique 422 (W. Brown & J. Halley eds., 2002) for a brilliant analysis of the limits of demanding rights of the law. Taking as her point of departure Gayatri Spivak's critique of the subject's position under liberal law as wanting 'that which we cannot not want', Brown spells out the several paradoxes of using the law. These include the fact that the law re-inscribes the very designations that have violated us, and because of which we came to it. It differentially empowers different social groups, and erases the compound production of subjects, conflating acts with identities. None of these paradoxes are engaged with in this report, let alone Brown's final question: "In other words, how might the paradoxical elements of the struggle for rights in an emancipatory context articulate a field of justice beyond that which we cannot not want? And what forms of right claims have the temerity to sacrifice an absolutist or naturalized status in order to carry this possibility?".
36. PUCL-K, *supra* note 30, at 68.
37. *See* Lisa Duggan, The Twilight of Democracy: Neoliberalism, Cultural Politics, and the Attack on Democracy (2004); Jasbir Puar, Terrorist Assemblages: Homonationalism in Queer Times (2007); A New Queer Agenda (Defilippis et al. eds., 2012), https://sfonline.barnard.edu/a-new-queer-agenda/.
38. For a critique of these larger contexts in Europe see Hegemony and Heteronormativity: Revisiting 'The Political' in Queer Politics (Maria do Mar Castro Varela, Nikita Dhawan & Antke Engel eds., 2011).

CHAPTER 3

Continental Drift

Queer, Feminism, Postcolonial

Brenda Cossman

The relationship between feminism and queer theory has long been a contested one. From its genesis in the works of Eve Sedgwick and Gayle Rubin, queer theory emerged as a project of theorizing sex and sexuality in an analytic framework independent of feminism. As Rubin wrote in 'Thinking Sex': "In the long run, feminism's critique of gender hierarchy must be incorporated into a radical theory of sex, and the critique of sexual oppression should enrich feminism. But an autonomous theory and politics specific to sexuality must be developed."[1] Others, like Judith Butler, have resisted the bracketing of gender and the break from feminism, insisting instead that neither feminism nor queer theory should have such clearly delineated proper objects, and that more is to be gained from a kind of 'intellectual trespass' between them.[2] Indeed, Butler's work on gender performativity, so foundational to queer theory, was itself an intervention in feminist debates.

In this article, I tell a story of drifts—of continental drifts from feminism to queer theory, drifts between continents, from West to East and back again. Much of my own work has been located in these drifts. It is located in the drift away from feminism to queer theory. I turned to the sex-radical work of Rubin and became more engaged with questions framed by Michel Foucault, Eve Sedgwick, and Judith Butler.[3] Yet I never fully repudiated feminism: I remained committed to the idea of its continued analytical purchase.[4] My drift away from feminism to queer theory also involved going back again. Much the same can be said of my work in terms of drifts between continents. It has been located in the West and in India,[5] sometimes sequentially, sometimes simultaneously.[6] The temporal, spatial and theoretical drifts back and forth have produced a slightly dislocated and disoriented body of work that sometimes speaks parochially, and at other times speaks between and across. In this article, I seek to bring that continental drift to the question of queer theory's relationship with feminism and its location in the postcolonial. While the story starts in the West, where queer theory first emerged, it drifts eastward (or westward depending on one's flight route). But continental drift is not a story of movement from West to East; it is a story of the movement of the Earth's continents relative to each other. Shifting tectonic plates produce more than a little deep structural change. So too does the drift of queer theory toward the postcolonial and the postcolonial toward the queer.

QUEER THEORY?

Queer theory is a tough thing to pin down. Its deconstructive nature defies any simple definition or synopsis and, from its inception, it has refused the definitional.[7] However, if we go back to its roots, to the foundational writings of Eve Sedgwick, Gayle Rubin, and Judith Butler amongst others, it is possible, and I believe useful, to identify several basic themes or perhaps predispositions.[8] Its genesis can perhaps be seen to lie with Foucault's argument that sexuality is a discursive production rather than a natural condition.[9] Queer theory has developed as an interrogation and deconstruction of the multiple discursive productions of sexuality, seeking to denaturalize the assumed connections between sex, gender, and desire. Teresa de Lauretis, the first to coin the term and one of the first to denounce it, described queer theory as "a refusal of heterosexuality as the benchmark for all sexual formations".[10] It was a critique directed to "recast or reinvent the terms of our sexualities, to construct another discursive horizon, another way of thinking the sexual."[11] Perhaps at its most general, queer theory can be seen as an interrogation and denaturalization of the sex, gender, desire matrix. As Annamarie Jagose has described it:

> Broadly speaking, queer describes those gestures or analytical models which dramatise incoherencies in the allegedly stable relations between chromosomal sex, gender and sexual desire. Resisting that model of stability—which claims heterosexuality as its origin, when it is more properly its effect—queer focuses on mismatches between sex, gender and desire.[12]

Judith Butler's groundbreaking work in *Gender Trouble* and *Bodies That Matter* took aim at the identity and essentialist constructions of gender, insisting that chromosomal sex, gender and sexuality are discursively produced and performed. In *Epistemology of the Closet*, Eve Sedgwick centred the critical analysis of the homosexual/heterosexual dichotomy. Through these works, queer theory deconstructed the dichotomy between gay and straight, homosexual and heterosexual, suggesting that these dichotomies were themselves part of the problem. The homo/hetero distinction normalized heterosexuality and reinforced very static and essentialist conceptions of sex, sexuality and desire. It was similarly a critique of identity—specifically, gay and lesbian identity claims—arguing against the essentialization of gay identity against a heterosexual norm.

Secondly, queer theory was positioned as a critique of the normal, and by extension, of normative sexuality. David Halperin described queer as, by definition, whatever is "at odds with the normal, the legitimate, the dominant. [...] Queer demarcates not a positivity but a positionality vis-à-vis the normative–a positionality that is not restricted to lesbians and gay men but is in fact available to anyone who is or who feels marginalized because of her or his sexual practices."[13]

Michael Warner, for example, in *The Trouble with Normal,* focused the queer on resistance to regimes of normal, particularly to sexual regimes of normalization.[14] This critical positionality against regimes of sexual normalization and normative sexualities teeters at times towards a more normative celebration or affirmation of sex, particularly of 'non-normative' sexual practices. Although this normative pro-sex affirmation sits uncomfortably with queer theory's critical and more poststructuralist tendencies, it gestures towards an underlying, if not always stated normativity. Indeed, some, like Gayle Rubin, argue for an ethics of sexual pluralism that expressly affirms the non-normative.[15] While the underlying normativity of queer theory remains contested and unresolved (perhaps even irresolvable), the interrogation of normative sexuality and the implicit embrace of non-normative sexualities can be seen as a thematic gesture that runs through much of queer theory.

Thirdly, queer theory seemed to emerge as a lens to focus on sex and sexuality independent of gender. It was articulated by Rubin and Sedgwick as a kind of break from feminism and the colonizing lens of gender, arguing that much could be gained from exploring sex and sexuality through its own unique lens. Rubin challenged feminism's claim to have occupied the field of sexuality and argued that it was essential "to separate gender and sexuality analytically to more accurately reflect their separate social existence".[16] It was time, she argued in 1984, to develop an "autonomous theory and politics specific to sexuality".[17] Sedgwick picked up on Rubin's call and argued in *The Epistemology of the Closet* that it was axiomatic that "the study of sexuality is not coextensive with the study of gender; correspondingly antihomophobic inquiry is not coextensive with feminist inquiry":[18] "the question of gender and the question of sexuality, inextricably from one another though they are [...] are nonetheless not the same questions, that in twentieth century Western culture, gender and sexuality represent two analytic axes that may productively be imagined as being distinct from one another."[19] The emerging body of queer theory was demarcating an area that studied sexuality without gender and without feminism, producing a sophisticated body of work on sex and sexuality that troubled heteronormativity independent of feminism's focus on male/female relationships.

Some have since declared queer theory as over, dead or passé.[20] Yet others continue to work with a queer lens. Given Lee Edelman's work on queer time,[21] Judith Halberstam's on queer time and space,[22] Elizabeth Freeman's on queer temporalities and histories,[23] and Kathryn Bond Stockton's on the queer child,[24] to name but a few of the more haunting works of the last decade, queer still appears to have more than a little intellectual energy pulsating through its veins, rendering its pronouncement as dead a bit premature. Queer is still in the process of being written. It remains, as Judith Butler has argued, "a category in constant formation": "It will have to remain that which is, in the present, never fully owned, but always and only redeployed, twisted, queered from a prior usage and in the direction of urgent and expanding political purpose."[25]

These themes or analytic predilections, which no doubt oversimplify the contested terrain of queer theory, remain compelling and analytically useful. I believe that they can usefully be brought to bear on what passes for queer theory these days, which in its less complex modalities, borders on reconstituting queer simply as gay. Indeed, this is where I risk becoming an un-reconstituted queer theorist, or Sedgwickian, insisting perhaps a little too strongly on some of queer theory's originalism as an anti-identitarian project. Eve Sedgwick once said that almost every attempt to deploy Foucault's repressive hypothesis has gotten it exactly wrong. I think that the same may be said of Sedgwick's work. Queer theory was intended to trouble identity: to explore and deconstruct the discourses producing gay identity.[26] Yet, today, the word 'queer' has been muted and transformed. While I agree with Butler and others that queer theory itself is a contested terrain, an ongoing critical project, without ownership, I cannot help but recoil from the deployment of queer as a mere synonym for 'gay', only hipper. Queer parenting, queer marriage, queer community—while I do not suggest that the practices of parenting or marriage or community could not in fact be queered, I question the extent to which the mere insertion of queer as an adjective in front of these practices does so. For me, queer theory offers a powerful, anti-identitarian lens to explore sex and sexuality. If this makes me an un-reconstituted Sedgwickian, so be it, but acknowledging it may allow the reader to make their own judgments.

FEMINISM?

The rupture between feminism and queer has, as I have suggested above, been productive. Yet there is also a way in which it has been stultifying. As Judith Butler has argued, each has been given its proper object: gender is allocated to feminism while sexuality is allocated to queer theory. The two are cast in an antagonistic relationship, their differences incommensurable. For queer theory, feminism is reduced to one side of the sex wars—those that seek to regulate the harms that sexuality presents for women—while casting itself as a more liberatory politics that seeks to destabilize the disciplinary regulation of sexuality. For feminism, queer theory is reduced to a sexual libertarian and representational politics, overly male in orientation, devoid of ethicality, unconcerned with the material conditions of women and the role of sexuality in producing inequality. This is an unproductive dichotomy, trafficking in caricatures and stereotypes, that fails on the one hand to recognize the contribution of different currents of feminism, while erasing debates within queer theory around gender, ethicality and political engagement on the other. Feminism becomes equated with dominance feminism. As Butler has argued: "feminism becomes identified with state allied regulatory power over sexuality [...] and these feminist positions which have insisted on strong alliances with sexual minorities and which are skeptical of the consolidation of the regulatory power of the state have become barely legible as 'feminist'".[27] It is a divide that fails to interrogate the more productive potential of analyses that might lie in the interstices of gender and sexuality, feminism, and queer theory.

In a more recent intervention in the feminism/queer theory debates, Janet Halley has provocatively argued that it is time to "take a break from feminism". Halley has demonstrated the conflicts between dominant variants of feminist critique and queer theory in the context of sexual harassment law, with feminist "victories" producing queer theory losses. She argues that it may be time "to urge feminists to learn to suspend feminism, to interrupt it, to sustain its displacement by inconsistent hypotheses about power, hierarchy and progressive struggle".[28] She defines feminism as having three shared features: "First, to be feminism, a position must make a distinction between M and F (male and female)", and second, "a position must posit some kind of subordination between M and F, in which F is the disadvantaged or subordinated element".[29] Finally, a position must advocate against this subordination, or in Halley's words, it must "carr[y] a brief for F".[30] This concern with the distinction and subordination between male and female, men and women, particularly as it has sedimented in dominant or 'governance' feminism,[31] operates to preclude a range of alternative insights into the workings of sexuality that could be seen through an alternative theoretical lens, such as queer theory.[32]

Halley's methodology allows her to produce counter-narratives of the operation of power on the terrain of sexuality, narratives that were obscured from within feminism's male/female binary. Yet, as a methodology, taking a break from feminism runs the risk of reproducing some of the problematic effects of the feminism/queer theory rupture. While Halley recognizes the diversity within feminism, and the deep ideological divisions within feminism on issues of sexuality, thereby avoiding the simplistic feminism/queer theory, gender/sexuality dichotomies, "taking a break" from feminism risks leaving in place rather than "moving between" the polarized worlds.[33]

In my debates with Halley, I argued that a return to feminism might mitigate these risks.[34] I argued that feminism's focus on gender as an axis of power continues to have analytic purchase. Gender, when understood broadly as, in Joan Scott's words, "a primary way of signifying relationships of power",[35] a way in which material and symbolic resources are produced and distributed in asymmetrical ways, remains an important foundational and analytical frame for feminism. Gender still matters in the world in real and symbolic, discursive and material ways. But in keeping with the influence of queer theory, I argued that it should not be an exhaustive analytic frame: "Feminism, as an analytic lens on gender as an axis of power" could "be supplemented, challenged, and confused by other theoretical and analytic frames".[36]

Gayle Rubin gestured towards a possible *rapprochement* of sexuality and gender "in the long run".[37] Others, notably Butler, have mused on whether the long run has since arrived. My argument with Halley would suggest that I agree. But I must admit to a continuing apprehension. If the long run has arrived, and it is time for more "intellectual trespass" between the two, the *rapprochement* must be a careful and contingent one. Gender still has—has always had—analytic purchase in the study of sex and sexuality. But feminism has not always been a humble discourse. It can no longer seek the first and last word. It should begin by recognizing the limits of its own imagination. It simply cannot see everything in its lens or mind's eye. I have argued that it may be theoretically productive to leave feminism—and its expertise on gender—behind, to allow for a critical engagement beyond its own borders. Queer theory allows for, indeed demands, a multiplicity of readings that bring a different set of questions into sharp relief.

POSTCOLONIAL?

It has not escaped my attention that my discussion has been focused exclusively on Western texts and located exclusively within Western debates on feminism and queer theory. The invocation of the 'we' has been in terms of the arguments that I have made in my work, engaging a predominantly Anglo-American audience. And so what, if any, purchase should any of this discussion have in the postcolonial, post-globalizing, post-*Naz* mobilization moment in India? One entirely legitimate response would be 'absolutely nothing at all'.

Admitted, at the heart of queer theory, in its Sedgwickian origins, is an assertion about Western culture, and the overwhelming focus has been on the production and deconstruction of heteronormativity and queerness in Western culture. Foucault's work, including the *History of Sexuality*, has been thoroughly criticized for its failure to engage with the histories, knowledges, and subjects of colonial/postcolonial experiences.[38] Yet the most basic insights of Foucault-inspired queer theory, that is, the social and regulatory production of sexual subjects in historically-specific discourses, are worthy of analytic pursuit beyond this massive failure. Queer theory's traction, at a minimum, might lie in the questions that it can ask: how are sexual subjects produced? What are discourses of inclusion and exclusion? How, if at all, are subjects produced through discourses of heteronormativity?

Not all would agree. Joseph Massad in *Desiring Arabs* takes a postcolonial aim at the universalizing Western discourse of gay and lesbian rights.[39] Following in the intellectual tradition of Edward Said, Massad argues that the promotion of the concept of gay rights in the Arab world has been an orientalizing and colonizing one, a missionary campaign by Western gay activists, "produce[ing] homosexuals, as well as gays and lesbians, where they do not exist".[40] Massad argues that it is not that same-sex activity does not exist, but that homosexual identity did not exist prior to the intervention of the 'Gay International':

> The new and redefined universal human subjectivity that they are proselytizing to the rest of the world is not that of including the homosexual but that of instituting the very binary [...] which will exclude the homosexual that it created in the first place, and all that is carried out in the name of 'liberation' for oppressive cultures and laws.[41]

Massad's critique is not intended to be particularly queer-friendly. Yet I would argue that it is one with queer overtures. His rejection of the essence of homosexual identity and interrogation of the multiple discourses producing the gay subject in the Arab world is one consonant with queer theory's insistence on the artificiality and centrality of the homo/hetero dichotomy in Western culture. While it stands as perhaps the most controversial and damning postcolonial critique of the emergence of the postcolonial gay and lesbian subject, theoretically it does not do the work to displace the critical moves of queer theory.

Other postcolonial and transnational theorists are rather less overtly hostile to the critical manoeuvres and analytic gestures of queer theory. Many scholars have in recent years begun to interrogate both the limitations of Western queer theory and the electrifying challenges of transnational sexuality and queer studies.[42] Gayatri Gopinath, for example, offers a provocative and compelling deployment of queer in a postcolonial context. In *Impossible Desires*, Gopinath sutures 'queer' with 'diasporic' as a corrective lens for both queer and diasporic studies.[43] Her deployment of queer is, on one level, quintessentially queer: "On the most simple level, I use queer to refer to a range of dissident and non-normative practices and desires that may very well be incommensurate with the identity categories of gay and lesbian."[44] Yet Gopinath's deployment of the queer diaspora is expressly intended to move beyond the "homonormativity of certain strands of Euro-American queer studies that centre white, gay, male subjectivity" and is part of the collective project of decentring whiteness and dominant Euro-American paradigms in theorizing sexuality both locally and transnationally."[45] She challenges the 'Gay International', yet she does so through the deployment of a more nuanced and postcolonial queer rather than in Massadian opposition to it.

Gopinath's work also foregrounds the feminist alongside the queer, insofar as she centres queer female diasporic subjectivity. She seeks to uncover articulations of queer female desire in a range of diasporic cultural representations, often in places where such desire would seem most impossible. Gopinath builds on the work of postcolonial feminist scholars who have revealed the discursive role of women in the projects of nationalism but have failed to interrogate the particular role of "heterosexuality as a key disciplinary regime".[46] She is explicit about her theoretical location:

> while this project is very much situated within the emergent body of queer of color scholarship [...] it also parts way with much of this scholarship by making a queer female subject the crucial point of departure in theorizing a queer diaspora. In so doing, *Impossible Desires* is located squarely at the intersection of queer and feminist scholarship and therefore challenges the notion that these fields of inquiry are necessarily distinct, separate and incommensurate. Instead the book brings together the insights of postcolonial feminist scholarship on the gendering of colonialism, nationalism and globalization with a queer critique of heteronormativity of cultural and state nationalism formations.[47]

Her work is postcolonial, queer, and feminist, pushing each beyond their own blinders.

Jasbir Puar similarly propels queer theory beyond many of its self-imposed boundaries to explore the role of heteronormativity in US nationalism and its production of the terrorist subject as an insidious, violent outsider.[48] Queer is deployed as a regulatory norm which, in the post-9/11 war on terrorism, becomes implicated in the racialization of Muslim terrorist subjects. Puar develops the idea of queer assemblages, a kind of Deleuzian assemblage "of dispersed but mutually implicated networks" in which "queerness [comes] forth at us from all directions, screaming its defiance".[49] For Puar:

> Queerness as an assemblage moves away from excavation work, deprivileges a binary opposition between queer and not-queer subjects, and, instead of retaining queerness exclusively as dissenting, resistant, and alternative (all of which queerness importantly is and does), it underscores contingency and complicity with dominant formations.[50]

Amongst her many critical moves and insights, Puar observes an archetypical failure of Foucault's repressive hypothesis of the sort identified by Sedgwick. In her critical reading of the Abu Ghraib "sexual torture scandal", Puar demonstrates the ways in which queerness colluded with American nationalism in many gay/lesbian/queer commentaries. The photographs were framed

> as 'evidence of rampant homophobia in the armed forces,' with scarce mention of the linked processes of racism and sexism. Even more troubling was the reason given for the particular efficacy of the torture: the taboo, outlawed, banned, disavowed status of homosexuality in Iraq and the Middle East, complemented by an aversion to nudity, male-on-male contact, and sexual modesty with the rarely seen opposite sex.[51]

Puar notes the stunning failure to recognize the most basic of Foucault's insights: "in the uncritical face-value acceptance of the notion of Islamic sexual repression, we see the trenchant replay of what Foucault termed the 'repressive hypothesis': the notion that a lack of discussion or openness about sexuality reflects a repressive, censorship-driven apparatus of deflated sexual desire".[52] It is but one of her countless deployments and redeployments of queer theory, highlighting the potential analytic purchase of queer assemblage in engaging the postcolonial. Puar's is an exhilarating, high-voltage intellectual assemblage, taking the queer to unchartered territory, with multiple intellectual trespasses across a broad range of critical theoretical interventions.

Gopinath and Puar present but two particularly brilliant visions of the queer in the postcolonial and counter-narratives to Massad's rather more negative prognosis. Queer theory—even in its narrower pre-Puar/Gopinath instantiations—has a range of questions apposite for the postcolonial context. Without presupposing the range of intellectual frameworks that the answers may need to deploy, queer theory can ask questions about the discourses through which contemporary postcolonial sexual subjectivities are constituted. How are sexual subjects naturalized? What ideologies of nationalism, postnationalism, colonialism and postcolonialism are deployed in naturalizing some sexual subjects, and exiling others?

What discourses of resistance are deployed? And in a more post-Puar, post-Gopinath modality, queer theory might ask about the multiple ways that queer assemblages are ever-present in producing citizens and racialized deviants, postcolonial nationalisms and their sexualized, racialized others.

QUEER INDIA?

Queer has recently emerged as a site of scholarship and activism in India.[53] Ruth Vanita's ground-breaking edited collection *Queering India* was the first to put the sign of queer on the Indian academic map.[54] Several recent and important anthologies have invoked the queer as well, most notably perhaps, Brinda Bose and Subhabrata Bhattacharyya's *The Phobic and the Erotic: The Politics of Sexualities in Contemporary India*[55] and Arvind Narrain and Gautam Bhan's *Because I Have a Voice: Queer Politics in India.*[56] The essays that make up these volumes have produced diverse critical genealogies of sexual identities and practices in India. Narrain and Bhan specifically invoke 'queer' both in their title and in the framing of their theoretical lens. Although contested and evolving, a certain usage of queer appears to be emerging in much of the existing literature. Consider, for example, the glossary entry in a recent article on transgender rights in India.[57]

> Queer: The word queer is increasingly being used in India to connote a diversity of ways of living that contest the embedded nature of heterosexism in law, culture and society. The term denotes a diversity of sexual orientations and gender identities in the Indian context that includes hijra, kothi, transsexual, and intersexed persons.[58]

Narrain and Bhan deploy queer in not dissimilar terms, careful to insist that it is not synonymous with LGBT. Queer, they argue:

> captures and validates the identities and desires of gay, lesbian, bisexual and transgender people, but also represents, for many, an understanding of sexuality that goes beyond the categories of

> 'homosexual' and 'heterosexual'. It speaks, therefore, of communities that name themselves (as gay and lesbian, for example) as well as those who do not, recognizing the spaces for same sex desire and sexuality that cannot be captured in identities alone.[59]

Queer politics, they insist, is not simply a minority issue of communities defined by their sexual orientation, but a broader questioning of normative assumptions around sexuality and gender.[60]

Bose and Bhattacharyya pick up from this usage of queer, both affirming it as a place to locate current discussions of LGBTQ identities, practices and politics in India while also mobilizing a more theoretically complex engagement with the genealogy of queer theory and its transnational machinations.[61] They frame their project as one of interrogating the contemporary politics of sexualities in India, seeking to highlight the emerging politics of non-normative sexualities. Bose and Bhattacharyya transitively deploy the concept of alternative sexualities but replace 'alt' with queer along the way. While noting the many sexualities and practices that lie outside the "narrow berth" of the normative in India, they adopt the term queer more narrowly:

> For the particular political usages of this anthology, we shall take, in the main, the sexual constituents of queer–lesbian, gay, bisexual, transgender–as the primary signifier of the 'other' of sanctioned sexual identity as the LGBT movement quite justifiably exposes the absence of a level playing field whenever its battles are seen as analogous to those amongst the heterosexual community who feel beleaguered for a variety of impediments in the pursuit of their desires.[62]

Bose and Bhattacharyya's subsequent questioning of the appropriate theoretical framing for these interrogations engages the fraught relationship between sexuality and gender and seeks to locate the work within an emerging cosmopolitanism, attentive to both global processes and local heterogeneities. The volume is ultimately framed as one of sexuality studies wherein the queer, as signifying LGBT identities, politics and practices, are in the sharpest relief. The essays that follow—richly textured genealogies of queer sexualities across cultural and literary studies—engage these heterogeneities; sometimes explicitly invoking the queer theory of the West, often assuming familiarity but moving to more cosmopolitan and culturally-specific interrogations.

Not all of those working on sexuality in India have embraced the sign of the queer. Ratna Kapur's work on the sexual subaltern, while having a decidedly queer bent, never invokes queer theory.[63] Indeed, Kapur gets to the sexual subaltern through a different theoretical trajectory. Her work is located within postcolonial theory, feminism, and subaltern studies. Kapur defines the "sexual subaltern" as capturing the diversity of counter-heteronormative sexual identities and sexual practices in India, including:

> gay, lesbian, bi-sexual, transgendered, *khush*, queer, *hijra*, *kothis*, *panthis* and many more. They have has *also* included sexual practices and behaviours such as adult and consensual pre-marital, extra-marital, non-marital, auto-erotic/masturbatory, promiscuous, and paid-for sex, as well as MSM (men who have sex with men). It is this diversity of identities and range of practices that cannot be captured within the acronym 'LGBT,' and why there is a need to articulate the politics of sexual subgroups from within a postcolonial context rather than to borrow theories or politics from elsewhere, a move that is both decontextualised and dehistoricised.[64]

Kapur has eschewed the sign of queer in favour of the sexual subaltern because of its better historical fit in the Indian context.[65] Yet, there is an obvious way in which her ground-breaking work on non-normative sexualities in Indian law, culture and history evokes theoretical hauntings not dissimilar to queer theory. While explicitly located in the subaltern tradition,[66] Foucault, Rubin and Butler make their appearances. My point in drawing out the resonance between Kapur's sexual subaltern and queer theory is not to suggest that her work is really queer. It is rather to suggest that critical genealogies of sexual identities and practice consonant with queer theory may be found in many places.[67] The very theoretical orientation of queer theory has been to find non-heteronormative identities, practices, discourses and possibilities at the margins of culture and history. It need not claim these critical genealogies under an imperializing sign of the queer.

AND BACK AGAIN?

So, what of the queer and what then might be learned from these multiple encounters? What is the relationship between the deployment of queer in India and queer theory in the West? I ask this question not to measure queer studies in India against the norm of queer theory in the West. Rather I am seeking to interrogate and compare the theoretical assumptions and heuristic twists and turns in each. Comparison is a multidirectional exercise.[68] If we turn the comparative gaze back on itself, what might queer theory in the West learn from its encounter with the postcolonial?[69]

I began by highlighting three basic themes or analytic predictions of queer theory in the West that I argued continue to have purchase. But what becomes of these ideas in the continental drift? First, there was the interrogation of the sex/gender/desire matrix, which is of course a central dimension of sexuality studies in India, sometimes naming its intellectual influences in Western queer theory and other times seeking to unmoor the inquiry from Western scholarship, to produce more culturally and historically-specific knowledges. Again, this is not about claiming such knowledges as 'queer theory'. It is rather to unearth the continuing traction of explorations into this matrix. But, the queer theory I described is one that is avowedly anti-identitarian in its exploration of this matrix. As Ratna Kapur has argued in her article in this volume,[70] there are visions of identity being reinscribed in the deployment of queer in India. On this count, there is indeed some considerable conflation with the usages of queer in the West where, despite its anti-identitarian roots, queer has often become an identity. As I confessed above, this is to me a problematic deployment of queer, analytically at any rate. I believe that the more anti-identitarian spirit of queer theory continues to have explosively subversive potential.

Inspired, as always, by Foucault, I would suggest that the exploration of the proliferation of sexualities challenging the sex/gender/desire matrix is not enough. Queer, as it is emerging in the literature, although producing some wonderfully rich genealogies of sexual subjects, past and present, under its sign, could be pushed to more critique. As I have argued elsewhere,[71] critique is about identifying the many ways that power and knowledge produce the objects, discourses, and fields under study. But it is also about pushing those fields of knowledge to their "breaking points", to:

> the moments of [their] discontinuities, the sites where [they fail] to constitute the intelligibility for which [they stand]. What this means is that one looks both for the conditions by which the object field is constituted, and also for the limits of those conditions, the moments where they point up their contingency and their transformability. In Foucault's terms, 'schematically speaking, we have perpetual mobility, essential fragility or rather the complex interplay between what replicates the same process and what transforms it.'[72]

The anti-identitarian impulse of queer theory, in interrogating and deconstructing the sex/gender/desire matrices, fits with this spirit of critique; of not only taking apart but of looking deeply at how the very subjects and practices under study produce the knowledges through which we are studying them and the limits of our field of vision. Queer theory, I believe, can help push our fields of knowledge to these productive, if disorienting, breaking points.

The second theme was the critical interrogation of the normal and the embrace of non-normative sexualities. On this theoretical count, queer studies in India has perhaps surpassed its Western counterpart. In the very descriptions of the queer, the non-normative repeatedly takes definitional precedence, often outweighing the identitarian tendencies of the term. Western queer theory has been rightly criticized as centring the gay male subject, despite its anti-essentialist claims. While, as Kapur has argued, there is an emerging identity in the deployment of queer in India, it is an identity that self-reflexively extends well beyond the gay male subject to a panoply of non-heterosexual subjects: lesbian, bisexual, transgender, hijra, kothi. Queer—in most of its iterations—interrogates these sexual desires and practices as non-normative. Only a few scholars, however, take it beyond the non-heterosexual. Kapur, uncomfortable with the term queer itself and preferring sexual subaltern, extends her analysis to the many forms of non-normative sexualities, homo and hetero alike, bringing sex workers and young straight lovers expressing their desire on screen, into the embrace. This is perhaps a common, unresolved tension in queer's meaning. Despite Halperin's assertion of the potential queerness of straight subjects who operate outside the norm, this has not—at least until very recently—been within the purview of most queer theory in the West. The anti-identitarian, anti-normative impulse of queer theory seems to stall at the very edges of the binary that queer theory initially set out to deconstruct.

The third theme—of examining sex and sexuality independent of gender and feminism—is in and of itself a more problematic one, given questions of temporality such as whether the long run has arrived, and whether continental drifts even occupy the same temporality. There is no doubt that sexuality/queer studies in India has emerged as distinct from feminism; although it has been produced by those who are located at the intersections of feminism and sexuality. It may also be that the historically and culturally-specific iterations of the sexual have produced a different kind of relationship with feminism. Narrain and Bhan speak of gender as a crucial dimension of queer inquiry yet do not deploy the language of feminism, nor do they often return to questions of gender per se. Kapur's work on the subaltern on the other hand is decidedly feminist, if also subversive of many of its orthodoxies. Bose and Bhattacharyya's volume speaks of the liminal and fraught space between sex and gender, which many of the contributors explore. Some point out the limits of feminism—indeed the outright heterosexism or homophobia of feminism—while also gesturing toward the need to integrate an interrogation of sexuality into feminism and feminism into sexuality.

These gestures toward the conversation between feminist and queer, and the resistance to their polarization articulated by many may be indicative of a nascent trajectory that sidesteps the fraught history of the West. Indeed, the very questions posed and the essays published in this volume are indicative of this emerging conversation.

What might be learned about feminism's relationship with the queer in and through the postcolonial? The postcolonial work of Puar and Gopinath is already located within a dialogue between queer theory and feminism, amongst a multiplicity of other critical lenses. Kapur's work on the sexual subaltern is one with more than a twist of Butlerian and materialist feminism. In these works, feminism and its analytic lens is present yet not privileged, decentred yet not disclaimed. Indeed, these are works that lead the way in intellectual trespass, richly weaving the threads of diverse critical theories into vibrant 'queer assemblages'. Turning the gaze back on itself, queer theory may well stand to learn that in the postcolonial the long run has indeed arrived.

Continental drift is, after all, a drift of tectonic plates in relation to each other. The continental drift of the postcolonial and the queer, of these shifting tectonic plates, creates permanent ruptures and seismic change. If we return for a moment to Butler's admonitions that queer is not to be owned but is a category in constant formation, we can see the postcolonial/queer encounter as precisely such a moment of the queer being "always and only redeployed, twisted, queered from a prior usage and in the direction of urgent and expanding political purpose".[73] The queer/postcolonial encounter is one that may be queering queer from its prior usage and is certainly taking it in urgent political directions.

NOTES

1. Gayle Rubin, *Thinking Sex: Notes for a Radical Theory of the Politics of Sexuality, in* Pleasure and Danger: Exploring Female Sexuality (C.S. Vance ed., 1984).
2. Judith Butler, *Against Proper Objects, in* Feminism Meets Queer Theory (E. Weed & N. Schor eds., 1997).

3. *See for example*, Bell et al., Bad Attitude/s on Trial: Pornography, Feminism and the Butler Decision (1997); Brenda Cossman, Sexual Citizens: The Legal and Cultural Regulation of Sex and Belonging (2007).
4. Brenda Cossman et al., *Gender, Sexuality, and Power: Is Feminist Theory Enough?*, 12 Colum. J. Gender & L. 601 (2003); Brenda Cossman, *Where Did Feminism Go? Reflections of a Slightly Lapsed Feminist,* 9 Issues in Legal Scholarship (2011).
5. Brenda Cossman & Ratna Kapur, Subversive Sites: Feminist Engagement with Law in India (1996); Brenda Cossman & Ratna Kapur, Secularism's Last Sigh: The Hindu Right and the (Mis)rule of Law (1999).
6. Brenda Cossman, *Returning the Gaze? Comparative Law, Feminist Legal Studies and the Postcolonial Project*, Utah L. Rev. 525 (1997).
7. David Halperin, Saint Foucault: Towards a Gay Hagiography 62 (1995); Annamarie Jagose, *Queer Theory,* 4 Austl. Humanities Rev. (1996), http://australianhumanitiesreview.org/1996/12/01/queer-theory/. David Halperin writes: "Queer [...] does not designate a class of already objectified pathologies or perversions [...] rather it describes a horizon of possibility whose precise extent and heterogeneous scope cannot in principle be limited in advance." Annamarie Jagose similarly writes: "It is not simply that queer has yet to solidify but rather that its definitional indeterminacy, its elasticity, is one of its crucial characteristics."
8. Judith Butler, Gender Trouble: Feminism and the Subversion of Identity (2nd ed., 1999); Judith Butler, Bodies That Matter: On the Discursive Limits of 'Sex' (1993); Rubin, *supra* note 1.
9. Michel Foucault, The History of Sexuality: An Introduction (R. Hurely trans., 1978).
10. Teresa de Lauretis, *Queer Theory: Lesbian and Gay Sexualities,* 3 differences iii (1991).
11. *Id.*
12. Jagose, *supra* note 7.
13. Halperin, *supra* note 7, at 62.
14. Michael Warner, The Trouble with Normal: Sex, Politics and the Ethics of Queer Life (2000); *see also*, Michael Warner, Fear of a Queer Planet: Queer Politics and Social Theory (1993).
15. Rubin, *supra* note 1, at 283. "A democratic morality should judge sexual acts by the way partners treat one another, the level of mutual consideration, the presence or absences of coercion, and the quantity and quality of the pleasure they provide".
16. Rubin, *supra* note 1, at 308.
17. *Id.*
18. Eve K. Sedgwick, The Epistemology of the Closet 27 (1990).
19. *Id.*
20. *See for example* Jeff Nunokawa, *Queer Theory: Postmortem*, 106 South Asian Quarterly 553 (2007). Others, less quick to declare its death, have explored its

present and future. *See for example,* Special Issue, Social Text: What is Queer About Queer Theory Now? 84-86 (David Eng, Judith Halberstam & Jose Esteban Munoz eds., 2005); After Sex: On Writing Since Queer Theory (Janet Halley & Andrew Parker eds., 2010).

21. Lee Edelman, No Future: Queer Theory and the Death Drive (2004).
22. Judith Halberstam, In a Queer Time and Place: Transgender Bodies, Subcultural Lives (2005).
23. Elizabeth Freeman, Time Binds: Queer Temporalities, Queer Histories (2010).
24. Katheryn Bond Stockton, The Queer Child, or Growing Sideways in the Twentieth Century (2009).
25. Butler (1993), *supra* note 8, at 228.
26. Sedgwick, *supra* note 18, at 48. "My first aim is to denaturalize the present, rather than the past–in effect, to render less destructively presumable homosexuality as we know it today".
27. Butler, *supra* note 2.
28. Janet Halley, *Sexuality Harassment, in* Left Legalism/Left Critique 80, 102 (J. Halley & W. Brown eds., 2002); *see also* Janet Halley et al., *Gender, Sexuality, and Power: Is Feminist Theory Enough?*, 12 Colum. J. Gender & L. 601 (2003); Janet Halley, *Take a Break from Feminism?*, *in* Gender and Human Rights 57 (K. Knop ed., 2004).
29. Halley et al., *supra* note 28, at 604.
30. *Id.*
31. *See* Janet Halley et al., *From the International to the Local in Feminist Legal Responses to Rape, Prostitution/Sex Work, and Sex Trafficking: Four Studies in Contemporary Governance Feminism*, 29 Harv. J. L. & Gender 335, 340 (2006). Janet Halley coined the term "governance feminism" to "refer to the incremental but by now quite noticeable installation of feminists and feminist ideas in actual legal-institutional power".
32. Halley, *supra* note 28, at 604. Halley's idea of "taking a break from feminism" is *not* a renunciation of feminism, nor an anti-feminist position. It is simply a bracketing of feminism's questions and its focus on the masculine/feminine distinction. Although she is extremely critical of "governance feminism"—the alliance of liberal, radical, and cultural feminism that has informed a range of regulatory approaches—she does not condemn all feminism with the same brush stroke. Her argument is often misconstrued as an anti-feminist renunciation. A more careful reading of her work reveals that it is not.
33. Biddy Martin, *Sexuality Without Genders and Other Queer Utopias, in* Femininity Played Straight: The Significance of Being Lesbian 3 (1996). The idea of "moving between" polarized positions is borrowed from Biddy Martin's piece. Halley's focus on governance feminism—radical and culture feminism—similarly runs the risk of obscuring the potential insights of the multiple variants of more marginal feminisms that live closer to the porous borders between the feminist and the queer.

34. Cossman et al., *supra* note 4, at 601; Brenda Cossman, *Sexuality, Queer Theory and Feminism After: Reading and Rereading the Sexual Subject,* 49 McGill L. J.. 847 (2004).
35. Joan Wallach Scott, Gender and the Politics of History 42 (1988).
36. Cossman, *supra* note 34, at 853.
37. Gayle Rubin, *supra* note 1, at 170.
38. *See for example,* Ann Stoler, Race and the Education of Desire: Foucault's History of Sexuality and the Colonial Order of Things (1995).
39. Joseph Massad, Desiring Arabs (2007*); see also,* Joseph Massad, *Re-Orientating Desire: The Gay International and the Arab World,* 14 Pub. Culture 361 (2002).
40. Massad (2007), *supra* note 39, at 163. "The categories gay and lesbian are not universal at all and can only be universalized by the epistemic, ethical, and political violence unleashed on the rest of the world by the very international human rights advocates whose aim is to defend the very people their intervention is creating."
41. *Id.* at 41.
42. *See for example* Inderpal Grewal & Caren Kaplan, *Global Identities: Theorizing Transnational Studies of Sexuality,* 7 GLQ 664 (2001); Elizabeth A. Povinelli & George Chauncey, *Thinking Sexuality Transnationally,* 5 GLQ 439 (1999); Martin F. Manalansan IV, *Diasporic Deviants/Divas: How Filipino Gay Transmigrants 'Play with the World', in* Queer Diasporas 183-203 (C. Patton & B. Sánchez-Eppler eds., 2000); 2 Yukiko Hanawa, Circuits of Desire (1994); Phillip Brian Harper et al., Queer Transexions of Race, Nation, and Gender (1997); Dennis Altman, Global Sex (2001).
43. Gayatri Gopinath, Impossible Desires: Queer Diasporas and South Asian Public Cultures (2005).
44. *Id.* at 11.
45. *Id.*
46. *Id.*
47. *Id.* at 16.
48. Jasbir Puar, Terrorist Assemblages: Homonationalism in Queer Times (2007); *see also,* Jasbir Puar, *Queer Times, Queer Assemblages,* 23 Social Text 121 (2005).
49. Puar (2005), *supra* note 48, at 127.
50. *Id.* at 121-122.
51. *Id.* at 123.
52. *Id.* at 125.
53. *See* Arvind Narrain, Queer: Despised Sexuality, Law and Social Control (2004); Arvind Narrain, *The Articulation of Rights around Sexuality and Health: Subaltern Queer Cultures in India in the Era of Hindutva,* 7 Health Hum. Rts. 142 (2004); Arvind Narrain, *Rethinking Citizenship: A Queer Journey,* 14 Indian J. Gender Stud. 61, 62 (2007); Rinchin, *Queering Marriage and Family,* 40 EPW 718-20 (2005); *see* Shohini Ghosh, *Invoking the Imagined Spectator: Bombay Cinema and Queer Sexualities, in* Queer Theory: Law, Culture and

Empire (K. Brooks & R. Leckey eds., 2010). There has been a veritable explosion of writing invoking the word 'queer'. My discussion in this section is not intended to exhaustively survey this literature, but rather to more modestly highlight some of its emergent themes in the use of the term 'queer'.

54. Queering India: Same-Sex Love and Eroticism in Indian Culture and Society (Ruth Vanita ed., 2002).
55. The Phobic and the Erotic: The Politics of Sexualities in Contemporary India (Brinda Bose & Subhabrata Bhattacharyya eds., 2007).
56. Because I Have a Voice: Queer Politics in India (Gautam Bhan & Arvind Narrain eds., 2005).
57. *Id.*
58. Siddharth Narrain, *Crystallising Queer Politics: The Naz Foundation Case and Its Implications for India's Transgender Communities,* 2 NUJS L. Rev. 455 (2009).
59. Bhan & Narrain, *supra* note 56, at 4.
60. *Id.*
61. Bose & Bhattacharyya, *supra* note 55.
62. *Id.* at xxi.
63. *See* Ratna Kapur, Erotic Justice and the New Politics of the Postcolonial (2005); *see also*, Sexualities (Nivedita Menon ed., 2008). Menon argues in favour of the politics of 'counter-heteronormativity', in and through an expressly feminist lens. For Menon, counter-heteronormativity refers to a range of political assertions that implicitly or explicitly challenge heteronormativity and the institution of monogamous patriarchal marriage.
64. Ratna Kapur, *Out of the Colonial Closet, But Still Thinking 'Inside the Box': Regulating 'Perversion' and the Role of Tolerance in De-Radicalising the Rights Claims of Sexual Subalterns,* 2 NUJS L. Rev. 381, 385 (2009).
65. *Id.* at 383. Kapur argues that both LGBT studies and queer theory "are seen to emanate primarily from 'the West', and neither captures the nuances and complex histories within which the sexual subaltern has emerged".
66. Subaltern Studies I: Writings on South Asian History and Society vii-viii (Ranajit Guha ed., 1982); Sumit Sarkar, A Critique of Colonial India (1985); Dipesh Chakrabarty, Provincializing Europe: Postcolonial Thought and Historical Difference (2000); Dipesh Chakrabarty, *Radical Histories and Question of Enlightenment Rationalism: Some Recent Critiques of Subaltern Studies,* 30 EPW 751 (1995); Mapping Subaltern Studies and the Postcolonial (Vinayak Chaturvedi ed., 2000); Dipesh Chakrabarty, Habitations in Modernity: Essays in the Wake of Subaltern Studies (2002); Vinay Lal, Empire and Knowledge: Culture and Plurality in the Global Economy (2002).
67. Indeed, it is precisely this kind of move that Kapur makes in her intervention in this volume; in shifting to a more explicit engagement with the sign of the 'queer' in the postcolonial and Indian context, Kapur explores the dissident and regulatory potentials of queer.
68. *See* Cossman, *supra* note 6.

69. Nishant Shahani, *After the Fire: India is Burning,* 15 GLQ 180 (2009). As Nishant Shahani writes in his review of Bose and Bhattacharyya's edited volume *The Phobic and the Erotic*: "if queer politics in India can learn something from queer theory in the West, can queer theory in the West learn anything from politics in India?"
70. *See* in this issue, Ratna Kapur, *Multi-tasking Queer: Reflections on the Possibilities of Homosexual Dissidence in Law.*
71. Brenda Cossman, *Feminism in Hard Times: From Criticism to Critique, in* Feminisms of Discontent: Global Contestations (A. Barnes ed., 2015).
72. See Judith Butler, *What is Critique? An Essay on Foucault's Virtue, in* The Political: Readings in Continental Philosophy (D. Ingram ed., 2002); Michel Foucault, *What is Enlightenment, in* Ethics, Subjectivity and Truth 14-15 (P. Rabinow ed., 1997).
73. Butler, *supra* note 72.

CHAPTER 4

Section 377 and the Myth of Heterosexuality

Zaid Al Baset

"For sake of convenient reference, they would hereinafter be referred to as 'homosexuals' or 'gay' persons or gay community."[1] This apparently innocuous sentence rests self-assured on page six of the historic July 2009 Delhi High Court judgment of *Naz Foundation v. Government of NCT*. But, of course, it is convenient: this collapsing of a constellation of terms that connote a multiplicity of sexual identifications and proclivities. I admit, nevertheless, that putting homosexual and gay in quotes is smart, suggestive of how this convenience is rather inconvenient, of how something is already lost—an insurmountable gap of difference has been mounted on a page.

It is also telling that gay, when juxtaposed with community, loses its decorative quotation marks. One wonders, why? What does the word 'community'—such a 'social', 'harmonious' and 'stable' term—do to the word 'gay' that it becomes unproblematically gay? Or am I reading too close for comfort, for it may well be just an editorial slip? One cannot be certain, but since uncertainties demand questioning, I shall continue. What the sentence manages to achieve, violently yet almost naively, is a collapse of history, a terrible error in the conflation of identities, locations, and desire and, most significantly, an attempt to naturalize the 'unnatural'. In absenting history, nature is reified: the homosexual/gay[2] becomes a naturally occurring 'unnatural' phenomenon. It is precisely this closeting of history, its camouflaging as natural, that produces the hegemonic heterosexual.[3] In other words, the 'naturalness' and omnipresence of heterosexuality is manufactured by an elimination of the historical specificities of the organization, regulation and deployment of sexuality across time and space.

This essay will 'look' at such innocent sentences, will search for gaps and contradictions, will make silences on the pages of the judgment speak. This is not an effort to nullify the significance of the judgment, rather, one to ascertain the various ways in which it constitutes the becoming of queer selves and their articulation in contemporary queer politics in India.[4] I will argue through the course of this paper that the *a priori* de-historicization of the queer subject forces any expression of queer politics to evoke the spectre of a closet. And in so doing, every 'outing' is simply another act of closeting, reiterating the naturalness of the only natural sexual category—the heterosexual. The 'closet' is a site of the construction of a tautology—heterosexual is natural, or as it were, the myth of the heterosexual.

This condensation of queerness, this censure of terms on the pages of the judgment, where 'gay' or 'homosexual' is used as a metonym for the entire spectrum of sexual and gender difference, carries with it the charge of concealing an 'essentially' variegated experience. One cannot help but register the rare occurrences of terms such as lesbian, *kothi, hijra* and so forth in the text of the judgment.[5] This 'erasure' has a two-fold consequence: firstly, sexual and gender differences which have historical and contextual importance are effectively lost, and this loss is conveniently forgotten. 'Homosexual' and 'gay' then begin to function as universal signifiers of homosexuality, which itself appears as a homogenous, general (natural) phenomenon, easily understood and uncomplicated. Secondly, the historicity of the terms 'homosexual' and 'gay' is undermined; these words are uprooted from their context of deployment and emptied of their cultural content. The term 'gay' connotes a specific historical intersection of class, gender, region, and even race. Likewise, the 'homosexual' has traversed an arduous history in the pages of late nineteenth and twentieth century medical and psychiatric journals and writings on sexology.[6] In the judgment, however, and arguably in the broader political context, these terms simultaneously erase the histories of other terms, as well as their own specific trajectories. Roland Barthes, in his essay 'Myth Today', likens a myth to a second-order semiological system wherein "a sign in the first system becomes a mere signifier in the second." He notes:

> the signifier of myth presents itself in an ambiguous way: it is at the same time meaning and form, full on one side and empty on the other [...] As a total of linguistic signs, the meaning of the myth has its own value, it belongs to a history. [...] in the meaning, a signification is already built and could very well be self-sufficient if myth did not take hold of it and did not turn it suddenly into an empty parasitical form. The meaning is *already* complete, it postulates a kind of knowledge, a past, a memory, a comparative order of facts, ideas, decisions. When it becomes form, the meaning leaves its contingency behind; it empties itself, it becomes impoverished, history evaporates.[7]

For Barthes, myths have a specific schematic deployment. In a myth, "the sign in the first system becomes a signifier in the second system"[8] such that the materials of mythical speech (the language itself, photography, painting, posters, rituals, objects and so on), however different at the start, are reduced to a pure signifying function as soon as they are caught by the myth.[9] The signifier of the myth is at once meaning (the signified or the final term of the first system of sign) *and* form (the signifier of the myth). What is signified by the myth is the *concept*. Just as the correlation between signifier and signified in language is termed *sign*, the relationship between *form* and *concept* is termed *signification.*[10] In simple terms, in the case of a myth, symbols may have specific meanings in themselves but myth erodes or distorts such specific meanings to posit *itself*, thereby emptying out the specific content of the symbols it uses. Keeping this schema in mind, I intend to show how heterosexuality as a *concept* employs terms such as 'gay' and 'homosexual' (and many others), transforming their *meaning* into *form* to create a specific *signification*, that is, heterosexuality as natural (normal) and homosexuality as unnatural (abnormal) or, simply put, the *myth* of heterosexuality.

There is but an 'abnormal regression' of the words 'homosexual' and 'gay' as they are transformed from *meaning* to *form*. Both words as meanings contain a geography, a history, a morality (or its lack), a literature, a pathology and so forth. 'Gay' conjures up mental images of Western subcultures of the 1960s, the Stonewall Inn riots, the birth of the gay movement in the US and its mimesis all over the world from the mid-twentieth century onwards, gay communities, gay individuals (most often white, male, and middle class), gay identifications the world over, gay rights, gay men of colour often Westernized and middle class (again), the 'plague' of AIDS, gay marriage, gay adoption, even gay promiscuity. The term 'gay' is rich, value–loaded, and pregnant with meaning. So, too, is the 'homosexual' born of the 'temporary' aberration that the sodomite was, evolving into a pervert 'species',[11] a naturally occurring anomaly. Although this anomaly was so named only as late as 1869,[12] the richness of meaning that 'gay' and 'homosexual' connote have to be depleted to sustain the myth of heterosexuality.

Barthes points out "[t]hat the form does not suppress the meaning, it only impoverishes it, it puts it at a distance, it holds it at one's disposal [...] It is this constant game of hide-and-seek between the meaning and the form which defines myth."[13] 'Gay' and 'homosexual' when deployed as forms (as in the case of the judgment) have their meanings placed at a distance, have their richness tamed, and are intentionally made the accomplices of a *concept* (what the form signifies). This concept is heterosexuality. The terms are used interchangeably and appear to simultaneously connote sexual acts, sexual orientation, sexual behaviour and sexual identities (each a different register of analysis). Barthes asserts that "this history [that is drained] out of the form [is] wholly absorbed by the concept."[14]

The concept, far from being an abstracted form, is suffused with history. It *is* history, a totality of our existence and our knowledge of reality. Heterosexuality intentionally employs 'gay' and 'homosexual' in tamed form in order to reinstate itself and assert its own ubiquity in history. In doing so, it robs these terms of their historicity. The word 'heterosexuality' appears only thrice in the judgment, although the concept pervades each line of it as much as it pervades all societal structures. The concept intentionally deforms meanings to ensure that the signification "appears both like a notification and like a statement of fact."[15] The 'naturalness' of heterosexuality imposes itself on us as a fact, uncontested, frozen in time and eternalized.

For Barthes, mythical signification is made possible by a motivated analogy. Unlike the sign, in which the signifier and signified are but arbitrary, mythical signification is never arbitrary; the relationship between concept and form is one of analogy, however partial. For instance, to appropriate the image of a mother loving a child as form demands that an analogy be established between the mother and heterosexuality; the mother is heterosexual. A mother is *naturally* heterosexual. A mother is *always* heterosexual. What is interesting to note is that the signification of heterosexuality is made possible not simply by motivated analogy but through motivated opposition as well. As forms, 'gay' and 'homosexual', and indeed all queer terms (including the term 'queer' itself), are not simply devoid of their particularities, they are naturalized in opposition to the concept of heterosexuality. They operate as empty signifiers enabling the very constitution of heterosexuality as the norm. The effect of this naturalization is that they become eternally frozen as 'naturally unnatural', and the means through which the eternal naturalness of heterosexuality is realized. The myth of heterosexuality does nothing more than depoliticize and dehistoricize sexuality, thereby sustaining the natural image of heterosexuality. The 105-page Naz judgment is a mere testimony to the successful career of the myth. Within the text, queer terms operate only as form veiling history wherein homosexuality and heterosexuality appear as naturally occurring phenomena, the former hitherto criminalized and the latter the foundation of society.

THE (UNNATURALLY) NATURAL HOMOSEXUAL

Probing the myriad ways in which the judgment resurrects the heterosexual myth, despite intending its dissolution, calls for a summary of the judgment itself. The judgment, which has been the cause of much celebration, holds that "Section 377 IPC, insofar as it criminalises consensual sexual acts of adults in private, is violative of Articles 21, 14 and 15 of the Constitution".[16] The concluding paragraphs endorse the inclusiveness of the Constitution of India, and assert that "those perceived by the majority as 'deviants' or 'different' are not on that score excluded or ostracized" and that misconceptions about LGBTs (lesbian, gay, bisexual and transgender persons) should not inform law.[17] The rest of the document is, of course, how the court arrives at this 'historic' judgment. Section 377 was born out of a desire to sexually discipline the colonial subject, imagined as erotically perverse in 1860. It criminalizes "unnatural offences" which include voluntary "carnal intercourse" against the "order of nature" with any man, woman, or animal. Section 377 further explicates that penetration sufficiently constitutes 'carnal intercourse'. 'Carnal intercourse' in this instance has been interpreted as anal sex and oral sex and other non-procreative but penetrative sexual acts.[18]

Interestingly, then, the law does not discriminate between 'homosexuals' and 'heterosexuals'; both stand implicated and are potentially capable of going against nature. Please note that the words 'homosexual' and 'heterosexual' were yet to be invented when this law was drafted by Lord Macaulay and have not been incorporated in the law. Section 377, then, technically speaks to the image of the sodomite alone. The sodomite is a man of wayward morality and aberrant sexual predilections; at least, by Christian standards (to be precise, all salvation religions condemn sodomy). Although the sodomite eventually becomes a homosexual, conflating a sodomite with a homosexual would be a discursive sin. A sodomite indulges in sexual acts that invite religious condemnation and legal proscription whereas a 'homosexual' is a person with an aberrant sexual identity.

Sodomy connotes acts of transgression whereas the homosexual is constituted with a transgressive subjectivity.

The subjectivity of the sodomite, however, remains more elusive and interestingly generic; generic in the sense that it implies an immoral, perverse, 'satanic' disposition which can wreak havoc on any mind (minds are yet to be heterosexualized/homosexualized). This anti-sodomy law puts into place certain stable equations. The natural is not criminal. It cannot be so, for the natural also appears to be involuntary (an edict of the divine, if you will). The unnatural is an act of volition, hence the sodomite *chooses* to sin; sin is not yet his constituting essence. The sodomite is a mere rupture, a momentary rupture in the form of an interdicted sexual act in the otherwise natural world and naturalized being. Nature, in this case, can be restored. The sodomite can be converted to his naturally moral self (arguably through punitive measures). One must never forget that the natural is also always moral, and one must also take cognisance of the fact that the moral is constituted as ahistorical. So, the law puts into place the naturalness of coitus between a man and a woman.

Carnal intercourse between a man's penis and a woman's vagina is so natural that it did not even require an act of naming. Sodomy then serves a dual function: it named a desire that nobody dared name, but also alluded to a desire so natural, moral, and obvious that it needn't have a name at all. Sodomy is appropriated to speak for *the* natural desire. While the former was an 'open secret', the latter was an objective, universal, religious fact. 1869 is the year when the terms 'homosexual' and 'heterosexual' came into being, underscoring a specific shift in European understandings of sexuality.

Sexuality began to operate, not through a calculus of prescribed and proscribed sexual acts, but through a classification of persons and identities. Sexuality became a science. And science confirmed that homosexuals are a separable species altogether; not a temporary aberration but a naturally occurring anomaly, and until the late twentieth century, medical/psychiatric science was steadfast in its reparative stance of fixing this anomaly.[19] The faith that nature could be restored remained intact, and nature had a new name:

heterosexuality. Some more stable equations follow: heterosexual = natural, and homosexual = unnatural (but naturally occurring); natural = normal, and unnatural = abnormal.

I am deliberately bypassing the nature/nurture debate on sexuality, especially homosexuality, because I am interested not in the causation of the phenomena but in their deployment. Whether homosexuals are born or created, they are deployed as always already present across history and society. It is not the issue of causation that naturalizes the homosexual subject. It is not that if homosexuals are born, they become natural entities, and if they are created, they become historical subjects. Homosexuality remains an 'unnatural' natural occurrence whether born or created. History is always *arrested* so as to make the category of the homosexual a natural universal.

Section 377 operates through the accomplishment of this arrest and so does the text of the judgment. Section 377 becomes the site at which heterosexuality is produced as natural, first simply through the evocation of the temporary sodomite and then through a construction of an *essential* homosexual. Section 377, in the way that it is worded, establishes two other 'facts' as intended afterthoughts: (a) men are *the* sexual subjects, therefore sex is always phallocentric (this, as we shall see, will be reiterated in the text of the judgment), and (b) a lesbian slip (unlike a Freudian one) is where a woman's 'right' to sexual subjecthood is playfully ignored/missed. Both these 'facts' have far-reaching consequences.

THE HOMOSEXUAL ERASURE FROM THE PUBLIC AND THE PRIVATE

Section 377 has seldom been applied in court judgments,[20] but its very existence has thrust criminality on same-sex desiring individuals, forcing them 'underground' and burying them under the edifice of a nation that excludes them and stymies their ability to avail of opportunities leading to a dignified life. One must eschew suggesting an absolute causal link between Section 377 and homophobia in India, yet the law provides a fecund site for the articulation of homophobia and responses to it. It renders any form of queer identification always already deviant. Not surprisingly then, the two-decade-old queer movement in India has largely been a struggle against Section 377. In 1994, ABVA (AIDs Bhedbhav Virodhi Andolan)—a left–wing, non-funded group—filed a petition against Section 377 in the Delhi High Court questioning its constitutional validity. The petition was filed at the behest of a medical report which confirmed that Tihar Jail had become a sodomite's haven. The World Health Organization (WHO) had recommended the distribution of condoms to inmates. Fearing that it would add fuel to the fire (or desire) and promote what the law prohibits, jail authorities refused. The case came up for hearing in 2001 and was dismissed without ABVA even knowing, as it had failed to keep track of it.[21]

In 2001, the Naz Foundation,[22] in collaboration with the Lawyer's Collective,[23] filed a public interest litigation (PIL) to 'read down' Section 377 "to the extent that the said provision criminalises consensual sexual acts between adults in private".[24] The petition was initially dismissed on the grounds that the Naz Foundation had no *locus standi* in the case. However, following a review by the Supreme Court, the case came up for hearing before the Delhi High Court in 2009. Prior to this, in 2006, the petition was fortified by a coalition of NGOs—Voices Against Section 377—which campaigned vociferously against the 'draconian' law. The culmination of this struggle is the 105-page text which details responses to the provisions of Section 377, most notably by the Naz Foundation, NACO (National AIDS Control Organization) and Voices against Section 377.

The petitioners argued that Section 377, insofar as it implicates consensual sex between adults in private, infringes upon the fundamental rights guaranteed under Articles 14 (right to equality), 15 (right to non-discrimination), 19 (freedom of speech and expression), and 21 (right to life) of the Constitution of India. The right to privacy, the petitioner noted, is implicit in the right to life and liberty, and "since private, consensual, sexual relations or sexual preferences figure prominently within an individual's personality and lie easily at the core of the 'private space', they are an inalienable component of the right to life."[25]

The petitioner further submitted that the use of 'sex' in Article 15 cannot be read as restricted to 'gender', but rather includes sexual orientation within its ambit, and hence equality on the basis of sexual orientation is implied in the right to non-discrimination. It was argued that the classification of sexual acts into procreative and non-procreative (as manifest in Section 377) is based on "stereotypes and misunderstanding[s] that are outmoded and [enjoy] no historical and logical rationale."[26] Such classifications are necessarily 'arbitrary and unreasonable' and violate the provisions of Article 14 of the Constitution. The petitioner further surmised that Section 377 negates the freedoms guaranteed under Article 19 since "an individual's ability to make personal statement about one's sexual preferences, rights of assembly/association and right to move freely so as to engage in homosexual conduct are restricted and curtailed." The petitioner also makes a strong case against Section 377, arguing that efforts towards HIV/AIDS intervention and prevention are severely hampered because of the discriminatory attitudes towards the gay community, which is particularly vulnerable to the disease. To support the above arguments, various court cases were cited, provisions of international law were quoted, and snapshots of the nature of the oppression that same-sex desiring individuals face in India were provided. The verdict that came in favour of the petitioner in effect de-criminalized consensual adult sex in private.

The 'private' in this case demands scrutiny. What does the right to privacy entail? In the text of the judgment, in a section titled 'Section 377 as an Infringement of the Rights to Dignity and Privacy,' various definitions are available. Privacy has been understood as "a private space in which man may become and remain himself" or as the "right to be left alone".[27] The right to be left alone is not understood simply as a negative right against government intrusion but also as a right to "get on with your life, your personality and make fundamental decisions about your intimate relations without penalization."[28] It also entitles people to "a sphere of private intimacy and autonomy which allows individuals to nurture relationships without interference from the outside community."[29]

It is noteworthy that any reference to privacy is always juxtaposed with the family or home. For instance, Article 12 of the Universal Declaration of Human Rights (cited in the text) states that "no one shall be subjected to arbitrary interferences with his privacy, family, home or correspondence nor to attacks upon his honour and reputation. Everyone has the right to the protection of the law against such interference or attacks."[30] Article 17 of the International Covenant on Civil and Political Rights is also worded in a similar vein where privacy, family and home appear together.[31] Likewise a reference is made to the case of *R. Rajagopal v. State of T.N.* (1994) where the court stated that "a citizen has a right to safeguard the privacy of his own, his family, marriage, procreation, motherhood, child bearing and education among many other matters."[32]

Privacy, then, is concurrently deployed as a spatial metaphor and a metaphor for personal autonomy. As a spatial metaphor, it is telling that 'privacy' is aligned with the family or home so that it connotes a physical space—the private sphere. The notion that 'privacy' implies the 'private sphere' is strengthened by proclamations such as the one provided by NACO, which states that the

> enforcement of Section 377 IPC against homosexual groups renders risky sexual practices to go unnoticed and unaddressed inasmuch as the fear of harassment by law enforcement agencies leads to sex being hurried, particularly because these groups lack 'safe place', utilise public places for their indulgence and do not have the option to consider or negotiate safer sex practices.[33]

Clearly, 'safe place' must mean the private sphere. The word 'risky' is worthy of note. Are same-sex acts 'risky' because they take place in the public sphere (in a hurried manner) and invite censure, or are they 'risky' because of the very nature of such acts (apparently more prone to HIV infection)? Which same-sex sexual acts are particularly 'risky'? Is homosexuality 'risky' *per se*?

Moreover, the notion of 'public places' needs qualification.[34] 'Public places' in this case could refer to public toilets, parks, and even public transport. Undoubtedly, one needs to make a distinction between sex in public and exhibitionism. Gay sex in public is often veiled. There are rituals of practice which may well be invisible to anyone other than the practitioners themselves. This public space is at least partially closeted. Often queer readings of space begin with the insight that public spaces are "produced as ambiently heterosexual, heterosexist and heteronormative."[35] Although one can question this presumption, it cannot be dismissed altogether. If one were to accept that public places are heteronormative, and same-sex sexual acts are, at least partially, closeted, then, by intending to relegate 'homosexual' acts to the private sphere or 'safe places', the judgment would effectively reiterate the ambient heterosexism of public space.

The outcome is an erasure of the 'homosexual' from the public. Counter-intuitively speaking, when queer acts are 'caught' in public, the seamless heterosexuality of the space is ruptured; the judgment aims to suture the same by rendering invisible the possibility of public spaces being tainted by markers of same-sex desire. Allowing queer sex in private is deeply problematic too. As the aforementioned articles show, there is an unconscious conflation of the private with the home and family, even marriage. The family as a space is always already heterosexual. In most liberal discourses, it is also imagined as a natural/biological unit. Adding the two together, the family becomes a site for the reproduction of heterosexuality as natural. For most queer Indians (if not all), the family or home functions as public space too. The heteronormativity of the Indian family can force queer Indians inside the closet even within the private sphere. The judgment then rests on a utopic notion of a 'private' space which is erased from the public and does not exist in the private. The space then provided to 'homosexuals' in India is in effect a non-space, or simply an erased space.

Privacy also, as suggested earlier, implies personal autonomy. Relegating one's sexuality to the domain of the private also runs the risk of it being perceived as something innate, instinctive, and outside the social, allowing it once again to slip into the abyss of the natural. Personal autonomy cannot be exercised in a social context. The social context for queer Indians is overtly heterosexist. The argument against the 'reading down' of Section 377 forwarded by the Additional Solicitor General submits that the "right to privacy is not absolute and can be restricted for compelling state interest."[36] He contends that India has a higher standard of morality than the West and likens homosexual sex to "gross male indecency". Moreover, the Ministry of Home Affairs stated that the deletion of Section 377 could "open the flood gates of delinquent behaviour and can possibly be misconstrued as providing unfettered license for homosexuality."[37]

That public morality is steeped in homophobia needs no reiteration. But the fact that the homosexual is always excluded from and stands outside the moral public is an issue that cannot be ignored. Personal autonomy will not make any sense unless 'homosexuals' become a part of the moral public. It is precisely at this point that the notions of privacy as space and privacy as autonomy intersect. The former presupposes the latter and vice versa. Queer Indians are spatially and structurally erased and morally excluded from the public. The right to privacy does not ensure inclusion in the moral public.

Not surprisingly, one of the strategies that NACO adopts for the prevention of (HIV/AIDS) infection reads thus: "reinforcing the traditional moral values of abstinence, delayed sexual debut till marriage and fidelity among the youth and other impressionable groups of the population."[38] 'Tradition', 'marriage' and 'fidelity' appear as words from a heterosexual script and 'impressionable groups' is an instance of just how cryptic and vague language can be. An assertion of personal autonomy by queer individuals runs the risk of ensuring their exclusion from the public (morality), which they were never a part of in the first place. It's a catch-22 situation: public morality does not include the 'homosexual' as part of the public and an assertion of personal autonomy invariably excludes the 'homosexual' from the public, since the public is always already imagined as heterosexual.

Consensual same-sex acts between adults 'in private' functions only as a *form* (as a historical and structural impossibility) usurped by the concept of heterosexuality. To the extent that it is framed in opposition to heterosexuality, homosexuality signifies the heterosexual myth by erasing its own signification. The judgment is peculiar precisely because queer Indians are closeted by the logic of the judgment at the very moment of their 'outing'. The judgment then evokes the spectre of a closet.

ALL THE WORLD'S A CLOSET

What, then, is a closet? Or more specifically, what does the closet hide? The closet seems to be a space whose boundaries, although continuously porous, are a defining feature of queer lives. Closets exist, and they hide social information. They hide certain socially proscribed sexual desires, certain unnamable sexual acts deemed 'unnatural' by cultural context and law, certain identities which dare not speak their name, and certain forms of behaviour which can make an individual susceptible to stigma and oppression. The closet does not simply hide this susceptibility; it hides stigma and oppression itself. It marks the silencing of different voices, a silence which is achieved by a gross violation of the lives that inhabit the closet, through violence and pain inflicted by significant others both within and without the closet, as well as instances of self-inflicted pain and violence. The closet also hides pleasure, and myriad sexual expressions and furtive encounters that gratify the self. The closet also conceals the possibility of disease and death. Asserting that the closet is "the defining structure of gay oppression", Sedgwick states that the "gay closet is not a feature only of the lives of gay people. But for many gay people it is still the fundamental feature of social life and there can be few gay people, however courageous and forthright by habit, however fortunate in the support of their immediate communities, in whose lives the closet is not still a shaping presence."[39]

Taking this a step further, I wish to argue that the closet is not simply a feature of queer lives; rather all lives in a hetero-patriarchal context have a relationship with the closet. The closet is maintained both from within and outside, but more prominently from the latter. The closet represents an unknowing, an ignorance, a forgotten secret which, if tampered with, can challenge the naturalness or the inevitability of compulsory heterosexuality. The closet then functions as a space in which to imprison the signs and signifiers that pose a threat to compulsory heterosexuality. The closet is that empty form in which a history of desire is locked and then forgotten. The relationship that heterosexuality shares with the closet is one of *denial*—a denial that ensures the systematic opposition between the 'normal' heterosexual who occupies the outside of the closet and the deviant 'homosexual' who occupies the space within. The boundary of the closet then circumscribes the homosexual as well as the heterosexual; one lives inside it, the other remains ignorant of it. But, of course, this ignorance is painstakingly maintained.

The tragedy of the homosexual resides in the fact that not only must they must exist within the closet but they must also deny the closet altogether and perpetuate the myth of heterosexual normalcy. While occupying the closet, the homosexual also erases it by creating a non-space and pretending to be outside the closet. Interestingly, then, the closet acts as a double bind in a homosexual's life: they are supposed to exist within it by feigning an existence outside it. The closet is a feature of all lives: both heterosexuality and homosexuality erase its epistemology through structural homophobia. The closet is a ubiquitous space; it does not exist as a marker of homosexuality, rather as an erasure of it to ensure the pervasiveness of heterosexuality. In a subverted sense, the closet represents the site where heterosexuality is in effect made compulsory.

A movement steered toward securing the rights of queer individuals must then confront the closet, and by that logic compulsory heterosexuality. Confronting the closet would mean reclaiming the markers of all the desires, identities and acts which challenge it.

A political dismantling of the closet has often been described as the process of 'coming out'. The phrase 'coming out' underscores a closed space but, as I have argued, the closet is a non-space and connotes an erasure of a space. In this sense, 'coming out' would imply reclaiming a space which never existed in any real way.

'Coming out' is never a finished process; it is always a work in progress, a matter of degree. An individual who 'comes out' has to keep 'coming out' and offer social information about themself. Hence, the metaphor of 'coming out' itself reifies the concept of the closet, for outing oneself appears as an act of vacating the closet, which is always already an empty form. The relationship between the closet and 'coming out' is a relationship of opposition between two forms which serve the concept of heterosexuality. The heterosexual is always exempt from this terrible and perpetual state of repetitive coming out to which the homosexual is doomed. The heterosexual is always already outed, ever present, always known.

MINORITIZING MANOEUVRES

A section titled 'Section 377 IPC Targets Homosexuals as a Class' in the *Naz* judgment holds that:

> Sexual acts which are criminalised are associated more closely with one class of persons, namely, the homosexuals as a class. Section 377 IPC has the effect of viewing all gay men as criminals. When everything associated with homosexuality is treated as bent, queer, repugnant, the whole gay and lesbian community is marked with deviance and perversity. [...] The result is that a significant group of the population is, because of its sexual non-conformity, persecuted, marginalized and turned in on itself.[40]

The clubbing of homosexuals into a class of persons is a minoritizing exercise, [41] and an act of single vectored interpellation.[42] It creates a picture of a concomitance between sexual acts and sexual identity. Locating personhood is imperative for a liberal discourse on rights, for acts cannot have rights, *individuals* have rights. Acknowledging homosexuals as a specific class/species that indulges in certain acts that follow from their essential being ensures the reification of its privileged other—the heterosexual.

If the homosexual is a distinct person, then so must be the heterosexual. Whatever the terms and conditions of the negotiation between the majority (heterosexual) and the minority (homosexual) may be, the two always occupy mutually exclusive spaces. In such a situation, the closet as a non-space which reiterates compulsory heterosexuality is no doubt altered. It no longer remains a non-space or an erasure but a space filled with variants of sexual identities. An easier way of putting it would be that the minoritizing discourse propels the 'coming out' of identical homosexual selves as distinct from the heterosexual who exists outside, hitherto colonizing the closet.

The closet stands colonized insofar as it continues to render coherence to the heterosexual who stands outside it. But this 'coming out' is also a 'filling in' of the closet to the extent that the closet is a non-space whose ontology is established only through the act of 'coming out', for the closet does not exist before this act. But this filling of the closet with homosexuals is what I call a form of 'heterosexual condescension'. The closet, in such an instance, does become a signifying economy for homosexual desire but only insofar as the already privileged heterosexual provides this space for such sexual variance. It is important to note that in a heteronormative context, the heterosexual is always already privileged; the minority homosexual, as he comes out, remains secondary, if not inferior, to the heterosexual. Yes, a space is created. The closet is marked and it posits homosexuality, but at what cost? The closet then reinforces what appears to be outside of it—compulsory heterosexuality.

Ranjita Biswas notes in her essay 'The Lesbian Standpoint':

> Heterosexuals are called upon to acknowledge homosexuals and understand their lives to give them space within the hegemonic. But never do we question the dominant order. It is important to note that against a backdrop of institutional primacy and legitimisation of the middle class monogamous reproductive heterosexual framework;

> in particular homosexuality would emerge as deviant and marginal, at best variant. The hegemony of the heterosexual order functions through a securing of its boundaries. And to do so it has to create it's 'other'. Without a certain precipitation of the deviant, heterosexuality cannot posit itself as normal; without the image of a copy gone bad, heterosexuality cannot be called original.[43]

With this as a focal point, I argue that a minoritizing gesture (as ennobled as it may be) is only a function of heterosexual condescension, which is equivalent to saying: 'Look, you poor homosexual. I understand you are an anomaly (of nature/culture or whatever) but in my self-proclaimed privilege, I give you some space.' Such a space remains marginal, a million homosexual outings notwithstanding. A 25-year-old gay man who I interviewed told me, "I do feel I'm abnormal in a way and I wish I was straight."[44] A minoritizing discourse sustains this wish rather than wiping it out, and it is precisely at the site of this sustenance that compulsory heterosexuality reigns supreme.

Contrastingly, an argument in favour of reading down Section 377 holds:

> According to NACO, those in the High Risk Group are mostly reluctant to reveal same-sex behaviour due to fear of law enforcement agencies, keeping a large section invisible and unreachable and thereby pushing the cases of infection underground making it very difficult for the public health workers to even access them. The situation is aggravated by the strong tendencies created within the community who deny MSM behaviour itself. Since many MSM are married or have sex with women, their female sexual partners are consequently also at risk for HIV/infection. [...] Clearly, the main impediment is that the sexual practices of the MSM and gay community are hidden because they are subject to criminal sanction.[45]

Such an argument, possibly more effective, nevertheless poses two problems. One, a politics framed on the medicalization of same-sex sexuality comes dangerously close to the nineteenth century medical construction of 'homosexuality' as a deviant or aberrant sexuality; and two, even though medical science and psychiatry have now relented from alleging that homosexuality is a 'sickness',[46] a politics linking same-sex practice to AIDS (as valid as the link may be) retains this homosexuality and disease nexus, which is counter-productive to a more positive view of same-sex desire. In India, where the common-sense perception of homosexuality remains one of sickness, even among medical practitioners,[47] such framings do more harm than good to queer persons.

The idea that gains currency is: even if homosexuals are not themselves sick, they are still carriers of grave sickness. Such framings retain the easy dichotomy between the healthy 'heterosexual' and the potentially sick and polluting homosexual. They affirm the notion that homosexuals are natural aberrations, mistakes made by nature. By highlighting the possibility of married men who have sex with men transmitting the disease to women and children, such a framing also appears to strengthen the heterosexual family and constitutes 'homosexuals' as a threat to the health and vitality of wayward heterosexual males and their families.

In a masterstroke, heteronormativity allows the normative male—who does not identify his same-sex practice—to put the entire onus of a sexual act on the non-normative male for his *masti*/discharge/sex,[48] just as it allows the normative male to put the onus of a woman's sexual assault on the woman herself. The category MSM—men who have sex with men—marks a universalizing attempt whereby sexual acts are privileged over sexual identities, and is itself problematic on various counts. In his essay 'MSM, HIV/AIDS and Human Rights in South Asia', Shivananda Khan asserts that MSM signifies "a range of masculinities and gendered behaviour(s) with differing contextualization of sexual practices, sex partner choices, perceived sexual needs, pleasures and desires."[49] He also problematizes the use of 'male', for the term straddles both normative males (who can easily pass off as 'heterosexual') as well as 'non-males' or effeminate men who, in a hetero-patriarchal context, would not qualify as men at all.

The term's inclusivity is made possible by a series of exclusions and omissions that ignore the specificities of gender, class and sexual orientation among men who engage in same-sex practices. Such a term then conflates identities with acts without doing adequate justice to either. For instance, how does one read a sex act between a *kothi* (a feminized male who is penetrated) and *parik/panthi* (a manly male who penetrates), where what appears to be a homosexual act has overtly heterosexual connotations when gender identifications and role-taking are taken into account. The kothi disturbs the alignment between sex and gender by coalescing a male body with a 'feminine' subjectivity, whereas the panthi iterates the alignment between the male sex and masculinity. It is precisely because the panthi does not disturb the sex-gender alignment—that of masculinity with penetrative sex—that he is able to 'pass' as normative, while the kothi fails to do so. Can a sexual act between a kothi and panthi, whose gender identifications reiterate heteronormative standards of desire, be reified as homosexual simply by divorcing it from the subjectivities of the actors performing the act? Would this not simplify the question of what constitutes a homosexual act in the first place? Is this not a violently reductive exercise which underplays the possibility of interesting slippages in the way homosexuality and heterosexuality are employed as opposing categories?

In emphasizing the transience of same-sex acts and implicating them within the discourse of fun/masti or casual encounters, the term MSM plays upon another trenchant dichotomy between procreative sex and recreational sex, where the former is privileged. It functions to trivialize same-sex sexuality as opposed to the more 'responsible' heterosexual act of human reproduction. I do not wish to trivialize reproduction itself, but aim only to assert that the easy equation 'heterosexuality = procreative = meaningful = responsible = natural' versus 'homosexuality = hedonistic = meaningless = irresponsible = naturally unnatural' is untenable and only reinforces a distaste for queer persons. Given the heteronormative context in which such 'deviant' acts are located, it reinforces the allegedly direct correspondence of heterosexual acts, identities and behaviours, thereby justifying the heterosexual claim to normality and naturalness.

From the above discussions, it is amply clear that queer politics simultaneously employ a minoritizing discourse of persons with a universalizing discourse of acts. What are the consequences of such an exercise on the closet? The closet 'appears' as a hitherto hidden space emptied of its contents—a secret typification of identities and register of acts, of contestations of the heterosexual matrix. This 'appearance' conjures an image of dismantling the closet itself. On the contrary, I argue that the closet is a space marked by the absence of homosexual signification; it is not emptied of its content, rather content is attributed to it. Homosexuality, conceived either as a compendium of identities or an assortment of acts, is articulated in a way that ends up supporting heterosexual hegemony. Far from being dismantled through queer politics, the closet is reconfigured as a space of the 'other' simply as a form, devoid of content, emptied of the complex social histories of 'othering', which by virtue of its opposition to the concept of 'heterosexuality' crystallizes it as a myth, eternal and foundational to sociality.

POSTSCRIPT

This essay was originally published in 2012 and has been republished here without further changes. This essay was cited by the Supreme Court in its verdict on Navtej Singh Johar v. Union of India that decriminalized homosexuality in India on the 6th of September, 2018.

NOTES

1. Naz Foundation v. Govt. of NCT of Delhi, (2009) 160 DLT 277, at 6.
2. I use homosexual/gay interchangeably to suggest that de-historicizing these terms allows one to use them as though they mean the same thing, when they necessarily do not.
3. My use of 'hegemonic heterosexual' implies the ideological construction of a particular alignment of sex, gender, and desire that posits itself as natural, inevitable, and eternal. Heterosexuality is the site where the male-sexed masculine man's desire for the female-sexed feminine woman is privileged

over all other forms of sexual desire, and this becomes a pervasive norm that structures all societal structures.

4. The term 'queer' is fraught with contradictions. It has had a chequered history, from being a derogatory term for 'homosexual' males to a term that connotes, in theory, the impossibility of fixed essences and identity locations and a refusal to envisage a formulaic relationship between one's sex, gender, and desire. The resistance to any closure of meaning is what makes the term polemical and allows for continuous revisions. 'Queer' is fashioned as an inclusive term while acknowledging, at the same time, that any act of inclusion will create its own set of exclusions. The term, arguably, is used in at least two senses: (a) as a noun, where it functions as an 'umbrella' term aiming to bring together diverse sexual proclivities, gender identifications and sexual practices as an opposition to heterosexuality (this meaning of queer is commonly employed in political practice); and (b) as a verb which poses a theoretical critique to the crystallization of sexual identities into fixed essences. I use queer in this essay, whether as a noun or a verb, as a term of resistance against the discourse of sexuality that privileges the heterosexual as natural and constructs all 'others' as unnatural.
5. Naz Foundation, supra note 1, at 382. The term kothi features only once in the text of the judgment, in a section titled 'Responses of Other Respondents'. Respondent No. 8 is the coalition 'Voices against Section 377 IPC' which includes kothi persons who are then subsumed within the LGBT category. The term hijra is used five times in the text; firstly, as a part of 'Voices against Section 377 IPC', only to be subsumed within the LGBT category. The term is also invoked while citing the case of *Jayalakshmi v. The State of Tamil Nadu*, which addresses a hijra who committed suicide due to custodial torture, in order to highlight police violence against hijras. Interestingly, this section begins with the sentence, "Then there is a reference to 'Bangalore incident, 2004' bringing out instances of custodial torture of LGBT persons." Again, an attempt is made to erode the specificity of the hijra person by including her within the LGBT category.
6. *See* Sibaji Bandyopadhyay, *Approaching the Present—The Pre-Text: The Fire Controversy, in* The Phobic and the Erotic 42-61 (B. Bose & S. Bhattacharya eds., 2007) for a historiography of the terms 'homosexual' and 'gay'.
7. Roland Barthes, Mythologies 140-141 (2009).
8. For an elaboration of the nature of a linguistic sign is detailed in *see* Ferdinand De Sassure, Course in General Linguistics 65-67 (W. Baskin trans., 1981). Sassure writes, "The linguistic sign unites not a thing and a name but a concept and a sound image". A sign, therefore, is an amalgam of the signifier (that which expresses) and the signified (the concept). For instance, the sign 'tree' is a two-sided entity composed of the word 'tree' (signifier) and the concept of a tree (signified).
9. Barthes, *supra* note 7, at 137.
10. *Id.* at 140.

11. Michel Foucault, The History of Sexuality: An Introduction 1 (1990).
12. *See generally* Bandyopadhyay, *supra* note 6.
13. Barthes, *supra* note 7, at 141-142.
14. *Id.* at 142.
15. *Id.* at 148.
16. Naz Foundation, supra note 1, at 382.
17. LGBT as an acronym gained political currency in the 1990s. It refers to communities based on sexuality and gender-based identities.
18. Alok Gupta, *Section 377 and the Dignity of Indian Homosexuals*, 41 EPW 4815 (2006).
19. *See* Foucault, *supra* note 11, at 1; Bandyopadhyay, *supra* note 6.
20. Geetanjali Misra, *Decriminalizing Homosexuality in India*, 17 Reproductive Health Matters 20 (2009).
21. Arvind Narrain, *Queer Struggles Around the Law: The Contemporary Context, in* Sexualities 56-57 (N. Menon ed., 2007).
22. The Naz Foundation Trust is a New Delhi-based NGO (founded by a parent organization in Britain) that has worked on HIV/AIDS and sexual health since 1994. It endeavours to sensitize the public on matters of sexual health and provide support to people living with HIV/AIDS. It has a rights-based approach to issues pertaining to sexual health.
23. Established in 1981, the Lawyers Collective is a 'public interest service provider' in the field of human rights advocacy, legal aid and litigation, especially issues relating to women's rights, HIV/AIDS, and so on. Its members include professional lawyers, law students and human right activists.
24. The Naz petition was filed following police raids of NGOs working on HIV/AIDS and with the MSM community in Lucknow. In July 2001, the police arrested 10 people, one of whom was an activist from Bharosa (an NGO working with the MSM community) and raided the offices of Naz and Bharosa in Lucknow, seizing safe sex materials. An FIR was registered under Section 377, Section 120B (conspiracy to commit an offence), Section 109 (abetment) and Section 292 (sale and so on of obscene material) of the Indian Penal Code, 1860. The incident was widely reported in the media and the NGOs were accused of running gay clubs and polluting young minds. For a detailed account of the Lucknow case, *see* Narrain, *supra* note 21.
25. *See* Naz Foundation, *supra* note 1, at 285.
26. *Id.* at 286.
27. *Id.* at 311.
28. *Id.* at 310.
29. *Id.* at 311.
30. *Id.* at 104.
31. G.A. Res. 2200A(XXI), U.N. Doc. A/RES/2200(XXI); *European Convention on Human Rights*, European Court of Human Rights, https://www.echr.coe.int/documents/convention_eng.pdf. Article 17 of the International Covenant on Civil and Political Rights states that, "No one shall be subjected to arbitrary

or unlawful interference with his privacy, family, home or correspondence nor to attacks upon his honour". In a similar vein, the European Union Convention on Human Rights states that, "Everyone has the right to respect for his private and family life, his home and his correspondence."

32. *See* Naz Foundation, *supra* note 1, at 309.
33. *Id.* at 283-291.
34. I use 'public places' to refer to specific geographical locations whereas 'public spaces' is used to refer to space in the notional/ideological sense of the public-private.
35. David Bell & Gill Valentine, *Introductions: Orientations, in* Mapping Desire 16-17 (1995).
36. Naz Foundation, *supra* note 1, at 300.
37. *Id.* at 287.
38. *Id.* at 291.
39. Eve Kosofsky Sedgwick, Epistemology of the Closet 68 (2008).
40. Naz Foundation, *supra* note 1, at 355.
41. Sedgwick, *supra* note 39, at 86. Sedgwick notes "to be gay [...] is to come under the radically overlapping aegises of a universalizing discourse of acts and a minoritizing discourse of persons. Just at the moment, at least within the discourse of law, the former of these prohibits what the latter of them protects; but in the concurrent public-health constructions related to AIDS, for instance, it is far from clear that a minoritizing discourse of persons ('risk groups') is not even more oppressive than the competing, universalizing discourse of acts ('safer sex')."

    Sedgwick intends to highlight the simultaneous yet contradictory strands of separatist (referring to an essentialist discourse of persons) and integrative (referring to a constructionist discourse of acts) understandings of sexuality that inform the public discourse of same-sex desire coupled (more often than not) with the discourse of HIV/AIDS. Her analysis is particularly germane to understanding the contradictory arguments in favour of reading down Section 377 and the ways in which they speak to the metaphor of the closet.
42. I use 'single vectored interpellation' to suggest a subject interpellated by only a single vector, sexual desire in this case. Such an interpellation is always a reductive exercise since subjects are interpellated through multiple vectors such as class, race, gender, region of birth and so forth, which intersect in complex ways.
43. Ranjita Biswas, *The Lesbian Standpoint, in* The Phobic and the Erotic: The Politics of Sexualities in Contemporary India 274 (B. Bose & S. Bhattacharyya eds., 2007).
44. This interview was part of my research for my M.Phil. dissertation titled 'Truth and Other Lies: Telling Queer Stories', which was based on accounts of gays and lesbians living in Kolkata and Delhi. The interview was done after the Delhi High Court judgment of 2009. My MPhil was supervised by Professor Sibaji Bandhopadhyay at the Centre for Studies in Social Sciences, Calcutta.

45. *See* Naz Foundation, *supra* note 1, at 326.
46. Arvind Narrain & Vinay Chandran, *'It's Not My Job to Tell You That It's Okay to Be Gay': Medicalization of Homosexuality: A Queer Critique, in* Because I Have a Voice 55 (A. Narrain & G. Bhan eds., 2005).
47. *Id.* at 59-62.
48. Shivananda Khan, Making Visible the Invisible: Sexuality and Sexual Health in South Asia 32 (1996). Masti/discharge/sex refer to sexual 'play' which doesn't necessarily impinge upon the sexual identity of those involved. Khan notes: "The word [masti] is not easily translated but in a sexual context it means sexual 'playfulness,' and is usually used in the context of sexual play between males. It is not seen as a serious act, because it does not involve a woman. Nor is it really seen as sex. To some extent it is even socially permissible, 'Young men letting off steam'. So long as it remains invisible. This does not differentiate this form of sexual playfulness from others, for all sexual behaviour, whether socially legitimate (sex between married partners) or otherwise must also remain invisible."
49. Shivananda Khan, *MSM and HIV/AIDS in India,* 4 (2004), https://www.semanticscholar.org/paper/MSM-and-HIV-%2F-AIDS-in-India-Khan/1c6c94faa5f428b6f74a0d8e8725c5a85217c48e.

CHAPTER 5

Claiming Citizenship, Contesting Civility

The Institutional LGBT Movement and the Regulation of Gender/Sexual Dissidence in West Bengal, India

Aniruddha Dutta

INTRODUCTION

In July 2010, an article in a national English daily titled 'Let's Keep the Pride' marked the first anniversary of the 2009 Delhi High Court judgement that decriminalized private sexual activity between consenting adults of the same sex[1] The article approvingly described a commemorative event at Delhi[2] that demanded equal rights for the "LGBT community".[3] However, while the article supported the political legitimacy of 'LGBT' persons as equal citizens and thus echoed an increasingly common stance in Indian print media, it also singled out "a few transgenders" for "inappropriate behaviour" during the event that "threatened to mar the atmosphere".[4] Even as the report approvingly cited "cheerful slogan shouting by gay rights supporters" and "provocative images" such as two men kissing, it berated the aforementioned "transgenders" for dancing while "lifting up their skirts and shouting swear words", which apparently embarrassed even "their own community".[5] The author quoted leading gay activist Ashok Row Kavi in support:[6] "We must use our rights responsibly [...] We have to go a very long way to convince society that we are equal citizens with equal rights."[7]

His words uncannily echoed those of Akash,[8] a community leader and activist in the small town of Berhampore in the eastern Indian state of West Bengal. During a conversation in 2007, soon after the establishment of Madhya Banglar Sangram, the local community-based organization (CBO) for 'sexual minorities', Akash told me that the public behaviour of certain members of socio-economically marginalized and stigmatized gender/sexually-variant communities like *kothis* and *hijras* provoked adverse social reactions and made working for their rights difficult.[9] Speaking as a community member and leader, Akash said: "If one wants acceptance and respect from society, one will have to act in a respectable manner." The stern caveat about 'respect' (*shomman* in Bangla) was not surprising. During my ethnographic fieldwork in the city of Kolkata and other small towns in West Bengal,[10] I heard similar comments about the unruly and disreputable behaviour of some gender/sexually-variant persons in both casual conversations with activists and more formal contexts, such as meetings of non-governmental organizations (NGOs) that work with 'sexual minorities' (*jounoshonkhaloghu* in Bangla). Various actions collectively designated as *bhel kora* (acting flamboyantly) or *bila kora* (creating trouble) in the regional intra-community code or argot—including specific gestures used to solicit money (*chhalla*) or perform sex work in public (*khajra*), and more broadly, any overly assertive or aggressive public display of gender non-conformity—were critiqued for exacerbating 'mainstream' perceptions of these communities and even provoking abuse, thus hampering the struggle for equal rights and against societal discrimination. According to one activist who spoke against such public behaviour in a meeting preceding the 2007 Kolkata Rainbow Pride Walk: "the action[s] of some of the participants such as dressing up during [last year's] walk was indecent and lowered the dignity of the walk. It was also detrimental to the objective of the movement [...] establish[ing] the rights of community people."[11] This led to an unwritten consensus among NGO representatives on the need for greater surveillance of such 'indecent' behaviour: for instance, the *thikri*, a loud clap used by hijras and some kothis for public assertion, came under censure during subsequent walks.[12]

The systematic interconnections between the above instances suggest that at the very moment when 'sexual minorities', the 'LGBT community', and/or their constituent identities are constructed as intelligible and legitimate citizen-subjects deserving equal rights, a range of practices and subject positions at the intersections of class/caste and gender marginality—particularly gestural manifestations of public assertion and gendered flamboyance by working-class and/or Dalit (oppressed caste) subjects—are sought to be excluded or disciplined by emergent modes of sexual/political subjecthood. Such practices may be condemned both as flouting cultural norms of respectability through their indecency or disreputability, and as interrupting the process of gaining formal equality within civil society through their unruliness or incivility.

In this article, I locate and examine these regulatory tendencies as part of the contested processes through which institutions and activists in India in general, and West Bengal in particular, construct and assimilate 'sexual minority' groups into legitimate citizenship, and into an aspirationally cosmopolitan middle-class civil society, through claims upon both cultural nationhood and transnational discourses such as LGBT and human rights. As I will argue, even as institutional LGBT activism in India contests restrictive narratives of national culture where gender/sexual variance is portrayed as alien and corruptive to the nation, it might reinscribe a normative relationality between socio-cultural hierarchies of respectability and exclusive forms of civility and citizenship, such that certain forms of queer resistance or dissidence are condemned both for social indecency and for violating civic equality through excessive provocation or aggression. While the process of claiming citizenship via liberal discourses of equal rights visibilizes some LGBT subjects as deserving citizens, it might further entrench or reiterate extant social stigma against non-elite groups and subject positions, such that associated forms of difference, resistance and subjectivity are rendered uncivil, illegitimate and/or politically unintelligible—'subaltern'[13] in the sense of speech and resistance that cannot be heard or recognized within dominant discourses of equality and rights.[14] Moreover, hierarchies of civility and respectability fuel identitarian splits between categories such as gay and transgender, MSM (men who have sex with men) and transgender, and even good and badly-behaved transgender, though many 'community people' inhabit multiple and overlapping subject positions.

These arguments resonate with a growing literature in the West that maintains that LGBT recognition and visibility has incorporated relatively elite queers into nationality, citizenship and socio-cultural respectability ('homonormativity' and 'homonationalism') at the cost of continuing or increasing the marginalization and deprivation of racial and socio-cultural others.[15] While Indian institutional activism may mirror some trends in Western LGBT politics, I argue that attempts to legitimize LGBT groups into cultural nationhood and civic equality become internally contested and contradictory in the postcolonial context of India and, moreover, come into friction with various forms of gender/sexual agency and class/caste resistance associated with working-class and non-metropolitan subcultures and communities, which may not be easily recuperated into narratives of national culture and liberal discourses of citizenship.[16] These frictions result in contested tendencies within the movement to control the domain of civic participation and regulate the involvement of working-class and Dalit gender-variant people through imputations of their indecent, disreputable or uncivil behaviour. Such regulatory tendencies are particularly applied to publicly visible trans feminine people (feminine-identified people assigned male at birth) belonging to hijra and kothi communities or subcultures, which evokes parallels with the ways in which these communities have been criminalized by colonial-era laws meant to safeguard public order and decency.[17]

I do not suggest that such regulatory tendencies are necessarily concerted institutional policies enforced by organizations or activists from above, or that they can simply be blamed on particular actors. Rather, this chapter analyzes conglomerations or assemblages of societal, institutional and intra-community forms of hierarchy and stigma that do not have any singular agent, and indicates the structural limitations of liberal discourses of citizenship more than specific individual or organizational intentions. As I will attempt to demonstrate, regulatory modes of public and political visibility, organized around the liberal democratic ideal of formal equality and the modern interiorized and privatized conception of gender/sexual identity, interact with and reinscribe social and intra-community hierarchies based on 'traditional' ideas of decency and respectability (shomman in Bangla). These processes are not merely internal to the LGBT movement but evidence a broader structural dynamic of postcolonial citizenship where cultural ideologies of class, caste, and gender intersect with the legacies of Enlightenment humanism and colonial governance, which promised the universalization of equality and rights while withholding citizenship and political sovereignty from subjects deemed insufficiently civilized.[18]

In its aspirational trajectory towards equal citizenship, the movement seeks to pedagogically assimilate working-class groups into norms of civility and respectability, seeing them as inadequate subjects who need to be trained in order to become worthy of rights. These attempts reflect the contemporary iterations of a long history of dominant-caste/class reformist endeavours to "recast" subordinate groups within hegemonic constructions of national identity or culture.[19] As Akash's equation between gaining social equality and acting respectably suggests, abstract political ideas of civic equality and exchange are expressed through particular cultural ideas of respectability, demonstrating convergences between regulatory ideals of political and cultural citizenship that restrict working class/Dalit participation in civil society.

CIVIL VS. POLITICAL SOCIETY?

As I will describe, these politico-cultural convergences create a structural rift between those relatively privileged subjects who may claim equal participation in both civic and cultural realms (usually middle or upper-class LGBT activists), and those who do not gain the position of full/proper citizens, but rather become positioned as recipients of the welfare and training provided by middle class-led NGOs, particularly as 'target groups' or low-tier staff in HIV/AIDS prevention interventions undertaken by many (though not all) NGOs.[20] This rift may seem analogous to Partha Chatterjee's distinction between 'civil society' and 'political society', the first being the domain of equal citizenship entitled to a stable set of constitutional rights, the second the sphere of both welfare and the regulation/surveillance of excluded sections through governmental technologies.[21] According to Chatterjee, "civil society" in postcolonial nations is restricted to the urban middle classes, and aspires to be an "orderly zone" of law and rights in congruence with "normative models of bourgeois civil society."[22] It is both "sequestered" from and threatened by the messy practices of "political society", where different subaltern groups negotiate their demands through "temporary, contextual and unstable arrangements" with governmental power.[23]

However, I will deploy an ethnographic analysis of the movement for 'sexual minority' rights to suggest that both the 'real' spatial boundary and the conceptual distinction between civil and political society may be subject to contestation, rather than marking the separation of neatly "sequestered" domains.[24] NGOs advocating for 'sexual minorities' invoke constitutional rights to enter mainstream civil society, and in turn seek to regulate the participation of non-elite 'target groups' in this expanded civic space—a contradictory dynamic that cannot prevent further challenges from below. Such challenges often expose the lie of civic order and its disavowed moments of contingency, instability and excess.

In the following sections, I elaborate on this process with reference to my ethnographic fieldwork as a participant-observer in several organizations associated with 'sexual minorities' in West Bengal between 2007 and 2012.[25] The location is prompted by my familiarity with the Bengal region as a native speaker of Bangla, and by the access afforded by my gradual inclusion as a friend and community member in both middle- and working-class contexts over the years. West Bengal also provides an appropriate site because of its early growth of an institutionalized LGBT movement (including India's first pride walk in Kolkata in 1999), its links with the national LGBT movement, and the expansion of NGOs across non-metropolitan and metropolitan areas, allowing contact across socio-economic and geographic locations.[26] While I approach mainstream discourses of citizenship operative at the national level through a media analysis, I also analyze forms of political expression and dissent in West Bengal (such as pride walks and musical/dance performances) to provide a regionally-situated example of how excluded sections negotiate or challenge the civil/uncivil distinction that polices the boundaries of civil society. Although my ethnographic analysis is specific to West Bengal, I contend that there are parallels with broader national trends and indicate this at several points in this chapter to bring light to the larger context and scope of my arguments.

In the third section, I demonstrate how contemporary Indian civil society—within which the movement aspires for inclusion—simultaneously negotiates cultural-nationalist formulations of the ethically responsible citizen and the transnational figure of the citizen-consumer, resulting in a complex (and at times conflicting) ethos of civility and citizenship. This challenges the conceptual abstraction of civil society as an ordered domain of civic interactions that actualizes ideals of liberal democracy and citizenship, and shows how these idealized norms are inevitably entangled in elite (and contestable) conceptions of proper civility and (trans)national culture. As feminist critiques and revisionist historiography have shown, the "distinctive culture of civil society" emerged in Europe with an associated ethos and style of public behaviour that drew from and furthered bourgeois and male dominance.[27] Thus, rather than comprising an external disorderly domain such as 'political society', contingent political negotiations and claims by privileged subjects were internal to the constitution of normative forms of civility and citizenship from their moment of emergence. Further, the putatively rational discourse of civility is profoundly gendered and contingent upon a disavowal of 'feminine' excess and irrationality.[28]

In the fourth section, I examine how disparate tendencies within the dominant culture of civil society, while contradictory in themselves, unite to delegitimize certain subjects' citizenship—especially those identified with disreputability, irrationality, or aggression—exacerbating forms of stigma and fuelling identitarian divides within minoritized communities. On the other side of this exclusion, forms of middle-class cultural expression, such as specific genres of music and dance, are used to assimilate and include unruly subjects through a pedagogical process of disciplining and containment.

The fifth section studies how subaltern encroachments and appropriations continually challenge the boundaries of civil society, interrupting the restricted spaces of civility and broadening its permitted ethos by mixing 'high' and 'low' culture. Again, musical and dance performances become a crucial site of these crossings and mediations. As Bourdieu argues in his influential sociology of culture, the media of cultural expression (such as music) index class, and social position can play crucial roles in the struggle over cultural capital and social mobility.[29] I investigate how contestations and crossovers in the realm of 'culture' might reclaim models of equality and citizenship beyond middle-class civil society spaces, and permit situated demands far beyond the 'original' provenance of the liberal political tradition.

Before moving on, a note on categories of identification might be useful. The cross-cultural emergence and adaptations of modern identity-based conceptions of sexuality have inspired complex academic debates that are beyond the scope of this article.[30] Given the transnational circulation of the term 'gay' in the media and the urban emergence of visible gay- and lesbian-identified communities, the Indian movement commonly uses the 'LGBT' schema of identities for civic activism and media representation directed at middle-class audiences.[31] 'Queer' too is increasingly used in the sense of an umbrella term for LGBT identities[32]—even though, academically, 'queer' may be deployed as a *critique* of identity-based politics.[33] However, many NGOs active in LGBT activism also undertake state- and donor-funded interventions for sexual health and human rights which interact with and draw lower-level staff from working-class and non-metropolitan communities that, as I observed during my fieldwork, may not identify as 'gay' and are usually even less familiar with 'queer'.[34] NGOs draw upon transnational HIV/AIDS prevention discourse and use 'sexual minorities', 'MSM' and 'TG' (transgender), rather than LGBT, to denote 'target groups' and staff in HIV/AIDS interventions.[35] MSM and TG include and subordinate terms like kothi and hijra, which become positioned as 'vernacular'.

Institutional attempts to classify these terms as MSM or TG have resulted in unstable cartographies of identity. While hijras are usually categorised as a 'third gender' TG group organized into marginalized clans, kothi communities comprise a spectrum of feminine-identified people including feminine males, third gender identified persons and trans women, some of whom may also join hijra groups. Thus, there are institutional disagreements on whether kothis should be classified as feminine MSM or transgender women, as described in the fourth section.[36] Analytically, these non-elite forms of gender/sexual difference may be understood as 'queering' or blurring identitarian boundaries between categories like MSM and TG, even though the word 'queer' is largely absent in such contexts. All terms should be read as if in scare quotes, denoting unstable formations of identity rather than essentialized or historically unchanging subject positions.

THE JUNCTURE OF LIBERALIZATION: CONTESTED ETHOS OF CIVILITY AND CITIZENSHIP

The story I tell here begins in the 1990s, a complex period in the history of independent India, marked simultaneously by socio-economic liberalization/globalization and the political rise of Hindu right-wing nationalism.[37] As Arvind Rajagopal has argued, these are not simply contradictory tendencies but rather there is an "elective affinity" between consumerist liberalization and Hindu nationalism, which utilized commoditized forms of mass culture for the purposes of propaganda and monetary support from diasporic Indians in the US and the UK.[38]

However, one contested locus where this "elective affinity" is ruptured seems to be non-normative genders and sexualities. This decade was marked by visible representations of same-sex desiring and gender-variant subjects in the media, even as dominant discourses of national identity attacked such representations as foreign to 'Indian culture' and threatening national sovereignty and security.[39] The most publicized instance would be the 1998-99 controversy over *Fire,*[40] a feature film depicting a sexual relationship between two housewives, where the Hindu right wing entered the fray with virulent proclamations of lesbianism as a Western import, not only un-Indian but also corrupting Indian womanhood and family values.[41] Such discourses show how patriarchal and dominant-caste definitions of a gendered familial order become constitutive of normative definitions of 'Indian culture' and national identity[42]—thus forming, in Lauren Berlant's terms, an "intimate core" of national culture and citizenship.[43] However, there has also been a wave of 'positive' media coverage in multiple languages, decrying these conservative trends and foregrounding, even celebrating, emergent gay and lesbian subjects and subcultures as signs of progress connected with the trajectory of economic liberalization and cultural globalization, here seen as desirable. For instance, a characteristic article in the Kolkata newspaper The Telegraph cites an LGBT pride walk in 2005 as evidence of changing social mores and states:

> One doesn't have to look too far for the reasons for this change in attitudes. The City of Joy itself is changing. Shopping malls [...] have mushroomed [...] satellite television and multiplexes have added spice to life [...] call centres have engaged a brigade of young workers [who] are making money and willing to spend it.[44]

In response to these contradictory currents, dominant LGBT activism has sought equal status within the national citizenry through a *double* move—both contesting and re-claiming the "intimate core" of national culture and identity on the one hand, and evoking transnationally circulating models of liberal democracy and metropolitan culture on the other. For example, in response to the *Fire* controversy, lesbian activists highlighted the historical tolerance of same-sex desire within 'Indian culture', breaking down a monolithic and conservative view of Indian identity but also sometimes deploying essentialisms of their own—like a nostalgic idealization of a libertarian Hindu antiquity, or of the purported pre-colonial tolerance of different sexualities.[45] Since then, a common strategy has been to cite revisionist readings of pre-colonial India and to depict homophobia as an alien imposition by Victorian legislators.[46] While undeniably important in claiming silenced or marginalized histories, scholars have noted how such claims are often articulated with reference to high or 'classical' culture and can be Hindu-normative,[47] sometimes even attributing the historical rise of homophobic attitudes to Muslim invasions and thus mirroring a classic trope of Hindu-right nationalism.[48] For instance, an exhibition of photographs of temple art/sculptures by Giti Thadani at the 2009 Annual Calcutta LGBT Film & Video Festival was advertised thus: "Homosexuality is very much part and parcel of Indic histories [...] these histories have been ignored, ravaged by different monotheistic invasions."[49]

Contradictorily, homophobia is also depicted as an anachronistic and embarrassing reminder of conservative Indian tradition compared to 'advanced' societies, and events of public activism such as pride marches and film festivals are indexed as ways to catch up with Western levels of equality and acceptance.[50] Thus, contemporary

LGBT activism can be placed within a simultaneously national and transnational moment, evidencing overlaps between cultural nationalism and aspirational cosmopolitanism, symptomatic of the larger situation of the Indian middle classes.

This complex moment corresponds to an ideological juncture between 'old' and 'new' modes of middle-class citizenship: the post-independence Nehruvian citizen who is oriented towards civil service, austerity, and a moral responsibility to the nation, and the rising citizen-figure who fulfils the social contract by virtue of being a consumer driving the economy and thus need not shy away from excess.[51] As Leela Fernandes and William Mazzarella point out, these are less accurate descriptors of middle-class reality and more "idealized images" or "normative positions" that mark out the contested contours of civic discourse.[52] Even as commentators like Praful Bidwai have lamented the alleged decline of the former moment of civic culture,[53] English-language media has increasingly celebrated the rise of the latter.[54] These contrasting pulls are diffracted onto public forms of LGBT activism.

On one hand, there is an ambitious rhetoric of humanism and the moral struggle for a better society, including references to nationalist songs from the pre-independence period, as seen in the case of the Kolkata pride walk. This idea of an ethically engaged citizenship is cross-fertilized by discourses of universal human rights and transnational civil society shared through NGO and activist 'advocacy networks' across the world.[55] In the Bengali context, this is manifested in the close association between the elevated rhetoric of *monushotto* and *manobota* (humanity/human dignity) drawn from pre-independence humanism (including both cultural nationalist and anti-nationalist/cosmopolitan strains within the literary/cultural legacies of the 'Bengal Renaissance'), and *manobadhikar*, a more contemporary transnational formulation from the English 'human rights' framework, disseminated through NGO networks, UN agencies, and state discourses. The coalitional slogan for the pride walks from 2007 through 2010, *Chai manusher adhikar niye banchte*, or 'We want to live with the rights/dignity of the human', references both these spheres of influence. As a phrase, manusher adhikar—'rights of the human'/'human rights'—has an exact precedent in the poetry of Rabindranath Tagore (1861-1941), arguably the central figure of Bengali literary/cultural production in the first half of the twentieth century. Tagore's poem *Apoman* (Insult/Disgrace, dated 1900) protests centuries of denying 'manusher adhikar' to the oppressed and outcaste sections of Indian society and indicts dominant culture for this millennia-long disgrace against humanity,[56] concluding with a "programmatic [...] call to all" for social transformation.[57] As both cultural capital and political strategy, Tagore's poetry and music have been appropriated and frequently performed in pride marches and associated cultural programs.[58] But the phrase 'manusher adhikar' also marks the insertion of this Bengali humanist inheritance into NGO and state technologies of governmental power directed at the welfare and upliftment of excluded sections under the aegis of middle-class leaders. As noted at the outset of this chapter, the pride march is also a space where working-class/Dalit sections are sought to be educated into civic norms, both to maintain the "dignity of the walk" and to "establish the rights of community people"[59] claimed within the transnational rubric of manobadhikar ('human rights'). Thus, the evocation of cultural-nationalist ideals and the human rights framework might collude with the pedagogical disciplining of subaltern groups, aimed at making them respectable, dignified and deserving rights-bearing citizens, as I further detail in the fourth section.

On the other hand, there is also the desire to keep up with transnational patterns of conspicuous consumption and display that have become a hallmark of metropolitan gay/lesbian culture. This is evidenced by events such as the 'Pink Rupee Party', organized by the Delhi-based queer group Nigah in the summer of 2009—a fundraising event preceding a week-long 'QueerFest' comprising film screenings, performances, workshops and so on that asked members of the 'queer' community to attend a dance party at a prominent city pub, requiring a 'donation' of Rs. 400: "The pride of Nigah QueerFest is that it is funded by the Queer Community

[…] The last 2 years have been a great success with your love and support […] Yet again, we invite you to the fundraiser party to show your support and dance the night away with us."[60] While the use of the term 'queer' immediately indexes the class privilege and discursive access of Nigah and its constituency (as distinct from many organizations working with kothi/hijra subcultures and communities in West Bengal), similar events in pubs and dance clubs have been occasionally undertaken by NGOs in Kolkata, with the agenda of fundraising and/or creating 'safe spaces'.[61]

Such events draw from and celebrate the rising economic presence and visibility of the big city gay/lesbian consumer and their purported ability to contribute to social transformation (you can "show your support") without necessitating further ethical or political commitment (just "dance the night away with us"). This fits in with a lot of media coverage that maps gay/lesbian visibility onto the cutting-edge of urban lifestyle and consumerism, which is celebrated both for its rejuvenation of the economy on the global stage and for being gender/sexually progressive.[62] While spaces like parties do permit the flaunting of queer difference to an extent, access to these spaces is limited by class, which leads to another kind of containment and exclusion, in addition to the aforementioned national/cultural mode. Thus, as I argue in the subsequent section, despite their apparent contradiction, both of these normative modes of claiming citizenship—cultural and nationalist ideals of citizenship, and a Westward-looking consumerism and cosmopolitanism—may jointly function to stigmatize and/or discipline non-elite forms of public resistance.

These conflicting modes of citizenship demonstrate that while middle-class LGBT activism does interrupt civil society, it can also get assimilated into the contradictory moments of its dominant ethos, based on the contingent nature of upper/middle-class manoeuvres within structures of power: balancing the historical hegemonic aspirations of a nationalist vanguard with a newer economic leadership related to changing labour patterns and occupations (such as the rise of information technology and service industries) and the concomitant rise in upper/middle-class purchasing power.[63] Just as its 'originary' moment in Europe, the domain of proper citizenship hardly emerges as abstract or neutral laws of rational communication and arbitration of interests, [64] but is established through changing upper/middle-class strategies of establishing their dominance, as manifested in relatively elite forms and spaces of cultural expression.[65]

PEDAGOGY AND CONTAINMENT: CONFRONTING NON-ELITE SUBJECTS

However fraught and internally conflicted, these various modalities of middle-class citizenship might be consolidated through attempts to guard the putatively "orderly zones of civil society"[66] from encroachment by disruptive working-class/Dalit sections. While this could take many forms, perhaps the most direct and visible manifestation is the spatial regulation of urban modernity. As William Mazzarella contends via Dipesh Chakrabarty and Sudipta Kaviraj:

> Indeed, a zone in which the 'new' and the 'old' middle classes increasingly appear to find common cause is in an urban politics of 'livability'–a concern, above all, with neighbourhood order, cleanliness, and decency–a politics that loudly decries the lack of 'civility' that mars the modernity of the third world metropolis.[67]

The resultant criminalization of groups such as squatters, slum-dwellers, and street-hawkers is usually achieved through the invocation of property rights, which foregrounds their illegality as encroachers while conveniently eliding their structural necessity within informal urban economies[68]—and as one might extend the argument, such strategies of positing disruptive 'others' to urban modernity permit a tentative consolidation of middle-class civility through the externalization of disorder onto disruptive 'others'.

Similar dynamics of exclusion are evident in the intersection of class/caste and gender/sexual marginality as well. In media discourse, the more visible subaltern groups such as the hijra community (often inaccurately termed eunuchs in the media) are often targeted for their occupations of begging and extortion and are seen as violators of civic space, in marked contrast to the token celebration of middle-class les-bi-gay subjects as markers of a transforming urban culture. In typical reports, we read, "Eunuchs [sic] [...] have been causing great harassment to people, barging into homes and extorting money, reports our special correspondent from Agartala"[69] or "They gatecrash weddings and childbirths, sing lewd songs and make extortion demands."[70] Here, it merits emphasis that the nominal inclusion of hijras through an invocation of constitutional rights serves to simultaneously condemn them as disrupting the same model of formal equality. That is to say, on the one hand they may be acknowledged as Indian citizens, deserving rights as such: "If eunuchs are participating members of a polity, there is no reason why they should need to 'adopt' either of the official genders [... there is a] need to rethink the boundaries of 'official' society, whether in the census figures or in electoral policy."[71] But by the same token of equal citizenship, hijra practices like chhalla or *badhai* (ritualized demands for money during events like childbirths or weddings, or in public spaces like trains, in return for blessings) are understood as acts of extortion or encroachment that violate middle-class privacy and property rights,[72] and are thus condemned as disruptive, aggressive or (most innocuously) comical. Hijras and kothis may, however, contest this limited model of formal equality, pointing out how it conceals the larger context of injustice—as Disha, a kothi-identified community member told me during my fieldwork, "People say kothis harass people during chhalla, but don't acknowledge that they are harassed three times more!"

What structural imperatives or motivations might prompt such widespread and anxious condemnation and/or trivialization of hijras? As Gayatri Reddy argues in her ethnography of kothis and hijras in South India, hijras are often pejoratively characterized by middle-class society through ascriptions of lack—firstly, by the literalized lack of the procreative phallus, as hijras may be castrated (evident in pejorative constructions of hijras as 'eunuchs' which ignore other aspects of hijra identities),[73] and, moreover, by a lack of shame (*sharam*) and/or respectability.[74] Such ascriptions, of course, serve to naturalize and maintain gender/sexual and class/caste order and their attendant hierarchies. Yet, in recent years, hijras have utilized such constructions of themselves (as outside of the gendered/sexualized familial order, and 'lacking' class/caste positions and the concomitant worldly attachments) to gain visibility in the public sphere, especially through contesting electoral politics.[75]

While hijras have proclaimed that such 'lacks' render them less susceptible to corruption and nepotism than more socially mainstream politicians,[76] Reddy cautions that such a strategy may only serve to 'remarginalize' them by reinscribing hegemonic frameworks of marginalization.[77] While the caveat is well taken, such a neat containment within a hegemonic framework would not serve to explain widespread anxieties about hijra presence and visibility. Rather, there is also a different dynamic at play in hijra assertions—hijras may inversely ascribe their 'lack' to broader political and societal structures. Hijras may be seen as marking the failure of normative forms of citizenship and politics by ascribing their political ascent to the *kaliyug* of postcolonial modernity (in Hindu cosmic chronologies, kaliyug is the current era of decadence).[78] In re-ascribing their purported 'impotence' to corrupt politicians and failing political structures, Lawrence Cohen argues that "*Hijra* leaders [...] entertain a reflexive practice of citizenship in which *hijras* uniquely address the problem of a political lack at the core of postcolonial nationalism."[79] We may extend Cohen's point to observe how this plays out beyond the arena of electoral politics and critiques civility itself.

Instead of being bound by a formal definition of rights governing civic and economic exchange, hijras and some kothis may perform their 'lack' as an entitlement to special privileges—Cohen notes how hijras may describe their "wound" (of castration) as an "all-India pass" entitling them to ticketless travel on public transport.[80] As I observed during my fieldwork, non-operated kothis may also claim this exemption while traveling or doing chhalla (blessing for money) in trains; as Disha, the aforementioned community member pointed out, she felt that this was their just due from society, given the lack of employment opportunities and equality. By inverting ascriptions of 'lack' to society itself and justifying their entitlement to special concessions, hijras and kothis challenge models of both formal equality and governmental technologies that seek to conflate the subjects of economic interest and productivity with that of juridical rights,[81] even though their agency is severely circumscribed by their interstitial location and structural dependence within the same broader order.

Further, as I observed during my fieldwork, both hijras and kothis may employ provocative and flamboyant displays of gender/sexual difference as a response to situations of public harassment or abuse in ways that disrupt liberal models of equality and rights. In scattered conversations over the course of my fieldwork, several community members have described how assertive non-verbal gestures such as the thikri or the threat to reveal their genitalia (or their castrated 'lack') by lifting up their saris, function as 'weapons' (*astro*) to produce an affective response of fear and shock in mainstream audiences, and permit their escape from situations of public violence better than just a verbal defense would. Similar assertions of campy or flamboyant (*bheli*) behaviour have been recorded in Anirban Ghosh's *Diaries of Transformation*, a documentary film on gender-variant communities in Kolkata, where Bini, one of the protagonists, claims: "Our clap is our weapon [...] without the clap even if we shake our hips [that is, walk in a flamboyantly feminine manner] people don't care [...] when we clap people get intimidated and don't mess with us. The clap and the hair [...] the longer our hair, the more people respect and fear us."[82] In this strategically aggressive use of non-verbal affective 'weapons' that foreground gender/sexual difference, kothis and hijras may be read as challenging liberal models of equal citizenship that advocate the rational arbitration of conflict based on juridically defined rights to ensure a measured equality between citizens in civil society.[83]

Given that the movement is precisely about claiming space within civil society through the discourse of equal rights, this translates into a deep discomfort with hijra and kothi performances of gender/sexual difference and resistance. At the same time, the institutional movement in West Bengal (and India, more broadly) is heavily dependent on the low-tier involvement and support of such sections: especially for the crucial (and underpaid) labour of outreach work and peer education within NGOs and CBOs' state- and donor-funded HIV/AIDS intervention programmes.[84]

Besides acting as staff in HIV/AIDS interventions, working-class communities also serve to shore up the requisite sexual minority populations to show to the state and foreign donors as 'target groups' and to provide mass participation in civic events like pride walks.[85] Thus, rather than outright exclusion, there are tendencies within the institutional movement that seek to include them within civil society through pedagogical training into citizenship. The marginal hijras must be weaned away from traditional occupations such as chhalla and public soliciting for money (commonly described in terms of extortion/aggression, as we saw above) through IGPs or 'Income Generation Programmes' that aim to provide their 'self-sufficiency' through training in specialized labour and skills. IGPs are a staple but often unfulfilled programme objective within many NGOs and CBOs—as Akash in Berhampore complained, hijras are often resistant to such well-intentioned activist efforts at mainstreaming them: "M. [a well-known transgender activist] had gone to hijra colonies to persuade them to take up occupations like making *bidis* [hand-made cigars], but they beat her up and sent her away."

For sections like kothis who occupy more intermediate positions vis-à-vis the 'mainstream', there is a condemnation and desired containment of excessive or aggressively campy behaviours (collectively called *bhel* and *bila*). This is especially evident during pride meetings, where there have been repeated complaints against disruptive practices such as thikri. In the pride walks between 2007 and 2011, such concerns led to an unwritten consensus on the censure of this particular gesture, accompanied by greater self-policing of excessive flamboyance, public cruising and so on through appointed members of the 'community'. This is an extension of governmental technologies used in targeted interventions for HIV/AIDS control, such as 'behaviour change communication' (BCC) and 'information, education, communication' (IEC)—'target groups' are to be educated not just on health issues such as safer sex (the standard functions of BCC and IEC), but also on civic behaviour during public events.[86] The complex hierarchical structure of peer educators, community advocates, shadow leaders, outreach workers and so on, established by NGOs within the community in the process of administering BCC/IEC, is utilized for this extended purpose as well. In 2007, community members occupying relatively senior administrative ranks were designated to police the walk and control errant behaviour. People who used thikri in response to perceived taunts from surrounding crowds or used vulgar or foul language were disciplined by senior community members. Such disciplining finds support in the attitudes of middle-class community members and allies. As a local celebrity and LGBT icon, the singer Siddharta, put it in an interview to a community magazine: "It's great to express oneself, and there is nothing objectionable should someone choose to cross-dress, for that is their personal gender choice; however, one shouldn't do it so loudly that it trivialises the issues of the movement."[87]

Thus, the activist demand for freedom of gender/sexual expression is simultaneously raised and contained in terms of the constitutional right to privacy ("personal gender choice") linked to the modern conception of an interiorized gender/sexual personhood that does not challenge the broader public ordering of intimacy and gender. ("The state has no business in the bedrooms of the nation."[88]) Through policing gender/sexual excess, prominent tendencies within the movement conform to the 'intimate core' of national culture and citizenship (that is, sexual expression should be familial, private, and restrained so as not to be too 'loud' and disrupt civic exchange and serious communication—an injunction especially applied to cisgender women, and to trans feminine subject positions like hijra or kothi).

At the same time, in tension with the aforementioned tendency of assimilation to extant ideals of cultural citizenship, certain modes of difference, display and flamboyance might be valorized in terms of aspirational ideals of metropolitan (particularly 'Western') gender/ sexual progressivism. This is illustrated by the Hindustan Times article cited in the opening paragraph of this chapter, which merits more detailed analysis:

> The [LGBT] community in Delhi got together at Jantar Mantar on Friday evening to mark the first anniversary of the landmark court judgment decriminalising consensual gay sex.
>
> The party that began […] with loads of cheerful slogan shouting by gay rights supporters, ended a tad bit sourly when […] some decided to indulge in inappropriate behaviour. Dancing in the middle of the road, a few transgenders started lifting their skirts and shouting swear words — enough to embarrass those of their own community [...].
>
> 'They are spoiling the moment's sanctity,' said a bystander. [...] Looking visibly disturbed, one participant […] said, 'This kind of a behaviour at a place like Jantar Mantar is so unacceptable. [...]'
>
> 'The gay community […] has to show whether it can behave responsibly,' says Ashok Row Kavi, India's leading gay rights activist […].
>
> Prior to the ruckus, the evening had its fair share of cheering, singing and dancing, in good fun. Men kissed men. Women hugged women […] Some participants were wearing t-shirts bearing provocative images (two London Bobbies kissing), or words ('Unf**k the world').[...]
>
> 'We have to go a very long way to convince the mainstream society that we are equal citizens with equal rights,' said Kavi. '[…] we must learn how to use our rights sensibly.'[89]

While the middle-class visibilization of queer difference with reference to metropolitan LGBT culture (for example, "London

Bobbies kissing" and "unfuck the world") is "provocative" and "in good fun", acts typical to hijra and kothi modes of public visibility ("lifting up skirts" while dancing) serve to "embarrass" the "LGBT community" and the reporter as its ally, both "marring the sanctity" of a monument of national culture (the Jantar Mantar), and interrupting the process of civic equalization ("convince[ing] mainstream society that we are equal citizens with equal rights"). At the same time, the valorization of middle-class 'provocation' speaks to the contradictions within dominant LGBT evocations of cultural-national and political-civic citizenship, which must disrupt nationality and civility (through "provocative images [...] or words"), but *not too much*—establishing a delicate balance between normative culture and LGBT difference by precluding acts too aggressive, excessive or crass for middle-class 'provocation'.

These tricky negotiations between claiming and disavowing dissidence feed into the formation of identitarian divides that seek to exclude or guard against unruly forms of gender/sexual variance. For instance, a group such as GayBombay, intended to form a safe space for gay-identified men, has repeatedly policed the borders of 'gay' by banishing actions such as cross-dressing ('drag') from its events: "Drag is a strict no-no. For the simple reason that though GayBombay doesn't mind drag, the places that host us do. There are also may be [sic] many attendees who will prefer being discreet [...] This is a discreet event being held as a clean, safe & social get-together of a non-sexual nature."[90] This seeks to establish a clear distinction between GayBombay's "clean" and "discreet" gay space and more overtly transgender spaces/communities, even as the very need to have an explicit injunction against drag points to the anxiety-inducing overlaps between 'gay' and 'transgender'. These anxieties recur within non-metropolitan kothi subcultures and communities that have been mapped as both MSM and transgender by different state and foreign agencies. The National AIDS Control Organization maps kothi as feminine MSM—"males who show varying degrees of femininity"[91]—while a 2009 consultation supported by the United Nations Development Programme (UNDP) maps them as "the most common local identity" for transgenders, defining a male-to-female transgender as "one who is biologically male but loves to feel and see herself as a female."[92] As observed during my ethnographic fieldwork, kothi subcultures and communities encompass people inhabiting a wide spectrum of gender variance who are often sought to be classified into rigid identitarian divisions that are fuelled by anxieties around gender/sexual and class/caste difference.

For example, when Akash's organization in the Berhampore region was awarded an HIV/AIDS control project under the rubric of 'MSM' in 2011, a senior community member suggested that, now that they were officially an MSM organization, those community members who were too bheli (campy, unruly) should either control themselves or stay out. Furthermore, such divides might be extended even within the 'transgender' category. For instance, Kalki Subramaniam, a prominent South Indian transgender activist, authored a protest petition in November 2011 against railway police force action in western India that rounded up poor hijras, in which she included the lines: "I know how some of the transpeople who go for begging behave in public. Not all. When will people stop generalising about us?"[93] A few years later, at a 'Hijra Hubba' (meet) organized by an NGO in Kolkata in September 2015, the actress Moon Moon Sen, speaking as an invited guest, cautioned transgender people to dress 'soberly' and not behave too loudly or aggressively in public in order to gain social acceptance, and hailed trans people who had completed their formal education as positive examples for the community.

Thus, even in protests against transphobia or at activist events for transgender/hijra rights, a division may emerge between the innocent and victimized transgender and unruly trans people (particularly hijras and kothis) who behave badly in public. Such anxieties thus inform a double split in identity—the first between MSM/gay and transgender, involving MSM/gay-identified groups distancing themselves from public effeminacy or gender variance, and further, between civil and unruly trans persons. But as signalled by the kothi's ambivalent positioning between MSM and transgender and the dangerous association between gayness and drag, many individuals can and do cross these divides, prompting the policing of identitarian boundaries.

However, such processes of division and exclusion are accompanied by simultaneous processes of inclusion and assimilation: especially the education of unruly community members (whether understood as MSM, kothi or transgender/hijra) in more disciplined and civil forms of expression and dissent. In the aforementioned context of pride rallies in Kolkata, senior activists led participants through pre-set slogans and iconic songs in the 2008 and 2009 walks. At designated points during the rally, activists sang inspirational songs ranging from the Bengali version of 'We Shall Overcome' to iconic nationalist-era songs such as Tagore's *Ekla chalo re* ("If no one comes in answer to your call, walk alone!"); everyone was encouraged to join in if they knew the words. At other moments, slogans were raised in a call-and-response fashion, reminiscent of mainstream political rallies with their multi-tiered hierarchy among party leaders and cadres.

Beyond the specific case of pride walks, forms of middle-class culture such as classical or 'fusion' dance, art songs and theatre come into play as safe and contained valves for gender/sexual expression, where the display of non-conformity need not interrupt the ethos of civility but can rather find space within it. This is strikingly evident in an open letter in the spring 2008 issue of *Swikriti Patrika*, the magazine of the Dum Dum Swikriti Society.[94] Addressed to the broader 'community', the letter struck a cautionary note when talking about the behaviour of certain community members which, it predictably argued, was coming in the way of the struggle for acceptance and rights. It especially targeted kothis who adopted aspects of hijra subcultures:

> Please remember, all our problems will not disappear if Section 377 is revoked. When people come to truly understand the problems of kothis, only then the real purpose of our movement would be fulfilled. And to accomplish that task we need reason, education, skill, self-respect and the sense of humanity. Remember, certain

> strange behaviours employed by [some] kothis—such as doing bila or giving thikri in public spaces—is not seen in a good light even by other kothis, let alone the mainstream.[95]

The letter thus highlights the need to become proper economic and rights-bearing subjects by acquiring "reason, education, skill". But it doesn't stop there. The letter goes on to state that there is a lot of talent within the community which needs to be foregrounded: "I have seen that a lot of kothis tend to be very talented. Through their talent they can become exemplary for the rest of society [...] then they will truly take part in the struggle for rights."[96] Given that the author, Anirban, signs off as a *shongeet-shilpi* (musician), and is in real life a singer of both Hindustani (North Indian) classical and Tagore songs, it cannot be in doubt what kind of "talent" is referenced here. Anirban belongs to a small-town, middle-class, yet upwardly mobile family living in the outskirts of Berhampore, and has been active in the local CBO, Sangram, since its inception in 2006. Soon after his 'open letter' was published in the Kolkata magazine,[97] he sought my help in writing an abstract for a paper to be presented at an international AIDS conference on how 'cultural' activities like music and dance could help bring the community together across class and behavioural splits: "As you know, there is a huge fissure between bheli [flamboyant, campy] kothis and the rest of the kothi community," he told me while we drafted the abstract. "But *cultural programmes* with music and dance can bring them together and can also be a space for awareness-raising and expression," he continued.[98] Thus, as he argued in the abstract, these forms of cultural advocacy needed more attention from funding agencies, as current targeted intervention programmes on health issues like safer sex were not enough.

Another activist in the same organization, Asaf, is a professional Bharatnatyam dancer who organized a 'dance drama' on the broad theme of 'marginalization' in 2007, a year before Anirban's open letter. One evening during rehearsals he told me: "Our dance is not going to have any depiction of vulgar taunting on the streets."

"Nor any kothis giving thikri in response to the taunting," interjected another prospective performer.

"Yes," replied Asaf, "We are going to show everything, but in a much more *abstract* manner. Else," he continued, "it looks distasteful, of low standard [*nimno-maner* in Bengali]." Artistic 'abstraction' here signals a safe distance from the actual on-street resistance undertaken by many kothis and hijras, which is seen as distasteful and vulgar, even though the theme was the marginalization of these very subjects. Can one also sense here the necessary abstraction of intimate and embodied experience in order to ascend to the proper political culture of the liberal public sphere?[99] Asaf's 'dance drama' aspired to use abstract art to convey serious socio-political meaning without the vulgarity of embodied resistances—"The paintings of M.F. Hussain might be difficult to understand, but don't they mean anything?" he asked. Here, the different senses of abstraction that characterize civil society and high art become functionally conflated as ways to distinguish oneself from 'low standards'.[100]

For the music, Asaf chose a lushly orchestrated track *Jaage Hain* by the noted composer A.R. Rahman, from the film *Guru*. He said, "It shows a process of awakening, of coming together [of the marginalized]." In the film, the song is a rousing paean to an industrialist's efforts to build an entrepreneurial empire, a much-celebrated inspirational figure for the 'new' middle classes.[101] As the music developed, the dancers—initially scattered and debilitated by unspecified traumatic experiences—recover and gather together, hand in hand. Into this veritable *bildungsroman* of the awakening political subject, set to the theme song of an icon of middle-class aspiration, Asaf recruited some of the most bheli (flamboyant) kothis of the area. One of the most notorious is Mandira, who identifies as both transgender and kothi,[102] and who has been frequently upbraided for her inclination towards provocative public cruising, wearing flashy or revealing feminine attire, and aggressive responses to harassment or abuse. During the rehearsal, she told me: "I don't know why it is that kothis take to dancing so well [...] If I can dance, I don't want anything else." Asaf looked on as she spoke and illustrated the pleasures of dancing by gracefully performing *mudras* (ornamental gestures), reminiscent not so much of actual 'classical' (Bharatnatyam) gestures, but more their popularized versions in Hindi film dances. Clearly, this was a permissible forum for 'feminine' gender expression and flamboyance. Thus, the containment of potentially provocative or disruptive embodiments becomes a part of the pedagogical reform of gender/sexual subalterns, allowing their entry into cultural citizenship.

RE-CLAIMING CIVILITY: CONTESTATION AND REINVENTION

Kothi/hijra sections might resist both their confinement into a sequestered sphere of governmentality (Chatterjee's 'political society')[103] as 'target groups' of disease-control, and their pedagogical assimilation into civil society by contributing to and contesting the very definition of civility in their claims to citizenship. This is not to argue for a voluntarist or entirely self-conscious idea of their agency, but rather their potentially productive location within structural contradictions and possibilities. As discussed above, cultural and musical performances become important to these processes of contestation and reinvention.

It doesn't take long to perceive the contradictions in the leadership of the 'new' middle class, which contradictorily balances the disciplining of non-elite visibility, the performance of class distinction through consumption and display, and the provocative visibilization of LGBT difference. The Berhampore activist Akash, while herself censorious of kothi bhel, was struck by what she perceived to be the double standards of Kolkata leaders when attending NGO meetings in the city. Of one activist—who had been quite active in the censoring of thikri during the 2006 and 2007 pride—she said: "Sujit was so distracted with her make-up during the general meeting; about half an hour into it she took out her purse with a flourish, and started doing her face, showing off her fancy lipstick [...] What bhel!" Sujit's not-so-subtle marker of class distinction (expensive cosmetics) is thus reduced to merely another form of bhel—thus catching the hypocritical disavowal within middle-class attempts to discipline kothi camp. (This re-ascription of bhel is also reminiscent of hijras' re-ascription of their putative 'lack' onto broader structures of civil society and politics.)

This is a minute everyday event, but the same dynamic of re-ascription and reversal played out on a much bigger scale when some lower-rung transgender-identified activists rebelled against the leaders of AlterNet Bengal (name changed), a nodal NGO within the organizational networks of West Bengal, in an episode spanning the 2010-12 period. Amidst broad allegations of monetary corruption, hierarchy, a lack of transparency and so on, there was a telling attack on how one of the leaders had allegedly indulged in lavish "drink parties" using grant money. Even as the accused activist scoffed at the unidiomatic use of English—"I am unable to understand what 'drink party' means."—the imputation of profligate decadence and excess crystallised around "drink" is unmistakable.[104] In response, the accused activist made public a rigorous accounting of the expenditures undertaken as proof of his adherence to due procedure.

But beyond merely holding leaders to their ideals of discipline and subjecting them to the same kind of scrutiny the lower rungs of the 'community' themselves face, there may be a re-figuration of the very norms of civic engagement. This becomes evident in the working-class utilization of spaces like pride, which epitomize some of the contradictions around civility—on the one hand it is a protest march claiming equality in terms of the constitutional right to privacy and personal freedom, and on the other it is a celebratory pageant of difference, flamboyance and excess. This duality is reflected in its media reception, which typically mixes issue-based reports with photo-features. Some organizations, like the lesbian feminist front Sappho for Equality, cite this media commoditization and objectification of gender/sexual difference as one of the reasons they stayed away from participating in pride walks till the mid-2010s. As one of their senior functionaries told me during an interview: "We will go only once it is a walk about homosexuality, not homosexuals."

While their discomfort with the display and potential objectification of 'homosexuals' is understandable given their ideological stance as feminists, many kothis and hijras use this space precisely to foreground the embodied difference dominant activist discourse seeks to control by relegating it to the realm of personal gender expression. Beyond the demand for equality, then, what is being contested is the fairness of the extant gendered norms of civic participation. And just as in the project of disciplining, forms of cultural expression like music and dance become crucial to this contestation.

In the 2009 walk, I noticed a self-identified hijra, Sujata, walking among a cluster of people, including some senior activists. One of them, Ashim, is a good singer of *Rabindrasangeet* (Tagore songs) and *Adhunik* ('modern', that is, contemporary) Bangla songs, and has in the past led several performances of songs such as Tagore's *Ekla cholo re* ('Walk alone') during pride. This time, however, Sujata said that *she* would sing something. She began innocuously enough, with a somewhat lofty *Adhunik* song about human dignity and respect. However, even as the others started humming the song, she broke into a dance to the lines: "Time itself is changing / I have gotten my rights; You are changing yourself / I have been given my rights."[105] This was sung almost satirically, while executing Bollywood-style dance gestures along with the hijra gesture of thikri—with swaying hips and seductive hand gestures punctuated by loud claps provocatively directed at fellow walkers and roadside onlookers, all characteristic of typical bheli behaviour.

However differently and ambivalently one may read this performance—seduction, flirtation, resistance, explicit gender performativity, and so on—what at least seemed clear was the provocative imputation on the word 'you', referencing pride's 'mainstream' audience, as well as senior activists, who are hailed to respond to these forms of performance and communications of difference, combining the discourse of equal rights with the affective, non-verbal 'weapons' of bhel. Sujata's bold interpellation of her audience put the burden of change squarely on the mainstream and elite sections of the movement—rather than it being gendered labour (Anirban's injunction to acquire "reason, education, skill") to be performed by feminized kothis and hijras, as demanded within projects of reform. In as much as such a performance may be read as a gendered and sexualized political gesture, it might also be understandable through Lauren Berlant's concept of "diva citizenship", which "does not change the world", but is "a moment of emergence that marks unrealised potentials for subaltern political activity."[106] In this case, it challenges and refigures modes of civility by foregrounding and performing—indeed making a spectacle of—the realm of the 'intimate' or the 'private' (Siddhartha's "personal gender choice") so as to challenge the elisions engendered through the normative constitution of these terms (family-oriented, hetero- and homonormative) within public discourse.

Sujata's performance also points to the strategy of performing middle-class culture subversively, using pedagogical modes of music and dance to break into civil society spaces and undermine the normative distinctions that guard access to it. Thus, rather than outright rejection, there may be a reclamation and re-articulation of such cultural forms through mélanges with inappropriate civic behaviour or 'low' culture.

Let me describe here a particular event to do with the literal and metaphoric displacement of an iconic Rabindrasangeet, *Aguner Poroshmoni*—roughly translated as 'The Touchstone of Fire'. A rousing call for self-expansion by making sacrifices for a higher cause, this popular song has become a staple of Bengali middle-class, left-liberal circles, and is often interpreted as a revolutionary hymn and sung at public protest events (such as those in the wake of corporate land-grabs and related abuses in Singur and Nandigram). It has also been performed at several Kolkata pride walks that I have attended, either during the walk itself, or as a culminating gesture at the end of the walk and speeches.[107]

But I was surprised to hear it at a candlelight vigil in 2008 referencing the Transgender Day of Remembrance, organized by a CBO comprised mainly of kothis from working-class, migrant, non-Bengali backgrounds, most of them Hindi- or Bhojpuri-speaking. The CBO's location is significant; it's based in a worker's colony in North East Kolkata which is only slightly better than a slum in terms of living conditions, and yet is juxtaposed with a new and glitzy multiplex complex in the area. (The contradictions of 'new India' could not be more apparent). The vigil was held in a 'cruising' area around a lake called Subhash Sarovar, across the street from the colony. The lake is a disreputable and dangerous area after dark, and several kothis had been victims of sexual assaults and harassment there over the years. That summer evening, we—press, 'community' members, and senior NGO functionaries—arrived at the location only to be confronted by a power cut, then routine in low-income areas of the city. As a result, the event got off to a slow start, everything being chaotic in the dark. With much shouting of directions and jostling around of people (irrespective of the activists' rank), a semblance of a circle somehow formed, and candles were distributed. Some order and hierarchy was subsequently re-established, and two senior NGO leaders led the vigil with speeches in English and Bengali against Section 377 (the anti-sodomy provision of the Indian Penal Code, 1860),[108] and homo- and trans-phobic violence.

After these mandatory addresses, there was a hesitant pause, and we wondered what would be coming up next. Ashutosh, the CBO leader, called out: "Hey, what is that song we usually sing on such occasions?"

Someone piped up, "Do you mean *Aguner Poroshmoni*?"

"Yes, yes," replied Ashutosh. "Anyone who knows the song, please lead." So, people who knew the song started singing and the rest joined in, the tune familiar enough to permit collective singing, though many among the non-Bengali crowd scarcely followed the lyrics and would join in a beat or two after the ones who did. As is typical during such inspirational hymns, we linked hands during the performance—an uncomfortable procedure given that we were also holding on to our candles and stood on muddy ground, slippery after a recent shower. However precarious and tuneless the performance, all the senior functionaries stayed on until the end, awkwardly holding hands with the motley group of slum-dwellers, junior activists, and press.

As a symbolic event, the vigil signalled the arrival of Ashutosh—who was herself a resident of the colony, though better-educated than most of her CBO members—as an important player within the NGO circle of Kolkata (and thus, by extension, West Bengal; Ashutosh later played an important role in the insurrection against AlterNet Bengal, mentioned above). In that context, how do we read her evocation of *Aguner Poroshmoni*? Given the demographics of the group that sang it that night—mostly non-Bengali working-class migrants from UP and Bihar, with Bengali middle-class activists mixed in—the choice was odd, but also apposite. On one level, Ashutosh was merely indexing a culturally appropriate civic ritual and thus establishing the legitimacy of her CBO as a civil society organization. At the same time, this was done without mentioning the songwriter (the revered Tagore) or remembering the song's name, thus subverting its aura of middle-class respectability through the casualness of reference which, moreover, made the ritualistic and formal nature of the activity clear. This would indicate a strategic use of a middle-class cultural form, subverting its conventional use as a pedagogical device within the movement.

However, there could also be another and perhaps more radical reading. Even if Ashutosh was contesting modes of civility, her actions were also a call to middle-class activists and leaders to truly realize the potential of equal citizenship. As activists joined hands over the slippery, muddy ground to sing this familiar song, they were momentarily interpellated into an equalized, revolutionary community, however fragile, illusory, and temporary. Through that interpellation, middle-class leaders were made to depart from their comfort zones—quite literally—as they negotiated their way through a familiar song in an entirely defamiliarized and physically uncomfortable setting. The broader implication of such a defamiliarization might well be that the putatively inclusive and universal ideals of civil society could be achieved only in as much as they are displaced from their normative forms and reinvented in new contexts,[109] rather than being coerced onto recalcitrant subjects of disciplinary power under the guise of a pedagogical training for citizenship.

CONCLUSION

In the preceding sections, I have endeavoured to show that while there is widespread anxiety around and a regulation of civic participation both within queer communities and in the wider domain of middle-class society and the media, this anxiety cannot ensure the separation of 'sequestered' domains such as 'civil' and 'political' society. The contingency, instability and messiness associated with the latter constantly interrupt and threaten the apparent order and logic of the former. Moreover, modes of working-class/Dalit activism may simultaneously utilize and displace ideals and norms of civility and citizenship. Chatterjee's schema remains immensely useful as a diagnostic tool to chart the desired separation between civic activism and the governmental regulation and pedagogy of 'target groups', but more as a prescriptive/normative division that seeks to contain contradictions than as a reality given in political praxis.

The crucial importance of the realm of 'culture' within such praxis demonstrates the messy entanglements of putatively universalizable abstract norms and ideals of modern citizenship with particular histories and locations. Thus, cultural contestation becomes integral to the subversive re-fashioning of normative political forms to articulate the situated demands of marginalized sections. This process suggests how normative models of liberal democracy and bourgeois civil society need not remain external to the realm of popular politics and practice, to be used only strategically or instrumentally, but may be displaced, expanded and re-shaped in the encounter with subalternity as Chatterjee himself suggests in his analysis of Dalit constitutional politics.[110]

Analogously, subjects like the kothis and hijras of West Bengal may not be located merely as adversely affected by or external to trans-national articulations of LGBT equality and rights. Rather, in the very process of contesting their exclusion, they become integral to both the critique and the re-constitution of these discourses and political forms. Recognizing this might help us, privileged subjects in the academy, to advance on the difficult and fraught path of engaging a future politics more open to difference.

CODA

This essay was written in 2012. Since then, there have been notable developments such as the Supreme Court's NALSA judgment on transgender identity recognition and rights in April 2014. This has resulted in the West Bengal state government paying more attention to transgender/hijra issues, with the formation of a 'Transgender Development Board' in 2015. The central government has also introduced several successive drafts of the *Transgender Persons (Protection of Rights) Bill*, the 2019 version of which was ratified as an Act. With the increasing visibility of transgender activism, there are more transgender-specific events, and transgender networks like the Association for Transgender/Hijra in Bengal (ATHB) have organized separate pride walks. However, the aforementioned class/caste and gender/sexual hierarchies have remained very relevant despite a certain degree of apparent empowerment for trans-identified people.

After cutbacks of government HIV funding for community-based organizations in 2012, the process of organizing the Kolkata Pride

Walk was increasingly taken over by middle-class queer people in the absence of a structured network of non-metropolitan community-based organizations. This has meant declining participation by non-metropolitan and working-class/Dalit community members, even as there is an increase in the visibility of genderqueer and non-binary persons in Pride walks and rising assertions by urban Dalit activists. While this means that the overt policing of dress and flamboyance has become less acceptable, subtle and even blatant forms of discrimination continue. For example, during 2015's pre-Pride preparations, Pride organizers sought to provide overnight accommodation for non-elite participants from outside Kolkata, but stipulated that they should maintain "decorum" during their stay, which caused a small-town community-based group to protest the imputed lack of "decorum" among non-metropolitan participants. In June 2022, a transgender person was shamed and removed from a WhatsApp group meant for planning a summertime Pride walk (not the main Kolkata Pride walk, which now happens in winter) for playfully using slang in voice messages, which the organizers felt breached decorum and spoiled the atmosphere.[111]

Meanwhile, with the increased upward mobility of some transgender leaders, caste-class related hierarchies among hijra and kothi communities have become more pronounced. For example, dominant-caste hijra members of the Transgender Development Board such as the late Dipa Haji have publicly condemned kothis who do chhalla as illegitimate encroachers into hijra professions, claiming they harass the public and malign the reputation of hijras.[112] At the national level, hijra identities have been articulated in more Hindu-normative and nationalist ways by hijra activists such as Lakshmi Narayan Tripathi. The Sanskritized term *kinnar*, evocative of Hindu mythology, has become a widespread 'respectable' moniker for hijras, beyond its provenance in the Hindi belt—hijras in West Bengal, who in my ethnographic experience almost never used the term, now use it far more commonly as a term of public identification, and indeed, might prefer it to the pejorative connotations of 'hijra'. On another front, many activists have pointed out that the controversial and much-critiqued *Transgender Persons (Protection of Rights) Act* may intensify the surveillance of hijra livelihoods, which, as discussed above, have long been abjected and criminalized through models of civility, formal equality and neoliberal productivity. The ongoing transformation and reconfiguration of class/caste hierarchies and norms of civility in the post-NALSA period would necessitate a separate study. For now, it would perhaps suffice to say that the core problem studied in this essay, the exclusions accompanying inclusion within liberal rights-based frameworks, remains sadly relevant in contemporary LGBT politics.

NOTES

1. Naz Foundation v. Govt. of NCT of Delhi, (2009) 160 DLT 277. This judgment was subsequently contradicted by the 2013 Supreme Court judgment (Kaushal v Naz Foundation) which upheld the constitutionality of Section 377 of the Indian Penal Code (377 IPC). In 2018, the Supreme Court once again read down 377 IPC to exclude consensual same-sex relations from its purview.
2. The event, a gathering at the national monument of Jantar Mantar, was organized by an informal coalition of activists and organizations on July 2, 2010, exactly a year after the Delhi High Court judgment of July 2, 2009.
3. Zabeeh Afaque, *Let's Keep the Pride*, Hindustan Times (July 3, 2010, 3:20 AM), https://www.hindustantimes.com/entertainment/let-s-keep-the-pride/story-svsdfu8xq3GdNDRwj2SxIK.html.
4. *Id.*
5. *Id.*
6. *See* The Humsafar Trust's 'About Us' page: https://humsafar.org/about-us/. *See also* The Humsafar Trust, *Project Bolo: A Collection of Oral Histories of Indian LGBT Persons* (2011), http://humsafar.org/wp-content/uploads/2018/03/Project-Bolo-Write-Up-2.pdf. Ashok Row Kavi is among the most prominent gay rights activists of India. Kavi founded The Humsafar Trust in 1994, and it is one of the largest Indian NGOs working with GBT communities on issues of rights and male sexual health.
7. Afaque, *supra* note 3.
8. All personal names have been changed to maintain privacy and confidentiality, except when they are public figures (Ashok Row Kavi, for example) cited in media reports or other public documents.

9. Kothis comprise a spectrum of feminine-identified persons including same-sex desiring males and transgender women, while hijras are organized groups of feminine-identified persons assigned male at birth, often described as a 'third gender'. *See* Lawrence Cohen, *The Kothi Wars: AIDS Cosmopolitanism and the Morality of Classification, in* Sex in Development: Science, Sexuality and Morality in Global Perspective 269-303 (V. Adams & S.L. Pig eds., 2005) on the construction of the kothi category; *see also* Gayatri Reddy, With Respect to Sex: Negotiating Hijra Identity in South India (2005) on hijra and kothi communities and subcultures.
10. This chapter was originally written in 2012 and is based primarily on ethnographic fieldwork conducted at various locations in West Bengal between 2006 and 2012, when I worked as a participant observer with several community-based organizations and non-governmental organizations in the region. I have added a coda at the end of this chapter to reflect on subsequent developments.
11. Quoted from the English minutes circulated among participants after the meeting (e-mail correspondence, May 25, 2007).
12. The 'consensus' I mention here was not officially recorded in the meeting minutes; however, it was evident in attempts by senior community members and activists to regulate behaviours such as thikri, which I observed in the Kolkata Rainbow Pride walks of 2007, 2008 and 2009.
13. I draw from Spivak's influential theorization of the 'subaltern'; *see* Gayatri Chakravorty Spivak, *Can the Subaltern Speak, in* Marxism and the Interpretation of Culture (C. Nelson & L. Grossberg eds., 1988); Gayatri Chakravorty Spivak, *Scattered Speculations on the Subaltern and the Popular*, 8 Postcolonial Stud. 475 (2005).
14. I refer to the modern liberal democratic tradition of juridical/political equality through which the LGBT movement has often claimed constitutional and human rights; for a critique of this political tradition in the South Asian context, *see* Ajay Skaria, *Relinquishing Republican Democracy: Gandhi's Ramarajya*, 14 Postcolonial Stud. 203 (2011).
15. *See* Kevin P. Murphy, Jason Ruiz & David Serlin, *Editor's Introduction*, 100 Radical History Rev. 1 (2008); Anna M. Agathangelou, M. Daniel Bassichis & Tamara L. Spira, *Intimate Investments: Homonormativity, Global Lockdown, and the Seductions of Empire*, 100 Radical History Rev. 120 (2008); Jasbir Puar, Terrorist Assemblages: Homonationalism in Queer Times (2008); That's Revolting!: Queer Strategies for Resisting Assimilation (Mattilda B. Sycamore ed., 2004).
16. For an overview of the narratives of national culture that the Indian LGBT movement contests or assimilates, *see* Ratna Kapur, *'A Love Song to Our Mongrel Selves': Hybridity, Sexuality and the Law*, 8 Soc. & Legal Stud. 353 (1999). For a critical theorization of liberal citizenship in postcolonial societies, *see* Partha

Chatterjee, Lineages of Political Society: Studies in Postcolonial Democracy 1 & 12 (2010).

17. The regulatory tendencies described in this chapter primarily affect working-class or Dalit persons, and communities assigned male at birth. Working-class/Dalit communities of same-sex desiring women and transgender men have been much less visible within institutional activism in eastern India for complex reasons, including the lack of HIV/AIDS control funding for women (except female sex workers). For an overview of colonial-era laws on vagrancy, public order and decency, some of which still remain in effect and are used to criminalize hijras and kothis, *see* Human Rights Watch, *This Alien Legacy: The Origins of "Sodomy" Laws in British Colonialism* (Dec. 17, 2008), https://www.hrw.org/report/2008/12/17/alien-legacy/origins-sodomy-laws-british-colonialism.
18. Dipesh Chakrabarty, Provincializing Europe: Postcolonial Thought and Historical Difference 4-8 (2000).
19. Recasting Women: Essays in Colonial History 14 (Kumkum Sangari & Sudesh Vaid eds., 1989).
20. Grants for HIV/AIDS prevention from the Indian state and foreign or multilateral donors is a major source of funding for both large national NGOs like The Humsafar Trust and the Naz Foundation, and smaller community-based organisations working with 'sexual minorities'. *See* Akshay Khanna, *Taming of the Shrewd 'Meyeli Chhele': A Political Economy of Development's Sexual Subject*, 52 Development 43, 47 (2009) for a critical analysis of this 'HIV/AIDS industry'.
21. *See* Partha Chatterjee, The Politics of the Governed: Reflections on Popular Politics in Most of the World (2004); Partha Chatterjee, *Democracy and Economic Transformation in India,* XLIII EPW 53 (2008).
22. Chatterjee (2008), supra note 21.
23. *Id.*
24. *See* Chatterjee, *supra* note 16, at 90-93. In response to criticisms of the civil/political society binarism, Chatterjee's more recent work acknowledges overlaps between modes of political engagement in these two spheres, but does not provide any empirical analysis of how the distinction itself might be contested.
25. *See* supra note 10.
26. For a chronological account of the institutional movement in West Bengal, *see* Sherry Joseph, Social Work Practice and Men Who Have Sex With Men 99-100 (2005).
27. Nancy Fraser, *Rethinking the Public Sphere: A Contribution to the Critique of Actually Existing Democracy*, 25/26 Social Text 56, 59-60 (1990).
28. *Id.*; Joan Landes, Women and the Public Sphere in the Age of the French Revolution 2-4 (1988).

29. Pierre Bourdieu, Distinction: A Social Critique of the Judgment of Pure Taste 1-2 (R. Nice trans., 1984).
30. For an overview of these debates, *see* Peter Jackson, *Capitalism and Global Queering: National Markets, Parallels Among Sexual Cultures, and Multiple Queer Modernities*, 15 GLQ 357, 360 (2009).
31. *See* Anurag Varma, *Abhay Deol Extends Support to LGBT Community*, Indiatimes (Mar. 02, 2012, 11:57 AM), https://www.indiatimes.com/bollywood/abhay-deol-extends-support-to-lgbt-community-14616.html. For example, the Listserv <lgbt-india@yahoogroups.com> is the primary national online forum for activist discussion. The media too increasingly uses LGBT as an umbrella term.
32. *See* Queer Azaadi Mumbai's 'About' page: *About* (Jan. 28, 2012), https://queerazaadi.wordpress.com/about/.
33. *See* Teresa de Lauretis, *Queer Theory: Lesbian and Gay Sexualities*, 3 differences iii (1991); Annamarie Jagose, *Queer Theory*, 4 Austl. Humanities Rev. (1996).
34. In the years following this chapter, 'gay' and 'transgender' have both become more commonly used within working-class/Dalit communities, although kothi/hijra are still commonly used. The interactions between these terms deserves fuller analysis, and is beyond the scope of this chapter.
35. For the use of MSM and TG in HIV/AIDS discourse, *see* National Aids Control Organization, *Targeted Interventions Under NACP III: Volume 1 Core High Risk Groups* 13, Ministry of Health and Family Welfare (2007), http://naco.gov.in/sites/default/files/NACP-III.pdf.
36. *Id.*
37. Kapur, *supra* note 16; William Mazzarella, *Middle Class, in* Keywords in South Asian Studies (R. Dwyer ed., 2004).
38. Arvind Rajagopal, Politics After Television: Hindu Nationalism and the Reshaping of the Public in India 34 (2001); Mazzarella, *supra* note 37, at 8.
39. Kapur, *supra* note 16.
40. *See* Ratna Kapur, *Too Hot to Handle: The Cultural Politics of* Fire, 64 Feminist Review 53 (2000); Shohini Ghosh, Fire: A Queer Film Classic (2010).
41. Mary E. John & Tejaswini Niranjana, *Mirror Politics: Fire, Hindutva and Indian Culture*, 34 EPW 581 (1999).
42. *Id.*
43. Lauren Gail Berlant, The Queen of America Goes to Washington City: Essays on Sex and Citizenship 5 (1997).
44. Vishnupriya Sengupta, *Oh! Calcutta!*, The Telegraph (Aug. 7, 2005, 12:00 AM), https://www.telegraphindia.com/culture/style/oh-calcutta/cid/865723.
45. Kapur, *supra* note 16, at 358.
46. *See* HRW, *supra* note 17.
47. Akshay Khanna, *Us 'Sexuality Types': A Critical Engagement with the Postcoloniality of Sexuality, in* The Phobic and the Erotic: The Politics of Sexualities in Contemporary India 159, 177 (B. Bose & S. Bhattacharyya eds., 2007).

48. Kapur, *supra* note 16, at 46.
49. Excerpted from the website of one of the organizers; *see* Sappho for Equality, *Excavation of Feminine Memories: Allied Event of Dialogues 2009*, Sappho for Equality (2009), http://www.sapphokolkata.in/events/.
50. Phil Hazlewood, *India Gets Its First Mainstream Gay Film Festival*, Taiwan News (Apr. 7, 2010, 00:00 AM), https://www.taiwannews.com.tw/en/news/1235588. "Organizers [are] hailing it as a sign of progress after years of prejudice and discrimination. [...] Such events have been an established part of the cultural scene in Western countries for many years but in socially conservative India [...] it has been largely an underground activity."
51. Mazzarella, *supra* note 37, at 1; Amita Baviskar & Raka Ray, *Introduction, in* Elite and Everyman: The Cultural Politics of the Indian Middle Classes 2-3 (2011).
52. On "idealized images" of the new middle class, *see* Leela Fernandes, *Restructuring the Middle Class in Liberalizing India*, 20 CSSAAME 88 (2000); Leela Fernandes, India's New Middle Class: Democratic Politics in an Era of Economic Reform 60 (2006); *see* Mazzarella, *supra* note 37, at 4 on the "normative positions" involved in this debate.
53. Mazzarella, *supra* note 37, at 8.
54. Fernandes (2000), *supra* note 52.
55. Margaret E. Keck & Kathryn Sikkink, Activists Beyond Borders: Advocacy Networks in International Politics (1998).
56. Rabindranath Tagore, Gitanjali 140 (J. Winter trans., 1998).
57. Gayatri Chakravorty Spivak, *Ethics and Politics in Tagore, Coetzee and Certain Scenes of Teaching*, 32 Diacritics 19, 20-29 (2002).
58. *See* Part V of this chapter.
59. *Supra* note 11.
60. Nigah, *Nigah Invites You for the Pink Rupee Party !!!*, Nigah Delhi (Aug. 31, 2009), http://nigahdelhi.blogspot.com/2009/08/nigah-invites-you-for-pink-rupee-party.html.
61. For example, there was a combined gala organized by Pratyay and Sappho upon the conclusion of their own film festival in 2009, similar to Nigah's initiative in Delhi. Fund-raising parties were also organized prior to the 2011 Kolkata Rainbow Pride Week in July. Such events have only increased since this piece was written.
62. For an analysis of the media coverage of LGBT and 'alternate sexualities', *see* Aniruddha Dutta, *Narratives of Excess and Exclusion: Nationhood, Class and Queerness in the Indian English-Language Press, in* Out of Place: Interrogating Silences in Queerness/Raciality (E. Miyake & A. Kuntsman eds., 2008).
63. Fernandes (2000), *supra* note 52, at 92.
64. Fraser, *supra* note 27, at 59.
65. Fernandes (2000), *supra* note 52, at 92.
66. Chatterjee (2004), *supra* note 21, at 62.
67. Mazzarella, *supra* note 37, at 7.

68. Nivedita Menon & Aditya Nigam, Power and Contestation: India Since 1989 78-81 (2009).
69. *Eunuch Trouble*, The Telegraph (Sept. 21, 2005).
70. Shveta Bhagat, *Eunuchs Not Always Born But Made*, Times of India (Sept. 5, 2005), https://timesofindia.indiatimes.com/city/delhi/Eunuchs-not-always-born-but-made/articleshow/1219979.cms.
71. The Telegraph Online, *Gendered Roles*, The Telegraph (Feb. 10, 2003, 12:00 AM), https://www.telegraphindia.com/opinion/gendered-roles/cid/1017056.
72. *See* Reddy, *supra* note 9, at 2. Many hijras bless newborn children in return for money and gifts, and typically wear feminine attire on such occasions.
73. Gayatri Reddy, *Geographies of Contagion: Hijras, Kothis and the Politics of Sexual Marginality in Hyderabad*, 12 Anthropol. Med. 255, 257 (2005).
74. Gayatri Reddy, *"Men" Who Would be Kings: Celibacy, Emasculation, and the Re-production of Hijras in Contemporary Indian Politics*, 70 Soc. Res. 163, 166 (2003).
75. *Id.* at 165.
76. Cohen, *supra* note 9, at 278; Reddy, *supra* note 74, at 167.
77. Reddy, *supra* note 74, at 172.
78. *Id.* at 163.
79. Cohen, *supra* note 9, at 278.
80. *Id.*
81. Michel Foucault, The Birth of Biopolitics: Lectures at the College de France, 1978-1979 296 (G. Burchell trans., 2008).
82. Anirban Ghosh, *Diaries of Transformation*, 2011. (Directed and produced by Anirban Ghosh, digitization and distribution funded by the Pratyay Gender Trust.)
83. *See* Skaria, *supra* note 14, at 203. I draw on Ajay Skaria's critique of liberal democracy as 'measurable equality'.
84. In West Bengal, the non-governmental coalition MANAS Bangla served to route funds from the West Bengal State AIDS Prevention and Control Society (WBSAPCS) to its member CBOs in the 2007-12 period. *See* Karnataka Sexual Minorities Forum, *Chasing Numbers, Betraying People: Relooking at HIV Related Services in Karnataka*, CLAC (2011), https://clac.cab/sites/default/files/document_library/chasing-numbers-betraying-people-relooking-at-HIV-related%20-services-in-Karnataka.pdf for the utilization and exploitation of low-tier workers in HIV/AIDS interventions.
85. *See Rural Gays Dominate Rally,* The Asian Age (July 7, 2003). Targeted interventions for HIV/AIDS prevention and control are often the primary funding source for many NGOs and CBOs, and such funding has therefore also fed into pride organizing.
86. On the use of BCC and IEC in national health discourse, *see* National AIDS Control Organization, *National BBC/IEC Strategic Framework for HIV/AIDS Programme,* Ministry of Health and Family Welfare (2004) (on file with author).

87. *See* 5 Swikriti Patrika 14 (Surya Dipta Nag ed., 2008) [author's translation].
88. Pierre Elliott Trudeau, Canadian Minister of Justice, Remark to Newsmen, Ottawa, Canada (Dec. 21, 1967) reported in The Globe, Toronto (Dec. 22, 1967). Trudeau was commenting on the government's proposal to overhaul Canadian criminal law, giving new recognition to individual rights in several areas, including sexual behaviour.
89. Afaque, *supra* note 3.
90. *05 Jun '11: GB Sunday Meet*, Gay Bombay (June 05, 2011), http://www.gaybombay.org/index.php/2011/06/05-jun-11-gb-sunday-meet/.
91. NACO, *supra* note 35, at 13.
92. SAATHII, *Regional TG/Hijra Consultation in Eastern India* 16 (2009), http://www.saathii.org/orissapages/tg_hijra_issues_consultation%20.html.
93. Kalki Subramaniam, *Protest Transphobia from Railway Protection Force (Gujarat),* Orinam (Nov. 10, 2011), http://orinam.net/protest-transphobia-from-railway-protection-force-gujarat/.
94. A CBO in Kolkata.
95. Patrika, *supra* note 87, at 2-3.
96. *Id.* at 3.
97. I use male-gendered pronouns for most 'community' members who socially present as male (or did when this chapter was written in 2012), except when they explicitly identify as transgender. I use female pronouns for hijras and some feminine-presenting kothis. However, gender identity and presentation might be contextual and variable for each person.
98. The italicized words were originally in English. The same convention will be used in subsequent quotes.
99. Compare Berlant, supra note 43, at 4 & 5 and Fraser, supra note 27, at 60 with Jurgen Habermas, The Structural Transformation of the Public Sphere 28 (T. Burger & F. Lawrence trans., 1991).
100. For the abstract rationality of civil society as a mode of distinction, see Fraser, *supra* note 27, at 60; for art as social distinction, *see* Bourdieu, *supra* note 29, at 2.
101. Mani Ratnam, *Guru* (2007). The song is used in the climactic scene of the film, with the industrialist celebrating national leadership and pledging international success to a stadium full of staff, family and admirers.
102. *See* SAATHII, *supra* note 92, at 16. Kothi has been mapped as a sub-category of both MSM and transgender, terms which have percolated into communities.
103. *See* Michel Foucault, Security, Territory, Population: Lectures at the College de France, 1977-1978 108 (G. Burchell trans., 2007); Chatterjee (2008), *supra* note 21, at 57. While Foucault uses the term 'governmentality' to designate the entire complex of institutional apparatuses and knowledge that characterize the modern administrative state's relationship with its population, Chatterjee posits a separation between rights-bearing citizens in 'civil society' and subjects of governmental welfare/control.

104. Cited from correspondence sent to the LGBT-India list <lgbt-india@yahoogroups.com>. Given the unverifiable nature of and ongoing controversy around these accusations, I intentionally omit references to specific authors and emails.
105. My translation.
106. Berlant, *supra* note 43, at 223.
107. The words to the song are as follows (my translation and transliteration): *Aguner Poroshmoni* (The Touchstone of Fire), Rabindranath Tagore (1861-1941)

Place the touchstone of fire on the spirit	Aguner poroshmoni chhowao praane
Make this life blessed in its sacrifice to light.	E jibon punyo karo dohon daane II
Lift up and hold this body of mine	Amar ei deho khani tule dharo
Make it the lamp of your divine house	Tomar oi debaloyer prodip karo
Let the flame stay alight day and night in song.	Nishidin alok shikha jwoluk gaane II
Let your touch on the surface of darkness	Adharer gaye gaye porosh tabo
Make stars bloom anew, all through the night	Shararat photak tara nabo nabo
Darkness will melt from the sight of the eye	Noyoner drishti hote ghuchbe kaalo
It will see light wherever it may fall	Jekhanei porbe shethay dekhbe aalo
My suffering will rise as a flame upward.	Byatha mor uthbe jwole urdhopaane II

108. The text of Section 377 is as follows: "Unnatural Offences—Whoever voluntarily has carnal intercourse against the order of nature with any man, woman or animal, shall be punished with imprisonment for life, or with imprisonment of either description for a term which may extend to ten years, and shall also be liable to fine.

    Explanation—Penetration is sufficient to constitute the carnal intercourse necessary to the offence described in this section."
109. Samir Amin, Eurocentrism (1989); *see also* Chakrabarty, *supra* note 18. While I agree with the argument in Samir Amin's *Eurocentrism*, it need not necessarily go with an endorsement of his 'socialist universalism' in response to the seemingly universalizing logic of capital; rather these concepts may need to be interrogated for their pre-emptive universalizing move, which predicts what form such reinvention may take based on assumed universals such as 'capital'.

110. *See* Chatterjee, *supra* note 21, at 13-15.
111. The discussion on decorum preceding the 2015 Pride walk has been gleaned from an email thread that followed the public circulation of the minutes of a pre-Pride organizing meeting; names have been redacted to maintain confidentiality (email correspondence, October 12, 2015). The 2022 incident was narrated to me by transgender and kothi community members present in the aforementioned WhatsApp group.
112. *See* Tapas Pramanik, *Bhejal Brihannalader Julum, Atishto Shahar [City Faces Severe Harassment from Fake Hijras*], Ei Samay (Mar. 3, 2014) (on file with author).

CHAPTER 6

Complicating Privacy Further in the *Naz* Aftermath

Homonormativity and Queer Politics in India

Pawan Singh

The nexus of neoliberalism and queer politics has been subject to critique in the American context under the banner of 'homonormativity', defined variously as a gay politics that promises depoliticized, private domesticity without contesting heteronormativity,[1] and a sexual politics complicit with nationalism and white racial norms.[2] In the Indian context, however, the meaning of homonormativity has been emergent mainly in the post-*Naz* era that, albeit short-lived, marked a paradigm of queer visibility and ascendant political discourse in the twenty-first century. The *Naz* framework of human rights and its provisional decriminalization of homosexuality based on the private and consensual nature of same-sex conduct proved successful during its brief tenure (2009-2013) in nationally prominent cases of privacy violations, including the Siras case against Aligarh Muslim University and the TV9 sting operation on the gay dating service Planet Romeo. Yet the articulation of privacy as the basis for queer legibility and justice in these cases revealed the contradictions inherent in interventionist modes of empowerment for the Indian queer subject.

For instance, *Naz* formulated privacy in terms of a subject's decisional autonomy rather than what was seen by LGBTQ activists as the narrower vision of zonal/spatial privacy. However, decisional autonomy remains premised on one's public identification as gay or lesbian, a precursor to exercising the right to privacy—a disciplinary imperative that potentially situates the subject at the intersection of visibility and vulnerability. Drawing upon postcolonial critiques of neoliberalism, queer theory, media studies and political theory, this essay argues that privacy, whether decisional or spatial, as the basis for decriminalization is not merely a class-based formulation as argued by the critics of *Naz*. In addition to being available to only a privileged minority, privacy is a derivative right in the Indian Constitution that produces greater visibility for the violated figure, whose pursuit of justice in postcolonial India may bring empowerment with potential vulnerability. This paper further identifies the ways in which the homonormative impulse becomes accentuated post-*Naz*, especially following the Indian Supreme Court's disaggregation of Section 377 into sexual acts in the absence of a real subject of rights violation, or what Jacques Rancière has called the subject of a wrong that stages politics through disidentification.[3] It concludes with an analysis of privacy's correlates, mainly dignity and sexual autonomy, as advanced by the *Navtej Singh Johar* judgment of 2018 that decriminalized homosexuality in India once and for all.

INTRODUCTION

The 2009 *Naz* judgment in *Naz Foundation v. Govt. of NCT of Delhi* (*Naz* hereon) marked the start of an era of liberal LGBTQ politics through the privacy accorded to the same-sex conduct of consenting adults in the reading down of Section 377.[4] The ruling edified the notion of sexual personhood by recognizing sexual privacy as attached to persons and not merely places. In 2013, however, the Indian Supreme Court (SC) in *Suresh Kumar Koushal v. Naz Foundation*[5] (*Koushal* hereon) overruled *Naz* with the flawed observation that

LGBTQ rights were those of a miniscule minority, and that Section 377 was facially neutral in that it criminalized certain sexual acts deemed 'unnatural' irrespective of sexual orientation. Following this, a string of review and curative petitions filed by activists and advocates in the SC failed to generate further momentum until a landmark decision by a nine-judge bench of the same court ruled privacy to be a fundamental right in 2017 in *Justice K.S. Puttaswamy (Retd.) v. Union of India*,[6] popularly called the *Puttaswamy* judgment (*Puttaswamy* hereon). The explicit indictment of the 2013 *Koushal* judgment articulated by Justice Chandrachud lay the foundation for the final decriminalization of homosexuality in 2018 in *Navtej Singh Johar v. Union of India* (*Johar* hereon).[7]

This paper examines the various contestations around homosexuality's decriminalization in India between 2009 and 2018 to understand how Indian queer politics instantiate what various scholars have termed a kind of homonormativity in the articulation of sexuality-based rights through particular modes of political engagement by queer rights activists and individuals in the West.[8] The paper draws upon legal studies, queer theory and critiques of neoliberalism in postcolonial India to argue that the desire for privacy and dignity as the basis of the legal decriminalization of homosexuality in part imagines, and responds directly to, the concerns of the Indian queer subject with class privilege and the affordances of an uncloseted visibility. Based on an analysis of the various appeals to the courts registered by queer-identified individuals,[9] and cases in which the application of *Naz* secured justice for privacy-based wrongs, this paper proposes that there emerge three kinds of representational subjects that demonstrate the homonormative dynamics in the public demands for queer justice in India. These three subjects are the performative queer subject who is already visible, the violated subject whose public visibility is mediated in the moment of a privacy wrong and during subsequent legal representation, and the absent subject who never speaks for themselves..

The paper begins with a critical (not exhaustive) review of scholarship on homonormativity and queer politics in neoliberal times within the transnational context of LGBTQ rights. The next section offers an analysis of the *Naz* and *Koushal* judgments, which are key legal texts that mediate the performative representational subject's demands for queer justice. The next section takes up the issue of the violated subject of privacy wrongs in the post-*Naz* period before the 2013 re-criminalization of homosexuality by the SC. The conclusion offers reflections on the role of homonormativity in the Indian context with respect to the 2018 *Johar* judgment that finally decriminalized homosexuality in India.

NEOLIBERALISM AND QUEER POLITICS IN INDIA

Neoliberalism has been explained by social theorists in economic terms,[10] and in terms of its nexus with broader cultural politics,[11] mainly in the Western context. The articulation of a neoliberal queer politics has been advanced by the notion of homonormativity, defined as the cultural and sexual politics of neoliberalism in the American context.[12] In her analysis of advocates of the conservative gay movement in the US, also called the Independent Gay Forum (IGF), Lisa Duggan defines homonormativity as a politics that does not contest dominant heteronormative assumptions but upholds them while fostering a depoliticized gay culture based on privacy, domesticity and consumption. The Indian case of queer politics centred predominantly on the long-standing battle for homosexuality's decriminalization offers some overlap with homonormative modes of political engagement while also differing in certain ways.

Rupal Oza takes stock of neoliberal developments during India's economic liberalization in the 1990s, when India's encounter with global capital led to a loss of sovereignty, further resulting in attempts to control national culture and identity as manifested through the rigidification of gender and sexual identities.[13] It was in 1994 that the battle for the decriminalization of homosexuality began with a petition to repeal Section 377 of the Indian Penal Code in the context of facilitating HIV/AIDS-related healthcare among high-risk populations. The decade and a half long battle culminated in 2009, when the Delhi High Court read down Section 377 to legalize same-sex conduct among consenting adults in private, a decision that the SC overruled in 2013.[14] In their introductory piece to a special issue of the journal *Interventions*, Stephen Legg and Srila Roy note that the economic liberalization of the Indian economy has created spaces for the political expression of new gendered and sexual identities while also producing docile subjects for governance.[15] The queer legal mobilizations around Section 377 in particular, represent a form of 'civil society' or the urban, middle class and elites who, in the context of neoliberal capital, behave in a civil manner by, for instance, utilizing the formal workings of the law.[16] Debanuj Dasgupta and Niharika Banerjea draw upon Jasbir Puar's term, 'homonationalism', to observe that the desire for state recognition and acceptance on the part of the Indian LGBTQ movement has been expressed predominantly by upper-class, upper-caste Hindu men and women whose demands for personal liberty and privacy do not address important issues of larger social inequalities in Indian society and the redistribution of resources.[17]

Another aspect of the neoliberalism-queer nexus pertains to self-governing subjects who are worthy of rights as long as they perform codes of moral and respectable citizenship. While Oishik Sircar and Dipika Jain observe the rise of the queer consumer-citizen in the aftermath of the 2013 *Koushal* judgment, as corporate lifestyle brands interpellated Indian gay- and lesbian-identified individuals with progressive ads offering same-sex representations,[18] Debanuj Dasgupta and Ila Nagar see the *Naz* judgment as enabling the full economic and political potential of Indian gay and lesbian subjects through human rights, a conflation they critique as the interchangeability of constitutional rights with economic empowerment.[19] Dasgupta and Nagar cite the example of *kotis* and *jananas* in the city of Lucknow to suggest that certain non-normative bodies offer their own interpretation of carnality, unnaturalness and perversity to disrupt the dominant framings of homosexuality as a contest between the juridical subject of rights and cultural/religious forces that seek to reform 'perverse' sexuality. Others such as Aniruddha Dutta have offered ethnographic perspectives on sexually and gender-variant, lower-caste groups in West Bengal to demonstrate how their specific practices, experiences and identifications remain subject to dominant logics of legibility foisted upon them by institutional actors like NGOs, activists, and funders, who restrict their potential for political representation.[20]

The sections that follow offer readings of *Naz*, *Koushal*, and *Johar* to demonstrate the interplay of privacy, publicity, the public visibility of identity, and judicial constructions of sexual personhood in these texts. The analysis is particularly attentive to the dynamics of queer representation through the absence and presence of various subject positions in the legal drama of homosexuality's decriminalization.

NAZ AND *KOUSHAL*: VISIBILITY, ABSENCE AND HOMONORMATIVITY

The *Naz* judgment, delivered on July 2, 2009, was pronounced a landmark ruling for Indian LGBTQ subjects, among other sexual minorities. For the first time in Indian legal history, homosexuality was recognized in the affirmative terms of rights, including dignity, equality and, most importantly, privacy. A momentous departure from the cultural framing of same-sex relations as criminal and pathological, *Naz* remains an ocular-centric text that takes into account the long history of violence and violation inflicted upon gender non-normative bodies. We may also recall the primary rationale informing *Naz*'s humanitarian sensibilities—the HIV/AIDS needs of Indian men who have sex with men (MSM), a health demographic whose presence was recorded and presented through extensive NGO documentation, statistical data and health reports. Here I briefly review the *Naz* judgment to consider how a paradoxical politics of visibility informs its LGBTQ-affirmative spirit in its liberal abstraction of privacy. The *Naz* formulation of privacy does not hide the exposed bodies presented in the extensive evidentiary structure of human rights violations, nor does it fully account for their lived context, which is characterized by a profoundly public presence. This unaccounted for disproportionality between *Naz*'s vision of privacy and the acute public situatedness of certain bodies becomes more pronounced in the Supreme Court when the judges ask to see the bodies directly aggrieved by police misuse of Section 377.

The 105-page long *Naz* judgment demonstrates rigorous judicial labour to derive various secular principles of modern sexual personhood in India, which include key concepts like 'gay', 'privacy' and 'sexual orientation'. These three categories operate together in the judicial reasoning to discursively pivot the homosexual subject towards an imminent empowerment, mostly by requiring them to be visible as homosexuals, or to come out. The idea of coming out to take pride in an identity, to overcome shame regarding a sexual orientation, is crucial to understanding the liberal mandate of queer identity politics that disciplines the homosexual body through rights that entail greater public visibility when exercised.

Take for instance how, in the *Naz* judgment, the judges employed the terms "homosexual", "gay" and the "gay community" to refer to the behavioural category MSM "for the sake of convenience". The latter was claimed to be most susceptible to HIV/AIDS due to the operations of the law, a statement that reinforces the understanding that these categories, and by extension the LGBTQ spectrum, were being understood through the historical public health lens of HIV/AIDS, in which nondisclosure has been the norm in India.[21] Most significantly, MSM, a category into which many in India must default due to the very law in question, became a curious tacit erasure, insofar as members of this group would be unlikely to identify as gay and come forward in court. The blurring of these categories and the use of catch-all terms marks the courtroom as what feminist postcolonial scholar Ratna Kapur has described as a kind of "constrained, unreflective space" that is often constituted by the generic use of "queer".[22] The Indian sociologist Zaid Al Baset bemoans the historical evacuation of specificity in *Naz*'s use of the terms 'homosexual' and 'gay', noting that in this specific context these terms functioned as universal signifiers of unnatural desire foreshadowing other terms such as 'lesbian', '*kothi*' (a regional term for a visibly effeminate man who identifies as a receptive partner in anal sex), and '*hijra*' (transgender/eunuch).[23] Voices Against 377 similarly emphasized the public visibility of individuals with gender- and sexuality-based non-normative identities that had suffered both symbolic and material harm.

This conflation of a complex range of sexual practices and subjectivities was then further tamed, through the use of intimacy and sexuality as an unchanging core within the normative shell of privacy, and in the context of human relationships. This was particularly so in the judicial construction of privacy in *Naz*, informed by the 1998 South African decision to decriminalize homosexuality in *The National Coalition for Gay and Lesbian Equality v. The Minister of Justice*. The Yogyakarta Principles, 2007, a set of principles formulated by a group of human rights experts on matters of sexual orientation,[24] were also cited by the *Naz* judges to define sexual orientation and gender identity: "Sexual Orientation is understood to refer to each person's capacity for profound emotional, affectional [sic] and sexual attraction to, and intimate and sexual relations with, individuals of a different gender or the same gender or more than one gender."[25]

Another definition cited in the *Naz* text came from Professor Edwin Cameron, a Justice of South Africa's highest court who has written widely on HIV/AIDS, and who straightforwardly uses colloquial terms that understand sexual orientation as a matter of erotic attraction.[26] However, all of these definitions cast sexual identity in terms of an inaccessible interior realm that is immutable. In inscribing homosexuality into the legal definition of sexual orientation, the judgment eventually foreclosed any possibility of dwelling on a social constructionist understanding of sexuality.[27]

This was so despite the recurrence of MSM in the text, a category whose social constructedness never got addressed. Paradoxically, it was only by adducing the public aspects of homosexuality as a legible identity prone to social and cultural persecution that the judges could advocate for a right to privacy. In the *Naz* narrative of how homosexuals are mistreated in society at large, the public and private aspects of a homosexual identity remained irreconcilable. The logic at work goes this way: if sexuality is necessarily of interior essence, and a private matter, then that which becomes vulnerable to harm is the non-normative matter of the body. This model of the subject can be compared to what Judith Butler has called the "regulatory ideal" of sex, a model that functions to constitute the body's normativity.[28] By implication, sexual orientation is also rendered a regulatory ideal which, according to the judicial logic, is inaccessible as an interior core.

However, it isn't quite the fixed sexual orientation, the private core, that becomes vulnerable to harassment by police through the misuse of Section 377. Rather, the evidence of public violations of transgender bodies and other visibly effeminate gay men adduced to construct a narrative of harm under the misapplication of Section 377 told a story of a gender identity-based violence in public. Since sexual orientation, as the inner, unseen and unchanging core of a human, cannot be visually accessed, the police persecution of non-normative bodies was then based on their gender non-conformity. Given that, in this narrative, such harm is mostly inflicted on the public visibility of certain bodies, it is gender non-normativity (a citational and iterative act, in Butler's terms) as a public "expression" of sexual orientation—which, to reiterate, is private/interior—that comes to collapse the difference between sex and sexual orientation.

The persistently enthusiastic judicial empiricism in the *Naz* text on the vulnerability of homosexuals also referenced legal scholar Ryan Goodman's 2001 essay on the social panoptic effects of sodomy laws.[29] Goodman's essay, which is concerned with demonstrating the symbolic harm of sodomy laws even when they remain unenforced, advocates empirical research, especially field research, on the lives of gays and lesbians to assess the actual harm suffered by them. Based on open-ended interviews conducted with South African gay men and women in 1995 and 1999, Goodman's socio-legal approach, despite its laudable aims, relies on the normative assumption of progressive visibility embodied by the *out* LGBTQ subject. Particularly problematic is Goodman's empirical approach, whose results could only be substantiated by his research subjects forsaking their privacy to come out and speak openly about the symbolic harms of unenforced sodomy laws. These subjects could also be seen in the oxymoronic construction of the figure of the "unapprehended felon".

The figure of the "unapprehended felon", which signifies the symbolic harm of sodomy laws, also featured in the submissions by Voices Against 377, sharing this space of detriment with homosexuals, MSM, lesbians and gays, all of whom were denied full "moral citizenship" under the law's protean capacity to criminalize and discipline non-normative bodies.[30] More aligned with the liberal notion of moral and sexual citizenship in the Indian context, such a subjectivity translates into a class-based identity that can afford spatial privacy and also exercise personal autonomy, testifying to the elitist composition of the Indian LGBTQ movement.[31]

Jason Keith Fernandes contends that the harassment of subaltern men and sex workers at the hands of the police will continue despite the provisional reading down of Section 377 and the conferral of the right to privacy, primarily due to the public nature of their presence. Sex in public is clearly precluded under the right to privacy despite the recognition of privacy in the broader terms of decisional autonomy, transcending the supposedly narrower scope of its zonal or spatial aspects.[32] In contrast, Saptarshi Mandal argues that where public sex remains subject to prosecution under the sodomy law as well as public obscenity laws, the legitimacy of sex in private is configured by heterosexual marital norms that preclude sex workers and other public identities like hijras, often subsumed within the Indian LGBTQ movement.[33] As identities that are further distanced from any specificity of sexual subjectivity in the judgment, they are coded as what Geeta Patel calls "risky subjects", to be managed through humanitarian appeals based on risk and care. Concerned with the privatization of care within the framework of insurance and finance in India, Patel ponders the Naz Foundation's coupling of MSM, HIV and risk with the rights to health and life: what happens when the care of the self, the right to health, and the right to life are detoured through risk?[34]

Shivananda Khan, founder of the Naz Foundation, has extensively documented the lives of MSM in the context of HIV/AIDS outreach and prevention among lower-class and lower-caste vulnerable groups. With professions ranging from driving an auto-rickshaw or truck, sex work and other low-paying temporary jobs, these men, notes Khan, often don't subscribe to a Western gay identity, which remains more prevalent among English-speaking Western-educated affluent men in India. These men, who are often married and have children, mostly think of their desire in terms of sexual behaviour pertaining to the social context of cruising in parks, public toilets and other similar spaces.[35]

The judgment offered other grounds for the reading down of Section 377 as well. On the issue of public morality and the moral disapproval of homosexuality, the judges held that the invasion of the privacy of homosexuals did not serve any compelling state interest except in cases of non-consensual conduct and child abuse. As opposed to popular/public morality based on subjective notions of right and wrong, the judges defined constitutional morality as proposed by B.R. Ambedkar. Ambedkar's definition recognized that the tyranny of any one powerful minority might subvert the values of the constitution. Thus, in his estimation constitutional morality wasn't a natural sentiment but had to be cultivated for any society to be truly democratic.

Despite the Delhi High Court's coupling of privacy with decisional autonomy (an assumption of abstract agency) rather than zonal protection, which LGBTQ activists considered a narrower conception, all the evidence of abuse of the law pointed to spatiality as a more accessible realm within the evidentiary structure. No claim could be advanced on account of decisional autonomy if the court indeed reasoned correctly, because MSM are mere visible targets, not only subject to the law but also to health outreach. They never spoke for themselves in the *Naz* hearings. What does the right to privacy mean for those who figure as a health risk demographic and are constantly defined by their invisibility and inaccessibility? Given that they only appear in the courtroom through documentary evidence of their predicament, to expose how the application of Section 377 led to adverse health outcomes, the MSM are absent subjects on whose behalf the other performative representational subject speaks.

The extensive evidence on which the court relied to construct a transcendent notion of privacy as decisional autonomy pointed unequivocally towards public space where the decisional autonomy of the violated subjects did not mitigate the violence suffered. Such a public context for certain identities, whether they are self-identified or behavioural categories, remains fraught with a spectre of criminality that often exceeds the purview of the law. At the same time, spatial privacy, despite its fragility in the postcolonial Indian context, does offer a measure of material safety and protection from harm. Decisional privacy assumes a necessary identification as gay, lesbian or otherwise, and as such would only further expose the subject to potential violence, even if such exposure is in the service of empowerment, especially in the Indian context.

As a judicial text, *Naz*'s celebrated human rights spirit glosses over its conflations of identity with behaviour, the incongruity between the right to privacy and the public nature of violations, and ultimately, the invisibility of certain risky subjects, the hyper-visibility of gender non-normative bodies and the safe, normative visibility of the "unapprehended felons" who have been at the forefront of the movement to decriminalize homosexuality. Within this complex field of visibility, *Naz*'s privacy as decisional autonomy clearly privileged the homonormative minority that can invoke the lofty discourse of moral citizenship, claim pride, and stage dissent and political interventions.

More materially though, privacy as personhood stands aligned with the interests of the 'unapprehended felons'—the courtroom public of openly identified gay and lesbian men and women or, in the Supreme Court's reckoning, the "miniscule minority" that is indeed visible within the safely normative classed confines of both the private and the public. These, I argue, appear as the performative representational subjects who give an account of their self and its injury as gay or lesbian identified.[36]

A brief reading of the 2013 judgment in *Suresh Kumar Koushal v. Supreme Court of India* is instructive in unearthing the holes that *Naz* smoothly covered in its benediction of LGBTQ subjects' human rights and, by extension, all sexual minorities'. *Koushal*'s disaggregation of sexual identities—identities read into the prosecutorial economy of Section 377 by Indian LGBTQ activists and the *Naz* judgment—into an outdated yet expansive taxonomy of "unnatural sexual acts" is worth rethinking outside of the imperatively disciplinary model of "liberating" sexual identities through legal reform. Even as the judges observed that such acts could only be determined under the law with regards to the unique mechanics of each act—a technical deference to interpretation that allowed them to lay down no fixed standards of criminality under Section 377—their reasoning inadvertently and unwittingly aligned with what Steven Seidman would call the social constructionist troubling of an essentialist notion of identity. Seidman wrote in the early 1990s, during the emergence of a queer theory that took to task the mainstream gay and lesbian politics in America. This body of work noted the critical promise of the sign 'queer' in challenging the fixed and universalizing premise of LGBTQ identity politics.[37]

However, the Supreme Court's technical albeit flawed reasoning for deciphering the law's word as only concerned with certain "unnatural carnal acts" and not any identities in particular did belie the police's institutional misuse of the law to crack down on certain gender non-normative bodies and HIV/AIDS outreach work in a public context. *Koushal*'s various flaws notwithstanding, the Court's repudiation of this documentation as merely abstract academic appeals, which in their view were not a sound basis for repealing the sodomy law, may be read as a poignant moment that exposed the stark inequality between the reality of MSM and other gender non-normative bodies and the 'unapprehended felons' who were indeed present in the Supreme Court as concerned interveners. The absence of a real aggrieved body in the courtroom that could testify to suffering physical violence as a result of Section 377 demonstrated why *Naz*'s construction of privacy as decisional autonomy was fallacious.

Those who could exercise decisional autonomy as gay and lesbian subjects were present in the courtroom. However, their appeals of symbolic harm, particularly their status as "second class" citizens of India, were unfortunately rendered grand abstractions despite claims of symbolic injury. These were all publicly visible individuals who had indeed come out of the closet into the visibility of the courtroom's legal space to ask for their rights. It must be noted that this publicity does serve an important purpose: that of creating a queer counter-public that can demand fairness from structures of justice, and which, according to John Rawls' theory of justice, should stand up to public scrutiny.[38]

However, the public visibility afforded by the coming out of several self-identified gay and lesbian individuals—both in the Delhi High Court and the Supreme Court—was still within the confines of normative class-safety, a fact that undercut its radical potential. To reiterate, they served the important function of performative representational subjects who claimed a symbolic injury under the law to appeal for justice. Such a subject also overlaps with Partha Chatterjee's notion of the civil society whose upper-class and upper-caste credentials and cultural capital enable them access to legal representational spaces.[39]

Eric O'Clarke's examination of the function of publicity in the inclusion of homoeroticism and queer representations in the modern public sphere is also relevant here. Drawing upon Habermas's formulation of the public sphere, he argues that homoerotic life finds inclusion in the bourgeois public sphere through a heteronormative sanction of queerness, through proprietary codes that make queer subjects just like everyone else. Their public performance as rights-bearing subjects who demand equality under the law is required by what O'Clarke calls publicity's "subjunctive mood", which provisionally admits their normative self into the public sphere while deferring "demonized remainders: queer persons and interests that would doubtless seem slightly out of place on a city council or in an Ikea commercial."[40]

The emergence of this normativizing public culture to mediate privacy as safety represents an enfolding of vulnerable queer life into a seamless national culture of empowered visibility and public iconicity. Jasbir Puar ascribes the visibility of the queer agential subject to homonormativity. As part of the visibility and LGBTQ empowerment agenda, this subject functions as a regulatory ideal that insists on "freedom from norms" through access to an implicit understanding of queerness as cosmopolitan and elite, premised on various regimes of mobility.[41]

On the other hand, the absence of an actually violated subject—the second kind of representational subject, whose visibility is mediated in the courtroom as the embodiment of the sodomy law's wrongful application—then proved to be a Rancièrean subject. In his work on the aesthetics of politics, Jacques Rancière regards the moment of politics to be the one in which the subject of a wrong or violation effects the verification of social equality that has been constitutionally guaranteed under the law. By pointing to the absence of such a subject in the *Naz* court, the Supreme Court judges implicitly enacted Rancière's logic of the dispute that leads to the challenging of the normative supposition of equality.[42] Conspicuous in their absence in the Supreme Court were MSM and other gender non-normative violated bodies, except in documentary evidence. This absence severely attenuated *Naz*'s conferral of human rights at the same time as it framed the visibility of the 'unapprehended felons' as a form of homonormativity, a disciplinary logic of the dominant LGBTQ identity defined by liberal principles of sexual personhood, decisional autonomy and class-based privacy as a form of safety. Given these dynamics of public presence and critical absence, LGBTQ rights may be read, not as those of a "miniscule fraction" as the Supreme Court's ideological dismissal would have us believe, but rather as the rights of those who do have a part to play in the "distribution of the sensible", to borrow Rancière's description of the social recognition and counting of certain groups with their constituent parts and functions in a given social order.[43]

Thus, reading *Koushal* against the grain of *Naz*'s sensibilities and its homonormative rhetoric of human rights does open up a critical space in which to understand how privacy itself is deeply mired in the social inequality that also structures the logics of presence and absence in the Indian LGBTQ movement. This is unequivocally evident in the Supreme Court proceedings where the absence of MSM and other physically injured non-normative bodies appeared to overshadow the presence of those who were claiming a symbolic injury or, in the inadvertent estimation of the judges, those belonging to a "miniscule minority". However, this analysis is an interpretation of the Supreme Court's judicial logics, and not a literal decoding of the judges' intentions. That they unwittingly enacted fundamental tenets of queer theory is purely incidental, even if it is analytically fortuitous.

In the next section, I review two nationally prominent cases following the 2009 decriminalization of homosexuality. These cases further attest to the tenuousness of privacy as the basis of queer empowerment in India by illustrating how privacy as a right, a material affordance and a constitutional principle is entangled with queer visibility as a form of vulnerability. These cases further illuminate the absent subject and the violated subject whose visibility remains irrevocably mediated.

POST-*NAZ* PRIVACY: SIRAS AND THE TV9 STING OPERATIONS

On February 8, 2010, seven months after the legalization of homosexuality in India and the attendant triumphant optimism around LGBTQ liberation, Dr Shrinivas Ramchandra Siras, a professor of Modern Indian Languages at the Aligarh Muslim University (AMU) in Northern India, was filmed without his consent in the privacy of his bedroom by his university colleagues, with the assistance of local media persons. The camera caught Siras in a compromising position with his male partner. The following day, the illegally obtained video footage and images were circulated via the local newspaper and sent to the university administration, following which Dr Siras was suspended by the authorities on the grounds of his "immoral conduct" in his on-campus home. The incident caused national outrage among various LGBTQ activist groups and teacher communities, who demanded strict action against a university that, in their view, had breached the privacy of an employee in his own home. With the help of LGBTQ lawyers and activists, the professor sued the university, won, and was reinstated. However, in April 2010, shortly before his return to the university as ordered by the Allahabad High Court, he was found dead in his apartment under mysterious circumstances. His death, occurring a short two months after his reinstatement, was inconclusively ruled to be a suicide.

Prior to Siras's death, a team of lawyers and civil rights activists conducted a fact-finding mission called 'Policing Morality at AMU'. This report informs the examination of the incident in this section.[44] The fact-finding report reveals that AMU's extra-legal actions were rationalized by the orthodox Islamic institution's own local constitution. Under this constitution, the professor's sexual conduct appeared reprehensible, comprising the grounds for his suspension. This was despite the broader consensus among the various parties interviewed that such an invasion of privacy was unconstitutional. A close reading of the fact-finding report directs attention to the ways in which privacy as a legal principle and a socio-cultural affordance remains intricately entangled with notions of traditional beliefs, religious morality and vernacular media practices that reinforce the spatial or zonal logic of the private as more immediately urgent.

The fact-finding report compiled by lawyers and civil rights activists represents a profoundly public intervention that, though imperative, places its subject as in need of redress. The subject is, moreover, placed at an irrevocably public altar of visibility and appears as an exemplar of vulnerability. The report begins with Dr Siras's version of the events between February 8 and 10, 2010, leading up to his suspension from the university and forced eviction from university housing, a space rendered immoral in the university's view by Dr Siras's homosexual conduct, abrogating his right to access his own home. During local media persons' intrusion into Dr Siras's bedroom while he was with his male partner, the professor was photographed in a compromising position and threatened with public exposure. The following morning, not only were the photographs circulated to and published in the local newspaper, but the professor was also served with a suspension notice by the university. Under Section 40 (3) (c) of the *Aligarh Muslim University Act, 1920*, Siras was cited as having indulged in "gross misconduct and immoral sexual activity" in contravention of the basic moral ethics followed in university housing. As a publicly visible moral offender, he was stripped of his freedom of movement by the university through an order to vacate his university home and not leave Aligarh without permission from the Vice-Chancellor of AMU.

Imposing its own religious morality informed by a historical interpretation of Islam, the University acted with utter disregard for the *Naz* decision. Under *Naz*, the right to privacy was defined in individual terms as linked to decisional autonomy and sexual personhood, thus broadening privacy from its zonal/spatial configuration. As becomes evident from the divergent views of the various parties interviewed in the fact-finding report, it is the transgression into the professor's bedroom that constitutes the first order of the sting operation's violation of privacy. The professor's decisional autonomy upon undue public exposure for his "immoral" conduct remains tied to his private actions within the confines of his home, located on university premises. Decisional autonomy can be effectively invoked only if the subject openly identifies as gay or lesbian, claiming legal sexual personhood as the basis of their privacy. Such identification in the professor's case clearly follows, rather than *precedes,* the spatial privacy invasion.

Privacy as spatial security and freedom became even more acute in the sequence of events following Siras's suspension. The professor was told to vacate his campus housing with immediate effect. In order to expedite his evacuation, the university ordered the disconnection of his home's electric supply, depriving him of light and power, perhaps one of the most fundamental liberties of a middle-class private existence. Siras was thus forced out of his home, and by extension, quite literally forced out of his material zone of privacy and into the visibility of public subjecthood. This status preceded his search for another home; the publicity pre-empted his ability to secure housing anywhere in the city.

Thus, it becomes clear that this aspect of the case has several implications for an understanding of privacy as a state of potential vulnerability within the postcolonial context. It demonstrates the tenuousness of privacy as a legal principle in the service of LGBTQ empowerment in India. It renders the material geography of private existence more urgent. His unfortunate death notwithstanding, if Siras had indeed returned to AMU as per the Allahabad High Court's reinstatement order, how would his legally won professional life as a visible gay subject unfold in the continued environment of the Islamic institution's homophobia and denial of homosexuality's prevalence on the campus premises? The Siras case successfully put *Naz* to the test, yet would have placed Siras at the paradoxical juncture of empowered visibility with potential vulnerability in the event of his return to AMU. The late professor represents the violated subject whose public visibility, despite winning the privacy case, remains interminably mediated by legal archives, media reports and, saliently, a 2015 Hindi film made on the AMU incident, capturing his experience.

Only a year later, in February 2011, a regional Indian TV news channel, TV9, broadcasted a story in Telugu titled 'Gay Culture Rampant in Hyderabad' during prime time news in Hyderabad. Through a sting operation conducted on the users of a gay dating service called Planet Romeo, an undercover TV9 reporter contacted users of the website and engaged them in conversation, ostensibly for a sexual hook-up. The story replayed recorded conversations and exposed the profile pictures of Hyderabad users in sensationalizing overtones of moral panic. Indian LGBTQ activists called the episode a flagrant invasion of the service users' privacy, as well as a violation of media ethics and the code of conduct set forth by the News Broadcasters Association of India (NBA).

The story caused national outrage, especially among LGBTQ groups in India. Subsequent events culminated in the imposition of a $2000 fine on TV9 and a further issuance of an apology by the channel as ordered by the News Broadcasters Standards Authority (NBSA), an entity that governs the media code of ethics and broadcasting standards in India. Indian lawyers argue that this course of action became possible thanks to *Naz*'s reading down of Section 377.[45] TV9's sting operation on the city's urban gay culture and the legal framework within which the new channel's "investigative" practices became punishable suggest a disjuncture between the global discourse on LGBTQ rights and the local cultures of vernacular media in India.[46]

The TV9 sting operation was yet another instance of *Naz*'s success, albeit with one key difference. The privacy violation committed under the sting operation once again foregrounded the spatial logic of online spaces, in which user privacy is assumed to operate within a broader public context. Considering that none of the Planet Romeo profile users exposed in the sensationalized media reportage ever came forward to speak for themselves and demand justice, privacy as decisional autonomy—as an exercise of sexual personhood, representing oneself as a violated subject—was once again marked by a critical absence. It was, however, certainly exercised by the interventionist LGBTQ activists and lawyers who staged protests in their bid to rescue the violated but invisible subjects. The violated users' absence in the representational drama may be read as yet another form of privacy that instantiates the logics of personal discretion, silence or not being aware of or concerned by the violation. These are possibilities of course, given that an attempt to seek their perspective would unwittingly follow a homonormative impulse. This logic of privacy as silence and invisibility has indeed been cast in homonormative terms of repression and erasure, as a form of tacit violence by Indian LGBTQ activists. To be visible, then, by coming out, demanding justice and an identity-based affirmation is indeed reinforced as the linear logic of rights-based homonormativity that equates visible public presence with the teleological outcome of progress.

The final section of this paper examines the right to privacy in the post-*Koushal* context, a time when the homonormative interventionist logic implicitly undermines one of the bases of reading down Section 377 in 2009, that is, employing constitutional rather than popular morality to include homosexuality as a legal social difference in India. It also examines the 2018 *Johar* judgment that decriminalized homosexuality in India once and for all.

THE POST-*KOUSHAL* LANDSCAPE OF PRIVACY

The *Koushal* verdict's overturning of *Naz* reverberated globally, with queer communities staging a "global day of rage" event with proclamations of "no going back" to re-criminalization under Section 377 and, by implication, into the closet.[47] The progressivist staging of this collective rage at the taking back of LGBTQ rights is a metonymic event suggesting the grand narrative of queer citizenship and normative visibility as the dominant mode through which homosexuality's social acceptance may be accomplished in India. The visibility of same-sex desire, however, has been a richer and far more complex social, cultural and representational project, irreducible to a single dominant logic, as demonstrated by scholars of postcolonial sexuality studies.[48]

The post-*Koushal* context of queer visibility in India further complicates the legal grounds for sexual privacy, particularly of same-sex desiring men who are also situated within heterosexual marriage. Three prominent cases are of particular relevance here. I analyze them briefly in order to show, not just the unwitting reinvigoration of a law that had ironically been seen to suffer from desuetude, but also the humanitarian investment in privacy as grounds for the legitimacy of engaging in homosexual behaviour.

In October 2014, a Bangalore-based software engineer who was married to a woman was booked under Section 377 of the Indian Penal Code for having sex with another man. His encounters had been recorded by his wife on a secret surveillance camera that she had installed in their apartment after her suspicions about her husband's sexuality grew. The wife's suspicions were due to her husband's use of pink lip-gloss, face packs and his habit of taking long showers, as well as his effeminate mannerisms.[49] Following a police complaint filed by her, the husband was booked, not for adultery (Section 497), but under Section 377, which at the time carried a maximum sentence of life imprisonment for engaging in "unnatural" sexual behaviour. Sandip Roy, a San Francisco-based journalist, observes that the patriarchal nature of Indian society pressures a number of gay men into entering heterosexual marriages. However, Roy further notes that this was a software engineer who had financial independence; he could not rightfully evade his responsibility to his wife. Roy sees this as a case of a gay man trying to have his cake and eat it too.[50]

While Roy's observation about the patriarchal pressure on men to get married is certainly tenable in the Indian context, his prescriptive observations oddly mirror and recapitulate the popular moral logic repudiated by the Delhi High Court in favour of a more secular constitutional morality. Roy's assumptions about the husband's actions as self-centred in the absence of his side of the story are yet another iteration of the homonormative interventionist mode of corrective justice. However, privacy becomes murkier in this case, given that the culprit is a same-sex desiring man who was caught having sex on camera. If gay sex had been legal, how would we approach the question of the husband's privacy in a heterosexual marriage, considering the countervailing rights of the wife? The answers to this may be as varied as the moral logics around sexuality, marriage and gender in the postcolonial Indian context.

But let's look at another case dated June 2014, that of a married doctor and four youths with whom the former had sexual relations. The youths were booked under an extortion law and Section 377 for blackmailing the doctor for money by threatening to expose an alleged videotape of one of his sexual encounters. The police were also exploring the possibility of charging the doctor under Section 377, since he was technically guilty of having engaged in "unnatural" sexual relations with the men.[51] The case easily lends itself to the trappings of a public sex scandal within which the doctor, despite being the victim of a privacy violation, would be seen as a culprit because of his extra-marital relations with men.

In the most recent case, dated April 2015, an All India Institute of Medical Sciences (AIIMS) doctor committed suicide in a hotel room after she discovered that her husband was gay. She left behind an anguished Facebook note in which she claimed that her husband tortured her and hadn't consummated their marriage in the five years that they were together. In a vein similar to the Bangalore techie's story, Sandip Roy characterizes the wife as an "unwitting" victim, while the husband is simply unwilling. Roy believes that in this day and age of internet networking and the extensive resources available for LGBTQ-identified or struggling men, gay men have a responsibility to not cave in to the pressure to get married. Observing that the internet has made it easier for people to lead double lives, Roy holds that the least gay men can do is not get married, even if they don't want to come out or participate in pride parades.[52]

Implicit in Roy's moralizing take on the two stories—the Bangalore techie's and the AIIMS doctor's suicide—is an essentializing undertone that necessarily casts married gay men as victims of the patriarchy. Struggling with their sexuality, they must avail of the LGBTQ support resources offered by NGOs like the Humsafar Trust in Bombay and the Naz Foundation in Delhi. Roy also seems to subscribe to the idea that gay men with material resources at their disposal must not give in to the pressure to get married and potentially ruin a woman's life. Roy's prescriptions mirror the logic of individualism that Michel Foucault has critiqued as the "care of the self". Reflecting on the question of individualism in different epochs and societies, Foucault offers three distinguishing social facts about the cultivation of the self:

> (1) the individualistic attitude, characterized by the absolute value attributed to the individual in his singularity and by the degree of independence conceded to him vis-à-vis the group to which he belongs and the institutions to which he is answerable; (2) the positive valuation of private life, that is, the importance granted to family relationships, to the forms of domestic activity, and to the domain of patrimonial interests; (3) the intensity of the relations to self, that is, of the forms in which one is called upon to take oneself as an object of knowledge and a field of action, so as to transform, correct, and purify oneself, and find salvation.[53]

Inherent in Roy's prescriptive advice to gay men who are presumably trapped in heterosexual marriages is this Foucauldian insight of the self as an object to be cultivated in terms of a normative order of responsibility and social accountability so that no one is victimized. The making of the queer self, first through the *Naz* version of privacy as decisional autonomy, and then called upon in the post-*Koushal* cases involving Section 377, purposes the Indian homonormative project of cultivating a queer self that is true to its sexual desires and assumes that identity within an ethos of self-care and responsibility.

Another instance of setting in motion the discourse of rescuing the queer self was a post on the Alternative Law Forum (ALF) mailing list that advertised an event addressing the socio-legal implications of *Koushal* for gay men in troubled marriages. The following points were listed as questions for discussion:[54]

> How can we understand and talk about the responsibilities gay men have related to marriage without only vilifying them?
>
> How seriously should we take 'family and societal pressure' as reasons gay men 'choose' or are 'forced' to marry? What cumulative psychological effects do these daily pressures have over time? How to manage/deal with/combat them?

> What are the laws that protect women? Are there laws that would enable both the man and the woman to come out of the situation in an amicable way? Does non-consummation/depriving the wife of sexual intimacy amount to cruelty?
>
> Who is the victim in the case of these marriages? The unknowing wife? The gay man? Is victimhood equally distributed, or can they both be victims of hetero-patriarchal society and yet one still be more responsible than the other?
>
> What are the Do's n Don'ts for men in such marriages? Should they change their behavior? Tell their wives? Is it a case by case basis?
>
> Where are the voices of women in this conversation? Is there a way to bring women into the discussion, rather than discussing them passively as victims of male dominance (straight, gay, or otherwise)?
>
> Is a gay man married to a woman and having sex with other men on the side any different than a straight man who has sex with other women? If so, how? If not, why?

Yet another iteration of the interventionist mode of prescriptive queer politics, the calculus of distributing responsibility, assigning blame and socially adjudicating (public) morality advances the rehabilitative project of homonormativity in India. How can we make it better for everyone, including gay men, straight women, and the two as a married couple? Though not as extensively publicized as Dan Savage's *It Gets Better* campaign, which seeks to make the lives of queer youth more livable in America in a bid to prevent suicides caused by bullying and harassment,[55] the Indian queer political mobilizations in the wake of the aforementioned post-*Koushal* cases certainly recapitulate the eagerly concerned righteousness of modern queer normativity. They also ignore the vital aspect of privacy as decisional autonomy by not extending the same principle to gay men "trapped" in heterosexual marriages.

By indicting this prescriptive moralizing geared towards "helping" certain victims of patriarchy who cause further harm to other victims, the underlying motivation is not to condone or defend the gay men or other stakeholders by offering empathy masked as critique. It is instead to be cognizant of the interventionist advocacy impulse animated by a normativizing culture of rights-based empowerment that offers liberal identity-based imperative justice. While rights-based modes of justice rely on fixed markers of difference, the particular case of the right to privacy as the basis of the decriminalization of homosexuality is problematic insofar as it engenders greater publicity and masks social inequality. This is true insofar as same-sex relations and homosexuality continue to be pathologized culturally, medically and socially. Further the decisional privacy claims of same-sex desiring men—if legally tenable—become attenuated in the context of heterosexual marriage, which predominantly takes priority over one's sexual identification as gay in the Indian context. Although the outcomes in these cases are tragic and devastating, the prescriptive morality in these accounts is exactly the kind of normative impulse that marks the emergence of liberal homonormativity in India. This moral position insists that, at the very least, gay men should not marry and should come out with the help of NGO support resources. Popular or public morality was repudiated by the Delhi High Court as a basis for disapproving of homosexuality in culture and society. Instead the High Court made constitutional morality (defined as the secular gaze of the law that treats all minorities as equal) the basis of legalizing homosexuality.

The recourse to a similarly charged public morality that prescribes the adoption of an honest and self-affirming sexual identity to gay men unwittingly recapitulates and reproduces pathologizing narratives of homosexuality being in need of public intervention. This prescriptive impulse then aims to normalize homosexual behaviour to create a safe, open, honest and pure queer identity. This is a paradigm of visibility where the neoliberal commodification of queer culture partly depoliticizes queer politics while fostering inequality.[56] The implications of economic neoliberalism shaping queer consumer culture in India haven't been studied in any measure. However, homonormativity as the cultural politics of neoliberalism manifests as the remaking of queer subjects as they make an appearance in the field of visibility, whether as Rancièrean subjects of a wrong or Foucauldian figures of self-care. Whether it's the Naz MSM or Planet Romeo profile users as critical absence, Siras as an empowered gay icon or the pathological Bangalore techie, the dominant queer politics in India has sought to bring them into the normative fold of empowered visibility through normative interventions.

CONCLUSION

At one point during the Supreme Court hearings of the *Koushal* case, the *Naz* attorney Mr Anand Grover argued that Section 377 affected the dignity of homosexuals in India. The judges responded by asking if the affected homosexuals could be identified in the court of law. Instead of responding in the negative, Mr Grover posited the hypothetical case of a troubled teenager who could identify his desires at puberty but could not come out as gay due to the heterosexist culture within which he lived. The judges simply declared that there was no question of compromising dignity if the identity was not known. The attribution of a fully developed and reconciled gay identity to a teenager's initial stirrings of desire by Mr Grover is precisely the kind of liberal imposition that underlies the Indian homonormative project.

Yet dignity, freedom of expression and sexual autonomy were edified as fundamental planks of privacy in the 2018 *Johar* judgment. Building on the *Naz* and *Puttaswamy* judgments, *Johar* employed the concept of 'transformative constitutionalism'—the idea that the purpose of the Constitution is to transform society for the better—in safeguarding the rights of sexual minorities. The judges further defined individual autonomy as the ability to choose intimate partners and establish one's identity through dignity, which was deemed an inseparable facet of such identity. The judges were particularly sensitive to the petitioners' mental agony, loneliness and experiences of harassment, particularly Justice Chandrachud, who invoked the language of sexual citizenship while observing that terms like 'public' and 'private' were not as clear-cut. Demonstrating a particular sensitivity to those who cannot afford spatial privacy, he extended the right to privacy to those vulnerable on account of their sexuality and appearance. However, he also noted that sexuality could not be compartmentalized, it was fluid in that it grants individuals the freedom to ascertain their desires and proclivities. This minor detail remained patently at odds with observations made earlier in the judgment regarding the immutable nature of sexuality. The *Johar* judgment strikes all the right ethical chords and even covers its theoretical bases in citing Eve Sedgwick's *Epistemology of the Closet,* as well as acknowledging the blurring of public and private. However, the five petitioners' class backgrounds and positions, which included an eminent dancer, a journalist, a celebrity chef, and two hoteliers, is worth examining to understand how Section 377 affected their lives.

Journalist Sunil Mehra who filed a petition with his partner of 20 years, Navtej Singh Johar, claimed that he chose to opt out of a career in the civil services due to the criminalization of his sexual orientation. Similarly, business executive Ayesha Kapur attributed her decision to quit a lucrative business at the height of her career to Section 377 and her fear that her sexual orientation would be discovered. Further, she notes that "even today, she is unable to accompany or be accompanied by her committed partner at social and family occasions."[57] These are indeed the lived realities of not just upper-class Indians who have suffered prejudice because of their sexual orientation, but most other individuals in India who often perhaps lack the vocabulary to articulate their feelings and identity. Aside from the fact that these petitioners are from an upper-class background—one of them was even married to his partner in France—it wouldn't be far-fetched to assume that they are protected to an extent by their class privilege, or what I call the socio-economics of the closet. However, to attribute their injuries to the operations of the law would seem misplaced. Their injuries seem to be an upshot of social attitudes towards homosexuality in India and are only indirectly linked to the operations of Section 377, which have certainly impacted non-normatively gendered bodies and MSM, who are not always afforded spatial privacy. The petitioners may be understood to be exercising privacy as decisional autonomy through legal representation. Even if we consider the *Navtej* judgment to be an exercise in transformative constitutionalism, that is, it sought to transform society for the better, such a view would be utopian at best given that, despite legal protections and rights, other minorities like Dalits continue to be persecuted. An elaborate discussion of transformative constitutionalism is, however, beyond the scope of this paper.

The critique of the emergent homonormativity offered in this paper does not in any way imply that rights-based modes of empowering justice should be replaced with a less normative and more radical agenda, for that kind of proposition would still traffic in a prescriptive moralizing vision of imagining a queer future. Rather, the animating task here has been to delineate the coordinates of an emerging homonormative political culture in India that appears to be reliant on the liberal, teleological and progressivist principles of queer identity politics. Instead of the constant insistence on visibility and affirmative presence, for queerness to be recognized and celebrated publicly, queer politics may also take cognizance of alternative meanings of privacy as secrecy, absence, and ultimately a kind of safety in not being seen or represented. Wouldn't that also be a form of decisional autonomy afforded through privacy? Perhaps to the liberal investments of the modern queer identity in India, this may sound like a regressive suggestion, a step back into the regime of the closet, akin to silence and erasure. However, in the postcolonial Indian context, embodied queer visibility is fraught with unforeseen dangers of moral policing that may be rescued by privacy-based justice but only at the expense of begetting greater public exposure, what I have called the intersection of visibility and vulnerability.

In an online story published by *The Guardian*, New York-based Indian documentary filmmaker and writer Parvez Sharma describes the predicament of fraught queer visibility by citing a Hindi newspaper story from a small town called Saharanpur, which he characterizes as far removed from the urban realities of gay pride. The news story was titled 'Gay Party Has Been Exposed', published in the Hindi daily *Amar Ujala*, and included photographs of 20 frightened-looking men sitting on the floor trying to hide their faces. The story also included their first names along with the identity of the party organizer, in addition to salacious details of "used condoms" and guests in a "compromising position".[58] Sharma, who grew up in Saharanpur, notes the contradictions of gay pride in India:

> In so many countries, invisibility is the norm and the preferred option for those who have same-sex desires. I have no doubt that most of the men and women who were busy marching in Delhi waving their banners would not like to be seen at a downmarket venue like the *dharamshala* in Saharanpur and I am not even sure if many of these newly minted 'queer' activists from India's big cities would find common cause with the small-town types arrested at this 'gay party'.[59]

Sharma is scathing in his indictment of the urban bias of queer visibility which, in places far removed from the cosmopolitan and Westernized spectacles of queer culture, exists in alternative modes of communication and exchange without recourse to the legibility of labels. Again, the intent here isn't to altogether reject the deployment of a Western vocabulary to articulate queer desire in India, nor is it to celebrate invisibility as a safer option. The richness and complexity of the queer representational project in India affords a critical interpretation of invisibility, absence and secrecy as being as constitutive of sexual privacy (in a cultural sense) as the legal counterpart of the right is seen to be. However, some would argue against absence and silence as unviable sites of politics that come with their own power relations, but to mistake them for a political position is to unwittingly enter the trap of normativity. The silence and absence of the unrepresented subject lends itself only minimally to an interpretation of their invisibility as a kind of cultural privacy and decisional autonomy. To attribute political agency to their actions or suggest false consciousness on their part would be analytically inaccurate.

The liberal homonormative positions in the post-*Koushal* cases have impelled a victim narrative to be interpreted within the moralizing overtones of an interventionist project that seeks to unspool the entanglements of homosexuality with heteronormative mandates of marriage and obligations to family. Without hearing the voices of convicted same-sex desiring men exposed for their extra-marital homosexual conduct, the homonormative project is undergirded by a set of assumptions that see fit to script the exposed men and the women they cheated on as victims. The question of whether they see themselves as such or not is foreclosed by the urgency of justice and the will to empower. Or, in the words of Gayatri Chakravorty Spivak, the emancipatory justice of modern liberalism is an affordance "we cannot not want".[60] With *Naz* as well as with the political response to *Koushal*, the modality of visible rage and dissent may have steeped Indian queer politics in a liberal homonormativity. However dominant, we might also show resistance to the compelling exhortations of the homonormative project by not always insisting on its indispensability to our current political imagination and our pursuit of justice.

NOTES

1. Lisa Duggan, The Twilight of Equality?: Neoliberalism, Cultural Politics and the Attack on Democracy (2003).
2. Jasbir K. Puar, Terrorist Assemblages: Homonationalism in Queer Times (2007).
3. Jacques Rancière, Dissensus: On Politics and Aesthetics (2010).
4. Naz Foundation v. Govt. of NCT of Delhi, (2009) 160 DLT 277.
5. Suresh Koushal v. Naz Foundation, (2014) 1 SCC 1.
6. K.S. Puttaswamy v. Union of India, (2017) 10 SCC 1.
7. Navtej Singh Johar v. Union of India, (2018) 10 SCALE 386.
8. Lisa Duggan, *The New Homonormativity: The Sexual Politics of Neoliberalism, in* Materializing Democracy: Toward a Revitalized Cultural Politics 175-194 (R. Castronovo & D.D. Nelson eds., 2002). *See also*, Puar, *supra* note 2.
9. I use queer as an analytical term in lieu of gay and lesbian to advance my critique of homonormativity as well as the term's uptake in the Indian LGBTQ movement, which has often mobilized under the banner of queer.
10. David Harvey, A Brief History of Neoliberalism (2007).
11. Duggan, *supra* note 1.
12. Duggan, *supra* note 8.

13. Rupal Oza, The Making of Neoliberal India: Nationalism, Gender and the Paradoxes of Globalization (2012).
14. Danish Sheikh, *The Road to Decriminalization: Litigating India's Anti-Sodomy Law,* 16 Yale Hum. Rts. & Dev. L.J. 104 (2013).
15. Stephen Legg & Srila Roy, *Neo-Liberalism, Post-Colonialism and Hetero-Sovereignties: Emergent Sexual Formations in Contemporary India,* 15 Interventions 461 (2013).
16. Partha Chatterjee, The Politics of the Governed: Reflections on Popular Politics in Most of the World (2004).
17. Niharika Banerjea & Debanuj Dasgupta, *States of Desire,* Sanhati (June 06, 2013), http://sanhati.com/articles/7185/.
18. New Intimacies, Old Desires: Law, Culture and Queer Politics in Neoliberal Times (Oishik Sircar & Dipika Jain eds., 2017).
19. Debanuj Dasgupta & Ila Nagar, *Public Koti and Private Love: Section 377, Religion, Perversity and Lived Desire,* 23 Contemp. South Asia 426 (2015).
20. Aniruddha Dutta, *Legible Identities and Legitimate Citizens: The Globalization of Transgender and Subjects of HIV-AIDS Prevention in India,* 15 Int. Fem. J. Politics 494 (2013).
21. *See* Naz Foundation, *supra* note 4, at 6.
22. Ratna Kapur, *Multi-Tasking Queer: Reflections on the Possibilities of Homosexual Dissidence in the Law,* 4 Jindal Global Law Rev. 36 (2012).
23. Zaid Al Baset, *Section 377 and the Myth of Heterosexuality,* 4 Jindal Global Law Rev. 89 (2012).
24. Michael O'Flaherty & John Fisher, *Sexual Orientation, Gender Identity and International Human Rights Law: Contextualising the Yogyakarta Principles,* 8 Human Rights Law Rev. 207 (2008).
25. Naz Foundation, *supra* note 4, at 36-37.
26. Edwin Cameron, *Sexual Orientation and the Constitution: A Test Case for Human Rights,* 110 S. Afr. Law J. 450 (1993).
27. Steven Seidman, The Social Construction of Sexuality (2003).
28. Judith Butler, Bodies that Matter: On the Discursive Limits of "Sex" 3 (1993).
29. Naz Foundation, *supra* note 4, at 40-41. *See also,* Ryan Goodman, *Beyond the Enforcement Principle: Sodomy Laws, Social Norms and Social Panoptics,* 89 California Law Rev. 643 (2001).
30. Naz Foundation, *supra* note 4, at 41-43. The Delhi High Court borrowed the phrase "moral citizenship" from the 1998 South African decriminalization decision in *The National Coalition for Gay and Lesbian Equality v. The Minister of Justice.*
31. Ashley Tellis, *Disrupting the Dinner Table: Re-Thinking the 'Queer Movement' in Contemporary India,* 4 Jindal Global Law Rev. 142 (2012).
32. Jason Keith Fernandes, *The Dilemma After the Decision: Strays Thoughts After Gay Liberation,* DervishNotes (Aug. 18, 2009), http://dervishnotes.blogspot.com/2009/08/dilemma-after-decision-strays-thoughts.html.

33. Saptarishi Mandal, *Right to Privacy in Naz Foundation: A Counter-Heteronormative Critique,* 2 NUJS Law Rev. 525 (2009).
34. Geeta Patel, *Risky Subjects: Insurance, Sexuality and Capital,* 24 Social Text 25 (2006).
35. Shivananda Khan, *Culture, Sexualities, and Identities: Men Who Have Sex with Men in India, in* Gay and Lesbian Asia: Culture, Identity, Community (G. Sullivan & P.A. Jackson eds., 2011).
36. Judith Butler, Giving an Account of Oneself (2005).
37. Steven Seidman, *Identity and Politics in a "Postmodern" Gay Culture: Some Historical and Conceptual Notes, in* Fear of a Queer Planet: Queer Politics and Social Theory (M. Warner ed., 1993).
38. John Rawls, A Theory of Justice (1971).
39. Chatterjee, *supra* note 16.
40. Eric O'Clarke, Virtuous Vice: Homoeroticism and the Public Sphere 7 (2000).
41. Puar, *supra* note 2, at 22.
42. Rancière, *supra* note 3.
43. *Id.* at 36.
44. Arvind Narrain et al., *Policing Morality at AMU: An Independent Fact Finding Report,* Fridae (Mar. 10, 2010), http://www.fridae.asia/gay-news/2010/03/10/9724.policing-morality-at-amu-an-independent-fact-finding-report.
45. Sheikh, *supra* note 14, at 3.
46. Parvez Sharma, *Gay Pride Only Goes So Far in India,* The Guardian (Dec. 30, 2010), http://www.theguardian.com/commentisfree/2010/dec/30/gay-pride-india-queer-delhi-western.
47. Tasneem Nashrulla, *Activists Plan "Global Day of Rage" to Fight for India's LGBT Community,* Buzzfeed News (Dec. 13, 2013, 10:16 PM), http://www.buzzfeed.com/tasneemnashrulla/activists-plan-global-day-of-rage-to-fight-for-indias-lgbt-c#.xuZ4QEX8l.
48. *See for instance,* Queering India: Same-Sex Love and Eroticism in Indian Culture and Society (Ruth Vanita ed., 2002). *See also,* The Phobic and the Erotic: The Politics of Sexualities in Contemporary India (Brinda Bose & Subhabrata Bhattacharyya eds., 2007).
49. FP Staff, *Bangalore: Woman Films Husband's Gay Encounters, Police Book Him Under Section 377,* Firstpost (Oct. 30, 2014, 10:11 AM), http://www.firstpost.com/living/bangalore-woman-films-husbands-gay-encounters-police-book-him-under-sec-377-1779287.html.
50. Sandip Roy, *Booked Under Section 377: Bangalore Techie's Story Gets Extra Punch Thanks to Outdated Law,* Firstpost (Oct. 31, 2014, 10:02 AM), http://www.firstpost.com/living/booked-under-section-377-bangalore-techies-story-gets-extra-punch-thanks-to-outdated-law-1780029.html.
51. FP Staff, *Section 377: 7 Booked for Blackmailing Doc, Who also Faces Arrest,* Firstpost (June 23, 2014, 11:14 AM), http://www.firstpost.com/living/section-377-7-booked-blackmailing-doc-also-faces-arrest-1584263.html.

52. Sandip Roy, *AIIMS Doctor and Her 'Gay Husband': So Why Didn't He Stay Single?*, Firstpost (Apr. 20, 2015, 2:05 PM), http://www.firstpost.com/india/aiims-doctor-and-her-gay-husband-so-why-didnt-he-just-stay-single-2203766.html.
53. Michel Foucault, The History of Sexuality: The Care of the Self 42 (1988).
54. *Troubled Marriages: Socio-Legal Implications*, ALF. Accessed on email. Apr 22, 2015.
55. Jasbir K. Puar, *In the Wake of It Gets Better*, The Guardian (Nov. 16, 2010, 2:30 PM), http://www.theguardian.com/commentisfree/cifamerica/2010/nov/16/wake-it-gets-better-campaign.
56. Martin F. Manalansan IV, *Race, Violence and Neoliberal Spatial Politics in the Global City*, 23 Social Text 141 (2005).
57. Harish V. Nair, *5 Gay Celebrities Demand Right to Sexuality, Ask Supreme Court to Quash Section 377*, India Today (June 30, 2016, 9:09 AM), https://www.indiatoday.in/mail-today/story/5-gay-celebrities-demand-right-to-sexuality-ask-supreme-court-to-quash-section-377-17131-2016-06-30.
58. Sharma, *supra* note 46.
59. *Id.*
60. Gayatri Chakravorty Spivak, Outside in the Teaching Machine 46 (2012).

CHAPTER 7

You Can't Fix Us

Trans Citizenship and the Classificatory Anxieties of the State

Gee Imaan Semmalar

INTRODUCTION

In 2012, the National Legal Services Authority (NALSA)[1] filed a public interest litigation in the Supreme Court of India on providing third-gender status and affirmative action for hijras, among other issues. It is important to note that unlike the legal campaign against Section 377 of the Indian Penal Code (IPC)[2] (which was led by cis, dominant-caste LGB activists and NGOs), the legal initiative behind this petition did not come from trans communities. In 2013, the case was tagged along with a petition filed in the Supreme Court by the Poojaya Mata Nasib Kaur Ji Women's Welfare Society, an organization working for *kinnars*. Laxmi Narayan Tripathi, a Brahmin transgender rights activist who claims that caste does not exist among trans people,[3] filed an intervention at a later stage.

On 15 April 2014, Justices K.S. Radhakrishnan Panicker and A.K. Sikri of the Supreme Court passed a judgment on the litigation filed by NALSA. The judgment, popularly known as the '"third gender" judgment', grants transgender people the right to self-identify their gender as male, female or third gender, extends affirmative action in education and employment, calls for gender reassignment surgeries to be made freely available, among other things. However, eight years after the NALSA judgment, trans communities are still awaiting the implementation of the directions of the apex court. One of the major changes that has happened since the judgment is that individual trans people have started directly approaching courts for legal redressal in civil cases, and have been able to quote the Supreme Court decision to get favourable judgments.[4] For instance, in the cases filed by Jackuline Mary[5] and Prithika Yashini[6] in the Madras High Court, the petitioners were able to get favourable judgments regarding their right to be employed in government service. Almost all of these achievements in gaining legal rights through civil cases were won by trans people's relentless struggle within the justice system. However, in criminal cases filed against perpetrators of violence against transgender people, we are yet to see positive changes. For instance, when a trans woman named Pravalika was murdered in Hyderabad in 2015, instead of investigating complaints against the accused named by multiple trans women, the police picked up another trans woman, and stripped and tortured her for hours in the police station.[7] In 2016, a 28-year-old trans woman named Tara was burnt to death inside the compound of Pondy Bazaar Police Station in Chennai.[8] In spite of protests in multiple cities, the police have still not conducted a proper investigation into her death. Ironically, India has come to be seen as a beacon for trans rights internationally, and its right-wing government[9] has claimed credit for 'uplifting' us, even though the NALSA case, which is hailed as a victory, was filed before their term in office.

THE BATTLEFIELD OF LEGALITY: DIFFERENCES RELATED TO POSITIONALITIES

The unrestrained faith in and reliance on judicial processes among cis, dominant-caste LGB sections is not one that is shared by trans people across castes, who know only too well the oppressive nature of state institutions.[10] This distrust for judicial processes was clearly articulated by trans women in a meeting held in Bengaluru in 2011 to discuss legal action against Section 36A, which had been added to the *Karnataka Police Act, 1963*. Section 36A allowed for the Commissioner of Police, by notification in the official Gazette, to

> make orders for the preparation and maintenance of a register of the names and places of residence of all eunuchs residing in the area under his charge and who are reasonably suspected of kidnapping or emasculating boys or of committing unnatural offences or any other offences or abetting the commission of such offences.[11]

The meeting was attended by trans women/hijras/*mangalamukhis* who broadly belonged to traditional hijra family structures, as well as NGO activists and independent activists. These categories are not mutually exclusive, as many activists were also part of hijra families. The unanimous decision made by them was that since the Act was not being implemented, the matter must not be brought to the attention of state authorities, and hence no immediate legal action must be pursued.[12] In other words, they agreed to let sleeping dogs lie.

Given the plethora of criminalizing laws that are routinely used to disproportionately target hijras, trans women and gender non-conforming people, such as the *Immoral Traffic (Prevention) Act, 1956*,[13] Section 320 IPC (on grievous hurt),[14] and the anti-beggary[15] and public nuisance laws in Section 268 IPC,[16] the suspicious distance trans communities maintain from legal advocacy comes from a deep experiential knowledge of the largely oppressive nature of the State and its functionaries. The 2018 reading down of Section 377 by the Indian Supreme Court in *Navtej Singh Johar v. Union of India*[17] has had very little impact on the lives of the most vulnerable of trans people because of the ubiquitous nature of transphobia, casteist violence, the deliberate non-registration of offences against trans persons by the police, and a lack of remedial access to judicial systems or protective laws.[18]

Attempts by transwomen to enter state institutions or access political power have largely been thwarted by overt and covert exclusions. In fact, the history of trans women in the Indian political arena illustrates how legal cases have been used by political opponents to take away even the little that has been won through relentless struggle. In 2003, an order of the Madhya Pradesh High Court upheld an order of the Election Judge, which held that Kamala Jaan was not qualified to contest the elections from a seat reserved for women in Katni district and must step down from her post as mayor.[19] The election petitioners had argued that since the seat was reserved for a woman, Kamala, who was a hijra, was not eligible. Interestingly, Kamala argued that 'Hijra' was her nickname and that she was a woman. However, on the basis of identity documents, the fact that she succeeded another hijra guru named Nihora[20] and lived with other hijras, compounded by a refusal to submit to a medical examination and historical 'evidence' of hijras being 'castrated men' 'lacking' the reproductive parts of a woman, the judge ruled that regardless of how Kamala was registered in the electoral rolls, she would not be eligible for a seat reserved for women.[21] In this case, an association with collective "hijra-ness"[22] was concretized and imposed as an identity to be used as 'evidence' by the court. Similarly, Asha Devi's 2000 candidacy for the post of mayor in Gorakhpur, eastern Uttar Pradesh, was declared invalid in 2003 on the grounds that the post was reserved for a female, and that Asha was not female.[23] Kamla Bua, who won the mayoral election in 2009 as an independent candidate for a scheduled caste woman's seat in Sagar district of Madhya Pradesh, was also subsequently disqualified by a court order in 2011. The reasons for her disqualification, however, were twofold—she had not filed proof of scheduled caste status at the time of filing her nomination, and she was not considered qualified for a woman's seat.[24]

In comparison, the zealous advocacy around Section 377 comes from a position of caste and cisgender privilege. The arguments placed before the courts around "private consensual sex" ignored the reality of the publicness of the gender non-conformity embodied by trans people/hijras that is routinely targeted by law enforcement officials. The Supreme Court judgment in *Navtej Singh Johar v. Union of India* quoted the Supreme Court in *K.S. Puttaswamy v. Union of India* (2017) and opined that,

> The right to privacy is not simply the 'right to be left alone', and has travelled far beyond that initial concept. It now incorporates the ideas of spatial privacy, and decisional privacy or privacy of choice. It extends to the right to make fundamental personal choices, including those relating to intimate sexual conduct, without unwarranted State interference.[25]

Public acts of soliciting sex and the use of public spaces such as parks and toilets by street-based sex workers who are kothi/hijra/transgender, and these individuals' heightened vulnerabilities, were not addressed by the activists, although the petitions buttressed their demands by referring to the everyday violence faced by trans women and kothis in the streets of Indian cities.[26] Importantly, 'private spaces' are often sites of violence for cis women, queer and trans people rather than places of safety. The ubiquity of domestic violence against cis women, queer and trans people across castes hardly needs more elucidating. The instances of workplace harassment against domestic workers within the privacy of their employer's homes is also to be highlighted. Through an anti-performance dedicated to the memory of Sweet Maria, a trans sister murdered in her own home in Kerala in 2012, we critiqued this privileged notion of spatial privacy. Moreover, the concept of decisional privacy cannot be easily applied to gender rebellious persons when the state, medical establishments and societal surveillance are a crucial part of constructing, reifying and maintaining our gendered otherness. What is the nature and extent of the spatial or decisional privacy that can be claimed by people with experiences of 'othering' based on class, caste, gender, disability and religion?[27] The question of choice in feminist activism must be, and has been, complicated by anti-caste analyses of sex work as a continuum of the historical, sexualized caste oppression of Dalit Bahujan women.[28] Given the structural exclusions in employment faced by trans women across caste and the complex ways in which power and desire interact, questions of choice, privacy and consent must be rigorously and critically interrogated in this context.

FOILED ATTEMPTS AT FIXING US

The first point in the operative part of the *NALSA* judgment of 2014 says, "Hijras, Eunuchs, apart from binary gender, be treated as 'third gender' for the purpose of safeguarding their rights under Part III of our Constitution and the laws made by the Parliament and the State Legislature."[29] Through mainstream media reports, the judgement has consequently, and problematically, come to be known as the 'third gender judgement'. The second point in the operative part of the judgment grants trans people the right to self-identify as male, female or third gender. It says, "Transgender persons' right to decide their self-identified gender is also upheld and the Centre and State Governments are directed to grant legal recognition of their gender identity such as male, female or as third gender."[30] In this judgment, there is a contradictory interplay between the language of constitutional rights, an overdetermination of sexual characteristics as the defining feature of trans people (with its attendant pathologization), a move away from the aforesaid with a provision for the self-declaration of gender, and an attempted synthesis of the individualizing, colonial modernity of the binary gender model with the collectivized, "local" third-gender model. The Supreme Court also advocated for trans people's inclusion in the socially and economically backward classes so that they can avail of affirmative action, without taking into account the caste differences that already exist within trans communities.[31]

The judgment is clear about the need for administrative legibility in order to provide state support. It says, "In order to translate the aforesaid rights of TGs into reality, it becomes imperative to first assign them their proper 'sex'."[32] This question of assigning us our 'proper place' in the classificatory system of citizenship has long confounded the State. It becomes imperative to enquire into the history of state anxieties around the opacity of gender deviance in the subcontinent we now know as India, and the many classificatory regimes imposed to make this deviance legible to administrative control and disciplining practices.

In the most cited case tried under Section 377 in the British colonial period, *Queen Empress v. Khairati* (Allahabad, 1884),[33] after the accused was arrested dancing in women's clothes, a medical examination "revealed" corporeal marks ostensibly evidencing a 'habit' of anal intercourse. Mr. J. L. Denniston, sessions judge of Moradabad, pronounced the person guilty and noted "that while none of the three circumstances individually (wearing women's clothes, subtended anus, and the presence of syphilis) were enough to provide evidence of criminality, taken together they left no "doubt that the accused had recently been the subject of sodomy.'"[34] When the case was appealed under the Allahabad High Court, Khairati's earlier conviction was dismissed for lack of clarity on the particulars of the perceived offense, such as the exact time, place, and persons with whom these offenses were committed.[35]

In Anjali Arondekar's work on the colonial archive, they talk about the 'crisis of legal translation', pointing out that the colonial archive "fixes sexuality as both loss and abundance, as (forensic) invisibility and (anthropological) hypervisibility".[36] Thus Arondekar highlights the paradox of medical evidence (and legal evidence in general), in that it crumbles at precisely the very moments it self-referentially establishes its own authority. Thus the colonial records state that Khairati was "not a eunuch in the literal sense". But who indeed was a 'eunuch' historically? This was an issue which the British grappled with in the legal and administrative realms of the nineteenth century colonial state.[37] Contemporaneously, the Indian state and its legal systems struggle to fix trans and 'third gender' categories, although the colonialities impinging on the processes, motivations and strategies may converge/diverge from those of the British state in very specific ways according to contexts (a subject that warrants further enquiry). For now it is perhaps enough to highlight that it is indeed in the opacity of our porous (dis)locations and the diverse, conflicting nature of our subjectifications that the anxieties and frustrations of the classificatory exercises of the State are most apparent.

THE SAFFRONWASHING OF TRANS AND QUEER HISTORIES

Sources from the early nineteenth century show a growing anthropological interest within the colonial regime towards the deviants among the native subjects. In an essay titled 'On the Customs of Gosawees or Gosaeens' (published as an appendix to Arthur Steele's *Summary of the Law and Custom of Hindoo Castes*), John Warden's footnote reads,

> it may be observed that the lusus naturae, best known by the designation of Hermaphrodite, wears the female saree and the male, Ungreka. These persons whether born of the highest or the lowest caste are outcast from their birth: and considered the vilest and most polluted of beings; they live upon the alms which they exact from the Brahmin at whose door they press their request, and who is willing to purchase their absence at any price. Their condition is supposed to be induced by the debauchery committed by them on Earth before the transmigration of their soul.[38]

From this description, it can be inferred that it is perhaps those whose visible sexual characteristics are outside normative classifications who are outcasts from birth. The concept of 'pollution' that is entrenched in the caste system is used to describe prevailing attitudes towards these people, and the causal link between their gender deviance and karma is made explicit by making a causal connection between their gender and 'debauchery' committed in previous lives.

Many articulations on sexuality in the subcontinent, including the discourse around Section 377 IPC, blame British colonial powers for criminalizing laws and prejudiced attitudes. Such articulations present a mythical pre-colonial time when gender deviance was accepted, and sexual behaviours/practices were varied and expressed without censure. However, the description cited above clearly refers to oppressive attitudes and practices under the caste system, which pre-dated the British colonial period. Brahmanical texts like the *Manusmriti*, *Vishnusmriti*, *Arthashastra* and *Garuda Purana* characterize the hijra by her overdetermined gender characteristics/expression and uncontrolled sexuality, rooted in practices of caste punishment including ex-communication and notions of pollution.[39] Ahistorical readings or articulations that posit a pre-British golden period erase the history of the oldest colonization of the subcontinent, that of the caste system. It is the great tragedy of Indian academia that even scholars who are labelled as post-colonial have not sufficiently analyzed caste colonization in their scholarly work, perhaps due to their own dominant-caste status.

This often deliberately opportunistic reading of a pre-British period that supposedly embraced deviant gender and sexual practices is not limited to the domain of hegemonic knowledge production. Legal arguments and judgements relating to cases against Section 377 and the *NALSA* judgement also make references to Hindu myths in similar ways. In the *NALSA* judgement, a section titled 'Historical Background of Transgenders in India' makes references to the concepts of *tritiya prakriti* or *napunsaka* as integral parts of Vedic and Puranic literatures, links the tradition of *badhai* to the myth of trans women waiting for Ram to return from exile, and refers to the myth of Aravan in the Mahabharata.[40]

Apart from legal case records and academic writing, discourses by NGOs claiming to work on LGBTI issues present as 'evidence' Hindu religious myths like Ardhanareeswara, Shikandi and Aravani in an attempt to 'prove' the acceptance and omnipresence of non-normative gender and sexual behaviours and practices before the arrival of the British.[41] There are also similar assertions from trans feminine/hijra groups, possibly seeking to normalize gender deviance or prompt acceptance through references to Hindu myths and legends. For instance, relatively new identarian terms used as terms of self-reference in Tamil Nadu, like Aravani,[42] rely on these Hindu mythical stories. Historically, Jogtis, who are dedicated to Goddess Yellamma[43] in North Karnataka, perform stories from the Hindu epics, and sometimes, the stories they tell are counter-histories or alternate versions of Brahmanical myths. Hijra cultures in general have over time adopted and practiced a syncretic religious culture with influences from Islam and Hinduism. However, there is currently a notable shift in the link between performative religiousity and new power assertions.

Recent religious declarations by some trans communities could be read as assertions of caste power and alliances with right-wing groups/governments for power. Since 2016, the Kinnar Akhara has been attending the Kumbh Mela and seeking acceptance from the other religious Akharas.[44] In 2018, the Kinnar Akhara—which claims to work on the human rights, health and education of the transgender community—urged people to vote the right-wing BJP government back into power in the upcoming elections. "The Akhil Bhartiya Sant Samiti invited the Kinnar Akhara for the first time... This shows the openness of the Vedic sanatan dharma and that it is open to the transgender community. Today, it was clearly said...*jo Ram ka hai, woh hamara hai* (he who belongs to Ram, is ours too)," Acharya Mahamandaleshwar Laxmi Narayan Tripathi, head of the Kinnar Akhara, was quoted as saying in the news.[45] Subsequently, a statement was released by trans, gender non-conforming and intersex individuals and groups against the Kinnar Akhara's saffronization of trans history, condemning the fueling of communal hatred through the call for a Ram Temple at the site of the sixteenth century mosque, the Babri Masjid, which was demolished in 1992 amidst large-scale violence by Hindu mobs.[46]

This 'nativist' third-gender model is often invoked through Hindu religious identity, and the strategy of seeking legitimacy from the right-wing governments in power through such assertions is on the rise. Often, the groups that make such assertions are invited to government consultations on policy making. Thus, the demarcations between religious political domains and ostensibly 'secular' human rights domains do not exist in reality. In human rights meetings internationally, it is dominant-caste trans women who claim a nativist hijra identity and construct, gesturally and performatively through speech and 'traditional' clothes, a respectable version of the colonial imagination of hijra cultural codes. They are contradictorily individuated as spokespersons even as they claim representation for a social grouping (which they often disassociate from in the local context) through performative *hijrapan*. I was witness to this at the Philadelphia Transgender Health Conference held in 2015, where dominant-caste trans women from India performed hijrapan internationally, even as they distanced themselves from hijra kinship structures in India. Even as the term 'transgender' or the shorthand 'TG' gains currency in gender non-conforming communities across class, caste and regions in India, the exoticizing gaze of the West, particularly within international trans activist circles, is catered to by such performative enactments of hijrapan.

THE MODERN COLONIAL MATRIX OF CLASSIFICATORY REGIMES

The homogenizing tendencies of globalized activism and the circulation and usage of 'transgender' as an identity marker which seeks to replace local identity terms or ways of describing gender deviance also come with their own neo-colonial baggage. Stryker and Currah put forward a critique of the term transgender as one that originated within the context of white, Eurocentric modernity. "Because transgender can be imagined to include all possible variations from an often unstated norm, it risks becoming yet another project of colonization—a kind of Cartesian grid imposed on the globe—for making sense of human diversity by measuring it within a Eurocentric frame of reference, against a Eurocentric standard".[47] The interplay between judicial interventions, legislation, globalized activist and academic discourse, confessional psychiatric medical practices and their diagnostic frameworks, gender affirming surgeries and their attendant biopolitical project of gender recognition/change, and the NGO industrial complex, plays a key role in the linguistic and political production, control, disciplining and reproduction of the transgender subject in the current Indian context. These processes are mirrored internationally in documents like the World Professional Association for Transgender Health's (WPATH) international health guidelines and the *Diagnostic and Statistical Manual of Mental Disorders* (DSM). Can we, even as we are caught and often actively participating in these institutions and discourses, offer possibilities for the disruption of the very forces that attempt to produce and control us?

Aniruddha Dutta has analyzed attempts by NGOs to impart pedagogical training on citizenship to lower-class hijras, attempts by lower-class hijra groups in West Bengal to contest/conform to codes of civility to contest/claim citizenship, and practices of self-censoring/censoring the other(ed) in order to be respectable enough to claim citizenship rights.[48] At a macro level within the symbolic order of the nation state, the 'pure' morality of the cisgender, caste Hindu, often vegetarian,[49] heterosexual family which functions within the limits of caste endogamy is constructed in opposition to the public immorality/polluted-ness of the "barren", sexually promiscuous or asexual hijra.[50]

'WE ARE NOT LIKE THEM': RESPECTABLE QUEER CITIZENSHIP AND THE IMMORAL OTHERS

In the last few decades, HIV funding had been instrumental in the creation of the MSM (men who have sex with men) category under which cis gay men and trans feminine persons were clubbed for target intervention programmes. In urban settings, cis gay men with privilege are often anxious about being clubbed with hijras. I have observed statements of disassociation like, "We are not like them, they bring a bad name to the LGBT family by harassing the public and begging", being made by cis gay men with privilege in several meetings and social gatherings in Bangalore. This deliberate dissociation and distancing from feminine expressions is often linked to respectability, which is, in this context, produced and reproduced by caste patriarchy. Hijra communities also have their own hierarchies of respectability and *asli* (real) or *nakli* (fake) identifications. According to Gayatri Reddy, these are determined by the "performance of various embodied acts, within the arenas of kinship, (a)sexuality, sartoriality, and religion."[51] Institutional discourses around trans identification and state welfare promises tend to solidify and reify these internal divisions, as Aniruddha Dutta has argued.[52]

Dating apps like Grindr[53] often function in a way that strengthens hegemonic codes of desirability predicated on femme denigration and caste supremacy. Gay parties hosted in fancy clubs across Indian cities often impose bans on 'cross dressing' or femme wear (unless it is a pre-planned and sanctioned drag night). Normative assimilations into hegemonic citizenship models based on caste, class and gender privilege often come from dominant-caste, cis gay men (in India and in the diaspora) who marry endogamously in traditional Hindu ceremonies[54] or place advertisements seeking Brahmin grooms.[55] While 'same sex' marriages outside the socio-legal framework have happened for a long time in India, these recent, homonationalist[56] caste alliances are not just accommodated, but also celebrated by the grooms' families, who conduct the weddings with grandeur in the presence of Brahmin priests who preside over the rituals. For instance, the marriage of Amit Shah and Aditya Madiraju at a Hindu temple in New Jersey was not just conducted in the presence of their families, but was, to a large extent, designed *for* them. After getting married at City Hall in New York, they decided to have a traditional Hindu wedding at a temple. "Our parents have taught us a lot about religion and how to follow customs," Madiraju said, adding: "After we got married at City Hall, we knew we wanted something more traditional with our families and friends involved."[57]

Several critiques have emerged, especially of dominant-caste activists associated with the campaign against Section 377, who use the language of individuated selfhood, privacy, human rights and modernity to set a hegemonic discourse for what they claim to be 'queer' citizenship rights.[58] This rather normative claim for citizenship rights involves a simultaneous distancing from the deviant. "We are not talking about gender. Gay men and gay women don't call themselves something else, the issue is of orientation," Senior Advocate Mukul Rohatgi argued before a five-judge bench of the Supreme Court during the hearings against Section 377.[59] Orientation in this conceptualization is an easily understandable and manageable category, an innocuous 'personal choice' made in the realm of the private. Meanwhile, those who call themselves 'something else' are illegible, and so hyper-visiblized as erotic in public spaces and so diverse that it is impossible to even fix a name for us.

Nithin Manayath has argued that the delineation of sociality into erotic and non-erotic domains is a better way to understand erotic sociality (whether hetero or homo) than the language of repressed self-hood narratives and identitarian frames.[60] While critiquing the campaign against Section 377 for constructing a discourse of a non-erotic public domain and an erotic private domain, he says,

> The legal activist argument has been that legal culture cannot recognise a model of publicness that would allow for an erotic domain within it. But traditional red-light districts and dhanda (sex-work) cultures in various parts of urban and rural India have operated under precisely such diverse cultural logics and strategies for hundreds of years.[61]

Furthermore, in *Navtej Singh Johar v. Union of India*, the petitioners who were IIT alumni were projected as meritorious citizens, "each of whom has excelled in their fields but suffer immensely due to the operation of Section 377."[62] Citizenship rights that are claimed thus, on the basis of caste merit and productivity, immediately position the lowered-caste hijra who does street-based labour as someone not worthy of the same. There are multiple contestations and claims for citizenship rights and 'societal acceptance' through religious, caste and gendered practices and (im)positions. The performative religiousity exhibited by some kinnar groups at the Kumbh Mela and their claims to godliness through Hindu epics is ironically an extension of the same normative claim to citizenship predicated on caste markers, although the legal arguments cited above couch themselves in the language of constitutional rights and 'secularism', while the assertion by kinnar groups is perhaps more discernible as right-wing.

THE MODERNITY OF CASTE

> [N]eo-brahmanism in the avatar of Hinduism became the cultural-ideological foundation of the so-called nationalist politics. Despite differences of expressions and emphases, both the communal nationalism (Tilak-Savarkar's militant Hindutva) and the so-called secular one (represented by Gandhi and Nehru) shared an incestuous relationship on the issues of caste and brahmanism.[63]

The Indian nationalist movement built the myth of a unified India and an Indian citizenship ostensibly unmarred by caste or community divisions, a Brahminic myth consistently challenged by Dr. B.R. Ambedkar, political theorist, anti-caste leader and the first Law Minister of independent India, who sought separate electorates for Dalits.[64] The myth of equal citizenship across gender, caste, class and community divisions often seeks to mystify power relations or attack the other(ed). For instance, opposition to affirmative action based on the rhetoric of merit and the demand for a uniform civil code across religious communities is predicated on the "truth effect" created by this myth.

It can be argued that, ever since the inception of the Indian nation-state, full citizenship rights have been extended only to cisgender, Hindu, dominant caste, endogamously married and reproducing populations. Dr. B.R Ambedkar said, "There is an utter lack among the Hindus of what the sociologists call 'consciousness of kind'. There is no Hindu consciousness of kind. In every Hindu the consciousness that exists is the consciousness of his caste. That is the reason why the Hindus cannot be said to form a society or a nation."[65]

British colonialism in many ways strengthened and institutionalized already existing caste power. Anti-caste scholar G. Aloysius argues that, historically, British colonial rule elevated the "sectarian, scattered and exclusivist discriminatory Brahmanical castes and their way and view of life to structural cultural dominance in modernity by investing it with a universalizing and inclusive socio political garb of 'Hinduism'."[66] This resulted in the relegation of caste to the margins of public discourse and a simultaneous strengthening of the Brahmanical elite who gained control over public institutions after Indian independence. He further argues that the entire social polity was permeated by a universalized Brahmanical imaginary.[67] It is this Brahmin imaginary that is being summoned when normative claims to citizenship rights are made by groups that are marginal along many axes to that very imaginary.

THE BRAHMANICAL IMAGINARY: PAST AND PRESENT

Even during colonial rule, the Brahmanical imaginary of local elites informed much of the legislation enacted by the British—the *Criminal Tribes Act*, enacted by the British in 1871,[68] drew from a pre-existing Brahmanical imaginary link between criminality and caste rather than merely reflecting imported colonial anxieties.[69] The only two works so far on Part II of the Criminal Tribes Act, 1871 relating to the control of "eunuchs" under analyze caste.[70] However, both studies point to flexible interpretations of the category of the "eunuch", bringing people from lowered caste[71] performing communities like sakhis under the Act.[72]

A similar incoherence around the definition of who a trans person is can be seen in the *NALSA* judgment of 2014 and the many drafts of the *Transgender Persons (Protection of Rights) Bill* from 2015 to 2019. In the *NALSA* judgement, a section on definitions reads, "Eunuch: Eunuch refers to an emasculated male and intersexed to a person whose genitals are ambiguously male-like at birth, but this is discovered the child previously assigned to the male sex, would be recategorized as intersexe[d]–as a Hijra."[73] In various portions, the judgment tries to fix a trans person as displaying characteristics of emasculation, a "lack" of reproductive organs, cross dressing, "genital anatomy problems",[74] but predictably fails in this futile exercise conducted since the period of British colonial administration. However, these exercises involving medical jurisprudence and evidentiary paradigms of illegality and social associations dating back to the colonial period have been replaced in recent legal developments (such as the *NALSA* judgment) by a self-identification system. In other words, the State incites us to play the role of informants in the hope of accessing promised welfare benefits.

Although there are still laws that criminalize trans communities in twenty-first century India, and public perceptions still associate trans women or hijras with criminality (kidnapping, extortion, prostitution), the State cannot speak openly and in obviously identifiable colonial language any longer, especially in a context where, in the international arena, nations vying to become ambitious superpowers have to comply with the human rights frameworks set by global activism and international agencies like the United Nations. Hence, the State ostensibly extends welfare schemes and speaks the language of constitutional or human rights whilst simultaneously placing the onus of identification on the citizens it seeks to administer. This can be seen in how the controversial biometric Aadhaar card was rolled out by the right-wing government in power. It was initially the ease with which you could be granted an identification card that was highlighted; later, it was made a mandatory prerequisite to accessing essential services like LPG gas connections, state-subsidized rations for citizens below the poverty line, and finally, to file income tax returns.

ILLEGAL CITIZENS: ILLEGAL KINSHIPS

Predictably, this moment when we have been granted the right to the self-determination of gender is a double-edged sword. Trans people have been missing in state registers due to migration, non-registration of gender markers, or name changes in official documents (due to tedious bureaucratic procedures, lack of access, discomfiture with state authorities, and a resistance politics involving a refusal to submit to state processes), and the lack of any ties with natal families who disown us. For instance, many trans people have been left out of the National Register of Citizens (NRC) for Assam because of a mismatch between the gender and name registered on their birth certificates and other documents.[75] Since the completed draft of the NRC was released on 30 July 2018, trans people in Assam have filed a case in the Supreme Court calling for a separate document verification process. With the building of detention centres to imprison "illegal" persons whose names are not in the NRC, the panic among those left out is grave. Moreover, the pre-1971 legacy data that needs to be shown as proof that a person's ancestors lived in Assam before 24 March 1971 is also impossible for trans people disowned by their natal families to access.[76]

Relatedly, the *Transgender Persons (Protection of Rights) Act, 2019* defines 'family' as "a group of people related by blood or marriage or by adoption made in accordance with law".[77] Additionally, in a later chapter it states, "Where any parent or a member of his immediate family is unable to take care of a transgender, the competent court shall by an order direct such person to be placed in rehabilitation centre."[78] By these measures, the Act continues to deny a consistent demand made by activist groups since the earliest version of this bill, to recognize hijra households as 'families' since, historically, these have been the only protective spaces for trans, intersex and gender non-binary people disowned by their natal families. Recognizing hijra family lineages will address the 'legacy issue' of at least some of the trans folks excluded from the Assam NRC. However, the State has long realized that an exercise in identifying and fixing large trans populations that are so diverse in religious affiliations, caste, gendered expressions, bodily differences and culture is an impossible task. Trans people who live on the peripheries of Indian citizenship have to struggle to register themselves or face the consequences of being labelled "illegal" and being deported or detained.

I SCREEN, YOU SCREEN, WE ALL SCREEN GENDER

Activists (myself included) protested against the screening committees which were to provide certificates of being trans in earlier versions of the *Transgender Persons (Protection of Rights) Bill*, quoting the principle of self-declaration in the Supreme Court judgement. The proposal to have district screening committees with a nexus of NGO workers, government officials and medical practitioners deciding whether a person is trans was an invasive, humiliating and pathologizing system. Consequently, amidst large-scale protests, the State partially rolled back the screening process. Currently, Chapter III of the Act grants the right to self-identify gender only if the person identifies as transgender. The person has to make an application to the District Magistrate, who in turn "shall issue to the applicant under section 5, a certificate of identity as transgender person after following such procedure and in such form and manner, within such time, as may be prescribed indicating the gender of such person as transgender."[79]

However, if the person wants to change their legal gender markers to male or female, they have to undergo surgery and, along with a certificate issued by the Medical Superintendent or Chief Medical Officer of the medical institution in which that person has undergone surgery, make a submission to the District Magistrate for a revised certificate. Section 7 (2) says,

> The District Magistrate shall, on receipt of an application along with the certificate issued by the Medical Superintendent or Chief Medical Officer, and on being satisfied with the correctness of such certificate, issue a certificate indicating change in gender in such form and manner and within such time, as may be prescribed.[80]

This still remains a gross violation of the *NALSA* judgment granting the right to self-identify gender regardless of surgery or hormonal therapy. The judgment says, "No one shall be forced to undergo medical procedures, including sex reassignment surgery, sterilization or hormonal therapy, as a requirement for legal recognition of their gender identity."[81] Moreover, in the operative parts of the judgment it clearly states, "Centre and State Governments should seriously address the problems being faced by Hijras/Transgenders such as fear, shame, gender dysphoria, social pressure, depression, suicidal tendencies, social stigma, etc. and *any insistence for SRS for declaring one's gender is immoral and illegal*" (emphasis mine).[82]

Many have written previously about the complex ways in which NGOs dependent on HIV funding have discursively created, and perhaps consolidated, too neat a delineation between LGBTI identities, or have imposed Western categorical imperatives on local identity markers that were far more fluid when denoting femininities.[83] Nithin Manayath points out how the 'knowledgeable sexuality expert' in support groups and NGO groupings 'corrects' people who say 'we entered the field' or 'we were doing gay sex' by imposing a sexuality-identity framework as the dominant narrative in these groups.[84] So, what could be understood as erotic practices, or 'fields of experience' not necessarily causally linked to narratives of selfhood, are made normatively legible within a non-erotic, identity-orientated framework through such correctional pedagogical interactions.

Moreover, hierarchies of civility and respectability fuel identarian splits between categories such as gay and transgender, MSM and transgender, and even good and badly-behaved transgender, though many 'community people' inhabit multiple and overlapping subject positions.[85] Post the *NALSA* judgment and the *Trans Act*, the question of who an 'authentic' trans person is, who can claim and receive benefits from the State, has further intensified intra-community conflicts and definitional anxieties. 'Hijra-ness', which was often in practice a collective, porous and fluid grouping based on femininity, a shared experience of social exclusion and alternate kinship, is forced to further individuate and identify itself as a third gender, and police the claims of others through gatekeeping.[86]

The nexus between state power and capitalist technology, sustained through the sale of individuals' personal data for surveillance purposes, rigging elections and advertising, is well known post the Cambridge Analytica scandal.[87] Data is currently the most valuable commodity in the world, and by voluntarily providing information to social media platforms and other companies, large populations are either willingly or unwittingly participating in a system that is designed to watch, control and administer them. But how do we, as marginalized communities, withhold information when it is linked to our access to state benefits? The modern state tactic of having us self-declare our gender for the purposes of administrative control might not feel as oppressive as pathologizing medical frameworks, but the dangers of such a system have to be critically examined.

BACK TO THE FUTURE

Despite a deep distrust of the state and its mechanisms, trans-led political movements are caught in a situation where we have to simplify and flatten our gender incongruity and diversities in order to demand equality under the frame of constitutional rights. Additionally, there is a self-disciplining of the erotic while participating in such legal discourse and struggles, and a pressure to appeal on the basis of issues of marginalization and claims to human rights. Nithin Manayath identifies this non-erotic judicial system historically as the *jammat* within hijra cultures.

> Hijras also effected non-erotic domain delineation through tactics of building and sustaining nation-wide and even cross-border ties in which, following Islamic traditions of the subcontinent, jammats (assemblies/community meets) are held to address individual and group distress, dispute resolution, work allocation, modalities of networking and a host of other concerns, not least, negotiating for inclusion in politics and state fabrications and identifying sources of patronage.[88]

However, the structure, leadership and scope of the jammats have also changed over time. For instance, places like Tamil Nadu that never historically had hijra *gharanas*[89] are constructing new ones, with senior gurus declaring themselves *nayaks*.[90] Disputes related to the demarcation of areas for erotic and non-erotic forms of work—sex trade, begging, badhai and so on—are settled within jammats. Even disputes where younger *chelas* have given money to male lovers instead of to their gurus—in some hijra cultures, chelas are non-erotically married to the latter—are adjudicated in jammats. Erotic and non-erotic domains are not so easy to delineate, and it is when the erotic enters a domain that is supposedly non-erotic that radical disruptions (and corresponding state repression) are potentiated.

I believe that the historical (and current) association of criminality with hijra social groups, the hyper-sexualization and erotic power of hijra bodies in public spaces, the pushback from traditional Islamic hijra gharanas who disassociate from the erotic,[91] and the right-wing tendencies within a rights-based discourse (whether ostensibly 'secular' or religious) that construct and individuate personhood and claims to equal citizenship rights, must be read in all their compelling and contradictory tendencies and potential for disruption.

We could potentially disrupt the existing gender binary and challenge Hindu supremacist assertions of the third-gender model, aggravating the crisis of classificatory regimes that have failed to contain our identities and expressions through the centuries. There is growing criticism of binary-identified trans people, who wish to register themselves as male/female, for being 'conformist'. Stone argues that "juxtaposing medically constituted transsexual embodiments against the backdrop of culturally intelligible gendered bodies" generates "new and unpredictable dissonances" in which "we may find the potential to map the refigured body onto conventional gender discourse and thereby disrupt it".[92] There are particular ways in which medically transitioning trans bodies and trans bodies of persons who have not undergone/do not wish to undergo medicalized transition can embody and articulate disruptions of the status quo. All disruptive potential is, of course, highly contextual.

The Indian Passport Seva Kendra authorities in a small town in Kerala had no idea what documents to ask for from the author of this article, a trans man who sought a change in gender markers in 2014. While seeking to change one's passport was a claim to citizenship and legibility, a resignification of gender categories threw the state into crisis around its own classificatory systems. It is in that gap in administrative control that disruptive infiltrations are possible, destabilizing the very category of gender. The potential to do that through trans people's mass self-declarations as male/female or third gender is also huge in the current context. We must articulate gender "to take advantage of the dissonances" and to "fragment and reconstitute the elements of gender in new and unexpected geometries."[93] In 1884, by the act of wearing a saree and dancing in public, Khairati created an unexpected geometry of gender that the British colonial powers were not familiar with, which they tried, but failed, to fix.

Gloria Anzaldúa, the queer, Chicana feminist theorist and writer, says,

> The work of mestiza consciousness is to break down the subject object duality that keeps her a prisoner and to show in the flesh and through the images of her work how duality is transcended. The answer to the problem between the white and the colored, between males and females, lies in healing the split that originates in the very foundation of our lives, our culture, our languages, our thoughts.[94]

The hegemonic dualism and power relations of gender, race and caste can be challenged through the creation and exploration of a borderland consciousness which resists and challenges violently imposed conceptual, material and social boundaries. Historically, such a borderland consciousness was perhaps nurtured within hijra kinship systems, and we must critically examine new legal policies which offer very little in terms of benefits but impose self-surveillance, and an identification and policing of intra-community spaces that have defied and confounded classificatory regimes since

British colonial times, or perhaps even earlier. Only in a future where we can resist normative assimilation by retaining our disruptive potential, and simultaneously assert our right to access state benefits, can we hope for a sustainable, radical politics.

NOTES

1. Constituted under the *Legal Services Authorities Act, 1987* to provide free legal services to underprivileged sections of society.
2. Codified in 1860, in the era of British colonial rule, Section 377 IPC has long been interpreted as referring to homosexuality, although its wording, "carnal intercourse against the order of nature", does not specify what kinds of sexual acts it penalizes. According to Section 377, "Whoever voluntarily has carnal intercourse against the order of nature with any man, woman or animal, shall be punished with imprisonment for life, or with imprisonment of either description for a term which may extend to ten years, and shall also be liable to fine."
3. Simar Bhasin, *Our Community Has No Caste or Religion: Laxmi on Being a Hijra*, Hindustan Times (Jan. 29, 2016, 11:31 AM), https://www.hindustantimes.com/books/our-community-has-no-caste-or-religion-laxmi-on-being-a-hijra/story-bfqDSEjGKkKID7isZ7mmrM.html.
4. *See* the Madras HC judgments in the cases of *Jackuline Mary v. Superintendent of Police, Karur* (April 17, 2014), *Arunkumar & Sreeja v. Inspector General of Registration & Others* (April 22, 2019), and *K. Prithika Yashini v. The Chairman, Tamil Nadu Uniformed Services Recruitment Board* (November 3, 2015), and the Delhi HC judgment in the case of *Shivani Bhat v. State of NCT of Delhi and Ors* (October 5, 2015).
5. *Jackuline*, *supra* note 4.
6. *K. Prithika*, *supra* note 4.
7. Orinam, *Statement by Telangana Intersex Hijra Transgender Samiti on Sexual Assault of a Hijra Sister*, Orinam (Jan. 23, 2015), http://orinam.net/statement-telangana-hijra-transgender-samiti-to-condemn-police-brutality/.
8. Ajita Banerjee, *Justice for Tara: How Many Deaths Do We Need to Resist Police Brutality?*, The Wire (Nov. 15, 2016), https://thewire.in/gender/justice-for-tara-how-many-deaths-do-we-need-to-resist-police-brutality.
9. The Bharatiya Janata Party (BJP) in India openly espouses a dominant-caste Hindu nationalist model and is widely recognized to be a right-wing party.
10. Although individual trans petitioners have recently been filing cases in lower and higher civil courts to address grievances.
11. *The Karnataka Police Act, 1963*, Department of Parliamentary Affairs, Karnataka, http://dpal.kar.nic.in/4%20of%201964%20(e).pdf.

12. The Karnataka Sexual Minorities Forum, a CBO based in Karnataka, filed a writ petition in 2015 seeking the replacement of the word "eunuch", as it is a derogatory term. Section 36A of *The Karnataka Police Act, 1963* has since been amended to replace "eunuch" with "persons".
13. *The Immoral Traffic (Prevention) Act, 1956* penalizes all acts related to sex trade, including running brothels or giving permission to run brothels, sex trade in public places, living off money earned through sex trade, procuring, inducing or taking persons for the sake of prostitution, soliciting for the purpose of sex trade, and so on.
14. Section 320 IPC lists a series of hurts that are to be considered grievous, and for which there are enhanced punishments. Emasculation is first in this list.
15. In India, there is no central law which penalizes begging, although 22 states (including a few union territories) have their own anti-begging laws. The act which functions as the derivative figure for all the states' anti-begging laws is the *Bombay Prevention of Begging Act, 1959.*
16. A person "who does any act or is guilty of an illegal omission which causes any common injury, danger or annoyance to the public or to the people in general who dwell or occupy property in the vicinity, or which must necessarily cause injury, obstruction, danger or annoyance to persons who may have occasion to use any public right. A common nuisance is not excused on the ground that it causes some convenience or advantage" is guilty of public nuisance as per Section 268 IPC.
17. On September 6, 2018, the apex court unanimously declared Section 377 unconstitutional "in so far as it criminalises consensual sexual conduct between adults of the same sex".
18. Puja Changoiwala, *India: No Country for Transgender Women,* South China Morning Post (July 8, 2018, 1:01 PM), https://www.scmp.com/week-asia/society/article/2154077/india-no-country-transgender-women; Vartika Rastogi, *Transgender Community Face Increasing Violence Since 377 Ruling,* The Citizen (Sep. 17, 2018, 7:19 PM), https://www.thecitizen.in/index.php/en/NewsDetail/index/7/15000/Transgender-Community-Face-Increasing-Violence-Since-377-Ruling.
19. Kamala alias Kamala Jaan alias Hijrah v. Sadiq Ali and Others, 31077 IndLaw MP (2003).
20. Guru is a traditional role of motherhood/leadership/guidance in hijra kinship structures across the subcontinent.
21. Kamala, *supra* note 19.
22. A term used by Nithin Manayath in *The Shameless Marriage: Thinking Through Same-Sex Erotics and the Question of 'Gay Marriage', in* Conjugality Unbound: Sexual Economies, State Regulation and the Marital Form in India 267 (S. Basu & L. Ramberg eds., 2014).
23. Aditi Dharmadhikari, *India's Had More Transgender Mayors Than We Originally Thought,* Homegrown (Jan. 12, 2015), https://homegrown.co.in/

article/21045/retrospect-indias-had-more-transgender-mayors-than-we-originally-thought.

24. PTI, *Kamla Bua, First Eunuch Mayor of MP's Sagar Dies,* IndiaTV (Nov. 14, 2019, 7:54 PM), https://www.indiatvnews.com/news/india/kamla-bua-first-eunuch-mayor-of-mp-sagar-dies-563763.
25. Navtej Singh Johar v. Union of India 2018 (10) SCALE 386.
26. *Id.* Oishik Sircar (2008) Questions of Visibility, 2 Plainspeak 10-17 (2008); Anjali Arondekar, *Time's Corpus: On Sexuality, Historiography and the Indian Penal Code, in Comparatively Queer: Interrogating Identities Across Time and Culture* (W. Spurlin, J. Hayes & M. Higonnet eds., 2010.
27. For more on privacy in this context, read an alternative, feminist judgment by Gee Imaan Semmalar, Re-Cast(e)ing Navtej Singh v. Union of India, 13 NUJS L. Rev. 3 (2020).
28. Historically, anti-caste leaders like Ayyankali and Dr. Ambedkar urged women from lowered caste communities to give up and protest against sexualized work/slavery. Among contemporary anti-caste scholars, Anu Ramdas, Rekha Raj, Smita Patil and many others problematize the dominant-caste feminist notion of "choice" in sex work along the same lines.
29. National Legal Services Authority v. Union of India, (2014) 5 SCC 438.
30. *Id.*
31. Gee Imaan Semmalar, *Gender Outlawed: The Supreme Court Judgment on Third Gender and Its Implications,* Round Table India (Apr. 19, 2014), https://www.roundtableindia.co.in/because-we-have-a-voice-too-the-supreme-court-judgment-on-third-gender-and-its-implications/.
32. NALSA, *supra* note 28, at 102.
33. Queen Empress v. Khairati (1884) ILR 6 All 204.
34. Anjali Arondekar, Subject to Sodomy, in For the Record On Sexuality and the Colonial Archive in India 68 (2009).
35. *Id.* at 69.
36. *Id.* at 67.
37. Through court cases and laws like Part II of the *Criminal Tribes Act* which relied on an expansive definition of "impotent man" to denote "eunuchs".
38. John Warden, *Appendix B: On the Customs of Gosawees or Gosaeens, in* Summary of the Law and Custom of Hindoo Castes within the Dekhun Provinces Subject to the Presidency of Bombay (A. Steele, 1827). Cited in an unpublished thesis by Shane Patrick Gannon, *Translating the Hijra: The Symbolic Reconstruction of the British Empire in India,* (2009) (PhD dissertation, University of Alberta).
39. Referred to variously as *napumsa, shanda,* tritiya prakriti and so on in many Vedic Texts. There are also many disparaging references to "eunuchs" and "hermaphrodites" in the *Manusmriti.* For example, "A Kandala, a village pig, a cock, a dog, a menstruating woman, and a eunuch must not look at the Brahmanas while they eat." The Laws of Manu. Vol. 25 of The Sacred Books of the East, Verse 239, Chapter 3 (George Bühler trans., Oxford: Clarendon

Press, 1886). For a discussion on British colonial translations of Sanskrit terms related to this see, Shane Gannon, Exclusion as Language and the Language of Exclusion: Tracing Regimes of Gender Through Linguistic Representations of the "Eunuch", 20 J Hist Sex. 1 (2011).

40. National Legal Services Authority v. Union of India, (2014) 5 SCC 438, para. 12-14 & 16.

41. *See for example*, 'Hindu View of LGBT' on the blog of an NGO called Srishti in Madurai, Tamil Nadu. *Hindu View of LGBT*, Srishti Madurai, http://srishtimadurai.blogspot.com/2011/10/hindu-view-of-lgbt.html. *See also*, *HAF Policy Brief: Hindu Teachings Inclusive of LGBT People*, Hindu American Foundation (June 16, 2016), https://www.hinduamerican.org/press/haf-policy-brief-hindu-teachings-inclusive-lgbt-people. *See also* the Gay and Lesbian Vaishnava Association's website: https://www.galva108.org/.

42. In the Mahabharata, it was prophesied that the Pandavas would win the Battle of Kurukshetra only if they sacrificed a 'perfect' male from among themselves. Aravan, the virgin son of the Pandava prince Arjuna, offered himself up for sacrifice. But he had a request: that he be allowed to spend one night as a married man. No king was willing to give Aravan his daughter in marriage only to have her widowed the next day, so Lord Krishna assumed a female form and married Aravan and, after a night of sexual bliss, Aravan was beheaded. Some trans women in Tamil Nadu consider themselves the female form of Krishna and perform widowhood as Aravanis at the Koovagam festival conducted every year.

43. Similar to the devadasi system of ritualized sexual slavery of dalit women, some young children from lowered caste Hindu and even Muslim families who are raised as boys and express feminine behaviour become Jogtis, and are ritualistically dedicated to Goddess Yellamma. Many non-dalit trans feminine persons also become Jogtis when they are older.

44. Devdutt Pattanaik, *How a New Akhara of Transgendered People Stole the Spotlight at the Ujjain Kumbh*, Scroll (June 29, 2016, 11:30 AM), https://scroll.in/article/809995/how-a-new-akhara-of-transgendered-people-stole-the-spotlight-at-the-ujjain-kumbh.

45. Lalmani Verma, *Kinnar Akhara Bats for Ram Temple in Ayodhya, Second Term for PM Modi*, The Indian Express (Nov. 06, 2018, 7:30 AM), https://indianexpress.com/article/india/kinnar-akhara-bats-for-ram-temple-in-ayodhya-second-term-for-pm-narendra-modi-5435495/.

46. *Trans, Gender Nonconforming & Intersex Collectives Strongly Condemn Kinnar Akhara's Support for Ram Temple at Ayodhya, India*, Round Table India (Nov. 24, 2018), https://www.roundtableindia.co.in/trans-gender-nonconforming-gnc-intersex-collectives-strongly-condemn-kinnar-akhara-s-support-for-ram-temple-at-ayodhya/.

47. Susan Stryker & Paisley Currah, *Introduction*, 1 TSQ 1 (2014).

48. Aniruddha Dutta, *Claiming Citizenship, Contesting Civility: The Institutional LGBT Movement and the Regulation of Gender/ Sexual Dissidence in West Bengal, India*, 4 Jindal Global Law Rev. 110 (2012).
49. There are regional differences in the food consumption habits of dominant-caste people. In some places, they may eat meat and claim purity of status, while in others a large part of the claim to 'purity' relies on vegetarianism.
50. For more, *see* Gee Imaan Semmalar, *Why Trans Movements in India Must Be Anti-Caste,* Trans.Cafe (Dec. 21, 2016), http://www.trans.cafe/posts/2016/12/12/why-trans-movements-in-india-must-be-anti-caste.
51. Gayatri Reddy, *Geographies of Contagion: Hijras, Kothis, and the Politics of Sexual Marginality in Hyderabad,* 12 Anthropology and Medicine 255 (2005).
52. Aniruddha Dutta, *Legible Identities and Legitimate Citizens: The Globalization of Transgender and Subjects of HIV-AIDS Prevention in Eastern India,* 15 IFJP 494 (2013).
53. Grindr is advertised as "a geo social networking and online dating application geared towards gay, bi and trans people". However, it is mostly used by cis gay and bisexual men.
54. Kelsey Borresen, *These Two Grooms Got Married In A Strikingly Beautiful Hindu Wedding*, Huffpost (July 31, 2019), https://www.huffpost.com/entry/gay-wedding-hindu-temple-photos_l_5d407f74e4b0db8affaf5d82.
55. Harish Iyer, *The Boy's Caste: An Arranged Gay Marriage*, Outlook (Jan 02, 2017), https://www.outlookindia.com/magazine/story/the-boys-caste-an-arranged-gay-marriage/298292.
56. Homonationalism is a term coined by Jasbir Paur in Terrorist Assemblages: Homonationalism in Queer Times (2007). Nishant Upadhyay, *Hindu Nation and its Queers: Caste, Islamophobia, and De/coloniality in India*, 22 Interventions 464-480 (2020); Upadhyay adapts this as "homohindunationalism" while Huma Dar uses the term "Brahminic-homonationalism" to refer to this in the Indian context.
57. Danielle Zoellner, *Grooms Go Viral for Their Traditional Hindu Wedding in a Temple*, Daily Mail (July 31, 2019), https://www.msn.com/en-in/lifestyle/relationships/grooms-go-viral-for-their-traditional-hindu-wedding-in-a-temple/ar-AAFjXbC.
58. Scholarly critiques of neoliberal attempts at subsuming all local gender and sexually variant behaviours and practices under terms such as 'queer', imported from the Global North, are increasing. However, like this chapter warns, this must not result in a romanticization of so-called nativist terms that are often steeped in caste patriarchy.
59. FP Staff, *Section 377 Hearing in Supreme Court: Mukul Rohatgi Tells Bench IPC Section Based on Victorian Morals, Not Ancient India*, Firstpost (July 10, 2018, 2:30 PM), https://www.firstpost.com/india/section-377-hearing-in-supreme-court-mukul-rohatgi-tells-bench-ipc-section-based-on-victorian-morals-not-ancient-india-4705681.html.

60. Manayath, *supra* note 22.
61. *Id.* at 269.
62. Navtej, *supra* note 25.
63. Braj Ranjan Mani, *Neobrahmanism, Human Rights and Social Democracy*, Round Table India (Feb. 01, 2012), https://www.roundtableindia.co.in/neobrahmanism-human-rights-and-social-democracy/.
64. Dr. Ambedkar consistently put forward the issue of separate electorates for Depressed Classes at the Roundtable Conferences. In August, 1932, Ramsay MacDonald, the British prime minister, announced the Communal Award, which granted Muslims, Buddhists, Sikhs, Indian Christians, Anglo-Indians, Europeans and Depressed Classes (now known as the Scheduled Castes) separate electorates in India. Gandhi, who believed that separate electorates for Depressed Classes would break the Hindus' purported unity, began a fast-unto-death in Yerwada Prison, finally forcing Dr. Ambedkar to sign the Poona Pact on September 24, 1932, rescinding separate electorates for the Depressed Classes and effectively thwarting their political representation.
65. B.R. Ambedkar, Annihilation of Caste (Rupa, 2019).
66. G. Aloysius, The Brahminical Inscribed in the Body-Politic (2010).
67. *Id.*
68. The *Criminal Tribes Act, 1871* (amended in 1897 and 1911) classified specific tribes as criminal and required them to register at police stations at regular intervals, and to compulsorily notify the police in the event of any absence/change of residence. The presumption was that all members of the classified tribes were criminal by birth—a notion derived from the caste system rather than a British colonial import. Part II of the Act deals with the 'Registration of "Eunuchs"'. *Please see* Jessica Hinchy, Governing Gender and Sexuality in Colonial India: The Hijra, C.1850–1900 (2019) for a detailed study of the same.
69. Anastasia Piliavsky, The "Criminal Tribe" in India Before the British 57 Comp Stud Soc Hist. 323 (2015). See Anand Yang, Dangerous Castes and Tribes; The Criminal Tribes Act and the Magahiya Doms of Northeast India, in Crime and Criminality in British India (1985).
70. Jessica Hinchy, Governing Gender and Sexuality in Colonial India: The Hijra, C.1850–1900 (2019); an unpublished thesis by Shane Patrick Gannon, *Translating the Hijra: The Symbolic Reconstruction of the British Empire in India*, 349-350 (2009) (PhD dissertation, University of Alberta). For a detailed critique of the former, see *Gee Semmalar, Constructing Hijras as Colonial Subjects*, 56 EPW (2021).
71. I use "lowered" (verb form) rather than "lower" (adjective form) to emphasise the active subjugation of groups relegated to a lower status in the caste hierarchy, similar to the ways in which "enslaved" rather than "slave" is used in contemporary scholarship. I first saw this usage in Braj Ranjan Mani, *Debrahmanising History: Dominance and Resistance in Indian Society* (2005).

Mani credits Mr Arun Kumar for the usage in his preface but I have not been able to locate the citation for this.

72. Hinchy, supra note [number to be added], at 171. This was previously pointed out Gannon, supra note [number to be added], at 349-350.
73. NALSA, *supra* note 28, at 48.
74. *Id.* at 48 & 9 & 70 & 49 & 77.
75. The National Register of Citizens was first created in 1951 to stop the flow of illegal immigrants into Assam. However, there have been huge protests in Assam following the recent release of the NRC, where 1.9 million people were excluded. Following the amendment of the *Citizenship Act, 1955* in December 2019, Home Minister Amit Shah announced that the NRC would be applied across India. Under the prescribed rules, one has to provide the legacy papers of ancestors pre-1971 to prove one's residence in India, and to claim Indian citizenship. Although the Indian government claims that the *Citizenship Act, 1955* was amended to protect Hindu, Christian, Sikh, Jain and Parsi immigrants from neighbouring countries, the fact that Muslims have been left out altogether has created widespread outrage and resistance across the country.
76. Pranjal Baruah, *Assam NRC: Shunned by Families, Citizenship of Many Transgender Individuals at Stake as They Fail to Secure 'Legacy Data'*, Firstpost (Aug. 28, 2018), https://www.firstpost.com/india/assam-nrc-shunned-by-families-citizenship-of-many-transgender-individuals-at-stake-as-they-fail-to-secure-legacy-data-5062251.html.
77. Transgender Persons (Protection of Rights) Act, 2019, 40 of 2019, section 2 (c).
78. *Id.* at Chapter V, section 2 (3).
79. *Id.* at 3, Chapter III, section 6 (1).
80. *Id.* at 4, Chapter III, section 7 (1) & (2).
81. NALSA, *supra* note 28, at 20-21.
82. *Id.* at 110, section 5.
83. *See* Aniruddha Dutta, *An Epistemology of Collusion: Hijras, Kothis and the Historical (Dis)continuity of Gender/Sexual Identities in Eastern India*, 24 Gender & History 825 (2012); Themal Ellawala, *Legitimating Violences: The 'Gay Rights' NGO and the Disciplining of the Sri Lankan Queer Figure*, 14 JSAD 83 (2019).
84. Manayath, *supra* note 22.
85. Dutta, *supra* note 49.
86. Though this gatekeeping existed before, it has intensified post-NALSA, perhaps because of the question of access to welfare schemes and benefits.
87. The Facebook–Cambridge Analytica data scandal was a major political scandal in 2018, when it was discovered that Cambridge Analytica had used the personal data of millions of Facebook users without their consent for the purposes of political advertising during elections.

88. Manayath, *supra* note 22, at 265.
89. Gharanas are historical hijra houses, believed to be seven in number and spread across India. When you enter traditional hijra kinship systems, you become affiliated with the gharana your guru lays claim to.
90. Nayaks are senior gurus who usually have a lot of power and prestige within hijra kinship systems (they are often heads of gharanas) and wield considerable decision-making power within their communities.
91. Gayatri Reddy, With Respect to Sex: Negotiating Hijra Identity in South India (2005). A disassociation I have heard articulated by senior members of the bigger havelis of Hyderabad in 2015-2017.
92. Sandy Stone, *The Empire Strikes Back: A Posttranssexual Manifesto,* 10 Camera Obscura 150 (1992).
93. *Id.*
94. Gloria Anzaldúa, Borderlands/La Frontera: The New Mestiza (1987).

CHAPTER 8

Finding the 'Gay' in Ambedkar

Contesting and Breaking Lines Between Caste and Sexuality

Akhil Kang

INTRODUCTION

I started touching myself thinking, in school, of the boy who had bullied me. I imagined the lips which had abused me, biting my nipples instead. I was hard. That hardness felt strange. Unexpected. It was then that I started fantasizing about my abusers. I felt dirty… desiring those dirty men.

My mother called my queerness dirty, years later. This was not the first time she had used the word 'dirty'. You see, our caste was dirty. An untouchable caste. A dirty chamar.[1] *In the nights, that dirty queerness wrestled with my dirty caste. Re-defining what my desires meant to me. Continuing my ritual of fantasizing about the oppressor, I thought about a man who had slapped me at a recent political protest.*[2] *Remembering the disgust and anger evident on his face when he looked at me, I realized how messy my relationship with oppression was. I knew I was going to touch myself thinking of him later that night. And as I lay in my bed, imagining him punishing me, it suddenly hit me that he might be a lower caste too. My fantasies died. I felt dirty.*

Dirty for trying to take control through fictional desires. Dirty for wishing he wasn't the same caste as me.

There could be many ways to begin writing about caste and sexuality. As individual disciplines (of power as well as knowledge), both are so vast that talking about them together seems like a daunting exercise. Why did I choose to begin with such a personal (and as some might say, discomforting) account? Perhaps it is the unremarkable moments rather than the momentous ones where categories and/or identities unravel each other. Or maybe, it is the 'dirtiness' of it all which helps us (dalit-queer[4] individuals) make sense of our relationship with oppression. It is the unseen which offers us an insight into how intersectional lives are lived. Caste has curious ways of making itself known. Often, it is the ordinary moments in which our relationships with hierarchies make us realize how vulnerable and unwanted we are. It was not the slap, but the humiliation of being sexually involved with a lower-caste man that made me realize that I am yet to, at least sexually, come to terms with being a chamar. That 'dirtiness', as I point out, invaded me in my most private moments (of touching myself) and spoke deeply of both caste and sexuality.

While describing the relationship of dirtiness with caste, I use the word 'intersectional'. One of the ways in which scholars of gender, race and sexuality have tried to make sense of experiences arising from different identities and marginalizations has been through the framework of 'intersectionality'. While historicizing intersectionality, Jennifer Nash argues against the impulse to find the 'origins' of intersectionality and notes contributions by several thinkers, activists and scholars who helped develop intersectionality's multiple genealogies in both Black feminist and women of colour feminist traditions.[5] Nash cites the works of Anna Julia Cooper, the Combahee River Collective, Evelyn Brooks Higginbotham and many others to highlight the development of theoretical frameworks which understood the mutually constitutive nature of gender, race, class and sexuality.[6] Patricia Hill Collins understands intersectionality to be at the crossroads between critical analysis and social action, and offers many conceptual tools to root intersectionality within resistant knowledges.[7] In addition to multi-dimensionality, Vivian May says,

> developed in the context of struggles for social justice, intersectionality offers a means to questions and challenge dominant logics, to further anti-subordination efforts, and to forge collective models for social transformation that do not replicate or reinforce the inequalities, erasures, and distortions animated and buttressed by either/or logics.[8]

Among many other formulations of intersectionality, Kimberlé Crenshaw tries to centre discussions of legal frameworks on immigration and domestic violence laws in the American context around the experiences of Black women and women of colour.[9] Therefore, intersectionality avoids manifestations of any 'single axis framework' and avoids treating gender and race as two separate categories.[10] Intersectionality, both in theory and praxis, emphasizes the need to take into account the complexities of experiences of race and cautions against compartmentalizing social categories/ subjectivities.

In June 2015, I wrote an article on an anti-caste political portal which, in some ways for me, was almost a 'new' coming out moment.[11] In the days following this online coming out, I was quite intrigued by how my writing on caste-sexuality became, for many, the perfect example of 'intersectionality'. I hadn't made any attempt to channel that writing through the intersectionality framework or pretended that I understood the history of that theory at all. Yet, the language through which the public consumed it felt like an unwelcome intrusion. That article also became the moment through which my mother 'officially' knew that I was gay. Strangely enough, when my mother brought that piece up for the first time in front of me (saying that she agreed with the "caste bit, but not the gay bit") I found myself summarizing my entire life by using the word 'intersectionality' too! Seeing my mother's confused face, I realized minutes later that I could not possibly find a way to translate that word into Punjabi. In that moment, my own lack of vocabulary made me re-think my own (comfortable) tendency to fall back on the intersectionality framework. Even though this framework would easily explain to my mother how lives are lived in different permutations and combinations, I found myself drawing some distance away from it. Not only because I could not find the words in Punjabi to explain it, but also because I did not want the complications of my identities and my life to be summarized in just one word. Beyond these complications, I want to unpack this distancing from intersectionality in the context of caste as well.

This paper avoids looking at and invading lives which are expected to carry the weight of intersectionality. In Part II, I step away from finding 'intersections' between caste and sexuality,[12] and explore why I draw away from the framework of intersectionality without necessarily dismissing it. I argue for this distance in the larger context of investigating the caste *of* intersectionality. This paper is not a critique of intersectionality as a theory/framework but a critique of the particular ways in which intersectionality has been used in the context of caste. After setting up the need to explore the caste of intersectionality I argue how, in the discourse of caste, sexuality has come to be understood through the category of dalit women but fails to imagine its queer possibilities. I do not seek to investigate questions of 'dalit patriarchy' or 'dalit masculinities'.[13] Dalit men have often been the site at which marginalized articulations of masculinities and sex are studied. As I mentioned before, this paper does not seek out specific bodies through which I want to understand caste-sexuality. Nor do I want to take on the burden of policing what amounts to an authentic dalit-queer experience. By discussing the various ways in which gender has been complicated through caste, I attempt to further explore the category of dalit by exploring the possibilities of reading queerness into caste. Then, I move the discussion around caste-sexuality towards opening up a framework of 'queering dalit'.

At this point it is important to note that the queering dalit framework does not provide any *new* ways of analyzing caste-sexuality. Nor is it a new name for 'intersectionality'. 'Queering dalit' offers a critique of both queerness and caste, using one another's similarities and differences. It also opens up avenues to see how existing frameworks are not beyond internal reflections even when they offer radical disruptions to dominant discourses.

In Part III, I analyze what the categories of dalit and queer have to offer each other politically and academically, and explore the ways in which the queering dalit framework opens up possibilities for the category of 'dalit'. Pushing beyond finding specific points at which caste-sexuality engage with each other, I critically analyze how that very engagement vis-à-vis structures of power re-defines the categories of 'dalit' and 'queer'.

THE SEARCH FOR QUEERNESS

Caste of Intersectionality

The framework of intersectionality emphasizes lived experiences and realities. This framework, like many other theories (queer theory for instance[14]), has travelled many scapes, acquired its own meanings, and has come to be articulated in alternative ways. In India, some scholars note that the framework of intersectionality merely gives a new name to a pre-existing perspective.[15] Nivedita Menon argues that a single axis framework was never dominant or unchallenged in India, and that the category of women was always destabilized by the politics of caste, class, religious identity, and sexuality.[16] Intersectionality has also been seen as a 'phenomenon of commas', and Akshay Khanna argues for quantum physics as an alternative way to understand multiplicities.[17] Reading theories on matter and mattering, affect, forcers and energies, Jasbir Puar offers the framework of 'assemblages', to be read alongside intersectionality.[18] Critical of how intersectionality has been de-politicized by many, Sirma Bilge points out that there are multiple narratives and tensions surrounding intersectionality's conceptual origin.[19] She argues that hierarchies are created when foundational text(s) of a concept are established and, by extension, hierarchies are created based on who gets to introduce the concept or is empowered by it, and whose career benefits from or is sidelined by it. These struggles reveal intersectionality's "power struggles, opportunity structures and turf wars".[20] Is it then important to ask *who* is denying this framework?

On addressing hierarchies, not just within academic debates but amongst debaters, Anu Ramdas draws attention to the importance of 'calling out' the caste locations of individuals in academia.[21] She argues that because caste functions in highly complicated arrangements and structures to maintain its status quo, language becomes a powerful tool to be employed against the trespassing power-less. The way ideas and expressions around academic discourses are gated and shunned by a certain caste and class of individuals, over a period of time, reveals complex networks of hierarchies. Therefore, all conversations, consciously or unconsciously, are powered by caste. This 'trespassing' by lower-caste individuals into the language of the powerful and oppressive is limited, not just to discourses of caste, but to language around queerness and sexuality as well.

Interrogating the social locations of queer individuals, Akshay Pathak argues that queer individuals are often de-linked from their caste.[22] He notes how queer individuals are perceived as caste-less because sexuality is imagined as having nothing to do with caste. Disturbingly, this ends up reproducing the same caste supremacist and caste preserving structures. Who gets to articulate queer and what queer is, or whose experiences of queerness gain currency, reveals how discourses of/on queer are not bereft of structures of caste. When caste becomes such an integral and powerful mode of everyday transaction in our lives, the queer individual in India is far from being casteless. The framework of intersectionality would then argue that it critiques the very hierarchical nature of the articulation of queer in India, and that it reveals the multiple ways in which queer lives are lived. But it (intersectionality) fails to account for its own gaps. Taking off from Bilge, who argues that dominant white feminist interventions de-politicize intersectionality, I would add that there is also a tendency for it to be de-caste(d) by dominant upper-caste groups and/or individuals. Just as intersectionality is de-racialized by subtracting race from its point of analysis,[23] the savarna[24] use of intersectionality subtracts caste from it. But this subtraction is cleverly done. Elsewhere I argue that queer and feminist spaces in India that actively engage with intersectionality end up re-producing stereotypes and assumptions about lower-caste bodies and persons.[25] Intersectionality often gets used by upper-caste collectives and individuals to engage with the 'other'. It becomes a tool to introduce a dialogue between identities—identities which an upper-caste individual would see as outside or miles away from their own personhood. It would never be used for internal reflection. The upper caste would be the objective entity 'applying' intersectionality to the lower-caste 'other'. Developing a legal understanding of dalit transgenders, Sumit Baudh argues that there are many ways in which individuals with 'intersectional subordination' have conflicted memberships in two or more communities.[26] They co-relate the use of 'personal narrative' in critical race theory in the US and 'experience' in dalit theorizing in India to point out how self-advertising 'intersectional' civil society groups remain hostile and unwelcoming to dalit and adivasi folk precisely because of their overt and covert casteist practices and off-hand casteist jokes and remarks. The de-politicized and de-caste(d) savarna use of intersectionality manipulates the use of this framework to benefit savarna hegemony by performing an investment in opposing caste hegemony. The savarna has distanced itself from intersectionality and embedded itself within it at the same time.

The notion of 'distance' has an intimate relationship with caste.[27] The maintenance of distance between upper and lower castes through endogamy, *khap* panchayats, restricted access to public services and amenities, and other forms of violence continues to be practiced daily. The use of distance here denotes both the affective as well as the political implications of removing lower-caste bodies and experiences. The distance is felt by the lower caste in many registers: emotional, physical, psychological, economic, social and political. Not only is distance repeatedly established to separate lower castes from upper castes, but this distance is also differently experienced by people. A lower-caste individual's relationship with distance might be a denial of access to opportunities or loneliness or lack of intimacy. On the other hand, distance for an upper-caste individual could be distancing themselves from relating to caste itself, because caste is popularly understood to be found only in lower-caste bodies. That is to say, 'distance from caste' and 'distancing caste' places the discussion of caste only in and around lower-caste bodies. Therefore, this distance (both literal and not quite so) is tied to how caste functions. The use of intersectionality and distancing oneself from it also function in a manner similar to how caste operates politically. In fact, this savarna use of intersectionality distances itself from how intersectionality operates. The purpose of this section is not to theorize intersectionality or decide whether it needs to be fully accepted or rejected, but to highlight that its very usage is embedded in caste locations. I distance myself from intersectionality precisely because every articulation around intersectionality in India is mediated through caste. However, it is important to acknowledge that frameworks like these, despite their shortcomings and faults, have found ways to be used as tools of empowerment and are ways for the marginalized, particularly lower-caste individuals, to exercise agency. Dalit women feminists are using intersectionality to create powerful tools and modes of resistance. My paper does not seek to discredit that work.

In the introduction I wrote about (a) an interaction with my mother—which highlighted a failure to understand intersectionality, and (b) the public consumption of my writings on caste-sexuality within the language of intersectionality—which highlighted a reader's need to read intersectionality into a piece of work which did not use the language of intersectionality at all. Additionally, whenever I talked about caste-sexuality in public forums, social movement spaces, universities and so on, I noticed that people, especially savarnas/upper castes, pushed against unique articulations of dalit-queerness when those articulations did *not* use intersectionality. Common responses included, 'But what you are saying *is* intersectionality,' and 'Why aren't you talking about intersectionality?' This denial of dalit-queer knowledge and episteme on its own terms shows how intersectionality is used by savarnas to secure their own stake within sites of knowledge that are produced through dalit labor. The savarna invocation of intersectionality uses an interdisciplinary approach that is organized around the symbol of dalit and adivasi marginality, even as their use retains little interest in the materiality of dalit-queers' bodies, the complexity of dalit-queer experiences, or intellectual and creative production. Intersectionality thus becomes one of the many tools through which the upper caste practices dalit disposability. The response of 'but this is intersectionality' also shows how the savarna continuously tries to gate-keep which dalit/dalit-queer experiences should be counted as intersectional.

Interrogating Caste and Gender Together

I began this section, 'The Search for Queerness', by addressing the caste of intersectionality. Much like the coming out piece mentioned in the introduction,[28] this paper is also written with the anxiety that it may get mistaken for material on intersectionality. The reason I began this section talking about intersectionality is to step away from this particular conceptual framework and start developing dalit-queer knowledge on its own terms. The conversations around intersectionality, at least in India, are heavily monopolized by upper-caste theorists, NGOs,[29] and civil society members who imagine that intersectionality has nothing to do with their own caste.

Before beginning the conversation on theorizing caste-sexuality (without placing it within the framework of intersectionality), it is imperative to note the ways in which caste and gender are located and studied. Studies on gender and caste necessarily become one of the primary sites of understanding caste-sexuality. Looking at how dominant descriptions of both the literature and the movements and actions of dalit women in colonial India were meant to enhance the social image of upper-caste women, Charu Gupta comments that the construction of womanhood functioned in two ways, wherein "upper caste was what woman is and ought to be; dalit was what she had better not be."[30] Through both revivalist and nationalist agendas, the female body also saw its confinement to ideas of reproduction and utility to the nation.[31] In the process of these reforms, many forms of sexualities, including dalit sexualities (along with homosexuality) were seen to be deviant and a threat to civilized norms of sexual behaviour.[32] These norms focus on dalit women more than others. The exercise of patriarchal power by men to subjugate women manifests in dalit women's sexual and bodily integrity and interpersonal relationships with men (both in public and private).[33]

Understandings of how dalit women have come to voice their pain, marginality and the violence they face, however, do not really use the language of queerness. This does not negate the fact that there are many accounts of dalit women, by dalit women, theorizing gender. Besides academia, dalit women have been writing about their lives and experiences through poetry, art, autobiographies, music and prose, amongst other creative media, for quite some time.[34] The need to centre dalit-queerness in dalit literature also arises from long histories of queer scholars pointing out the importance of developing queer methodologies that are not rooted solely in gender studies.[35] In her influential piece 'Thinking Sex', Gayle Rubin provocatively argues that we must not assume that the theoretical tools feminism uses to analyze gender will be sufficient for the task of analyzing sexuality.[36] Eve Sedgwick builds on Rubin's work and notes how questions of both gender and sexuality could very well be expressed in terms of each other but are nonetheless not the same question.[37] She writes,

> just as one has learned to assume that every issue of racial meaning must be embodied through the specificity of a particular class position–and every issue of class, for instance, through the specificity of a particular gender position–so every issue of gender would necessarily be embodied through the specificity of a particular vice versa; but nonetheless there could be use in keeping the analytic axes distinct.[38]

It has been several decades since Rubin and Sedgwick wrote these texts and many scholars have since challenged the tension between gender and sexuality.[39] Most notably, Susan Stryker critiqued

'Thinking Sex' for creating several obstacles for the interdisciplinary academic field of transgender studies.[40] Rubin did re-visit their text, and highlighted a problematic sexual politics organized around moral sexual panic, anti-pornography and child sexual abuse.[41] On the point of proposing that gender and sexuality be analytically separated, Rubin writes that at the time gender and sexuality were commonly conflated, and their text challenged the assumption that feminism is the privileged theoretical and political framework with which to analyze all things sexual.[42] Rubin further notes that the rejection of feminism was not the intention with which they wrote 'Thinking Sex', and that the argument for developing specific tools to understand sexuality found its roots in Max Weber's analytic strategy for grappling with different kinds of social stratification. Seeing how integral the relationship between gender and sexuality is, how they analytically support each other and yet require context-specific tools, I argue that the framework of caste-gender alone cannot do justice to dalit-queerness and caste-sexuality. Other social movements around the world, such as anti-racist, Black liberation movements, have been engaging with Black-queer scholarship for decades, and we need to ask why anti-caste and dalit movements have wrongfully dismissed dalit-queers and caste-sexuality.

Queerness offers an alternative way of imagining the categories of dalit woman and dalit man by disrupting the narrative of binaries like woman/man and sex/gender. It challenges the dominant understandings of bodies, desires and intimacies, and conceptualizes changing and flexible femininities and masculinities. But is it important for the 'queer' to exist explicitly for an experience to amount to a queer experience? The categories of gender need not be investigated through the lens of queerness alone, but it is necessary to acknowledge that the very experience of *living* a caste is interspersed with sexuality.

It is also equally important to develop theorizations on caste-sexuality from dalit-queer and trans perspectives. Living Smile Vidya and Gee Imaan Semmalar develop an understanding of transphobia as a kind of brahminism.[44] In addition to navigating caste, class and gender structures in their own homes, both of them (Vidya as a Dalit transwoman and Gee as a savarna transman) talk about hierarchies and practices motivated by caste in trans collectives and households.[45] It is also important to note that their conceptualizations of caste-sexuality are not limited to questions of caste or sexuality. Its intimate relationship with labour, sex work, respectability, body politic and career mobility shows how dalit-queer epistemology organically re-shapes the boundaries of everyday politics and refuses to be articulated in a monolithic form. Bhawani Maa, a Kinnar politician, narrates her own negotiation of caste-sexuality while contesting elections in 2019.[46] In the context of rising right-wing mobilizations among trans, hijra and gender non-conforming individuals, Bhawani's personal move towards Hinduism is strategic. Contesting for the AAP (Aam Aadmi Party) in Uttar Pradesh, she says that people who would have turned her away for begging now touch her feet to seek her blessings. Her pride in using her surname is also a response to upper-caste transwomen's casteist displays of power. The life of caste-sexuality, therefore, takes its own contextual, strategic, complicated, and messy turns.

While writing a letter to their lover(s), Dhrubo Jyoti tells a story about caste-sexuality through their grandmother.[47] Their grandmother's troubled ties with loneliness and abandonment, and her memory of both tells a story, not just of caste and misogyny, but also of queerness.[48] Dhiren Borisa develops a theory of space, politics and caste by spatially mapping desires. Foregrounding a theory of working-class dalit-queers, he notes the importance of visibility in violent structures of institutions and theories, and says,

> women, queers, people of colour, Dalits, Adivasis and the like, that have conspicuously been absent or kept aloof the academy, can never produce theory. We are just storytellers reproducing from our memories–our experiences of the margins–that in order to sound theoretical we will need to base ourselves on theories which never spoke of us in honesty.[49]

Thus, Borisa asks us to re-look at theories which either render people like us (dalit-queers) without agency, or completely erase us.

I refer to these works without forcefully injecting 'intersectionality' into them. They develop their own unique theory and politics of caste-sexuality and show how dalit-queers, trans and gender non-conforming individuals represent innumerable complexities which refuse to be digested into a coherent form.

JoanScott argues that experiences offer a critique of normative practices, but doesn't indicate the extent of that critique; experiences expose the existence of repressive mechanisms, but not their logics.[50] While defending experience, on the other hand, Johanna Oksala argues that the political importance of experience should not be neglected in the demand for social change.[51] Leslie McCall points out how narratives position an individual's experiences within the broader social location they occupy.[52] Experiences of caste-sexuality and dalit-queer experiences do not just demand social change (the annihilation of caste and institutional re-structuring, for instance) but speak deeply and intimately on questions about the functioning of caste itself. A dalit-queer experience, therefore, is not just a reflection on caste-sexuality/caste-queerness but also a living, breathing critique of oppressive structures of power.

What is Queering Dalit?

Western queer theory has continuously challenged the notion of sexual identity as monolithic, obvious or dichotomous,[53] and contemplated the possibilities of looking beyond the hyphens of conjugated identities that appear together yet apart.[54] It also disputes the idea of unitary identities and denies that sexuality can be comprehended through a singular lens.[55] In many senses, queer theory has not only shaken theoretical spaces but also re-defined socio-political ones, stressing the importance of the multiplicitous and often contradictory lives and emotions of desire, conduct and identity. Reading the geopolitics of queer theory and the sexual politics of dalit studies together, through the accounts of devadasis, Lucinda Ramberg notes that dalit respectability often finds itself in the bodies of women.[56] She comments that the call for the reform of 'sexually illicit' women is strong amongst dalit men, and even Ambedkar urged devadasis to 'give up their degrading life'.[57] However, Shailaja Paik argues that while Ambedkar no doubt urged women to be more 'masculine' and assertive,[58] we must be mindful of the particular historical, political and cultural contexts in which self-respect, political strategies and discursive strategies sought to destabilize and resist brahmin norms.[59] The sexual control of women's bodies is very evident in these narratives and scholarship and, one way or another, queerness exposes how desires and sexual ways of being are perceived. Queer prevents the moral and social subtraction of the sexual from caste, and helps us realize the radical potential of our desires, our sexual (or asexual) selves.

But surely 'queer', just like other categories, has its white baggage? As noted above, Western theories (such as intersectionality) are easily accommodated in the Global South. The unquestioned transportation of the use of 'queer' into the South Asian context has been seen by some as problematic because the word arose in a very Western historical context.[60] In the context of globalizing LGBT and queer politics, Aniruddha Dutta argues that transformative interactions between vernacular and global identities not only position local marginalized communities as the 'vernacular' but, despite creating political possibilities, also constrain many contextually flexible lived practices.[61] Noting the importance of a queer of colour critique, Ashley Tellis and Sruti Bala, while exploring what queer theory from South Asia would look like, state that this exercise is not just about adding an indigenous ingredient to the Western notion of queer theory.[62] How is adding dalit to queer any different then?

Elsewhere, on exploring my same-sex desires with upper-caste men, I argue that, for many of us, queer becomes the language in which we embrace awkwardness, humiliation and shame.[63] By making and un-making the 'Western queer' in my own way, rather than seeing any clash or contestation between queer and dalit, I imagined my very queerness to be dalit. The process of queering dalit, therefore, is not just a mere addition or amalgamation of identities but is the ways in which these identities exist in different permutations and combinations while being conscious of the caste, class, and racial locations that we come from. The fluidity of being queer tries to make sense of how being dalit is not a frozen identity and, similarly, being dalit convinces queerness of how important it is to strongly hold on to identities while, at the same time, being critical of them. This also highlights the importance of dalit-queerness for discourses on identity formation. Dalit-queers are not just doing the political, emotional, and physical labour of re-articulating and subverting 'queer' from its Western contexts but also highlighting how dalit-queerness has rejected casteist upper-caste articulations of being queer. Dalit-queer is not just a marker of identity, but also a political category.

One of the most prominent moments in which the queering dalit framework presents itself is when we try and talk about the performativity of both caste and sexuality together. Could gender performativity tell us anything about performing caste?[64] In public meetings and lectures, I have often been told that I don't 'look like a dalit', or that I don't 'talk like one'. Besides the obviously offensive casteist overtones of these statements, what always strikes me is how my performance of queerness is perceived as a performance of caste by the upper-caste gaze. During meetings where I categorically decide to perform my queerness, that same performance gets translated to performing caste. The two possibilities are, either (a) the public gaze does not and cannot imagine the queer to be lower caste, or (b) the very idea of what a lower caste should 'look like' is intimately tied to how we racially imagine lower-caste individuals perform their caste. A queer reading of this performance would tell us how the very category of caste is volatile and fluid because one could perform it in any way, but a 'dalit' reading informs us of the determination with which lower-caste identities hold onto their histories, and that their identities are not as fluid as queer would make them out to be!

Paik reads the stage performances of dalit women Tamasha performers in rural Maharashtra to examine how they contest the categories of obscene-erotic and traditional-modern.[65] Seeing how many women negotiate patriarchal power to bend it to suit their own purposes, and engage in the sexual economy of erotic excess as well as normative societal structures of caste, gender, sexual and familial labor by manipulating their bodies, Paik argues that gender and sexuality emerge as generative activities involving particularities of source and exchange.[66] Much like my own performance of dalit-queerness (as mentioned above), I am particularly interested in reading queerness into Tamasha performers' imitation of upper-caste feminists. Paik documents how some of these dalit performers have twisted tradition and modernity to forge new moral meanings. For instance, wearing a *mangalsutra* (a Hindu upper-caste marriage tradition in which women wear a thread to symbolize their supposedly sacred heterosexual union) is "not merely imitating married women or seeking complicity with patriarchy as in the case of upper caste women. She [the dalit Tamasha performer] instead negotiates and renegotiates, selectively appropriating certain traditional Brahmani practices, mimicking them, and generating broad possibilities and power for herself."[67] This performance of gender through caste is also a performance of caste itself. Here, queerness helps us ask: what does performing upper caste-ness look like?

It is as easy to militantly hold on to an idea of what it means to be dalit as it would be to say that everyone is queer. Perhaps, queering dalit offers a way to understand how a fixation on certain identities and the letting go of others can co-exist. However, the mutation of different categories is not where queering dalit would begin or end. Some of the many questions anti-caste movements around India are grappling with are:[68] how can we annihilate caste? Are inter-caste marriages and dining enough? Do the teachings of Ambedkar help us imagine a caste-free utopia? Would deleting our surnames in print make them irrelevant? In neoliberal times, when many social movements are obsessed with questions of 'what next' or 'how to achieve more', it is also necessary to hold on to the idea that there often does not *need* to be a goal and that it is perfectly normal to admit that our politics are imperfect and that we often cannot make sense of them.

I wonder if we have even begun to think of languages in which to imagine a world where caste loses its meaning. Are we even ready to let go of our attachments to caste when our entire personhood is built through caste? For many, letting go of caste could mean letting go of the material benefits that come with caste (for instance, leaving positions of power one obtained access to because of caste networking, or donating ancestral property), and for others, letting go of caste could mean getting rid of the violence attached to it or the humiliation that comes with it. Are we willing to let go of the modes of empowerment granted by caste? How relevant is the question of letting go, given the reality that particular castes inherit empowerment generationally, while others have to fight for it over time?

I am not arguing that queerness gives us an 'Aha!' moment of resolution in these situations, but instead that it helps us at least contain the ambiguities of the arbitrariness of caste. In establishing solidarities, we are repeatedly failing to realize that we do not in fact have answers to difficulties that have not even begun to be articulated. Scholars of politics and social movements often have a tendency to categorize the chaotic and disorganized.[69] The messiness of emotional and physical connections gets lost in these categorizations.[70] The un-nameable get deleted from our imaginations because it does not fit into the neat structures of that which is easily named. Time and again, queerness helps us test the radical potential of letting the un-named stay un-named. Given the fervour with which queerness also opposes the structures of power that benefit the privileged,[71] the ambiguity that queerness infuses in identity and identification cannot be sustained if they operate to benefit the upper class and caste.

Through queering dalit I am trying to realize the possibilities of ambiguity and fantasy in anti-caste movements. The realm of fantasy has been recognized and imagined by many scholars vis-à-vis queerness.[72] While it might be easy to get lost within the fluidity that queerness offers, it is important to recognize the (im)possibility of borders too. If anything, the *Scheduled Castes and*

Scheduled Tribes (Prevention of Atrocities) Act, 1989 has shown us how the recognition and naming of certain categories and identities is extremely important for certain individuals to articulate and find redress for their hurt and grief. At the same time, it is important to acknowledge that some people are not allowed this ambiguity in the first place, because of their caste location. I am not arguing that queerness here signifies impossibility and that caste denotes possibility, or that queerness signifies flexibility and caste signifies rigidity, nor am I trying to flip that narrative. It is the recognition of the fact that both function in ambiguity/rigidity and are moving into each other at times and separating at others that makes it possible to understand caste-sexuality. Thus, I imagine queering dalit to hold not just an articulation of 'Dalit, Queer and Proud'[73] but also of 'Dalit, Queer and NOT Proud'.[74] As a queer-dalit person there are moments when I feel comfortable being queer but not so comfortable being a chamar, and then there are moments when I feel proud to be a chamar but do not necessarily draw inspiration from queerness. There could also be moments when both do not matter, and I function outside these paradigms.

These negotiations are telling of the ways in which separating the categories of queer and caste are not so fruitful. Rather than indulging in insulting exercises of comparing the untouchability of lower-caste individuals and the marginalization of non-Dalit persons (assuming that is even possible), one needs to interrogate the similar ways in which all experiences around caste and queerness try to make sense of both the fixity and arbitrariness of human relations. Thus, statements such as 'both the LGBTQIA+ community and dalits are discriminated against and that is why they are the same' or 'transgenders are also similar to untouchables because of the way they are treated' are extremely damaging. I began this section by articulating my distance from 'intersectionality'. The name of this section, 'The Search for Queerness', highlights how queerness ends up becoming just another category to be searched for in any kind of experience, rather than recognizing the ambiguous way in which caste-sexuality functions. Thus, the point of this section was not to interview or dissect dalit-queer individuals to show how caste and sexuality operate. My use of queering dalit points towards naming the caste of queerness and the queerness of caste.

DISSECTING 'DALIT': A QUEER PROJECT

The word 'dalit' has a complex political history behind it, and scholarship on caste offers important insights for a queer reading of dalit. The caste system in India has come to be understood in many complex ways: from being seen as a form of social stratification based on birth and legitimized by Hindu beliefs[75] to the varna model of social division based on four castes,[76] it has emerged as an organizing principle of colonial knowledge,[77] a characteristic peculiarity of endogamy,[78] an examination of identities vis-à-vis the idea of pollution,[79] and has been understood through its relationship with and subversion of 'purity'.[80] Gupta points out, quite rightly, that anthropologists and historians have provided us with so many different variations of facts that we could now possibly formulate an analytical perspective on caste which is faithful to its multiple vocalities.[81] However, rather than tracing the history of the study of caste in this section, I will focus on the ways in which the category of caste is felt with respect to the political category of 'dalit'. I argue that this exercise tells us about experiencing queerness in everyday transactions and interactions, and shows us how the lines between dalit and queer are blurred. Thus, I explore how dalit and queer *living* translate to dalit and queer *politics*.

Tracing the usage and origin of the word 'dalit' in Marathi, which comes from 'broken or downtrodden', Eleanor Zelliot observes that this term was used in its most contemporary sense by a Marathi professor, Pantawane, who said, "To me, Dalit is not a caste...... Dalit is a symbol of change and revolution."[82] Examining the importance of this term and how dalit literature tries to establish its identity as different from 'mainstream literature', Darshana Trivedi notes that many of the texts, autobiographies, poems and so on written by lower-caste individuals arise out of historic necessity, and speak volumes on oppression, trauma, pain and violence.[83] Popularized through the writings of nineteenth century social reformers, 'dalit' came to signify a denial of equality as well as the past and present oppression and marginalization of untouchables at the hands of brahmins/other upper castes.[84] Through the work of radical anti-caste groups such as the Dalit Panthers in the 1960s and 1970s, 'dalit' also includes more diverse and endogamous groups of scheduled castes, depressed classes and more.[85] This word also began to denote a certain materialist, rather than idealist, composition and structure of Ambedkarite thought,[86] paying special attention to the structural conditions producing caste, arising out of lived experiences.[87] Needless to say, the genealogy of 'dalit' has also seen innumerable explanations by sociologists, anthropologists, literary scholars and political activists, among many others. The abundant ways in which the term has been fixed or seen as fluidly linked with many emotions, characteristics and origins is quite telling of how 'dalit' gained both political and radical currency in the anti-caste movement.[88]

While looking at women's leadership in a predominantly lower-caste political party, the Bahujan Samaj Party (BSP), Manuela Ciotti notes the repudiation of 'dalit' by local women leaders in the state of Uttar Pradesh.[89] She comments that while the leader of the party, Mayawati, explicitly subverts upper-caste womanhood by openly boasting about her chamar status, many women do not want to be associated with the assumed victimhood of 'dalit' when navigating their political subjectivities. Recognizing different social divisions among dalit women in rural Uttar Pradesh, Radhika Govinda argues that positionality should not always be conflated with identity.[90] She says that not all ex-untouchable women would consider themselves 'dalit women', and that the label of dalit is a political one that should not be confused with a fixed social division.

If one were to assume that dalit *is* only a political category, could an upper-caste individual call themselves dalit if they wholeheartedly believed in the anti-caste cause? What does this say about *being* queer?

If queer is political, as much as personal, what would make one fall short of being called queer? One might argue that these two are very different registers of being and ought to be analyzed differently, but the underlying and fundamentally radical potential of both dalit and queer manages to both break and affirm social, *positional* identities.

Recently, I was at a conference recalling the dubious ways in which people occupy spaces on digital and social media platforms. Many accounts on Twitter are operated anonymously and I had re-tweeted a couple of anonymous accounts' tweets about upper-caste hegemony and social accountability. After a few days of tweeting, tagging and re-tweeting, a couple of 'real' (that is, non-anonymous) Twitter accounts belonging to dalit men and women privately messaged me to warn me about anonymous casteless accounts that were masquerading as dalit accounts but were operated by upper castes.[91] Without enquiring about how they knew the anonymous accounts were upper caste, I eventually tweeted about being suspicious of online anonymous accounts because I felt strange establishing solidarity with the accounts of persons I could only assume were lower caste. After the conference, one of the attendees came up to me and asked, "Why did you have a problem with those accounts? If what they were saying about anti-caste discourse was something you agreed with and supported, then how does it matter that they were not dalits?" The reason I bring this discussion up here is exactly what this enquiry triggers. I want to bring our attention to how malleable 'dalit' is assumed to be by some of these anonymous accounts. Is it enough for me as a dalit person to see an upper caste performing the political dalit? Is it enough for me to establish solidarity with them?

It is not uncommon, at least in today's day and age, for heteronormative individuals to identify as 'politically queer' or to be practicing queerness in their pedagogies. Could that be said about being dalit too? Interestingly, I started noticing certain 'markers' through which these anonymous accounts started 'passing'[92] as lower castes. Was it just their saying the right things about anti-caste movements, or was it citing Ambedkar's writings the right way? Is there a wrong way to cite Ambedkar? Or could it be that they were tagging famous and well-known upper-caste surnames and holding them accountable for their positions on such and such issue of caste? Why *did* I have a problem with them? I was perfectly fine with what they were saying. For me, somehow, the *political* dalit was not translating to *social* dalit, and I realized that I did not believe in boundaries around queerness but felt violated when dalit was used in these ways. Does my commitment to queerness falter in some ways then, as I am able to experiment socially, performatively, physically and emotionally with gender but not so much with caste? I realized that despite advocating for some 'messiness' vis-à-vis caste-sexuality, I was still not comfortable with this particular kind of messiness.

Rather than looking at how 'dalit' is being re-configured by upper castes, I look at how it is being experimented with by lower castes. In arguing and fighting for dalit as a separate political identity, AnupamaRao argues that Ambedkar's contribution, of dalit communities constituting a 'separate element in the body politic', reconfigured the signification of 'dalit'.[93] She observes that Ambedkar's critical re-thinking of secular and democratic categories constructed new meanings and infused political value into the de-humanized dalit.[94] Therefore, according to Ambedkar's vision, *political* dalit is not very far from *social* (untouchable) dalit. Sharmila Rege comments that if one were to look at Ambedkar's writings and speeches, he tends to focus on the 'processes' that define his personal experiences, rather than his personal justifying the social.[95]

In the previous section, I asked where one could start looking for ruptures in gender and sexuality through the intersectional dalit-queer. I suggest that one does not actually have to look very far. Just like queer pedagogies and queer theories have been reading queer subtexts in seemingly heterosexual narratives,[96] anti-caste thinkers and reformers like Phule and Ambedkar read lower-caste narratives into dominant upper-caste traditions and practices (as a mode of subversion). In his strategic and ideological battle against the brahmin domination of culture and traditions in the late 1800s, Phule re-read the ballads of the Maratha warrior Shivaji and purposefully appropriated his figure in order to construct a collective identity for all lower castes.[97] Critiquing patriarchy,[98] he provided alternative accounts of texts, myths and stories common in popular Hinduism.[99] How queer is that! Not only is Phule re-purposing upper-caste versions of histories, but he also makes them into realities which can be lived and felt by lower castes in transformative ways. Therefore the 'queer' potential of this reading is not limited only to a methodology, but is a disruption of the rigidity of caste. Phule made an attempt to use traditional social categories in new ways and helped lower-caste individuals make sense of the contradictions within their identities.[100] Similarly, by interpreting the history of the Aryan race to highlight how an upper-caste construction of it left people (like shudras) out of the social order and its benefits and entitlements,[101] Ambedkar 'queerly' re-read and re-channeled a history once so utterly dominated by upper and higher castes. Queerness, therefore, not just offers the potential to subvert and reject upper-caste norms, but shows us how the category of 'dalit' itself has queer potential.

What does a queer reading really mean? Building on Sedgwick's 'reparative turn' and José Muñoz's 'disidentification', Nishant Shahani looks to the past and future through 'queer retrosexualities'.[102] His retrospective, reparative reading of the past "insists on the materiality of the past on the present—the very act of turning back refuses any sense of futurity without a consideration of the constraints of the past."[103] I use this notion of queer retrosexuality to explore the queer potential of looking towards the texts of the past (texts by anti-caste thinkers) to imagine present and future dalit-queer potentialities. Some might say that the title of this paper is misleading because, so far, I have made no attempt to find out whether Ambedkar ever referenced non-heteronormative individuals. To realize the potential of Ambedkar, I think it is necessary to not trace every possibility back to him. I do not think that I needed Ambedkar to talk about a supposed 'caste theory of queer' to be able to articulate caste-sexuality. As I point out, the practices with which Ambedkar was pushing the boundaries of history, Aryan theories of race and caste,

Buddhism, and untouchability already demonstrate that he was radically shaking the status quo by thinking through identities and the dominant political philosophies of his time. Thus, the category of dalit was used (even before queer came to be conceptualized) to challenge upper-caste hegemony.

However, in a post-Ambedkar, Ambedkar-ite world, it is inevitable for certain lower-caste individuals to depart from Ambedkar in ways which might seem queer (strange). An articulation of caste cannot be rejected simply because it failed to make the 'right' connections with Ambedkar's teachings. No one has (or should have) the power to take away what Ambedkar has come to symbolize to millions of people. Yet, that cannot be the only way we make sense of our relationship to each other and to anti-caste politics. He cannot remain the only frame of reference to talk about caste. Living in dangerous times, where just the installation of Ambedkar's bust would have you killed, I realize the implications of what departures from Ambedkar could mean. To go back to holding the messiness together, I do not think experimenting with dalit-ness makes one any less of an Ambedkar-ite or a traitor to anti-caste movements. It is precisely because of queerness, and experiments with the fluidity of being queer, that many dalit-queers could articulate different ways of being Dalit. As I highlight in the previous sections, by imagining queer and dalit together, in no way do I urge thinkers to suddenly collapse both identities and merge them together, but instead to recognize the ways in which they give each other boundless freedom to explore and simultaneously provide a way to limit expectations and assumptions.

DALIT-QUEER ALLIANCE

'Dalit, Queer & Proud': Dhrubo Jyoti, Dhiren Borisa and I came together under this banner in solidarity with each other. All three of us, collectively and individually, knew that we did not necessarily feel proud of being dalit at all times but felt that we needed to say something about caste-sexuality in the 2015 Delhi Pride Parade, given that the image of queer in India was dominated by casteist queer individuals. I remember being extremely nervous the day before Pride, and Dhiren telling me that the mere presence of dalit-queer individuals was undoing the violent histories that have long been silencing us. None of us fully realized the power involved in that process of undoing and we did not anticipate the dalit-queer manifesto (that is, the public statement) that we made to receive such a touching and overwhelming response. In the following years, we tried to connect with many other dalit-queer and trans folks all over the country and pursued the hope of a 'queering dalit' collective. Soon enough, we realized that 'dalit' carried different meanings for all of us. As did being queer. The precarity of our dalit-queer positionality was heightened by our collective realization that there were no boundaries to what being queer meant and that, to some extent, boundaries around dalit experiences were being heavily monitored in anti-caste movements.

Caught up in so many questions of appropriation, misappropriation, gatekeeping and misrepresentation, we didn't know what to do! How were we to decide the membership of this collective? Were we cognizant of adivasi and indigenous histories? Did we know enough about 'bahujan' categories? All of us were going through complex queer journeys of understanding what being an Ambedkar-ite meant. Personally, I was realizing that my queerness wasn't enough to hold our different dalit histories. Coming from an untouchable caste of chamars and belonging to the ad-dharmi Ravi Dassia community in Punjab, I never grew up with Ambedkar. I grew up with Guru Ravi Dass. Growing up in the 1990s, my parents never knew the term 'Ambedkar-ite'. Seeing how different chamar socializing is in Punjab and its very peculiar relationship with Punjabi hypermasculinity and land politics, I just couldn't find the common dalit in my fellow dalit-queers. The savarna as the constant oppositional figure wasn't enough for me to mobilize with others. I was also realizing that I was a chamar first and dalit later, that is, my immediate contextual caste mattered more. For me, 'dalit, queer and proud' shifted to 'chamar, queer and…'.

Acknowledging that queerness just wasn't giving us enough strength, we—a few dalit-queers—decided to let the collective fade away. We didn't know how to perform dalit respectability. We didn't know how to create space for ourselves in painfully heteronormative dalit movements. We weren't nodding our heads with pain-filled eyes when heterosexual dalits would try to establish solidarity with us by saying 'we both are oppressed', implying that you (queer) and me (dalit) are oppressed together. It was as if our queer and dalit existed separately. How could we tell them that our dalit families haven't been too kind to the 'queer' part of us? I highlight this narrative not just to document a tiny piece of dalit-queer history but also to point towards different attachments to dalit-queerness. I do not have any desire to reconcile this narrative with earlier sections exploring what the 'queering dalit' framework does, because I am able to hold this messiness together. At a time when theorists of caste and gender are suddenly realizing the importance of queer sexualities, dalit-queers continue to fade. Dalit-queerness continues to voice itself and continues to oscillate between naming the un-named and figuring out a name for itself.

CONCLUSION

In this chapter, I neither reject nor celebrate the framework of intersectionality. Rather, I have tried to show that while the framework of intersectionality has many possibilities, it, in the course of time, may or may not have departed from its original meanings and taken its own journey. Like many frameworks—thanks to hierarchies of who gets to talk about them—the savarna use of intersectionality has becomes caste-less, thus rendering intersectionality hollow. As Bilge says, the point is not for people belonging to certain social locations to move over or stop doing intersectionality, but to stop doing intersectionality in ways that *undo* it.[104] The framework of queering dalit offers another way of imagining, studying and exploring the theoretical, as well as lived and political potential, of both queerness and caste. Queering dalit needs to be understood not just as a political, intellectual, creative, or erotic project, but also as a way of feeling. 'Queering dalit' is my attempt to talk about caste-sexuality in its own terms, and represents an important and necessary dalit-queer epistemology.

While one might argue that dalit feminist knowledge can engage with anti-brahminic intellectual trends within sexual minorities' assertions,[105] it fails to recognize the possibility that 'dalit' and 'sexual minority' might be one and the same. Feminist histories have taught us how queer scholars' interventions radically shifted the boundaries and debates around bodies, agency, sexuality and so on. Similarly, it is high time for anti-caste discourse to realize that queer dalit individuals and thinkers do not experience caste in a man-woman binary. It is time we recognize that femininities and masculinities are constantly re-shaped, and that *being* dalit is as much a queer question as it is a question of caste. The lives of dalit women have been mutilated and exposed enough in the name of studying gender through the decades but, because of the colossal silence around understanding sexuality and queerness, gender has not been complicated enough.

Reading queerness into caste and caste into queerness holds onto the ever-changing aspects of both without losing the critical ability to see the oppressive baggage both terms come with. As I have pointed out in previous sections, the categories of queer and dalit, together, have the potential to offer a unique and important mode of analysis and interpretation. Both these categories have been through political, social and academic journeys and have proven how each individual belonging to these categories has been able to re-shape their meanings, from *living* dalit-queer to practicing the *political* dalit-queer.

ACKNOWLEDGMENTS

I presented a part of this chapter at the 48th Annual Conference on South Asia at Madison, Wisconsin in 2019, on the panel 'Dalit Movement's Next Steps: Solidarity and Interaction with Others'. I worked through many of the ideas I write about in this paper in Professor Paola Bacchetta's course on 'Theory & Critical Research' at UC Berkeley during the Spring 2020 semester as an exchange PhD scholar. I am grateful for their insights and comments on my draft.

NOTES

1. Varnas form the basis of the caste system and classify society into Brahmins, Kshatriyas, Vaishyas and Shudras, within which there are castes and sub-castes. Chamars were outside the varna system, therefore deemed untouchable; that is, ones who should not be touched and are therefore excommunicated and ostracized. '*Chamadi*' translates to 'skin' in English, and 'chamar' is a term historically used for people who worked in professions dealing with the skin of dead animals—tanning, cobbling, and so on. *See* Ramnarayan S. Rawat, Reconsidering Untouchability: Chamars and Dalit History in North India (2011).
2. I conducted this field work (through participant observation) in the city of New Delhi from 2016 to 2018. I was part of a team that sought to understand gender and sexuality in the context of political processes, political leaders and political movements, and we looked at institutional student politics in Jawaharlal Nehru University (JNU) and Delhi University (DU). I attended an event called 'Cultures of Protest' at Ramjas College, Delhi University on the 21st of February, 2017. The right-wing student party ABVP had reservations against one invited speaker (Umar Khalid) because of his involvement with (alleged) anti-State sloganeering. Khalid eventually decided not to come, but the climate quickly turned very hostile, and several attendees (including myself) were slapped, assaulted and beaten up by members of the ABVP merely for being present at the event and pointing out the urgent need for dissent in university spaces.
3. I use a hyphen between caste and sexuality to position them together in a way that does not introduce any boundaries between them. As this paper will reveal, I do not draw a strict distinction between the two terms, and I argue for a framework that re-looks at popular idioms which try to hold multiple categories together.

4. I use the word dalit interchangeably with lower caste. The different meanings of this word are explored more in the third part of this chapter, 'Dalit-Queer Alliance'.
5. Jennifer C. Nash, Black Feminism Reimagined: After Intersectionality (2019).
6. *Id.*
7. Patricia Hill Collins, Intersectionality as Critical Social Theory (2019).
8. Vivian M. May, Pursuing Intersectionality, Unsettling Dominant Imaginaries (2015).
9. Kimberlé W. Crenshaw, *Demarginalizing the Intersection of Race and Sex: A Black Feminist Critique of Anti-discrimination Doctrine, Feminist Theory, and Antiracist Politics*, 1 U. Chi. Legal F. 139 (1989).
10. *Id.*
11. Akhil Kang, *Ambedkar Helped Me Embrace the 'Emotional' Within the Rational*, Round Table India (June 17, 2015), https://www.roundtableindia.co.in/ambedkar-helped-me-challenge-oppression-and-embrace-the-emotional-within-the-rational/.
12. *See* Nirantar, *A Critical Examination of Sexuality Discourses in India* (2016), http://www.nirantar.net/uploads/files/A%20Critical%20Examination%20of%20Sexuality%20Discourses%20in%20India%20pdf.pdf. This report notes that the approach of much of the scholarship and work studying caste and sexuality seems almost obsessed with finding the 'intersections' between the two.
13. *See generally* S. Anandhi, J. Jeyaranjan & Rajan Krishnan, *Work, Caste and Competing Masculinities: Notes from a Tamil Village*, 37 EPW 4397 (2002).
14. To understand how queer theory has travelled across borders and contexts, *see* Martin F. Manalansan et al., Queer Globalizations: Citizenship and the Afterlife of Colonialism (2002); B.J. Epstein & Robert Gillett, Queer in Translation (2017).
15. Nivedita Menon, *Is Feminism about 'Women'? A Critical View on Intersectionality from India*, 50 EPW 37 (2015). For a response to Menon's piece, *see* Mary E. John, *Intersectionality: Rejection of Critical Dialogue?*, 50 EPW 72 (2015).
16. Menon, *supra* note 15.
17. akshay khanna, Sexualness (2016).
18. Jasbir K. Puar, *'I Would Rather Be a Cyborg than a Goddess': Becoming-Intersectional in Assemblage Theory*, 2 Philosophia 49 (2012).
19. Sirma Bilge, *Intersectionality Undone: Saving Intersectionality from Feminist Intersectionality Studies*, 10 Du Bois Review 405 (2013).
20. *Id.*
21. Anu Ramdas, *Casteless Academe, Name-calling Dalits?*, Savari (Oct. 04, 2012), www.dalitweb.org/?p=1021.
22. Akshay Pathak, *Brahmins Preferred: The Caste of Sexuality*, Round Table India (May 22, 2015), https://www.roundtableindia.co.in/brahmins-preferred-the-caste-of-sexuality/.

23. Sirma Bilge, *Whitening Intersectionality: Evanescence of Race in Intersectionality Scholarship, in* 5 Racism and Sociology: Racism Analysis Yearbook 175-205 (W.D. Hund & A. Lentin eds., 2014).
24. I use the terms savarna and upper caste interchangeably.
25. *See* Akhil Kang, *Casteless-ness in the Name of Caste*, Round Table India (Mar. 04, 2016), https://www.roundtableindia.co.in/casteless-ness-in-the-name-of-caste/.
26. Sumit Baudh, *Invisibility of "Other" Dalits and Silence in the Law*, 40 Biography 222, 232 (2017).
27. B.R. Ambedkar, *Who Were Shudras, in* The Essential Writings of B.R. Ambedkar (V. Rodrigues ed., 2002).
28. *See* Kang, *supra* note 11.
29. For instance, Yuval-Davis points out how UN and NGO networks often analytically confuse the conceptual methods of intersectionality. *See* Nira Yuval-Davis, *Intersectionality and Feminist Politics*, 13 EJWS 193 (2006).
30. Charu Gupta, *Representing Dalit Bodies in Colonial India, in* Unsettling the Archetypes: Femininities and Masculinities in Indian Politics (M. Ciotti ed., 2017).
31. Charu Gupta, *Writing Sex and Sexuality: Archives of Colonial North India*, 23 J Women's Hist. 12, 12 & 14 (2011).
32. *Id.*
33. Aloysius Irudayam S.J., Jayshree P. Mangubhai & Joel G. Lee, *Dalit Women Speak Out: Violence against Dalit Women in India,* National Campaign on Dalit Human Rights (Mar. 2006), https://idsn.org/uploads/media/Violence_against_Dalit_Woment.pdf.
34. *See* Shantabai Kamble, The Kaleidoscopic Story of My Life (1983); Urmila Pawar, Weave of My Life (1988); Babytai Kamble, The Prisons We Broke (M. Pandit trans., 2009); Kumud Pawade, Thoughtful Outburst (1981); Bama, Karukku (2000); Vijila Chirappad, A Home Without a Kitchen (2006); Gogu Shyamala, Father May Be an Elephant and Mother Only a Small Basket, But… (2012); Urmila Pawar & Meenakshi Moon, We Also Made History: Women in the Ambedkarite Movement (2015); Vulli Dhanaraju, Caste, Tribe and Gender: Politics of Self and the Other (2017); S. Anandhi & Karin Kapadia, Dalit Women: Vanguard of an Alternative Politics in India (2017).
35. Imagining Queer Methods (Amin Ghaziani & Matt Brim eds., 2019).
36. Gayle Rubin, *Thinking Sex: Notes for a Radical Theory of the Politics of Sexuality, in* Pleasure and Danger: Exploring Female Sexuality (C.S. Vance ed., 1984).
37. Eve Kosofsky Sedgwick, Epistemology of the Closet (1990).
38. *Id.* at 31.
39. Historicising Gender and Sexuality (Kevin P. Murphy & Jennifer M. Spear eds., 2011).
40. Stryker notes how, in the early 1990s, the transgender movement posed a challenge to queer theory by asking whether the queer sexuality framework

could adequately account for transgender identities. *See* Susan Stryker, Transgender History (2008); Susan Stryker, *Stray Thoughts on Transgender Feminism and the Barnard Conference on Women*, 11 The Communication Review 217 (2011).

41. Gayle S. Rubin, Deviations: A Gayle Rubin Reader (2011).
42. *Id.* at 230.
43.
44. Living Smile Vidya & Gee Imaan Semmalar, *Transphobia is a Kind of Brahminism: A Conversation Between Living Smile Vidya and Gee Imaan Semmalar, in* Gender, Caste and the Imagination of Equality (A. Rao ed., 2018).
45. *Id.* at 71.
46. Neha Dixit, *Can Trans Woman and AAP Candidate Bhawani Counter UP's Feudal Patriarchy with Religion?*, The Caravan (May 11, 2019), https://caravanmagazine.in/politics/elections-2019-prayagraj-bhawani-ma-kinnar-aap.
47. Dhrubo Jyoti, *A Letter to My Lover(s), in* Eleven Ways to Love: Essays (2018).
48. *Id.* at 23.
49. Dhiren Borisa, Imagined Spaces of Freedom: Negotiating Queer Cartographies of Desires in Delhi (2017) (unpublished PhD dissertation, Center for the Study of Regional Development, School of Social Sciences, Jawaharlal Nehru University).
50. Joan W. Scott, *The Evidence of Experience*, 17 Critical Enquiry 773, 779 (1991).
51. Johanna Oksala, *In Defense of Experience*, 29 Hypatia (2013), https://onlinelibrary.wiley.com/doi/full/10.1111/hypa.12053.
52. Leslie McCall, *The Complexity of Intersectionality*, 30 Signs 1771, 1781 (2005).
53. *See* Annamarie Jagose, Queer Theory: An Introduction (1996).
54. *See* Judith Butler, Gender Trouble: Feminism and the Subversion of Identity (1990).
55. Francisco Valdes, *Queers, Sissies, Dykes and Tomboys: Deconstructing the Conflation of "Sex," "Gender," and "Sexual Orientation" in Euro-American Law and Society*, 83 California Law Review 1, 24 (1995).
56. Lucinda Ramberg, *Backward Futures and Pasts Forward: Queer Time, Sexual Politics, and Dalit Religiosity in South India*, 22 GLQ 223, 239 (2016).
57. *Id.*
58. Shailaja Paik, *Forging a New Dalit Womanhood in Colonial Western India: Discourse on Modernity, Rights, Education, and Emancipation,* 28 J Women's Hist. 14, 27 (2016).
59. *Id.* at 29.
60. *See generally* Because I Have a Voice: Queer Politics in India (Arvind Narrain & Gautam Bhan eds., 2006).

61. Aniruddha Dutta, *Globalizing Through the Vernacular: Gender/Sexual Transnationalism and the Making of Sexual Minorities in Eastern India* (2013) (unpublished PhD dissertation, University of Minnesota), http://hdl.handle.net/11299/161632.
62. Ashley Teliis & Sruti Bala, *Introduction: The Global Career of Queerness, in* The Global Trajectories of Queerness: Re-thinking Same-Sex Politics in the Global South 21 (2015).
63. Akhil Kang, *Queering Dalit*, Tanqeed (Oct. 2016), http://www.tanqeed.org/2016/10/queering-Dalit-tq-salon/.
64. Butler, *supra* note 54, at 146. Judith Butler sees gender as a performance. Using drag as an example, she argues that gender is like a costume, and the fact that men and women keep playing and experimenting with it creates a possibility that "there is no original from which gay, lesbians or transvestite subjects deviate; the original is itself a mythical figuration".
65. Shailaja Paik, *Mangala Bansode and the Social Life of Tamasha: Caste, Sexuality, and Discrimination in Modern Maharashtra*, 40 Biography 170 (2017).
66. *Id.* at 179.
67. Paik, *supra* note 66, at 185.
68. I use the plural (movements) because there are many different ways of being dalit and Ambedkarite.
69. J. Craig Jenkins, *Resource Mobilization Theory and the Study of Social Movements*, 9 Annu. Rev. Sociol. 527 (1983); Comparative Perspectives on Social Movements: Political Opportunities, Mobilizing Structures, and Cultural Framings (Doug McAdam, John D. McCarthy & Mayer N. Zald eds., 1996).
70. I credit Jaya Sharma for the term 'messiness', who argues for the need to talk about the messiness of queer fantasies, and for using the framework of the psyche and psychoanalysis to talk about this messiness.
71. Peter Drucker, Warped: Gay Normality and Queer Anti-Capitalism (2015).
72. *See* Caitlin Gladney-Hatcher, *Under the Fantasy of Sovereignty: Homonormativity, Relationality and the Potentialities of Queer Sex,* 37 Atlantis 6 (2015); Juana Maria Rodriguez, *Queer Sociality and Other Sexual Fantasies*, 17 GLQ 331 (2011); Lauren Berlant, Desire/Love (2012).
73. C Moulee, Dalit Queer Pride at Delhi Queer Pride 2015, YouTube (Nov. 30, 2015), https://www.youtube.com/watch?v=SsQIq2_Di7A.
74. V. Angayarkanni, *Queer, Dalit and Not Yet Proud: This Is My Story*, Youth Ki Awaaz (Nov. 05, 2017), https://www.youthkiawaaz.com/2017/11/queer-dalit-and-not-yet-proud-this-is-my-story/.
75. Andre Beteille, Castes: Old and New, Essays in Social Structure and Social Stratification 57 (1969).
76. *See* C. Hayavadana Rao, Indian Caste System: A Study (1931).
77. *See* Nicholas B. Dirks, Castes of Mind: Colonialism and the Making of Modern India (2001).

78. B.R. Ambedkar, *Castes of India, in* The Essential Writings of B.R. Ambedkar 245 (V. Rodrigues ed., 2002).
79. *See* Ishwarlal Pragji Desai, Untouchability in Rural Gujarat (1976).
80. *See* M.N. Srinivas, Dominant Castes and Other Essays (1987).
81. Dipankar Gupta, *Introduction: The Certitudes of Caste: When Identity Trumps Hierarchy, in* Caste in Question: Identity or Hierarchy? xiii (D. Gupta ed., 2004).
82. Eleanor Zelliot, *Dalit - New Cultural Context for an Old Marathi Word, in* 11 Language and Civilization Change in South Asia 77-97 (C. Maloney ed., 1978).
83. Darshana Trivedi, *Literature of Their Own: Dalit Literary Theory in Indian Context, in* Dalit Literature: A Critical Exploration 1-8 (A.N. Prasad & M.B. Gaijan eds., 2007).
84. Ambedkar, *supra* note 27, at 285. For a denial of the term 'Harijan' in Dalit politics *see*, Ramachandra Guha, *The Rise and Fall of the Term 'Harijan', The Telegraph*, Ramachandra Guha (June 10, 2017), http://ramachandraguha.in/archives/the-rise-and-fall-of-the-term-harijan-the-telegraph.html.
85. Sreya Chatterjee, *Dialectics and Caste: Rethinking Dalit Life-Writings in the Vernacular, Comparing Dalit Narratives,* 53 Comparative Literature Studies 377, 380 (2016).
86. Ambedkarite is a political term used for persons who identify with and believe in anti-caste ideologies and the commitments of B.R. Ambedkar. This term is used by both upper castes as well lower castes.
87. Chatterjee, *supra* note 86.
88. S.P. Punalekar, *Dalits, Dalit Consciousness and Sociology, in* 14 Social Sciences: Communication, Anthropology and Sociology 491 (Y. Singh ed., 2010).
89. Manuela Ciotti, *'I Will See the World': The Production of Political Subjectivities Among Local Dalit Women Leaders in Lucknow, in* Unsettling the Archetypes: Femininities and Masculinities in Indian Politics 193 (M. Ciotti ed., 2017).
90. Radhika Govinda, *Different Dalit Women Speak Differently: Unraveling, Through an Intersectional Lens, Narratives of Agency and Activism from Everyday Life in Rural Uttar Pradesh, in* Dalit Women: Vanguard of an Alternative Politics in India 219 (S. Anandhi & K. Kapadia eds., 2017).
91. I say casteless because they did not have any surnames in their Twitter usernames and spoke of upper-caste oppression while simultaneously mentioning that 'caste didn't really matter' for them.
92. I use the phrase 'passing' the same way LGBTQ individuals have come to understanding 'passing' as straight-acting in public.
93. Anupama Rao, The Caste Question: Dalits and the Politics of Modern India 122 (2010).
94. *Id.*
95. Sharmila Rege, *Introduction: Towards a Feminist Reclamation of Dr. Bhimrao Ramji Ambedkar, in* Against the Madness of Manu: B.R. Ambedkar's Writings on Brahmanical Patriarchy 29 (2016).

96. Susanne Luhmann, *Queering/Querying Pedagogy? Or, Pedagogy Is a Pretty Queer Thing, in* Queer Theory in Education 120-132 (W.F. Pinar ed., 1998).
97. Rosalind O'Hanlon, Caste, Conflict and Ideology: Mahatma Jotirao Phule and Low Caste Protest in Nineteenth-Century Western India 136 (1985).
98. Uma Chakravarti, *Reconceptualising Gender: Phule, Brahmanism and Brahmanical Patriarchy, in* Issues in Contemporary Indian Feminism: Gender & Caste 164-179 (A. Rao ed., 2003).
99. O'Hanlon, *supra* note 97, at 138.
100. Laura Brueck, *Questions of Representation in Dalit Critical Discourse: Premchand and Dalit Feminism, in* Dalit Studies 180-201 (R.S. Rawat & K. Satyanarayana eds., 2016).
101. Ambedkar, *supra* note 27.
102. Nishant Shahani, Queer Retrosexualities: The Politics of Reparative Return (2012).
103. *Id.* at 15.
104. Bilge, *supra* note 19, at 411.
105. Smita M. Patil, *Revitalising Dalit Feminism: Towards Reflexive, Anti-Caste Agency of Mang and Mahar Women in Maharashtra*, 48 EPW 37, 43 (2013).

CHAPTER 9

Law, Sexuality and Diaspora

Sonia K. Katyal

INTRODUCTION

On a hot summer afternoon in New York City in 2009, 62 years after the birth of Indian independence (which took place on 15 August 1947), a group of South Asians—clad in saris, sunglasses, t-shirts and colourful kurtas—stood behind a set of iron barricades as the annual India Day Parade unfolded in front of them along Fifth Avenue. Anyone who has been to the India Day Parade knows it is a sight to behold: a multiplicity of languages, religions, cultures; a cacophony of histories and legacies—all complicated, all diverse, and all wrapped up into one glorious package, multicoloured and multicultural. The India Day Parade marks a powerful moment each year for the South Asian diaspora which—with all of its cleavages, classes, and political affiliations—comes together to celebrate the largest democracy in the world.

As the parade route ended, however, it was impossible to miss a certain group standing prominently and fixedly in place behind a series of iron barricades that prevented them from marching. The group was the South Asian Lesbian and Gay Association (SALGA), and its members had, for at least the fifth time in a decade, been formally denied entry to the parade celebrating the birth of the same nation that had given birth to so many of them.[1] On several prior occasions, the Federation of Indian Associations (FIA), which organizes the parade, had denied SALGA the right to march, and had done the same to a women's anti-domestic violence group, Sakhi, on the grounds that both groups were "antinational".[2] In 2009, when contacted by an acquaintance for an explanation, Dipak Patel, the president of the tri-state FIA, stated that "anyone is welcome to march", but quickly added that there is an application process for organizations and, like college admissions, "some people get in, some people don't."

Like most stories that involve civil rights, there are some spectacular moments of irony in SALGA's exclusion from the 2009 India Day Parade in New York City. Just weeks before, the very same group had been invited to march, front and centre, in the city's annual gay pride parade. SALGA's presence at the pride event was punctuated by an event that most South Asians had not expected: the overturning of sodomy laws by the Delhi High Court, four days later, in a soaring, comprehensive declaration of equality in a case called *Naz Foundation v. Government of NCT*,[3] which became one of the most popular stories in the *New York Times* that week.[4]

In stark contrast, just a month after the opinion was handed down, at the India Day Parade, SALGA members held signs and chanted behind barricades to draw attention to their exclusion. One sign held by a young woman read, "Indian. Gay. Proud." Another person stood firmly in the middle while wearing a blush pink T-shirt with the words "Legalize Gay" written on the front in purple. Another picture, perhaps, said it best: "Queers (heart) Equality", the sign read, in large magic marker lettering, with an enlarged "Past Due" stamp placed conspicuously at the bottom.

For a moment, imagine the symbolism created by the juxtaposition of these two events. Both moments are about how themes of inclusion and exclusion operate as undercurrents in citizenship. SALGA's absence at the India Day Parade takes place at the very same moment that the Indian Constitution was interpreted in the *Naz Foundation* case to demand just the opposite. At the India Day

Parade just one month after the judgment, queer South Asians were relegated to the sidelines in New York City. One moment celebrates the international trajectory of gay and lesbian civil rights, whereas another traffics heavily in the domain of cultural disenfranchisement.

The juxtaposition of these events provides a painful, lingering reminder of the limits of the law in changing the face of culture and citizenship. For some of us, the summer of 2009 will probably remain the unique moment in which both areas collided, requiring us to contemplate the role of the dual trajectories of inclusion and exclusion in both constitutional law and culture. The confluence of events—a very public slap in the face by the South Asian community on Indian Independence Day, coupled with the landmark judgment on gay rights in India that same summer—is well worth considering, not merely for the civil rights issues that it embodies, but also because it highlights the fluidity of concepts like migration, citizenship, and diaspora in forming—and reforming—those issues for a broader legal community.

As this story suggests, we have arrived at a crossroads in terms of the intersection between law, sexuality, and globalization. Within the United States where, in prior decades, gays and lesbians offered radical critiques of family and marriage, today many have abandoned those positions in favour of all the rights and privileges associated with the conventional nuclear family. The claims for LGBT rights and equality, tied as they are to the state and to state-sanctioned equality within the legal system, thus also indirectly extend state regulation into the private sphere, unquestionably reifying the state's primary role in liberating the LGBT citizen.[5] Globally speaking, inasmuch as these claims are tied to the formal, neoliberal language of rights and recognition, they also run the risk of overlooking some of the limitations embodied in legal claims to equality, obscuring some of the deeper, distributive inequalities with respect to gender, ethnicity, class, and race that persist despite the opportunities that citizenship has to offer.

The rise of liberal claims to rights and recognition thus carries with it some important global considerations. Historically, and even today, "the majority of accounts of queer migration tend to remain organized around a narrative of movement from repression to freedom, or a heroic journey undertaken in search of liberation."[6] Within this narrative, the United States is usually cast as a land of opportunity and liberation, a place that represents freedom from discrimination and economic opportunity. But this narrative also elides the complexity that erupts from grappling with the reality that many other jurisdictions outside of the United States can be even more forward looking when it comes to recognizing the need for LGBT civil rights, as the Delhi High Court opinion demonstrates, and the fact that many immigrants to the United States may confront a political reality (either at the hands of fellow immigrants or others) that is far less welcoming than the enduring plasticity of the "American dream" itself.

Perhaps, however, we might consider these caveats, not as limitations on a singular theme of citizenship, but instead as formidable opportunities for undertaking a cultural reimagination of citizenship altogether. Towards this end, this chapter attempts to provide one vantage point in theorizing the bipolar classifications that characterize globalization narratives. It argues that the concept of a diaspora offers us a powerful theoretical lens with which to unpack the polarizing themes that often characterize the intersection of law, sexuality, and citizenship. It takes as its starting point this observation by Stuart Hall:

> The diaspora experience [...] is defined, not by essence or purity, but by the recognition of a necessary heterogeneity and diversity; by a conception of 'identity' which lives with and through, not despite, difference; by hybridity. Diaspora identities are those which are constantly producing and reproducing themselves anew, through transformation and difference.[7]

As Hall suggests, the notion of a diaspora forces us to confront the reality of cultural hybridities in motion, but his insights also help us contemplate how these cultural hybridities might aid us in re-envisioning citizenship itself.

In this chapter, I argue that the idea of a diaspora represents a useful vantage point for theorizing the intersection between sexuality, law, and globalization. I attempt to interrogate what the concept of the diaspora might hold for legal scholars contemplating both the cultural and constitutional architecture of citizenship, particularly as the diaspora intersects with global sexualities. In attempting to capture some of the new conflicts that have arisen in these realms, this chapter uses the notion of a diaspora both as a theoretical device and as a doctrinal tool with which to analyze some key constitutional developments in the global legal and cultural regulation of sexuality. Not only do considerations of sexuality transform the concept of a diaspora, but considerations of the concept of a diaspora transform our thinking on sexuality as well. The concept's particular utility stems from its privileging of hybrid possibilities, particularly in recalibrating and reimagining the lines that we draw between North and South, East and West, home and elsewhere, and the inside and outside of the law.

Towards that end, this chapter introduces two conceptions of a diaspora, one cultural, another constitutional. In the first part of this piece, I introduce the cultural notion of an LGBT diaspora among peoples and the communities, real or imagined, that flow from it. Later, I broaden this concept to introduce a secondary conception of a constitutional diaspora while evaluating the role of legal hybridity in the wake of India's notable sodomy jurisprudence. Through these, I evaluate what these two types of diaspora offer us in terms of reimagining the terrains of nationhood and citizenship.

THE QUEER DIASPORA

Recent scholarship, legal and otherwise, has elucidated the ways in which the diaspora destabilizes the fixedness of the nation state, the concept of citizenship, and the idea of a cultural identity itself. Pico Iyer writes, the diaspora—the concept—covers "people [who are] are strangers to everywhere including their homes." As a result, they "are rooted in ideas rather than places."[8] The notion of relying on diasporic outsiders to evaluate the utility of identity-based categories—precisely because they defy these classifications altogether—is not a new innovation.[9]

More recently, however, a few legal scholars have offered us a wealth of insights about the function of law and the diaspora in regulating and idealizing the concept of citizenship, and also about the function of culture in transcending legal fixtures.[10] Yet, for the most part, very little diasporic legal scholarship contemplates the global growth of the LGBT civil rights movement. The term "queer diaspora", for example, while heavily cited and discussed in humanities scholarship,[11] is nowhere to be found in the corresponding legal literature. A search on Westlaw reveals only a few citations to the term.

Yet in making their demonstration at the India Day Parade, SALGA sought to use the power of its political presence to make an important point about how the queer diaspora actually plays a formative role in crafting the idea of a dissenting community by occupying the interstices of the uninvited. In crafting their dissent, the SALGA organizers, in their own small ways, craft their own micro-perspective of what a nation includes and excludes, in ways only perceptible to those who are present to watch the spectacle unfold.

Like so many other outsider groups facing such challenges, the LGBT marchers were spurred into crafting a more complex—indeed, a much more transnational—statement of dissent. "The [Delhi] court stated powerfully and succinctly that intolerance is not an Indian value," SALGA said in its statement. "Despite such a monumental victory for sexual minorities in India, we are outraged and disappointed that [...] the FIA is once again trying to make Indian sexual minorities invisible through its discriminatory acts."[12]

Borders of national, cultural and juridical identity become transformed as a result of such dissenting actions. SALGA's statement explicitly links its vision of inclusion and citizenship to one that is offered, not by an American court, but by an Indian one. In other words, a moment of exclusion in the diaspora can compel greater ties to transnationalism, enabling a burst of emotional, cultural, and even socio-legal connections between diaspora and homeland.

Like the story that I told in the introduction, there is something quite poetic about LGBT groups marching, full of celebration, in the homeland, even when members of the diaspora refuse to acknowledge them elsewhere. As countless newspapers recounted, as the *Naz Foundation* decision was being filed in 2008, several cities across India—New Delhi, Bangalore, and Kolkata—played host to their own gay pride parades, for the first time in history. "Up until now, we've been in the public space protesting a violation, or someone being beaten up," stated Gautam Bhan, one of the New Delhi parade organizers in 2008. "Now we feel like we have enough of a foothold to celebrate a positive presence."[13] After the opinion was handed down a year later, hundreds of gay rights supporters marched, again in New Delhi, Chennai, Bangalore, and elsewhere. In cities across the United States and in other countries, members of the South Asian queer diaspora, like SALGA, gathered in watchful celebration of the singular legal moment that *Naz Foundation* produced.

As this story suggests, the very space of an LGBT diaspora is marked by a dynamic hybridity between nations, sexualities, and loyalties that often elides simple classifications. By creating a space between an immigrant and a place of origin, a diaspora also creates the opportunity to reimagine the boundaries of a nation altogether. Diasporas are located somewhere between the global and the local.[14] The classic literature defines a diaspora in terms of three main elements: (a) dispersion across space, usually comprising the crossing of a group of individuals across state borders; (b) some form of "homeland orientation", which posits a country of origin as a source of ancestry, identity, collective memory, and connection; and (c) some preservation of boundaries or separation from mainstream society, which usually takes the varied form of resistance to complete assimilation (at times but not always as a result of social exclusion).[15] Diasporic individuals live in the in-between, the liminal, the "third space" according to Homi Bhabha,[16] such that individuals who live "here" and "there" are "caught in the discontinuous time of translation and negotiation."[17]

But a diaspora is itself a contradiction in terms. It relies on a fixed conception of the nation state for its very identity between home and homeland, even as it challenges the concept of the nation state altogether.[18] Somewhat similarly for the individual, the concept of belonging to a diaspora can be a positive or a negative experience, and sometimes simultaneously so. James Clifford notes that the concept of the diaspora can be forged in a negative fashion, through experiences of discrimination and exclusion in the destination state, but can be forged positively too, through an increased identification with global cultural or political forces.[19]

Although the concept of a diaspora has become an integral part of immigration law and of citizenship studies, few legal scholars have attempted to mine the insights gleaned from diasporic studies in the humanities. This absence is somewhat puzzling, especially given that every moment of migration is heavily inscribed by the role of both international and domestic law in creating and regulating a diasporic identity. Further, when we apply the concept of diaspora to the notion of an LGBT or queer identity, we face even more complications and complementarities. One must simultaneously, then, engage in the act of "queering the diaspora", as well as "diasporizing the queer".[20]

The lesbian and gay civil rights movement has historically operated under the dual influence of opposites.[21] One tends towards a minoritizing discourse that looks towards an ethnic model of largely fixed LGBT identity; and the other, conversely, focuses on a universalizing view of sexuality that recognizes the fluidity and breadth of same-sex desires within all individuals.[22] And yet, the ethnic model, particularly because it is so deeply steeped in the scripts of civil rights claims, and so attractive for this reason, often requires a delicate crafting and re-scripting of identities, often overlooking the limitations of a rights-based, neoliberal framework.

An ethnic model of LGBT identity, which necessarily focuses on sameness rather than difference, can be useful in casting the legitimacy of group-based claims to civil rights in the United States. However, this model, as many have noted, tends to underestimate individual variations in the formation of identity, particularly where sexual identity is concerned. Alice Miller's powerful work on asylum points out how law's privileging tendency most often prefers "fixed identities", that is, identities that "map neatly and recognizably onto conduct".[23] The rights-based framework that law imposes often requires LGBT people to compartmentalize identities in order to allow for claims to be considered viable under existing civil rights discourses.[24] Somewhat similarly, David William Foster has written about the difficulty of applying the concept of a diaspora—originally used to refer to the forced dispersion of Jews, and later to any type of forced exile of a particular group—to the kind of individualized paradigm of solitary flight that usually characterizes the experiences of LGBT people.[25]

In one sense, then, it seems difficult to apply the idea of a "diaspora" to an LGBT identity, given the diversity and variance that each identity comprises. Where is the "homeland" that the queer citizen aspires to, when each country is fraught with limitations on LGBT equality, and when so many individuals have identities that diverge from a fixed and stable notion of LGBT identity within each? The moments of exclusion in each paradigm offer meaningful opportunities for cultural dissent for those excluded from participation, but they also facilitate the creation of new transnational connections between the place of migration and the homeland. Indeed, as applied to sexuality, the concept of a queer diaspora, in its multinational, multicultural architecture, can also offer the LGBT citizen a way to craft an identity that does not necessarily require the adoption of a singular, fixed identity connected to citizenship. Thus, just as the idea of a diaspora challenges the fixedness of a nation state and place of origin,[26] the notion of a *queer* diaspora challenges the idea of a diaspora that presumes heterosexuality within its community. As the political theorist Simon Watney explains, the metaphor of a diaspora is "seductively convenient to contemporary queer politics."[27] He continues:

Unlike the tendency of seventies and eighties lesbian and gay theory to develop overly monolithic notions of identity and cultural politics, the concept of diaspora is suggestive of diversification, of scattering, fracturing, separate developments, and also, perhaps of a certain glamour. It also suggests something of a sense of collective interest, however difficult this may be to pin down. It implies a complex divided constituency, with varying degrees of power and powerlessness.[28] In this sense, the concept of a diaspora can operate both as a site of legal regulation but also as a site of theoretical resistance to and contestation of a unitary LGBT identity.[29]

Furthermore, the very idea of the diaspora might provide us with a better framework to understand the racial and sexual identity formation of immigrants of colour, who are often shaped between the domestic and the diasporic worlds that they inhabit.[30] Consider SALGA as one example. As Svati Shah explains, back in the early 1990s, the FIA explained its refusal of SALGA's request by claiming that "homosexuality does not exist in India", suggesting that the group's "participation would not accurately depict the reality of Indian communities."[31] At that time, then, SALGA's inclusion in the parade was about redefining these political scripts, by insisting on other ways of defining and understanding community, culture, and affiliation, outside of a logic of religious nationalism. Shah writes,

> [i]f SALGA's exclusion was emblematic of the ways in which the Indian Right had attempted to dictate a unilateral notion of 'authentic' Indian culture, SALGA's participation represented the undeniable existence of the life that exists outside the bounds of that representation.[32]

An additional audience, however, involved a certain puncturing of the conventional image of the "gay" citizen—the largely white, upper-class image of the gay community in the United States. Queer South Asian activists didn't draw inspiration purely from the mainstream US gay and lesbian civil rights movement, with all of its marginalization of issues of class and race, but rather a broader, transnational platform that placed a spectrum of issues of international disenfranchisement on the table, whether they involved race, national origin, religion, class, AIDS, or sexuality. By enabling SALGA's overall mission to bring these concerns to the fore alongside other issues of sexual orientation, SALGA, along with other groups, articulated a profound divergence from more mainstream (but certainly not all) gay and lesbian civil rights organizations in the United States.

As these two audiences demonstrate, the sort of compartmentalization that is required to build a constituency among gay- or lesbian-identified people also limits it in important ways as well.[33] Especially for queer people of colour, the prominence of a single model—are you in or are you out?—makes it more difficult to negotiate ways of thinking about sexualities that are compatible with the various subcultures of family, neighborhood, ethnicity and culture.[34] Yet this reality can also be a source of fertile possibilities, as these cultural hybridities enable a person to belong to a variety of different communities—a mainstream host culture, a diasporic community, a dominant queer community, and a diasporic LGBT community—simultaneously challenging the stereotypes associated with each one.[35] As an Asian American activist has written:

> We who occupy the interstices—whose very lives contain disparate selves—are, of necessity, at home among various groups that know little of each other [...] We have a deep hunger for a place in which we can be, at one and the same time, whole, and part of something larger than ourselves.[36]

Ten or more years after these words were written, the concept of the diaspora still provides a great deal of fruitful terrain for scholars writing at the margins of identity and globalization.

The notion of a queer diaspora thus captures an oppositional set of themes stemming from the intersection of transnationality and sexuality, one involving homogenization and another involving differentiation. As some of my prior work has argued, the typical concepts of gay and lesbian do not always capture the complexity of sexual identity formation, particularly in cultures with a strong sense of separation between one's sexual behavior and one's outward identity.[37] Thus, by emphasizing a particularized, singular idea of lesbian and gay identity, Western activists often miss some of the more complicated hybridities and identity formations within same-sex sexualities, particularly (but not exclusively) in the non-Western world.

A brief glimpse at this context therefore exposes some limitations in translating gay identity paradigms to cultures that lack Western assumptions regarding the centrality of sexuality to personhood. Nevertheless, popular discussions of sexuality in Asia and elsewhere tend to suggest the West as the source of sexual modernity, where "queer Asia has tended to be recognised to the extent that it articulates with first world metropoles, for example, through queer life in diasporic communities, or through northern consumption of select cultural products from the global south."[38] At times, LGBT advocates stress the "homophobia of third-world traditions", implying that "modernisation will make the non-Western world more liberated for queers."[39] As scholar Ara Wilson argues, "Even when they are critical of Western dominance in the world, as is the case with nationalists and many sexual-rights advocates, this interpretation recapitulates Western hegemony, by locating the origin and agency of modern queer life squarely in the West."[40] The logic of import/export often informs these discussions, suggesting that legible identities are derived from Western concepts of sexuality.

Again, however, the concept of a diaspora may be useful in navigating these conflicts. First, the idea of a queer diaspora captures the broad connections forged between LGBT-identified individuals across jurisdictions between North and South, East and West, helping to shed light on some of the limitations of a singular global model of gay or lesbian identity. Second, it also suggests the idea that each locality offers in its own decentralized interpretation of those connections, sometimes even in opposition to the dominant identity categories of gay and lesbian.

At times, what emerges from the constellation of transnational loyalties between those in the United States and India is also the birth of a diasporic community with experiences that recognize, at times, the need to challenge the typical progression from "in" to "out" that characterizes so many gay and lesbian narratives. The concept of a queer diaspora, as one example of this trend, enables the creation and study of alternative identities and communities that not only demonstrate different forms of subjectivity, culture, citizenship, and loyalty, but also, in some ways, bear "little resemblance to the universalized 'gay' identity imagined within a Eurocentric gay imaginary."[41] Within this narrative, for example, a queer diaspora tends to re-write colonial constructions of third world sexualities, demonstrating that they are not "anterior, premodern and in need of Western political development," as Gayatri Gopinath points out, but rather reconstitute conceptions of nationhood, identity and citizenship.[42]

The architecture of the queer diaspora thus extends from the private sphere of the home to the global, public sphere of the transnational, reworking the idea of home and homeland in the process. Indeed, within the diaspora, particularly the queer diaspora, members are constantly rethinking—and reconstituting—their relationship to the concept of home.[43] According to Martin Manalansan, the everyday is a crucial site that enables queers in the diaspora to both create new selves and forge new relationships among marginalized groups.[44] "Diasporic queers in particular refuse the assimilative framework," explains Manalansan, "they not so much carry with them the baggage of tradition but rather are in constant negotiation [...] selfhood and belonging are framed in the process of cultural translation and transformation."[45] Not only do these narratives demonstrate that we must view nation, diaspora, and citizenship as crucially connected, but we must also see how each reinforces, reimagines, and reconstitutes the other.

THE CONSTITUTIONAL DIASPORA: THE EMERGENCE OF CONSTITUTIONAL REGIONALISM

In the previous section, I highlighted some ways in which persons within the diaspora are able to traverse various boundaries and craft particular forms of hybrid identities between the point of destination and the homeland. In similar ways, legal doctrines and legal agendas can also migrate to other jurisdictions, producing a variety of generative effects that can be either progressive or regressive in nature, depending on the context. They can also engender a revolution of constitutional borrowing across jurisdictions, giving rise to multiple doctrinal hybridities, as demonstrated by the *Naz Foundation v. Government of NCT* opinions.[46]

In sum, the same themes that we examined above—notions of home, nation, the dyad between the domestic and the transnational, the theme of migration in the era of transient borders—are not just suited to examining the transnational movement of peoples, but may also be appropriate in examining the circulation of legal principles as well. Indeed, the legal issue in *Naz Foundation*, India's anti-sodomy law Section 377, was a product of British colonization, an exportation that was enacted in a variety of colonies, and then, in the case of India, Singapore, and others, has persisted long after the demise of colonialism. As a historical matter, among the 80 states that have sodomy laws, over half of them, like India and Uganda, inherited them as a byproduct of British colonialism.[47] For this reason, queer activists have often linked their efforts to overturn Section 377 to the legacy of Indian independence.[48]

Earlier, I suggested that the dominant theme of LGBT migration tends to offer a polarizing view of the United States and the West as a site of gay and lesbian liberation, often eliding the complexities faced by many immigrants and people of colour, who navigate a complex intersectionality between race, citizenship and sexual orientation.[49] The same trend translates to the realm of law, where, at times, non-Western jurisdictions are often painted as premodern and constitutionally less developed, in comparison to the West.

The migrations of legal principles, particularly, as they often occur, from Western to non-Western jurisdictions, also tend to facilitate a similar kind of simplistic polarity that at times offers the West as analytically and constitutionally more sophisticated than other, non-Western jurisdictions, thus suggesting that Western legal principles are deserving of an unparalleled level of exportation.

For this reason, it is important to see how the notion of a *constitutional* diaspora can engender further legal developments that also help to deconstruct the bipolar divides between East and West, North and South, that often complicate the discussions surrounding gay and lesbian equality. Perhaps most importantly, polarizing accounts that focus on the primacy of the West in gay liberation struggles miss powerful opportunities to learn from other developments outside of the West in terms of imagining LGBT equality. Indeed, one might consider *Naz Foundation*, because of its heavy reliance on non-Western treatments of sexual orientation in law and culture, a jurisprudential emergence of a constitutional regionalism, signifying the development of a new direction in the regulation of sexuality in the Global South.

The trend among LGBT activists is to presume that activists elsewhere can learn much from law and theory in the West; I think it is far more instructive for us to explore what the West can learn from the trend towards constitutional borrowing *within* non-Western nations and the creation of an alternative constitutional diaspora in the process.[50]

The Emergence of Constitutional Regionalism

In some very important work, Holning Lau has pointed to a variety of progressive developments throughout Asia, arguing that it is important to challenge the "imagination of Asia as a region void of any protection of sexual orientation and gender identity rights." He points to a chapter published in the William and Mary Law Review, where two authors argued that Justices Kennedy, in drafting

Lawrence, decided not to cite cases from Asia on the grounds that "gay rights are nonexistent" there.[51]

Yet as Lau points out, contrary to this perception, by the time *Lawrence* was handed down in 2003, a variety of Asian nations had already decriminalized sodomy laws; Japan (1882), Thailand (1956), Hong Kong (1991), and Fiji (1997) respectively. He points, in addition, to a recent South Korean Supreme Court ruling that held that transsexuals have a right to the recognition of their gender identity as one powerful example of how non-Western jurisdictions can be much more forward looking and far less monolithic in their perceived opposition to sexual minorities than those in the West might perceive. In Hong Kong, Lau notes several recent decisions that demand equal treatment for same-sex couples under public indecency laws, a case imposing anti-discrimination protections against a broadcasting authority that objected to a television documentary on same-sex couples, and a transgender marriage case that is moving through the judicial system.

Compared to the United States, which has yet to extend federal protections to individuals on the basis of sexual orientation, in 2008, Taiwan amended its employment discrimination law to include protections based on sexual orientation.[52] In addition, while the United States has almost no federal protections based on gender identity, in 2009, the Pakistan Supreme Court held that transgender individuals, known as *hijras*, had the right to be recognized as a third sex and to be free from police harassment.[53] All of these examples discount the perception that LGBT rights are nonexistent in Asia.

Many of these developments culminated in the Delhi court opinion, *Naz Foundation*, handed down in 2009. As I suggest below, *Naz* is an important opinion, not just for its rejection of sodomy laws, but also for its studied integration of non-Western comparative constitutionalism, which one might argue offers an example of regionalism that serves as a counterpart to the perception of LGBT rights as a Western import.

The first legal challenge to India's law banning 'crimes against the order of nature', Section 377, was filed in 1994, pursuant to an observation by one official, Kiran Bedi, who observed that she could not distribute condoms in prison to prevent the spread of HIV because she would be abetting a violation of Section 377.[54] The petition was dismissed at first, but several high-profile lawyers from the Lawyers Collective, and others, undertook another challenge to the law in 2001. When the Delhi High Court handed down its judgment in the *Naz Foundation* decision on 2 July 2009, one activist noted, "It was as if a weight had been lifted from our shoulders and one was finally set free."[55]

While the Delhi High Court's *Naz Foundation* decision relied in part on the United States' *Lawrence* decision on sodomy and other cases from the West, it also transcended these decisions by relying on a wider host of non-Western jurisdictions, particularly South Africa, in reaching its conclusions. This is an incredibly important demonstration, I would argue, of constitutional hybridity. Indeed, the *Naz Foundation* opinion can be read as a uniquely powerful example of cosmopolitan constitutional borrowing, balanced with a deep attention to Indian originalism. Not only did the *Naz Foundation* court rely on US jurisprudence, but it drew on decisions from Fiji, South Africa, Hong Kong, Canada, and Nepal.[56] It paid particular attention to Nepal, which enacted constitutional protections based on sexual orientation and gender identity, and which in 2009 actually set up a government panel to study same-sex marriage laws in order to reform its own laws.

Although the court relied on *Lawrence* for critical propositions regarding the role of privacy and autonomy, it relied on many other jurisdictions, as well as on broader United Nations human rights declarations on sexual orientation. Unlike *Lawrence*, which was grounded in notions of privacy and substantive due process, the *Naz Foundation* decision was motivated by four explicit platforms: the rights to privacy, dignity, equality, and non-discrimination.[57] In each of these platforms, in important ways, the Delhi court went far beyond *Lawrence* in its willingness to specify the precise benefits that might flow from decriminalization, and in its willingness to articulate why sodomy laws are contrary to international human rights principles, and unconstitutional under India's own privacy jurisprudence.

Perhaps the first leap from *Lawrence* involved a simple matter of tone and length. Rather than the detached, somewhat impersonal, brief, value-neutral position that the US Supreme Court took in *Lawrence*, the Delhi High Court in *Naz Foundation* displayed not just a cosmopolitan embrace of inclusion, but also an apparent indignance that sodomy laws still stood in India, particularly in light of its detailed discussion of the jurisdictions that had overturned them.[58] As Vikram Raghavan observes,

> *Naz Foundation*'s foreign references include materials from the usual suspects, the United States and the United Kingdom, as well as decisions from unlikely places, such as Hong Kong, Fiji, and Nepal. Those latter decisions are particularly important because they remind the cynic that gay rights aren't some luxurious Western construct.[59]

In the filings surrounding the case, the *Naz Foundation* lawyers drew attention to a number of prominent Indians who are said to have engaged in same-sex affective conduct, as well as "[a]nthropological research [that] has found homosexual subcultures in Native American cultures, ancient Greece, Chinese traditions, sub-Saharan Africa, and the Samurai traditions in Japan."[60] According to one expert, Arvind Narrain,

> It is the [references to same-sex sexuality throughout Indian history that provide] the strongest rebuttal to the notion of queer rights being a western disease—a careful drawing of a narrative that traces the queer as part of 'out' history and embodying a set of practices which exist at times unacknowledged, at others hidden, at yet others struggling to become 'visible'. In more simple terms, queer rights is an issue for Indians because there are queer traditions, queer practices, and queer people in India and rights language is one mode of making this history visible.[61]

Another major difference from the legacy of sodomy opinions in the West involves the comparably heavy absence of identity-based rhetoric in the arguments surrounding the Indian case relative to

Lawrence. The term 'men who have sex with men' (MSM) figured much more prominently than 'gay men', along with the court's willingness to articulate a set of cultural and public health concerns that avoid, and indeed actively transcend, the need for sexual identity and categorization.[62] The opinion spends paragraph after paragraph detailing the goals and objectives of public health education on HIV in an astonishingly comprehensive manner, finding that Section 377 is a powerful impediment to HIV education and the right to health.[63]

Along with the focus on MSM and public health, the opinion also spent a great deal of time and attention on the particular challenges faced by hijras.[64] Siddharth Narrain has argued that the opinion puts transgender equality on a platform that is comparable with sexual orientation equality.[65] For example, *Naz Foundation* cites the Yogyakarta Principles, which detailed the need for protection on the basis of gender identity, in addition to sexual orientation, and discussed cases from Pakistan and Nepal that dealt substantially with the rights of transgender persons. The court details several similar cases affecting a gay man, a lesbian woman, and a transgender person in the same manner, conveying their unacceptable treatment at the hands of the Indian authorities due to Section 377.

Turning towards sexual orientation discrimination, the court evinced a clear transnational impulse in recoding sexual orientation, not just as a powerful characteristic of personhood, but also as an attribute meriting human rights protection. Explicitly borrowing language from the South African Constitutional Court, the Delhi High Court noted that LGBT persons are denied "moral full citizenship", and then launched into an extensive discussion of almost every major case that has overturned sodomy laws—from *Dudgeon v. United Kingdom*[66] to *Norris v. Republic of Ireland*[67] to *Toonen v. Australia.*[68] Returning extensively to South Africa, the court quoted the United Nations High Commissioner for Human Rights, who compared sodomy laws to apartheid and noted their inconsistency "with international law and with traditional values of dignity, inclusion and respect for all."[69]

Not only did the court conclude that Section 377 violated the Indian Constitution based on a spatial notion of privacy, but it also made this conclusion because Section 377 criminalized "individual choices which are central to personal *dignity*."[70] The court then defined the concept of dignity with reference to the Universal Declaration of Human Rights, the International Covenant on Civil and Political Rights, the European Convention on Human Rights, and, most notably, a host of US Supreme Court opinions. While the opinion drew heavily on India's own rich sources of jurisprudence on privacy and dignity, it also drew upon cases from South Africa and related scholarship by Ryan Goodman on how sodomy laws shape a person's identity and self-esteem.[71]

Yet, in contrast to *Lawrence*, which limited its observations to the context of mostly spatial privacy, and only tangentially alluded to the issue of equality, the *Naz Foundation* opinion put equality front and centre—and established a strong claim for equal protection on the basis of sexual orientation in the process. In doing so, *Naz Foundation* transcended *Lawrence* by treating discrimination on the basis of sexual orientation as analogous to sex discrimination, and chose to apply strict scrutiny to Section 377, in stark contrast to *Lawrence*.[72] Towards the end of the opinion, the court emphasizes its role as a guarantor of fundamental rights. In doing so, the *Naz Foundation* court lent itself to the belief that its role was not just to protect citizens from the state, but also to protect citizens from one another. In sum, we can see how in each of the aspects I have mentioned—an offering of an affirmative notion of privacy, a willingness to consider sexual orientation discrimination as sex discrimination, and a refusal to diminish the meaning of same-sex relationships to the value of personhood—*Naz Foundation* transcends a great deal of Western jurisprudence in powerful ways.

Recall, for example, that *Lawrence* refused "morality" as a basis for legal provisions by citing a line in Stevens' *Bowers* dissent: "[T]he fact that the governing majority in a state has traditionally viewed a particular practice as immoral is not a sufficient reason for upholding a law prohibiting the practice." In stark contrast, the *Naz Foundation* opinion *reforms* rather than *abandons* morality in powerful ways. In an interesting twist, the *Naz Foundation* court noted, "If there is any type of 'morality' that can pass the test of compelling state interest, it must be 'constitutional morality' and not public morality."[73] In making this statement, the court notes that it is the stigmatizing and criminalizing of the LGBT community that is against constitutional morality, not the act of sodomy.[74] The court observed that the Indian Constitution "recognizes, protects, and celebrates diversity", and that the stigmatization or criminalization of gay people "would be against the constitutional morality".[75]

In short, the Delhi court offered human rights advocates and the nascent LGBT movement in India a triumphant win, both for the forcefulness of its findings as well as for its relentless eloquence in favour of the civil rights and equality of sexual minorities. Indian legal scholar Lawrence Liang observed that *Naz Foundation* is India's *Roe v. Wade*—as Vikram Raghavan echoes, "a rare opportunity for activists to reshape public opinion and influence a wider social debate about gay rights", a point that is particularly poignant, given that wider support from the legislature is needed as well.[76]

TOWARDS TRANSNATIONAL CITIZENSHIP

As I have suggested throughout this chapter, both types of diaspora—of persons and of constitutional principles—are movements that rewrite the meaning of the nation state and citizenship.[77] Both narratives also illustrate the ways in which the two types of diaspora transcend borders and remake the idea of nationhood in the process.

Benedict Anderson's famous book *Imagined Communities* powerfully postulated that a nation is conceived, not as a reality, but as a collective work of imagination that has emerged from the circulation of capital and the rise of print communication.[78] Regarding global sexualities, law assists in the process of imagining the nation by mapping a highly generalized series of identities onto the diversity of human experience, even as those identities reveal themselves to be highly dependent on context, time, and place. And although cases like *Lawrence* and *Naz Foundation* represent a particular moment in the development of gay and lesbian civil rights, they can also offer other jurisdictions particular insights about the utility and universality of particular categories and principles. The architecture of each opinion often charts the path to future challenges regarding the ultimate trajectory of LGBT civil rights and offers a vantage point to those of us contemplating the limitations and possibilities of citizenship.

For some activists, *Naz Foundation* represented the emergence of the idea of "sexual citizenship"[79] in South Asia. One might argue that in the court's painting of the notion of LGBT equality in India in such broad, lofty strokes, especially through the employment of Nehru's timeless statements about the need for inclusion, the *Naz Foundation* court was essentially extending the hand of citizenship—utterly unmistakably so—to queer minorities. One of the most prominent leaders of the gay rights movement in India, Arvind Narrain, writes of the "radical potential" of the idea of citizenship "to represent the rights of groups that have historically been marginalized."[80]

Even outside of India, elsewhere in the globe, *Naz Foundation* might signify the emergence of a new form of regional cultural citizenship that is based, in part, on the transnational loyalties that a diaspora facilitates. "As queer South Asians in the diaspora," Gopinath has asserted, "'citizenship', queer or otherwise, is not something that we can ever take for granted." Instead, as Gopinath suggests, the queer diaspora creates a multiplicity of collective spaces in the face of state regulation—spaces that are always mobile, always contingent, and always dynamically formed in relation to the nation.[81] A case like *Naz Foundation*, inasmuch as it relies on constitutional principles from both within and outside of the West, can signify the migration of those principles and be embraced by the diaspora elsewhere, as SALGA's experience suggests. The migration of legal principles that informs both *Naz Foundation* and *Lawrence* also further facilitates the forging of new global possibilities through a dynamic borrowing of legal principles.

Note, however, that although *Naz Foundation* opens a new world of possibility, it is still circumscribed by many of the limitations of formal claims to LGBT equality. As Ratna Kapur has pointed out, the dominant theme of tolerance, so apparent in the *Naz Foundation* opinion, does not always pave the way towards LGBT equality, nor does it offer a transformative kind of emancipation.[82] When claims to LGBT equality seem based on a universal logic, Kapur writes, "tolerance becomes the tool for handling that difference that formal equality is unable to accommodate or address."[83] Thus, Kapur suggests that, rather than actually advancing the cause of sexual liberation, *Naz Foundation*, along with other court cases and concomitant rights claims, may be limited in their victory.[84] Tolerance, she writes, "does not offer any vision of transformation, but becomes a substitute for justice, where the difference of the 'Other' is accommodated rather than her injury addressed."[85] Further, "while there is an appearance of magnanimity on the part of the majority or the state, in fact the extension of tolerance constitutes a way in which to sustain dominant sexual, familial and cultural norms."[86]

Indeed, Kapur is certainly asking the most important question: What are the limits of tolerance within a legal framework? Both forms of diaspora—of peoples and of legal principles—give rise to transnational loyalties that indirectly tinker with the fixed notions that we attach to citizenship, and help us reimagine a liberation that can be just as dispersed across jurisdictions as the diaspora itself. These transnational loyalties have transformative potential. Just as SALGA's protests reformed the presumed heterosexuality of the Indian diaspora, they also reformed the stereotypes associated with the gay and lesbian movement in the United States. And *Naz Foundation*, as it becomes reframed as a commentary on—and a transcendence of—*Lawrence*'s limitations, helps us imagine a more regional and inclusive approach to comparative constitutional interpretation. Our path to the future will be informed by the success—or failure—of this transnational possibility.

CONCLUSION

On 15 August 1947, precisely at midnight, the Constituent Assembly, which consisted of representatives selected by the Indian people, took a solemn oath of office to serve the people of India. "The appointed day has come, the day appointed by destiny—and India stands forth again after long slumber and struggle—awake, vital, free and independent," Pandit Jawaharlal Nehru said on that morning. For those who remember that day, it was marked by the newfound awareness that this crowded, populous nation—poor, fledgling, and plagued by its own civil strife—could rise up against the edifices of colonization, and successfully give birth to what stands today as the largest democracy in the world. Even to this day, India's victory over Britain—indeed, over the very legacy that ruled India for centuries—remains an unparalleled, even dazzling, moment in global history, one that marked the triumph of the meek, the poor and the colonized over a monastic imperiality.

Let us briefly fast forward to another moment 62 years later. A group of queer South Asians have gathered at the Stonewall Inn in New York City at 7:30 p.m. precisely, to mark another historical moment in the birth of gay rights. As they gather, clinking glasses, celebrations have been underway in every major city in India to mark the Delhi High Court's decision to overturn sodomy laws in India. The moment is crucial, not just for its legal importance, but also for its cultural significance in the non-Western world. The strident extension of equality and civil rights to sexual minorities in India is a powerfully emblematic moment—just as the photographs of hundreds of queer activists standing outside of the Delhi High Court suggest.

NOTES

1. Minal Hajratwala, *"Gay Hind": NY India Day Parade Draws Protesters*, Minal Hajratwala (Aug. 16, 2009), http://minalhajratwala.com/gay-hind-ny-india-day-parade-draws-protesters/.

2. Several chapters have explored the history of SALGA's exclusion from the India Day Parade. *See for example* Gayatri Gopinath, *Local Sites/Global Contexts: The Transnational Trajectories of Deepa Mehta's Fire*, *in* Queer Globalizations 149 (A. Cruz-Malavé & M.F. Manalansan IV eds., 2002); Svati P. Shah, *Out and Out Radical: New Directions for Progressive Organizing*, 14 Samar (2001); Minal Hajratwala, *Gays Shut Out of the Parade*, ColorLines (Aug. 19, 2009), https://www.colorlines.com/articles/gays-shut-out-parade.
3. Naz Foundation v. Govt. of NCT of Delhi, (2009) 160 DLT 277.
4. *See* Law and Social Sciences Research Network, *Vikram Raghavan on Naz Foundation–Part 1*, LASSnet (Oct. 07, 2009, 9:09 AM), http://lassnet.blogspot.com/2009/07/vikram-raghavan-on-naz-foundation-part_10.html. This notes that the New York Times' story on the Naz Foundation judgement was among the top 10 most popular stories on the newspaper's website.
5. For an excellent discussion of this point, see David L. Eng, *Freedom and the Racialization of Intimacy*, *in* A Companion to Lesbian, Gay, Bisexual, Transgender, and Queer Studies 38–59 & 41 (G. Haggerty & M. McGarry eds., 2007).
6. Eithne Luibhéid, *Introduction: Queer Migration and Citizenship, in* Queer Migrations: Sexuality, US Citizenship, and Border Crossings xxv (E. Luibhéid & L. Cantú Jr. eds., 2005).
7. Stuart Hall, *Cultural Identity and Diaspora*, *in* Identity: Community, Culture, Difference 235 (J. Rutherford ed., 1998) (emphasis omitted).
8. Pico Iyer, *Living in the Transit Lounge*, *in* Unrooted Childhoods: Memoirs of Growing Up Global 11 (F. Eidse & N. Sichel eds., 2004).
9. For a discussion on the notion of diaspora, *see* Robin Cohen, Global Diasporas: An Introduction (1997); Paul Gilroy, The Black Atlantic: Modernity and Double Consciousness (1993); Gabriel Sheffer, Modern Diasporas in International Politics (1986); James Clifford, *Diasporas*, 9 Cult. Anthropol. 302 (1994); Hall, *supra* note 7; Rogers Brubaker, *The 'Diaspora' Diaspora*, 28 Ethnic & Racial Stud. 1 (2005); John Lie, *From International Migration to Transnational Diaspora*, 24 Contemp. Soc. 303 (1995); Bhikhu Parek, *Some Reflections on the Indian Diaspora*, 3 J. Contemp. Thought 105 (1993).
10. For some examples of this work, *see* Kim Barry, *Home and Away: The Construction of Citizenship in an Emigration Context*, 81 N.Y.U. L. Rev. 11, 26–27 (2006); Anupam Chander, *Diaspora Bonds*, 76 N.Y.U. L. Rev. 1005, 1006 (2001); Robin Cohen, *Diasporas and the Nation State: From Victims to Challengers*, 72 Int'l Aff. 507, 517 (1996); Symposium, *A Tribute to the Work of Kim Barry: The Construction of Citizenship in an Emigration Context*, 81 N.Y.U. L. Rev. 1 (2006).
11. There is a large body of scholarship on the concepts of queer diaspora, migration, and globalization. For an excellent collection of essays, *see* Eithne Luibhéid, *Queer/Migration: An Unruly Body of Scholarship*, 14 GLQ 169 (2008); and Queer Migrations, *supra* note 6. *See also* M. Jacqui Alexander, Pedagogies of Crossing: Meditations on Feminism, Sexual Politics, Memory,

and the Sacred (2005); Lionel Cantú Jr., The Sexuality of Migration: Border Crossing and Mexican Immigrant Men (N.A. Naples & S. Vidal-Ortiz eds., 2009); Oliva M. Espín, Women Crossing Boundaries: A Psychology of Immigration and Transformation of Sexuality (1999); Anne-Marie Fortier, *Queer Diaspora, in* Handbook of Lesbian and Gay Studies 183 (D. Richardson & S. Seidman eds., 2002); Anne-Marie Fortier, Migrant Belongings: Memory, Space, Identity (2000); Martin F. Manalansan IV, Global Divas: Filipino Gay Men in Diaspora (2003); Martin F. Manalansan IV, *In the Shadows of Stonewall: Examining Gay Transnational Politics and the Diasporic Dilemma, in* The Politics of Culture in the Shadow of Capital 485 (L. Lowe & D. Lloyd eds., 1997); Passing Lines: Sexuality and Immigration (Brad Epps et al. eds., 2005); Postcolonial and Queer Theories: Intersections and Essays (John Hawley ed., 2001); Queer Diasporas (Cindy Patton & Benigno Sánchez-Eppler eds., 2000); Simon Watney, *AIDS and the Politics of Queer Diaspora, in* Negotiating Lesbian and Gay Subjects 53 (M. Dorenkamp & R. Henke eds., 1995).

12. Hajratwala, *supra* note 1.
13. Heidi J. Shrager, *India's Gay Rights Movement Comes Out*, San Francisco Chronicle (July 2, 2008, 2:10 PM), https://www.sfgate.com/news/article/India-s-gay-rights-movement-comes-out-3206262.php.
14. Avtar Brah, Cartographies of Diaspora: Contesting Identities (1996).
15. *See* Brubaker, *supra* note 9, at 5-6; Clifford, *supra* note 9, at 302-308; William Safran, *Diasporas in Modern Societies: Myths of Homeland and Return*, 1 Diaspora 83 (1991); Anthony Smith, The Ethnic Origins of Nations (1986).
16. *See* Homi K. Bhabha, The Location of Culture 1–5 (1994).
17. Homi K. Bhabha, *Cultural Diversity and Cultural Differences, in* The Post-Colonial Studies Reader 208 (Ashcroft et al. eds., 1995).
18. *See* Fortier, *supra* note 11, at 184. "Defined as decidedly anti-nationalist within critical cultural theory, it has been widely argued that the presence and experiences of diasporic subjects puts any normative notion of culture, identity, and citizenship in question by their very location *outside* of the time-space of the nation."
19. *See* Chander, *supra* note 10, at 1024 (citing James Clifford, *Diasporas*, 9 Cultural Anthropology 302, 311 (1994)).
20. *See* Jasbir K. Puar, *Transnational Sexualities: South Asian (Trans)nation(alism) s and Queer Diasporas, in* Q & A:: Queer in Asian America 405 (D.L. Eng & A.Y. Hom eds., 1998).
21. *See* Alan Sinfield, *Diaspora and Hybridity: Queer Identities and the Ethnicity Model*, 10 Textual Prac. 271 (1996) (citing Eve Sedgwick, Epistemology of the Closet 84–90 (1991)).
22. *See Id.*
23. *See* Alice M. Miller, *Gay Enough: Some Tensions in Seeking the Grant of Asylum and Protecting Global Sexual Diversity, in* Passing Lines: Sexuality and Immigration 137, 137–38 (Epps et al. eds., 2005).

24. Sinfield, *supra* note 21, at 272 (quoting Didi Herman).
25. David William Foster, *The Homoerotic Diaspora in Latin America*, 29 Latin Am. Persp. 163, 163 (2002).
26. *See* Fortier, *supra* note 11, at 189.
27. *Id.* at 185 (quoting Watney).
28. *Id.* (internal quotations omitted).
29. *See* Luibhéid, *supra* note 6, at xi.
30. For writings on the notion of a queer diaspora, particularly regarding Asian sexualities, see Monisha Das Gupta, Unruly Immigrants: Rights, Activism, and Transnational South Asian Politics in the United States (2006); A Lotus of Another Color: An Unfolding of the South Asian Gay and Lesbian Experience (Rakesh Ratti ed., 1993); Gayatri Gopinath, *Funny Boys and Girls: Notes on a Queer South Asian Planet, in* Asian-American Sexualities 119 (R. Leong ed., 1996); Puar, *supra* note 20; Q & A: Queer in Asian America (David L. Eng & Alice Y. Hom eds., 1998); Martin F. Manalansan IV, *In the Shadows of Stonewall*, 2 GLQ 425 (1995); Sonia Otalvaro-Hormillosa, *The Homeless Diaspora of Queer Asian Americans*, 26 Soc. Just. 103 (1999).
31. Shah, *supra* note 2 (internal quotations omitted).
32. *Id.*
33. Sinfield, *supra* note 21, at 272.
34. *See Id.*
35. *See* Ahmet Atay, *Identities in Motion: Cyberspace and Diasporic Queer Male Bodies in the Context of Globalization* 48 (May 4, 2009) (unpublished PhD dissertation, Southern Illinois University) (on file with UCLA Law Review).
36. Karin Aguilar-San Juan, *Going Home: Enacting Justice in Queer Asian America, in* Q & A: Queer in Asian America 25, 37 (D.L. Eng & A.Y. Hom eds., 1998).
37. Sonia Katyal, *Exporting Identity*, 14 Yale J.L. & Feminism 97, 153 (2002).
38. Ara Wilson, *Queering Asia*, 14 Intersections: Gender, Hist. & Culture in the Asian Context, ¶ 3 (2006), http://intersections.anu.edu.au/issue14/wilson.html.
39. *Id.* at ¶ 4.
40. *Id. See also* Inderpal Grewal & Caren Kaplan, *Global Identities: Theorizing Transnational Studies of Sexuality*, 7 GLQ 663, 669 (2001). "[T]he United States and Europe are figured as modern and thus as the sites of progressive social movements, while other parts of the world are presumed to be traditional, especially in regard to sexuality or else are attributed with a kind of primitive sexual openness."
41. Gayatri Gopinath, Impossible Desires: Queer Diasporas and South Asian Public Cultures 12 (2005).
42. *Id.*
43. *See* Eng & Hom, *supra* note 30; Anne-Marie Fortier, *'Coming Home': Queer Migrations and Multiple Evocations of Home*, 4 European Journal of Cultural Studies 405 (2001).

44. *See* Martin F. Manalansan IV, *Migrancy, Modernity, Mobility: Quotidian Struggles and Queer Diasporic Intimacy, in* Queer Migrations, *supra* note 6, at 147.
45. *Id.* at 155.
46. Naz, *supra* note 3.
47. *See* Gupta, *supra* note 30. *See also* Douglas E. Sanders, *377 and the Unnatural Afterlife of British Colonialism in Asia*, 4 Asian J. Comp. L. 1 (2009).
48. Human Rights Watch, *This Alien Legacy: The Origins of "Sodomy" Laws in British Colonialism* 2 (Dec. 17, 2008), https://www.hrw.org/report/2008/12/17/alien-legacy/origins-sodomy-laws-british-colonialism.
49. Jasbir K. Puar, Terrorist Assemblages: Homonationalism in Queer Times (2007).
50. *See* Nishant Shahani, *After the Fire: India is Burning*, 15 GLQ 180, 182 (2009).
51. *See* Holning Lau, *Grounding Discussions on Sexuality and Asian Law*, 44 U.C. Davis L. Rev 773, 774 & 776-777 (2011) (citing Stephen G. Calabresi & Stephanie Dotson Zimdahl, *The Supreme Court and Foreign Sources of Law: Two Hundred Years of Practice and the Juvenile Death Penalty Decision*, 47 Wm. & Mary L. Rev. 743, 804-805 (2005)).
52. *Id.* at 779.
53. *Id.* at 780.
54. There is a vast array of literature on sodomy laws in India and the history of same-sex sexualities, much of which is cited in Katyal, *supra* note 37, and Sonia Katyal, *Sexuality and Sovereignty: The Global Limits and Possibilities of* Lawrence, 14 Wm. & Mary L. Rev. 1429 (2006). A few recent pieces are Alternative Law Forum, *The Right That Dares to Speak Its Name: Decriminalizing Sexual Orientation and Gender Identity in India* 5 (Arvind Narrain & Marcus Eldridge eds., 2009), http://altlawforum.org/publications/the-right-that-dares-to-speak-its-name/; Because I Have a Voice: Queer Politics in India (Arvind Narrain & Gautam Bhan eds., 2005); Ruth Vanita, *"Living the Way We Want": Same Sex Sexualities in Contemporary India, in* The Phobic and the Erotic: The Politics of Sexualities in Contemporary India 342 (B. Bose & S. Bhattacharyya eds., 2007); Alankar Sharma, *Decriminalising Queer Sexualities in India*, 7 Soc. Pol'y & Soc'y 419 (2008); Sumit Baudh, *Human Rights and the Criminalisation of Consensual Same-Sex Sexual Acts in the Commonwealth, South, and Southeast Asia*, The South and Southeast Asia Resource Centre on Sexuality (May, 2008); Jigna Desai, *Homo on the Range: Mobile and Global Sexualities*, 20 Soc. Text 73 (2002). There is also an excellent set of chapters in a symposium by the National University of Juridical Sciences in India: *see* volume 2, issue 3 in the NUJS archives at http://nujslawreview.org/articles-archives/.
55. Alternative Law Forum, *supra* note 54, at 7.
56. *Id.* at 27.
57. *Id.* at 12.

58. Vikram Raghavan, *Navigating the Noteworthy and Nebulous in Naz Foundation*, 2 NUJS L. Rev. 391, 401-402 (2009).
59. *Id.* at 402.
60. Katyal, *Sexuality and Sovereignty*, *supra* note 54, at 1458 (citing the Naz Foundation brief).
61. *Id.* (quoting Arvind Narrain, *Queer People and the Law*, Seminar (Apr., 2003), http://www.india-seminar.com/2003/524/524%20arvind%20narrain.htm).
62. *Id.* at 1457.
63. Naz, *supra* note 3, at ¶ 60-66.
64. Note, however, that the conflation of transgender and hijra has been subject to some debate. *See* Ashwini Sukthankar, *Complicating Gender: Rights of Transsexuals in India*, *in* Because I Have a Voice: Queer Politics in India 164–65 (A. Narrain & G. Bhan eds., 2005).
65. In addition, Siddharth Narrain has argued that *Naz Foundation*'s theme of protecting sexual minorities in public suggests that *Naz Foundation* can be extended to create a mantle of protection from harassment in public spaces for transgender individuals . *See* Siddharth Narrain, *Crystallising Queer Politics: The Naz Foundation Case and Its Implications for India's Transgender Communities*, 2 NUJS L. Rev. 455, 466 & 469 (2009) (citing Sunil Babu Pant making this observation).
66. Dudgeon v. United Kingdom, 45 Eur. Ct. H.R. (ser. A) (1981).
67. Norris v. Republic of Ireland, 142 Eur. Ct. H.R. (ser. A) (1988).
68. Press Release, Human Rights Committee, Views of the Human Rights Committee under chapter 5, paragraph 4, of the Optional Protocol to the International Covenant on Civil and Political Rights, U.N. Doc. CCPR/C/50/D/488/1992 (Apr. 4, 1994).
69. Naz, *supra* note 3, at ¶ 59.
70. Alternative Law Forum, *supra* note 54, at 14.
71. Ryan Goodman, *Beyond the Enforcement Principle: Sodomy Laws, Social Norms, and Social Panoptics*, 89 Cal. L. Rev. 643 (2001).
72. The court explained its reasoning for the choice: "Discrimination on the basis of sexual orientation is itself grounded in stereotypical judgments and generalization about the conduct of either sex." Naz, *supra* note 3, at ¶ 99. It went even further by concluding that "[a] provision of the law branding one section of people as criminal based wholly on the State's moral disapproval of that class goes counter to the equality guaranteed [...] under any standard of review." *Id.* at ¶ 113.
73. *Id.* at ¶ 79.
74. Raghavan, *supra* note 58, at 410.
75. Naz, *supra* note 3, at ¶ 80.
76. Raghavan, *supra* note 58, at 417 (citing Liang).
77. *See generally* Barry, *supra* note 10, who reaches similar conclusions.
78. *See* Benedict Anderson, Imagined Communities (1991). *See* Benigno Sanchez-Eppler & Cindy Patton, *Introduction: With a Passport Out of Eden*, *in*

Queer Diasporas, *supra* note 11, at 1 & 10 (discussing how the notion of an "imagined community" has sustained the creation of sexualities that are not only discursively mobile, but are also not specific to a particular time or place of origin).

79. *See* Geetanjali Misra, *Decriminalising Homosexuality in India*, 17 Reproductive Health Matters 20, 27 (2009) (quoting Shohini Ghosh).
80. *See* Arvind Narrain, *Rethinking Citizenship: A Queer Journey*, 14 Indian J. Gender Stud. 61, 61 (2007).
81. Gopinath, *supra* note 30, at 121–122.
82. Kapur, *supra* note 54, at 284.
83. *Id.* at 393.
84. *Id.* at 388.
85. *Id.* at 394.
86. *Id.* at 395.

CHAPTER 10

The Promise of an Event

Sexuality's Historiography

Anjali Arondekar

For the past few years, much ink (toxic and otherwise) has been expended on how to read historical archives. From a diatribe against the hermeneutics of suspicion or reading against the grain (where all readings are necessarily symptomatic readings of something that is missing and/or erased) becoming the new hegemony, to a rallying call for surface readings and/or readings along the archival grain (where the surface of the texts bears witness to the violence of the moment), there is a shared sense that how and why we make meanings out of the past must constantly be debated.[1] That these trenchant challenges to our consumptions of times past have overwhelmingly come from scholars working on histories of slavery, sexuality, and colonialism who are attentive to archival economies of loss, paucity and/or devaluation, is hardly surprising.

Even as I write this, archival economies of devaluation abound, as state-sponsored campaigns to purify India of cultural pollution (*sanskritik pradushan*) have become the mainstay of a Hindutva-fueled polity. Within such state formulations, the pollution of the Indian populace derives from its historical amnesia, from its refusal and/or erasure of proper historical vernaculars, cast in the loss of Sanskrit as mother-tongue, or in the aspiration of a *swachh bharat*, emptied of the corrupting forces of alternative sexualities. The past, now more than ever, founds the moral authority of the Indian nation-state where all forms of difference are coercively shunted aside to make way for a new 'India shining'. When it comes to historical evidence, any shoddy travesty of research appears to pass muster, as is evident in the recent appointment of Professor Y. Sudershan Rao as chairperson of the Indian Council for Historical Research (ICHR).[2] For Rao and his ilk, Indian historians need to abandon their Marxist and Western historiographical ways to make way for a Hindutva-infused empiricism that would eschew archival ambivalences and establish historical dates for the "factual" events of the Ramayana and Mahabharata.[3] Such concerns, with the manipulation, erasure and/or refusal of diverse pasts, are especially pressing for the lives of sexual minorities, as the legal and economic right to be here and now is often authorized by the evidence of histories past. One has only to recall the ongoing legal challenges facing the repeal of Section 377 that remain mired in debates around the presence/absence of alternative sexualities in India's past.[4] Thus, it behooves us, as scholars of sexuality, to be more judicious and dialectical about the past in the face of instrumentalist, bellicose renditions of it as fodder for a triumphalist Hindutva world-view.

To put it mildly, the reading of sexuality's past(s) has now clearly become a complicated affair, a balancing act between an embrace of sexuality's munificent incommensurability (divergent temporalities are fodder for theories of queer difference) and a capture of its genealogical sameness (the past surrenders lineages of our queer presents). The cornerstone of such writing is of course the idea of the archive, more specifically the archival trace, as the preferred value form through which we accrue meaning. Even as it is almost commonplace, particularly for those of us who work within colonial archives, to argue that historical archives must be read more as registers of selection than empiricism, there is less debate around forms of archival consumption and dissemination, particularly as they unfold in minoritized historiographies.[5] I want to begin then with one such narrative form that continues to inaugurate most historiographical and/or ethnographic projects: the problem event, the detail, the legal case, the anecdote—in other words, an archival trace that is often a tantalizing obstacle to clarity, which then comes alive through our reconstructive hermeneutics.[6] More often than not, the turn to such an inaugural problem event becomes an exemplifying narrative, pointing to something bigger, a critical encounter that opens up potentialities that we as scholars want to, and most often do, figure out.

For scholars working at the interstices of multiple minoritized historiographies, such as myself, the problem event often becomes a crucial way of resolving the crisis of marginality where the scarcity of historical evidence is refused by the hermeneutical performance of plenitude—where you recover the archival trace for the promise of historical precedence and futurity. In my previous work, I wrote about the pressing impasse that haunts our recuperation of the historical archive, about the hermeneutical demands placed on histories of sexuality, and about the double binds and possibilities that emerge from within such recuperative practices. In this essay, I want to think more about the analytical forms through which recuperative historiographies gather their salutary force, especially as they service minoritized communities that lack adequate rights and representation. The challenge here is to marshal a queer historiography, as I have previously argued, that "paradoxically adds value to a sedimented historical form (minoritized archives must be resurrected, found, produced for future gains) precisely by staging interest in its modes of reproduction."[7]

In what follows, I want to talk more about what exemplifying readings of problem events mean for the ways in which we encounter archives, particularly archives of sexuality, as is the case here. Simply put, I want to discuss what makes something an archival event/situation, and not merely a gestural instance, illustration or example, and following Lauren Berlant, to "query the adequacy of an object to bear the weight of an explanation worthy of attending to and taking a lesson from."[8] By this I mean to say, why does the writing of a history of sexuality, as will be the case here, take a particular narrative form, and what creates obstacles to its lithesome storytelling? What are the hermeneutic demands placed on its telling? The provocation of my title, "The Promise of an Event", is an invitation to track the archival trace without presuming it as a mode of historical stabilization or recuperation. My efforts here are directed at resisting the impulse (by now well-sedimented in sexuality studies) to over-read archival evidence (particularly in the historical past) as obdurately and enticingly sparse. Indeed, the seductions of such paucity accrue a certain value where you cede to historical difference precisely to lay aside the epistemic work such difference does. In other words, how might we relay something of the messy misalignments that the archival trace offers, without revisiting routinized habits of analysis, even as we attend to the generation of value/capital that is implicit in the form itself? After all, as Jacques Derrida reminds us, "every example must necessarily fail to do its job."[9]

MORE IMAGINED THAN REAL

Let me begin then with one archival problem event. A public meeting of the residents and ratepayers of Girgaum (in South Bombay) is hastily convened on 16 July, 1911 with the express purpose of protesting "against the growing evil of women of bad repute coming to reside in increasing numbers in Girgaum." Four unanimous resolutions are passed (under the leadership of Sir Bhalchandra Krishna) and in turn forwarded to the Secretary of Government, Bombay. The resolutions argue (a) that it is "highly objectionable that women of ill-fame should at all be allowed to occupy houses even on main roads and thoroughfares, and generally in quarters inhabited by respectable families and they emphatically deprecate the recent increase of this evil in Girgaum", (b) that "effective steps should be taken to induce house-owners to refuse to let their houses or premises be used for immoral purposes", (c) that the "Commissioner of Police should use all the powers given to him by law to reduce this evil" and "fresh legislation" should be passed to further "empower him", and last but not least, (d) that a committee consisting of the gentlemen from the association should be appointed to take any steps necessary to "carry out the object of the meeting."

Responding with some testiness, the Secretary to the Government, C.A. Kincaid, writes a long and disciplining letter (dated 13 November 1911) to the ratepayers of Girgaum. In the letter, Kincaid applauds the "spirit" of the resolutions against the "evil of prostitution", but cautions against the inflammatory rhetoric used by the ratepayers, and argues that "he has reason to believe that the growth of the evil is more apparent than real." He further adds that in the "absence of definite statistics" there is no indication that the evil of prostitution has in fact increased in Girgaum—the more obvious explanation for the threat being that "ill-houses of fame" had been shut down in North Girgaum and this forced the "women to scatter and invade the southern part of the ward." In case the ratepayers still thought it was incumbent on the Commissioner of Police to take action, the Secretary further added that the Commissioner could not use the "power invested in him by the law" to take action against a large proportion of these immoral women, who were more "kept mistresses/devadasis" than "common prostitutes". And further, even if the women had scattered and moved to other parts of the city, it would interfere with the goals of the City Improvement Trust, which did not have a particular investment in providing "harlots' quarters". To do so would be to endorse such vice, and perhaps, the letter snidely questions, that is what the ratepayers want?

The letter ends with a final flourish, saying that "prostitution in Girgaum is a subject which usually comes in for publicity during the monsoon season when there is not much going on in Bombay and the Government are away in Poona." Castigating the ratepayers for their own involvement in the "apparent" evil of this vice, Kincaid adds that the houses in which the women resided were owned and supported by the very ratepayers advocating these resolutions. And, moreover, that in his own "experiences" of Bombay, "the very gentleman who presided over the meeting recommended to [the] Government the other day to honour an individual who counts among his nearest female relations three ladies who, according to my Criminal Investigation Department, must be classed among those who, in Census parlance, are 'following dishonourable professions.'" In a last note, he also reminded the ratepayers that the Government must act "with great caution", especially as the Commissioner of Police was still recovering from "being hauled into court by a woman upon whom he has served a notice and told that he had acted *ultra vires* and that the woman is not a 'common prostitute'." To erase any doubts on this question, Kincaid writes that he himself had visited houses accused of being "disorderly brothels" in response to similar complaints, only to find that one of the people who visits the house is "a member of a Parsi Purity Brigade or Vigilance Committee."[10]

At the heart of the debate between the two sides is a rather peculiar crisis of representation embedded in an even more fascinating palimpsest of arguments. The hermeneutical demand on either side is to make visible and/or eradicate an object of sexuality that is, for all considered, "apparent"—a paradoxical term that traffics equally in the realm of the obvious and the elusive: we know the evil ladies exist but the force of their threat may or may not be real. For someone like myself who is writing a book on these "evil ladies of Girgaum", this exchange inevitably becomes an archival trace laden with the challenges and possibilities of historical visibility. Surely I must insist, fueled by a corrective historiographical impulse, that what is lost in the back and forth of this exchange are the material histories and contexts of the very object of knowledge that is being debated. The slipperiness of the arguments made on both sides (are they or are they not prostitutes, are they "kept mistresses" or *Devadasis*?) could become the perfect foil for the 'real' history of sexuality that needs telling: that to reduce these women to the confines of this debate is to limit our analytical horizons; to forget that these so-called evil ladies became, in the decade or so after this event, founders of one of the most successful collectivities in Bombay, the Gomantak Maratha

Samaj, earning them the moniker of a model minority, "*Bharatatil Ek Aggressor Samaj*".

Let me say more about what I mean. I am currently writing a historiography of a Devadasi diaspora, the Gomantak Maratha Samaj. 'Devadasi' is a compound noun, coupling *deva* or god with *dasi* or female slave; a pan-Indian term (falsely) interchangeable with courtesan, dancing girl, prostitute and sex worker. Often referred to as *kalavants* (literally carriers of *kala*/art), these women moved between Portuguese and British colonial India for over two hundred years, in search of artistic training and professional enhancement. The Gomantak Maratha Samaj (henceforth the Samaj) is an OBC (Other Backward Castes) community and was established as a formal organization in 1927 and 1929 in the western states of Goa and Maharashtra respectively. It officially became a charitable institution in 1936. The Samaj continues its activities to this day and has from its inception maintained a community of 10,000 to 50,000 registered members. Of singular importance is that the history of the Samaj never disappeared, nor was erased, as is the case in more well-known historical accounts of Devadasis, particularly in South India. Instead, the Samaj, from its inception, has maintained a continuous, copious, and accessible archive of its own emergence, embracing rather than disavowing its past and present attachments to sexuality. The Samaj's archives (housed in Panaji and Bombay) constitute an efflorescence of information in Marathi, Konkani, and Portuguese, ranging from minutes of meetings, journals, newsletters, private correspondence, flyers, programs, all filled with details of the daily exigencies and crises that concerned the community. Often referred to as Bharatatil Ek Aggressor Samaj (literally, 'an aggressive community in India'), this Devadasi diaspora is routinely lauded (by the left *and* the right in India) for its self-reform and progress. From the immortal Mangeshkar sisters (Lata and Asha) to the first Chief Minister of independent Goa, Dayanand Bandodkar, there are few sectors of Indian society where the presence of Samaj members cannot be felt.[11]

THE PROPERTIES OF EVIL

Several historical accounts from the period allude to the "evil ladies" of Girgaum as the progenitors of this successful and celebrated Samaj. Padma Anagol, for example, situates such community efforts to read the "evil ladies" as morally contagious within a larger respectability movement, orchestrated by largely middle-class (and mostly upper-caste) women. Within such narratives of reform and progress, the "evil ladies" become purveyors of a curiously fecund set of cultural threats. Here the evil of the ladies shifts from the corruptions of sex to the debasement of kala, a shift that needs to be rerouted (and stabilized) through a more heteronormative marriage economy. On the one hand, the "evil ladies" trouble cherished distinctions between kalavants/*naikins* and prostitutes; after all, if they are primarily repositories of the arts (kala), then their growing presence cannot be regulated by anti-prostitution regulation, and the resolution of the Girgaum ratepayers holds no ground. On the other hand, the rise of such "evil ladies" and their clientele demonstrates the need for a more robust cultivation of arts/kala within middle-class women themselves. In this vein, middle-class men become clients of "evil ladies", in search of artistic enrichment, not sex, a turn that rouses middle-class women to claim the domain of the arts/kala for themselves. For Anagol, groups such as the Maharashtra Mahila Mandal (1902) embody the tensions of such concerns as they plot efforts to both train in the arts, and organize against the presence of the "evil ladies". Vernacular newspapers of the day, such as *Bodh Sudhakar* and *Subodh Patrika*, Anagol writes, registered the scale of these efforts equally, carrying accounts of middle-class women trying to oust the "evil ladies" from their residences, even as others such as *Indu Prakash* and *Dnyan Prakash* ran editorials extolling the bravery of the naikins in resisting eviction.[12]

Ethnographic and travel accounts of late colonial Bombay similarly record the troublesome and vexing history of the "evil ladies". Govind Narayan's *Mumbaiche Varnan* (1863) documents the author's migration to Bombay from Madgaon through a series of lush accounts of the city's shifting urban landscape. In a chapter describing the rise of arts and theatre in Bombay (circa 1861), Narayan writes with great disgust about the rise of "dancing girls" who appear to have garnered clientele across the city, with their "numbers increasing daily". Of great concern to Narayan is the dancing girls' successful acquisition of property and their vulgar display of wealth. He writes of one, "she spent nearly four thousand rupees" on an initiation ceremony for her daughter to become a Devadasi, reminding him of the "stories of the matriarchates mentioned in the Puranas".[13] We see a similar articulation of shock and awe in K. Raghunathji's documentation of the rise of "Bombay Dancing Girls". Writing for the *Indian Antiquary* (1884), Raghunathji provides detailed descriptions of these dancing girls (who are both Hindu and Musalman) and their practices, noting that a large percentage of the Hindu girls appear to have migrated "from Goa and the places around it".[14] He notes that the "Hindu dancing girls are of four sects, viz: - Naikins, Bhavins, Murlis and Kasbins. Of these the first two belong to Goa and villages round it, being natives of that district." Unlike Narayan, Raghunathji paints a more flattering picture of these women, extolling their beauty and their generally "intelligent pleasing appearance".[15] While they arrive in Bombay speaking "Goanese" (which we are mysteriously told differs from the "language of Bombay"), they quickly acclimatize and soon read, write and even compose songs in Marathi. As in Narayan's account, Raghunathji too emphasizes the "large sums of money" that the women appear to have access to, describing in excruciating detail the gold ornaments the women routinely wear.[16] While such anthropological accounts are to be consumed with some trepidation (after all, we are rarely provided with any sources for the information that is provided!), references to the women's growing presence and appetite for wealth can also be found in other genres of archival records.

Of interest, for example, are several legal appeals filed on behalf of these "evil ladies" petitioning the state for support in their claims for maintenance from the families of dead patrons or *yajemans*, residing in or around Girgaum. As in the two accounts discussed above, the focus continues to be on the acquisition of ill-gotten wealth by the "evil ladies" and the threat it poses to the sanctioned circulation of capital within family formations. One series of appeals, in particular, stands out in its detailed listing of monies acquired and requisitioned from the family of an upstanding member of society (very much kin of the Girgaum ratepayers association I began with) after his untimely death in 1919. In *Bai Monghibai v. Bai Nagubai* (11 August, 1922), Bai Monghibai (widow of the deceased Vasanji Madhavji Thakar, who died on November 21, 1919) appeals a previous judgment by Justice Kanga that awarded monthly maintenance of Rs. 400 to Bai Nagubai Manglorkar as "the permanent concubine of the deceased." According to the details of the previous judgment, the deceased, who "possessed moveable and immoveable property of a very large value", had abandoned his family domicile in Vadgadi and had come to reside with Bai Nagubai, a Goan naikin, "in her house in Girgaum and [...] he continued to reside there until the day prior to his death." Bai Nagubai claimed monthly maintenance and "alleged that a sum of Rs. 25,000 was specially promised by the deceased" for the benefit of her and her daughter after his death.

In the series of legal skirmishes that followed the original judgment by Justice Kanga, much effort was made to determine if Bai Nagubai was the "exclusive mistress" of the deceased, and if she maintained sexual chastity even after his death. Bai Monghibai, the deceased's widow, argues that the deceased merely visited Bai Nagubai in her Girgaum residence, and was permanently domiciled elsewhere. Acting Judge Lallubhai Shah, who reviewed the widow's appeal, concurs with her claim even as he is "willing to admit that Bai Nagubai used to live in a house near Kennedy Bridge at Girgaon where the deceased Vasanji used to visit her regularly [...] prior to his death and used to pay her some monthly allowance." The crux of the appeal relies on the status of Bai Nagubai's residence in Girgaon/Girgaum: was it or was it not the primary residence of the deceased? For Shah, the true nature of the deceased's relationship with Bai Nagubai cannot be ascertained without "knowing the nature of his visits" to the Girgaum residence. True companionship, for Shah, can only be determined through open and continuous co-habitation with Bai Nagubai, something that the facts of the case do not appear to corroborate. Shah's judgment is appealed further by Bai Nagubai; she provides evidence that the deceased had rented the Girgaum residence "in her name [...] and that he was nursed there during his last illness and only removed shortly before his death."[17]

As the story of these evil ladies unfolds in multiple historical accounts of the period, it becomes "apparent" that the "real" archival substance of their evil unfolds in variegated scenes of capital. From their ostentatious displays of wealth, to their corruption of the family form, the evil ladies appear to play exemplary roles in what Mariam Dossal has called Bombay's "theatre of conflict."[18] At the time of the ratepayers' complaint against the evil ladies of Girgaum, the city of Bombay appears mired in various struggles around land expansion and reclamation, gentrification and the increasing demands of native franchise. Preeti Chopra, for instance, argues that the expansion debates pivot around the "joint public realm" where native elites collaborate with the colonial state (with varying degrees of success) to create public institutions of finance.[19] One key stage of such financial ventures circles precisely around the acquisition and control of lucrative land such as the properties the evil ladies of Girgaum inhabit.[20]

Prashant Kidambi reminds us that this is also the period when the Bombay Improvement Trust (BIT) emerges as the central force in shaping the city's physical landscape. BIT was an ambitious colonial enterprise that was largely a response to the sanitation risks of over-crowding that had come to the forefront in the devastating aftermath of the Bombay plague. One of its key projects was the construction of thoroughfares such as the Princess Street Scheme II and the Sandhurst Road Scheme III that opened up a wide corridor in the otherwise crowded locality of Girgaum. Such efforts, however, were continuously mired in multiple property disputes around land acquisitions as native landlords and homeowners rushed to capitalize on the increasing value of their assets.[21]

Also eluded in our focus on the evil ladies of Girgaum is their emergence in the context of a precarious and controversial period of property tax legislation in Bombay Presidency. The crux of the controversy revolved around the famous Girgaum Memorial Memorandum of 1870 that called for the abolition of occupier's and house taxes, and what more reformist newspapers at the time such as *Native Opinion* derisively called the "landlord's movement". The Memorandum principally involved the tax levied on house property by the colonial state and asked for a reduction in the taxes from 7% to 4%. The *Bombay Municipal Act* of 1872 further complicated matters by allowing the upper echelon of ratepayers (primarily landlords and businessmen) to be elected members of the Municipal Corporation. Leading up to 1911, the year in which the Girgaum residents' and ratepayers' association files the public resolutions against the evil ladies of Girgaum, the tax rate legislation on property continued to be heavily disputed, with property values escalating (as mentioned above) thanks to the redistribution of land due to the institution of the City Improvement Trust. In such a context, the evil ladies' occupation of homes in the main thoroughfares of Girgaum needs to be more carefully examined.[22] According to the census of 1901, the number of "prostitutes" in Girgaum had diminished significantly (dropping from over 1,200 or so in the late 1890s to about 235 in 1901—figures *cum grano* of course, given the unreliability of census reports of the time).[23] So, the Secretary to the Government is right in arguing that a statistical case cannot be made for the rise of evil ladies in Girgaum. Alternately, what the private archives of the Gomantak Maratha Samaj (which contain many property deeds and genealogies of inheritance and distribution) reveal is that the evil ladies of Girgaum occupied and then gradually took possession of the multiple residences they were inhabiting, thanks to their complex negotiations with their yajemans (patrons) for a payment system that bypassed cash payments for property deeds.

The association of Girgaum residents and ratepayers lists as its prominent members Saraswat *shetias*, Mohammedan merchants, and a few converted Christians and Eurasians—a motley crew of caste and race that is reflected in the current geography of Girgaum.[24] In the back and forth between the members of the Girgaum association and the Secretary to the Government, no such skirmish over tax rates and property values is made visible.[25] Instead, the repeated and "apparent" invocations of "vice" and prostitution seamlessly conceal the economics and exigencies of the Samaj women's day-to-day survival. It is thus with some irony that I add here that the economic success of the Samaj is also largely built on their acquisition in the early 1900s of prime property all over Bombay presidency, particularly in the area of Girgaum, Gamdevi and Chowpatty.[26]

Even as I write this, I continue to 'discover' new archival evidence that tells further of this problem event. Generous colleagues of mine who work on histories of policing and surveillance in colonial Bombay note (with great confidence, I would add) the presence of numerous classified files on these "evil ladies of Girgaum", that currently lie outside the realm of public consumption. As of now, such files remain sequestered within the bureaucratic walls of police archives; their content, like the material of this problem event, offering the promise of multiple readings. Such invocations of classified (and therefore potentially explosive) evidence further augment the value accrued by the problem event. After all, any new historical reading, especially of sexuality's pasts, surely benefits from the continued promise of archival evidence. To hold such evidence in narrative abeyance makes further heroic reconstructions of the event possible, bypassing any narrative-stopping closure of an always-impending authentic history.

In light of such concerns, the scandal now shifts from an evaluation or disputation of the "evil" of the ladies of Girgaum to the "apparent" entanglements behind their invocation. Let me be clear, I am not reading sexuality here as a cover-story merely to make the familiar but necessary argument for paying attention to sexuality's material contexts. I am instead attempting to think of these contexts as themselves being equally locked in the dialectic of the apparent and the real. Within such imaginaries, the matter of the evil ladies of Girgaum works not as an exemplary case that resolves historical ambivalence or loss through its successful recognition and emergence, but rather as a narrative that inserts epistemic discontinuity into how and why we write histories of sexuality. Even as the story of the evil ladies as it morphs into the successful emergence of the Gomantak Maratha Samaj is a crucial and inspiring one, it is more than just yet another exercise in recuperative and redemptive historiography. Rather, it pushes us to consider the archival trace, less as a marginalized, erased archival trace of sexuality, and more as evidence of the hegemonic intercalation of property, caste and sexuality. The exemplar of the evil ladies thus does not affirm nor erase their liminality as archival objects; rather it simply presses against our desire for an archival hermeneutics that will recover and restore value to a lost form/collectivity. In this case, the collectivity, as I have noted, is never lost or erased, nor missing an archive. As is clear by now, not only do these evil ladies exist in multiple archival forms, but they also maintain and sustain an archive of their own making. Instead, the evil ladies of Girgaum function (then and now) as a fetishistic screen whereby we return over and over again to the vice of sexuality as the familiar place of historical redress and reform. What would it mean to refuse such a narrative of occlusion, to uncouple sex from the safety of its "evil" form, and to summon its ordinary visibility within public discussions of culture, capital, and even Indian feminism?

NOTES

* This essay is a republication of Telling Tales: Archives of the Geopolitical, in Turning Archival: The Life of the Historical in Queer Studies (D. Marshal & Z. Tortorici eds., 2022).

1. *See* Stephen Best & Sharon Marcus, *Surface Reading: An Introduction*, 108 Representations 1 (2009); Paul Ricoeur, Freud and Philosophy: An Essay on Interpretation (1970); David Stewart, *The Hermeneutics of Suspicion*, 3 Literature and Theology 296 (1989).
2. For a prescient reading of this appointment, *see* Romila Thapar, *The Appointment of a Historian Whose Work is Unfamiliar to Most Historians Shows Scant Regard for the Impressive Scholarship that Now Characterises the Study*

of Indian History and This Disregard May Stultify Further Academic Research, India Today (July 11, 2014, 5:02 PM), http://indiatoday.intoday.in/story/romila-thapar-smriti-irani-old-history-baiters-of-bjp/1/370799.html.

3. FP Staff, *Historians Raise Questions About ICHR's New Boss Prof Y Sudershan Rao,* Firstpost (July 14, 2014, 1:51 PM), http://www.firstpost.com/living/historians-raise-questions-about-ichrs-new-boss-prof-y-sudershan-rao-1617971.html.
4. For an extended exegesis on the use of historical archives in the efforts to repeal Section 377, *see* Anjali Arondekar, *Time's Corpus: On Temporality, Sexuality and the Indian Penal Code, in* Comparatively Queer: Crossing Times, Crossing Cultures 143-156 (J. Hayes & W. Spurlin eds., 2010); Ratna Kapur, *Unruly Desires, Gay Governance, and the Makeover of Sexuality in Postcolonial India, in* Global Justice and Desire: Queering Economy 115-131 (Dhawan et al. eds., 2015).
5. Ann Laura Stoler, Along the Archival Grain: Epistemic Anxieties and Colonial Common Sense 32-33 (2010).
6. Lauren Berlant, *On the Case,* 33 Critical Inquiry 663 (2007).
7. Anjali Arondekar, *In the Absence of Reliable Ghosts: Sexuality, Historiography, South Asia,* 25 differences 98, 100 (2015).
8. Berlant, *supra* note 6, at 666.
9. Derrida: 1998, 47
10. All records of this event were found in an unmarked file at the Mumbai offices of the Gomantak Maratha Samaj. The file was buried in a box containing paperwork on the acquisition of the Samaj building in Girgaum. The available records contain type-written letters from the Residents and Ratepayers of Girgaum (dated 16 July 1911) and a response from the Judicial Department (dated 13 November 1911). What is curious about the contents of the file is that the letters contain corrections that have been penciled in, with no indication of whether the letters were revised and re-sent. I have not been able to locate a copy of these materials in the Maharashtra State Archives' Judicial Department papers as yet. The bulk of the archives are now housed at the Gomantak Maratha Samaj Society building in Mumbai, India. In 2004, the Samaj offices were moved from Gomantak Maratha Samaj Sadan, 345 V.P. Road, Bombay 400004 to Sitladevi Co-op. Housing Society Ltd., 7-16/B Wing, D.N. Nagar, New Link Road, Andheri (W), Mumbai 400053. A partial archive can be found at the Gomantak Maratha Samaj, Dayanand Smriti, Swami Vivekanand Marg, Panaji 403001, Goa.
11. For more historical detail on the emergence of the Samaj and the presence of Devadasis in Western India, see Anjali Arondekar, *Subject to Sex: A Small History of the Gomantak Maratha Samaj, in* South Asian Feminisms (A. Loomba & R.A. Lukose eds., 2012). Other texts that touch briefly on the history of the Samaj include Bhobe's *Kalavant Gomantak*, Khedekar's *Gomantak Lok Kala* and Satoshkar's *Gomantak Prakriti Ani Sanskriti.* The brief history of the Samaj I provide here is one that I provide repeatedly and verbatim in all work

that touches on the Samaj's exemplarity. Part of the challenge of writing about a collective that is known and not known all at once is that the historical details become routinized only through their constant repetition.

12. Padma Anagol, The Emergence of Feminism in India, 1850-1920 123-37 (2005).
13. Govind Narayan, Mumbai: An Urban Biography from 1863 261-62 (M. Ranganathan ed. & trans., 2012). The original Marathi text utilizes more lavish and efflorescent language.
14. K. Raghunathji, *Bombay Dancing Girls,* 13 Indian Antiquary 166 (1884).
15. *Id.* at 167.
16. *Id.* at 165-178.
17. Bai Monghibai v. Bai Nagubai, (1922) 24 BOMLR 1009 and Bai Nagubai v. Bai Monghibai, (1926) 28 BOMLR 1143. Other cases that deal with questions of maintenance and similar "evil ladies" include Bai Appibai v. Khimji Cooverji, (1936) 38 BOMLR 77 and Yashvantrav v. Kashibai, (1888) ILR 12 Bom 26.

    Kunal Parker, writing on similar questions, proposes that colonial courts in India augmented Devadasi reform through innovative and often unprecedented translations of the law. Legal norms that previously applied to different castes represented within Brahmanical taxonomies were extended to include an innovative set of patriarchal norms with respect to the sexual behaviour of Hindu women. For example, the Devadasi was cast less as a "temple dancing girl", and more as a Hindu girl engaging in sexual activities outside of marriage. Such a shift from the "tradition" of Devadasis to the aberration of their sexual practices allowed the courts to legislate against the Devadasis as prostitutes without engaging their more complex functions as repositories of art, culture and religion.

    According to Parker, these concerns substantially impacted the interpretation of the 1861 Indian Penal Code with reference to the Devadasis. By focusing on the prostitution of minors dedicated to temples, Parker suggests that Devadasi reform groups rerouted provisions intended to protect minors to nullify adoption by Devadasis, and to outlaw any and all dedications of girls to deities. Such a turn to the protection of minors became a crucial part of judicial reform movements aimed at eliminating Devadasis. *See* Kunal Parker, *'A Corporation of Superior Prostitutes': Anglo-Indian Legal Conceptions of Temple Dancing Girls, 1800-1914*, 32 Mod. Asian Stud. 559 (1998).
18. Mariam Dossal, Theatre of Conflict, City of Hope: Bombay/Mumbai, 1660 to Present Times (2010). *See specifically* Chapter 7, *Urban Planning or Crisis Management? 1860-1930.*
19. Preeti Chopra, A Joint Enterprise: Indian Elites and the Making of British Bombay (2011).
20. In a similar vein, Padma Anagol notes that "residents of various towns and cities often sent complaints to police authorities to remove *kalavantins* from what they considered as 'respectable neighborhoods', and house them outside

the city or town limits." Anagol, *supra* note 12. Anagol cites the example of a complaint submitted by Ahmadnagar residents against prostitutes. *See* Nagar Samachar, 23 February 1878 and Dandio, 22 March 1879, Vernacular Newspaper Reports (VNR).

21. Prashant Kidambi, *Housing the Poor in a Colonial City: The Bombay Improvement Trust, 1898-1918,* 17 Studies in History 57, 58-79 (2001). *See also* Prashant Kidambi, The Making of an Indian Metropolis: Colonial Governance and Public Culture in Bombay 70-76 (2007).
22. Nikhil Rao, *Community, Urban Citizenship, and Housing in Bombay, ca. 1919-1980,* 36 South Asia 415 (2013). *See also* Nikhil Rao,House, But No Garden: Apartment Living in Bombay's Suburbs 1898-1964 (2013). For a broader historical view of the twists and turns of the ratepayer/landlord's movement, *see also* Miriam Dossal, *A Master Plan for the City: Looking at the Past,* 40 EPW 3897 (2005).
23. Ashwini Tambe, Codes of Misconduct: Regulating Prostitution in Late Colonial Bombay 60 & 168 (2009).
24. (Pace *Elites in South Asia*, pg. 89)
25. S.M. Edwardes provides the following detailed description of the topography of Girgaum in 1 The Gazetteer of Bombay City and Island 41-42 (1909-10):

    "The Girgaum section is bounded on the North by Girgaum Back road, on the south by Thakurdwar road, on the east by Girgaum Back road and Bhuleshwar road, and on the west by Back Bay and Charni road. Like Chaupati and Phanasswadi its interior portion has arisen upon the side of ancient parts, such as Borbhat and Mugbat, with the old Girgaum village as its original nucleus. Its most noteworthy buildings are the Muhamadan sanitarium at the corner of Queen's road, the old Police Court on Girgaum back road, the Allbless Bagh on Charni Road and the Portuguese Church opposite the Trans terminus. The latter building which actually lies just outside the sectional limits was founded in 1773 and rebuilt in its present form in 1836. The neighbourhood of Charni road has of late years been taken up to some extend tof the building of middle-class Parsi flats; but the bulk of the section still retains its old character as a Brahman settlement."
26. A recently curated exhibition by Tejaswini Niranjana and Surabhi Sharma, 'Making Music, Making Space', documents the musical histories of Girgaum, giving its audience a small glimpse of the rich and networked worlds of these naikins and kalavantins. In the exhibition, the audience is also provided with an annotated map of Girgaum that marks all the residences and buildings occupied by collectivities such as the "evil ladies". *See* http://www.indiaifa.org/events/making-music-making-space-june-15-17-2015-studio-x-mumbai.html.

CHAPTER 11

Afterword

Rahul Rao

This book might be read as plotting the coordinates of a queer Indian public culture that has both made possible and been enabled by a succession of judicial pronouncements through which the recent queer legal history of India is often narrated: *Naz Foundation*, *Koushal*, *NALSA*, *Puttaswamy*, *Navtej Johar*. In their introduction to the book, Dipika Jain and Oishik Sircar argue that the narratives of queer emancipation that constitute and are engendered by these pronouncements need to be understood 'in the larger context of the rise of Hindutva, Brahminism and Neoliberalism'. A number of the essays in this volume offer accounts of how these discourses—foundational to the current ruling dispensation—are imbricated with queer emancipation, such as it is, in contemporary India.

While homonationalism in its original formulation by Jasbir Puar marked the global fault lines between the civilized and the savaged, given the increasing conflation of the Indian nation-state with its Hindu majority, constituted through a demonization of non-Hindu groups, it should not surprise us that these fault lines now run through the Indian body politic.[1] Gee Imaan Semmalar writes of the "saffronwashing of trans and queer histories" visible in legal arguments, judgments, as well as the discourse of NGOs and some trans activists themselves. Seeking inclusion within the Hindu nation by portraying it as always already accepting of transness and gender nonconformity until the arrival of colonial invaders, such discursive moves are typical of a savarna postcolonialism that ceaselessly reiterates its putative subjection to white European colonialism while obscuring its own coloniality in the perpetuation of caste supremacism in the subcontinent.[2]

As Puar has so persuasively demonstrated, such manoeuvres in the homonationalist assemblage perform a splitting function, separating race-, class-, caste- and gender-privileged queers from those in subordinate locations. Nowhere is this clearer than in the differential and uneven impact of those projects pursued most assiduously by the contemporary Hindu Right. Semmalar reminds us that trans people are disproportionately likely to have failed the documentation requirements of the mammoth and draconian exercise recently undertaken in Assam to prepare a National Register of Citizens (NRC) that is widely seen, in combination with the Citizenship (Amendment) Act (CAA), as a legal device with which to expel Muslim residents of the state. Often 'missing' in state records as a result of migration, the non-registration of gender marker changes or name changes, and the lack of strong ties with natal families who have disowned them, trans people face an exponentially higher risk of detention and deportation as a result of their inability to evidence their citizenship.[3]

Like Hindutva, the neoliberal discursive register of homonationalism operates to split off queers deemed deserving of inclusion from those seen as undeserving of this privilege. Written nearly a decade ago, the chapters by Ratna Kapur, Ashley Tellis, and Aniruddha Dutta are prescient in their identification of the elitism of the queer movement in India, with their arguments being vindicated by some of the more recently written chapters. Several contributors focus in particular on the implications of the centrality of privacy claims in arguments for the decriminalisation of queer sex. Semmalar points out that arguments premised on privacy ignore the publicness of gender nonconformity and are indeed grimly ironic given the intrusive and arbitrary involvement of the state, medical establishment and societal surveillance in constructing, reifying and maintaining gendered otherness. It is against these intrusions that the trans demand for the right to gender self-identification—disregarded by the *Transgender Persons (Protection of Rights) Act 2019* despite a direction to the contrary in the *NALSA* decision—acquires salience. Zaid Al Baset notes that in vindicating the right to the expression of one's sexual preferences in private, the law evacuates sexuality from the social and the queer from the moral public in particular .

It is often suggested that the *Naz Foundation* decision's clarification that privacy ought to be understood as entailing both zonal (spatial) and decisional autonomy detaches the concept from its more elitist connotations. Privacy here is not only the prerogative of those who own and control space, but is recognized as a broader universal right to make decisions about one's bodily intimacies. Yet in delineating the distinct figurations of what he calls the performative queer subject (the visible faces of the queer movement), the violated subject (thrust into visibility in the moment of violation) and the absent subject (always alluded to, but never visible), Pawan Singh demonstrates how inextricably spatial and decisional privacy are intertwined. Thus, decisional autonomy can be vindicated only if the subject identifies publicly or is spoken for by those who already identify as such. Far from assuring privacy, decisional autonomy seems to demand a certain publicness that can only be performed by those with the requisite material wherewithal, for which the possession of property is one index.

***

If queer emancipation has been complicitous with Hindu and neoliberal values, what remains to be theorized is the relationship between Hindutva and neoliberalism. Much ink has been spilled in analyzing the precise and shifting configuration of forces within the Hindu Right committed to these dual and intertwined projects. What interests me here is the relationship between strategies for queer emancipation that rely on Hindu homonationalism and neoliberalism respectively. In my book *Out of Time: The Queer Politics of Postcoloniality*, I suggest that we need to supplement the civilizationalist logic of Puar's homonationalism with the political economy logic of what I call homocapitalism.[4] I develop this argument out of a study of the global reverberations of the *Ugandan Anti-Homosexuality Act, 2014,* which earned notoriety for its draconian provisions as well as for the well-documented involvement of US-based Christian evangelical activists who lobbied for its passage. One of the most high profile global reactions to the law came from the World Bank which, three days after the Act's passage in February 2014, announced that it was withholding a $90 million loan to Uganda that was to have funded maternal and infant care and family planning.[5] India was also emerging as a key terrain for the Bank's interventions in LGBT rights. In the same month, it released preliminary results of a study estimating the cost of 'homophobia' to the Indian economy as between 0.1% and 1.7% of its 2012 GDP.[6] A subsequent study of 39 countries makes the converse argument that the 'inclusion' of LGBT people as measured by the recognition of rights enumerated by the Global Index on Legal Recognition of Homosexual Orientation (GILRHO) and the Transgender Rights Index correlates positively with increases in per capita GDP and a higher ranking on the Human Development Index.[7] Thus, the threat of capital withdrawal and the promise of capital infusion have begun to emerge in parallel with homonationalism's orientalist discourses of civilizational superiority and backwardness as proselytizing strategies for queer liberalism.

In many ways, the logics of homonationalism and homocapitalism resonate with one another. Just as homonationalism selectively incorporates within the nation gender-, race-, class- and caste-privileged forms of queerness while disavowing others who coalesce into figurations of monster-terrorist-fag,[8] homocapitalism holds out the promise of inclusion for those forms of queerness that can demonstrate themselves to be integral to projects of economic growth and productivity, while relegating others to fates of poverty and incarceration.[9] Besides splintering queer movements, both logics also operate to separate queer movements from what might otherwise appear to be likely allies. The increasing salience of what might be called the homocapitalist assemblage attenuates any investment that the queer movement might otherwise have had in the many ongoing anticapitalist struggles against displacement, deregulation and privatization.

Yet even as a shared commitment to liberal political and economic values allows homonationalism and homocapitalism to resonate with and reinforce one another as if they were components of the same assemblage, there are moments in which they part company. Indeed I would go so far as to suggest that these are instances in which homocapitalism does not simply supplement homonationalism in the sense of overdetermining its force, but begins to supplant it. There are three ways in which this might happen.

First, the tropes of civilization and barbarism on which homonationalism relies do not always work in the way that they are intended to. Faced with the suggestion that LGBT rights have become a new marker of civilizational superiority, it is open to targets of this discourse to argue—as some have done—that what some consider progress is, to them, a sign of civilizational decay, and indeed to champion alternative orderings of sex, gender and sexuality as vehicles for their own claims to moral and political leadership. Dominant versions of homonationalism can thus be opposed by counternationalisms that are structurally homologous with them even if invested with morally antithetical content. In contrast, as the space for alternatives to capitalism shrinks, it is arguably more difficult to resist the claim and seductions of homocapitalism. Insofar as survival is contingent on the accumulation of capital in a capitalist world system, it is more difficult for states and societies to disavow development trajectories that portend capital accumulation. While counterhegemonic forces have sometimes fantasised about countercapitalisms (think of early post-independence Third World aspirations to 'autonomous' capitalism or indeed discourses of Black and Dalit capitalism), the global and inescapably interconnected nature of capitalism makes it more difficult for such forms of 'resistance' to sustain their autonomous existence. This means that whereas the discursive weight of homonationalism can be—and is—sometimes opposed by counternationalisms, homocapitalism can be meaningfully resisted only in an *anti*capitalist register.

While homonationalism 'works'—when it does—through an arousal of anxiety in those stigmatized as barbaric for being stranded on the wrong side of modernity, homocapitalism relies on a strategy of seduction that promises full entry into a capitalist futurity for those who heed its dictates. Contrasted with the fullness and apparent generosity of homocapitalism's promise, there is something less than persuasive about homonationalism. We know from Homi Bhabha's influential theorization of the instabilities and contradictions of colonial stereotypes that the racial logic of colonial civilizing missions promise a future in which native mimic men get to be almost white but *not quite.*[10] In contrast, the capitalist logic underwriting homocapitalism holds out the promise, however unrealistic and unrealized in practice, of a future in which queer liberal subjects might enjoy full market citizenship.

Given the extent to which Hindu, and more especially Brahminic, homonationalism is underwritten by the category of caste, we can also observe clearly the closedness of this kind of homonationalism in contrast with the relative openness of homocapitalism. Ambedkar believed that the varna system was originally a class system in which individuals could change their class, but became a closed-door caste system when Brahmins enclosed themselves into a unit with the characteristics of a caste. Pondering the question of whether other castes were compelled to 'close doors' and become endogamous, Ambedkar suggests that "some closed the door: others found it closed against them."[11] These mechanisms of enclosure have profound material and psychic implications for how Hindu homonationalism operates today, as well as for how resistant identities such as Dalit are conceived and inhabited. In contrast with the theoretical promise of liberal equality extended by homocapitalist discourse, Hindu homonationalism functions in the way Hinduism has always done—through, at best, a grudging, politically opportunistic and hierarchical inclusion (recalling its modus operandi vis-à-vis subordinate castes and adivasis) and, at worst, outright exclusion and elimination (recalling its modus operandi vis-à-vis Muslims). Ambedkar's meditations on the openness and closedness of different kinds of categories and the historical routes by which they arrive at these states of porosity might give us a different way to appreciate Akhil Kang's poignant reflections on the tensions between his pleasure in the fluidity of queerness and his self-confessed attachment to the fixity of Dalitness.

In sum, whereas homonationalism relies to a greater degree on coercion and stigmatization for its persuasiveness—and even then never *quite* promises full inclusion—homocapitalism elicits consent with its promise of a rosy future of growth, productivity and full inclusion on liberal capitalist terms. This is not to suggest that homocapitalism lacks a coercive dimension (recall the Bank's punitive withdrawal of capital from Uganda, as well as other articulations of 'gay conditionality'[12] that preceded and followed this move). Yet the balance of coercion and consent in homonationalism and homocapitalism might be different. In language that Ranajit Guha might have used, we might say that whereas homonationalism tends towards dominance, homocapitalism tends towards hegemony.[13]

Second, the relative autonomy of these logics is particularly evident when homonationalist discourses do not succeed in persuading recalcitrant state institutions to embrace queer subjects, providing an opening for homocapitalism to exploit. In December 2013, major Indian corporations responded to the Supreme Court's devastatingly retrograde judgment affirming the constitutional validity of Section 377 with advertisements that underscored their opposition to the decision. The luxury jeweller Tanishq advertized a set of glittering earrings with the slogan 'Two of a kind always make a beautiful pair. #Sec 377'. Others invited their customers to 'come out of the closet'.[14] We can see a similar phenomenon at work, more recently, in the wake of Black Lives Matter protests against the state's racialized violence and incarceration, when corporations have extravagantly proclaimed their antiracist credentials. These are dangerous but analytically useful moments in which the non-identity of interests between the state and market become apparent. Vulnerable to attack by the state, radicals can be tempted into alliances with the market against the state. These alliances allow the market to accrue a form of moral capital with which to fend off state regulation, even when this is justified on progressive grounds. Meanwhile, some queers acquire a stake in the success of capitalism, seeing it as tied up in their own liberation.

Puar is deeply attentive to the triangular relationship between state, market and queer citizen/consumer, recognizing that "the market is a foil for the state, producing consumer subjects (as well as highly skilled laborers) that simulate (and experience simulated) affective modes of belonging to the state, modes that assuage the angst of unrequited love." Market privileges, she explains "masquerade as forms of belonging to the nation and mediate the humiliation of waiting for national love."[15] Yet there is a tendency later in the argument to fold market and national inclusion into one another, as "convivial and complicitous rather than oppositional entities".[16] By way of example, Puar discusses how gay and lesbian consumers in the US were hailed in the immediate aftermath of the September 11 terrorist attacks by the tourism industry, which reframed the act of going on holiday as a performance of patriotic consumption that would restore the nation's psychic and economic health. While I find this reading very compelling, I want to hold open the possibility that racial/caste/national and market logics may not always align, and that the prospects for emancipation might sometimes be contingent on deepening their contradictions.

Third, homonationalism and homocapitalism operate on distinct temporal terrains. Homonationalism's gendered and sexualized rewriting of the standard of civilization calls to mind earlier iterations of this standard as a barometer of fitness for sovereignty in international society.[17] As several commentators have pointed out, the most recent manifestations of this standard appear ironic in light of early colonial history: whereas the Orient was once denigrated for its sexual decadence and licentiousness, it is now castigated for its repression. Moreover, as we are often reminded, many of the antiqueer laws against which Global South activists struggle today are remnants of colonial penal codes. It is precisely because the past can be a somewhat embarrassing terrain for liberal white Western LGBT activists to engage with, as it precludes their assumption of a high moral ground in conversations about LGBT rights, that some have come to prefer the terrain of futurity on which the promises of homocapitalism are articulated. We can see analogous differences in temporal orientation in the queer politics of contemporary India. Whereas Hindu homonationalism, like Hindutva more generally, evokes a 'golden' Hindu past that is sullied by Muslim 'invasion' and, to a curiously lesser extent, British colonization, queer neoliberal discourses look forward to a Rising/emerging India whose entry into the club of great powers is eagerly anticipated but endlessly deferred.

***

It may be argued that the tensions between Hindutva and neoliberalism are less apparent in the ideology of the Indian middle classes that support the current ruling dispensation. As Aniruddha Dutta suggests in this volume, dominant strains of LGBT activism have sought equality through a double move, both contesting and reclaiming national culture and identity on the one hand, and evoking transnationally circulating models of liberal democracy and sexual identification on the other. And as Partha Chatterjee has long argued, the anticolonial nationalist project—of which contemporary middle-class ideologies are, in some sense, a successor—always combined a spiritual discourse of cultural supremacy vis-à-vis the West (but also vis-à-vis minorities within the body politic) and a materialist anxiety that fuels a drive to mimic and catch up with what are perceived to be the more 'advanced' parts of the world.[18] Certainly the Hindu Right has perfected an electoral strategy that appears to seamlessly combine the vicious cultural politics of Hindutva with a neoliberal commitment to deregulation and unrestrained capital accumulation by the most powerful actors in the economy. Yet we must be alert to and exploit the possibility that the electoral coalition forged on the back of one set of commitments might splinter in its encounter with the other.

For two successive winters, the Narendra Modi government has faced some of the largest and most determined mobilizations that the politics of the Hindu Right has ever elicited. The passage of the CAA in December 2019 precipitated what some commentators described as the most significant upheaval since the Emergency in protest against the law's unprecedented introduction of religious qualifications for Indian citizenship. Divya Dwivedi, Shaj Mohan and J. Reghu have argued in a recent essay that the BJP's anti-Muslim communal politics work to divert attention from caste antagonisms, effectively welding together a coalition of dominant and subordinate caste groups under the sign of the 'Hindu'.[19] Just as W.E.B. Du Bois read racial supremacism in the US South as providing the "public and psychological wage" to white labour that would suture it to the white planter class while obviating the formation of class alliances with Black labour,[20] we might view the 'wages of Hindutva' as cementing communal allegiances with a view to undermining caste antagonisms. Yet the stability of these allegiances is by no means assured.

Since September 2020, when the government hastily passed three farm laws that open up India's agricultural sector to large domestic and foreign agribusiness corporations while also dismantling state control of agricultural markets, farmers have organized massive protests. The mobilization of November 2020, when hundreds of thousands of tractors travelling from villages in Punjab and Haryana towards New Delhi converged with a general strike by an estimated 250 million people across the country, has been described as "arguably the largest in human history".[21] Although for over a century, ideologues of Hindutva have disingenuously claimed Sikhism (as well as Buddhism and Jainism) to be part of the fold of

Hinduism on account of territorial provenance,[22] Sikh identity (as much as left ideology) was openly invoked in these protests against a Hindu government—predictability evoking memories and charges of Khalistani separatism and antinationalism. More significantly, the pervasiveness of agrarian distress in Punjab that the new farm laws threaten to intensify has created openings for solidarities across fractures of class and caste between landowning Jatt farmers and landless Dalit labourers.[23] As Amardeep Singh Dhillon notes, while at least some of the Jatt farmers in the current movement have been implicated in violence against Dalit Muslim labourers in the past, particularly in Uttar Pradesh, there is every possibility that the ongoing *kisaan andolan* might persuade them that they have more in common with each other against the forces of neoliberalism and Hindutva.[24] At any rate, the actualization of these possibilities is the work of progressive politics in the present.

In sum, the creation and consolidation of counterhegemonic alliances might require us to locate and exacerbate the contradictions in the Hindu Right project. Viewed through the preoccupations of a queer politics, we might want to do the same with respect to homonationalism and homocapitalism instead of always and everywhere folding them into one another. Even as we have learned to discern the contours of the homonationalist assemblage, a sharper appreciation of its distinct logic may make us less vulnerable to the seductions of an emerging and sometimes autonomous homocapitalism. More ambitiously, we might begin to explore the contradictions between these frames with a view to evading and eluding the logics of both.

NOTES

1. Jasbir Puar. 2007. Terrorist Assemblages: Homonationanlist in Queer Times. Durham: Duke University Press..
2. Divya Dwivedi, Shaj Mohan and J. Reghu. 2021. 'How Upper Castes Invented a Hindu Majority', *The Caravan*, January, at 48–50.

3. See also Brian A. Horton. 2020. 'Hauntings of a Deadname: Proof, Ephemera, and Queer/Trans Citizenship', *Polar: Political and Legal Anthropology Review.*. https://polarjournal.org/2020/09/07/hauntings-of-a-deadname-proof-ephemera-and-queer-trans-citizenship/.
4. Rahul Rao. 2020. *Out of Time: The Queer Politics of Postcoloniality*. New York: Oxford University Press.
5. BBC News, *World Bank postpones $90m Uganda loan over anti-gay law*, (Feb. 28, 2014), https://www.bbc.co.uk/news/world-africa-26378230.
6. M. V. Lee Badgett, *The Economic Cost of Stigma and the Exclusion of LGBT People: A Case Study of India* (2014), https://openknowledge.worldbank.org/handle/10986/21515.
7. M. V. Lee Badgett, Sheila Nezhad, Kees Waaldijk and Yana van der Meulen Rodgers, *The Relationship between LGBT Inclusion and Economic Development: An Analysis of Emerging Economies* (2014), https://williamsinstitute.law.ucla.edu/wp-content/uploads/LGBT-Inclusion-Economic-Dev-Nov-2014.pdf.
8. Puar, *supra* note 1, at 46.
9. Rao, *supra* note 4, at 145–151.
10. Homi K. Bhabha. 2010. The Location of Culture. 122 (2010).
11. B. R. Ambedkar, *Castes in India: Their Mechanism, Genesis and Development*, 46 Indian Antiquary (1917), http://www.columbia.edu/itc/mealac/pritchett/00ambedkar/txt_ambedkar_castes.html.
12. Rahul Rao, *On 'Gay Conditionality', Imperial Power and Queer Liberation*, Kafila, (Jan. 1, 2012), https://kafila.online/2012/01/01/on-gay-conditionality-imperial-power-and-queer-liberation-rahul-rao/.
13. Ranajit Guha, Dominance Without Hegemony: History and Power in Colonial India (1998).
14. Tasneem Nashrulla, *15 Heartening Ways Indian Brands and Bollywood Stars Are Fighting for LGBT Rights*, Buzzfeed, (Dec. 13, 2013), https://www.buzzfeed.com/tasneemnashrulla/15-heartening-ways-indian-brands-and-bollywood-are-fighting.
15. PUAR, *supra* note 1, at 26–27.
16. PUAR, *supra* note 1, at 62.
17. Jasbir K. Puar, *Citation and Censorship: The Politics of Talking About the Sexual Politics of Israel*, 19 Feminist Legal Studies 139 (2011).
18. Partha Chatterjee, Nationalist Thought and the Colonial World: A Derivative Discourse (1993).
19. Dwivedi et al., *supra* note 2.
20. W. E. B. Dubois, Black Reconstruction in America 626 (2013 [1935]).
21. Thomas Crowley, *'This Is a Revolution, Sir'*, Jacobin, (Jan. 12, 2021), https://jacobinmag.com/2020/12/general-strike-india-modi-bjp-cpm-bihar.
22. Vinayak Damodar Savarkar, Essentials of Hindutva (1923).

23. Aditya Bahl, *The Postcolonial Autumn: Agrarian Capitalism and Resistance in India*, Spectre, (Jan. 29, 2021), https://spectrejournal.com/the-postcolonial-autumn/; Amandeep Sandhu, *Left, Khaps, Gender, Caste: The solidarities propping up the farmers' protest*, THE CARAVAN, (Jan. 13, 2021), https://caravanmagazine.in/agriculture/left-punjab-haryana-caste-gender-solidarities-farmers-protest.
24. Amardeep Singh Dhillon, *Kisaan Andolan and the Neoliberal Food Economy*, New Socialist, (Feb. 15, 2021), https://newsocialist.org.uk/transmissions/kisaan-andolan-and-neoliberal-food-economy/.

Acknowledgements

This collection traverses a long and concentrated period of landmark moments in queer politics in contemporary India, bookended by the Delhi High Court's 2009 *Naz Foundation* judgment and the Supreme Court of India's 2018 *Navtej Johar* judgment. Both of these judgments have been hailed as triumphs for the queer rights movement in India, which was able to sustain a campaign to decriminalize Section 377 of the Indian Penal Code in the intervening period, when the legal challenge to this discriminatory law faced a major setback in the Supreme Court's *Koushal* judgment in 2013, but also significant advances through the *NALSA* and *Puttaswamy* judgments of 2014 and 2015 respectively.

That we have been able to curate a set of works that critically engage with the queer movements' engagements with the law in India pre, during, and in the wake of *Naz* and *Koushal* is thanks to the authors who responded to a call that we put out in 2013 for a special issue of the *Jindal Global Law Review* (*JGLR*). Select essays from that special issue joined with a new set of contributions that have today taken the form of this significant collection. This collection, thus, has also traversed a lengthy period of gestation in terms of the sheer amount of time it has taken us to finally get it ready for publication.

We are especially grateful to all our contributing authors for "staying with the trouble" (hat tip to Donna Haraway) of the expansive temporal journey of this volume. Special thanks to Rahul

Rao for accepting our invitation to write the Afterword. We are so grateful to Urvashi Butalia and Zubaan for being extremely hospitable to this project, and to Zara Ismail's sharp and considered copyediting work on this volume. Our relationship with Zubaan began with the publication of our 2017 edited collection titled *New Intimacies, Old Desires: Law, Culture and Queer Politics in Neoliberal Times*, which was focused on the shifting dynamics of global queer politics. With *Desire and Its Discontents: Queer Politics in Contemporary India*, we zoom in and take a close, hard look at those very dynamics as they have unfolded in an ever increasingly violent India.

For the opportunity to work on the *JGLR* special issue on law and queer politics as its editors, we sincerely thank C. Raj Kumar, Dean of the Jindal Global Law School (JGLS) and the Vice Chancellor of O.P. Jindal Global University. We would like to thank Raj for his commitment to the cultivation of a critically oriented legal research culture at JGLS. This critical scholarly community is also massively owed to some of our wonderful colleagues who have supported the journey of this volume right from its early days. In this regard, we especially thank Saptarshi Mandal and Sagnik Dutta. We could never have completed this volume if it wasn't for the meticulous research assistance of Krithika Bali, Praveen Chacko, Gavin Gene Pereira, Shreyas Gupta, Kavya Karthik, Sanjana Hooda and Vrishti Sami. We also thank the peer reviewers—who we unfortunately cannot name—who read and shared their thoughts on each chapter.

DJ & OS
May 2024

Editors

Dipika Jain is Professor of Law, Vice Dean (Research), Vice Dean (Clinical Legal Education), and the Director of the Centre for Justice, Law and Society at Jindal Global Law School (JGLS), India. She served as a visiting faculty member at the Transnational Law Institute at Kings College London from 2017-2020. Her research was cited by the Supreme Court in the landmark decision of *Navtej Johar v. Union of India* (2018). In 2018, she was designated the first Research Professor at JGLS. In 2020, her research was cited in the legislative debate on abortion laws in the Indian Parliament. She has published in several prestigious journals, law reviews, and compendia internationally, and her work can be found at https://jgls.academia.edu/DipikaJain. She has consulted for the UNDP, Centre for Reproductive Rights (New York), ARROW, and IPAS Development on Reproductive Justice, Digital Health and Family Law. As the Director of CJLS, she has addressed various barriers in access to justice for marginalized persons in India.

Oishik Sircar is Professor of Law at Jindal Global Law School, and an associate member of the Institute for International Law and the Humanities, Melbourne Law School. Oishik is the author of *Violent Modernities: Cultural Lives of Law in the New India* (Oxford University Press, 2021) and *Ways of Remembering: Law, Cinema and Collective Memory in the New India* (Cambridge University Press, 2024).

With Dipika Jain, Oishik has previously co-edited *New Intimacies, Old Desires: Law, Culture and Queer Politics in Neoliberal Times* (Zubaan, 2017). With Debolina Dutta, Oishik is the co-director of the award-winning documentary film *We Are Foot Soldiers* (PSBT, 2010).

Contributors

Akhil Kang is a PhD candidate in Social Anthropology at Cornell University. They are building an anthropology of the elite and studying upper-caste victimhood and woundedness. Specifically, they are studying the upper-caste communities of brahmins and jats in North India. Before their PhD program, they were working as a human rights lawyer in New Delhi. They have previously worked on issues related to feminist law archiving, child marriage, masculinity, and student movements. They are also involved in queer and anti-caste activism. They work at the intersections of the anthropology of South Asia, postcoloniality, cultural and affect studies, and necropolitics.

Aniruddha Dutta is an Associate Professor of Gender, Women's and Sexuality Studies at the University of Iowa. Dutta's research interests include transnational sexualities, globalization, development, political economy, and the institutionalization of gender and sexual politics in India. Their work has appeared in journals such as *Transgender Studies Quarterly*, *QED: A Journal in GLBTQ Worldmaking*, *International Feminist Journal of Politics*, *Gender and History*, and *South Asian History and Culture*. Dutta also works as a volunteer and advisor with several collectives of gender non-conforming communities such as kothis and hijras in eastern India.

Anjali Arondekar is Professor of Feminist Studies and Founding Co-Director of the Center for South Asian Studies, University of California, Santa Cruz. Her research engages the poetics and politics of sexuality, caste, and historiography, with a focus on Indian Ocean Studies and South Asia. She is the author of *For the Record: On Sexuality and the Colonial Archive in India* (Duke University Press, 2009; Orient Blackswan, India, 2010), winner of the Alan Bray Memorial Book Award for best book on lesbian, gay, or queer studies in literature and cultural studies, Modern Language Association, 2010. She is co-editor (with Geeta Patel) of 'Area Impossible: The Geopolitics of Queer Studies', *GLQ: A Journal of Lesbian and Gay Studies* (2016). Her second monograph, *Abundance: Sexuality's History* (Duke University Press, 2023), grows out of her interest in the figurations of sexuality, caste and capital in colonial British and Portuguese India.

Ashley Tellis is an academic, journalist, editor, poet and LGBH activist. His first book of poems *A Turn of Breath* was published in 2021. He was the only gay man to appear on a hoax list of alleged heterosexual sexual harassers in India and he teaches Literature, Gender Studies and Women›s Studies, when he is employed. He is frequently sacked from educational institutions and the LGBT community rejoices when that happens. Together with his ex-colleagues at the Jindal Global Law School (JGLS), Amit Bindal (JGLS) and Dr. Latika Vashisht (Indian Law Institute), he runs a group called The Legal Unconscious, which discusses law in relation to psychoanalysis. He is completing his first novel and second book of poems.

Brenda Cossman is Professor of Law at the University of Toronto. Her teaching and scholarly interests include family law, law and gender, and law and sexuality. She is the author of *The New Sex Wars: Sexual Harm in the Age of #MeToo* (2021), *Sexual Citizens: The Legal and Cultural Regulation of Sex and Belonging* (2007), and the co-author of *Bad Attitude(s) on Trial: Pornography, Feminism and* *the Butler Decision* (1997) and *Subversive Sites: Feminist Engagements with Law in India* (1996). In 2012, she was elected as a Fellow of the Royal Society of Canada, and in 2009 she received the Mundell Medal for contributions to letters and law.

Gee Imaan Semmalar is Max Weber Fellow and Post Doc Scholar at the European University Institute. Gee is an activist, artist and scholar working on legal histories, queer epistemologies, archival studies, critical colonial studies and critical caste studies. He holds a doctorate in law from Kent Law School, UK. Gee's academic writing has been published in the *NUJS Law Review, WSQ: Women's Studies Quarterly*, and *Economic and Political Weekly*, among others. Gee is also interested in theatre, the performing arts and creative writing.

Rahul Rao is Lecturer in International Political Thought at the University of St Andrews. He is the author of *Out of Time: The Queer Politics of Postcoloniality* (2020) and *Third World Protest: Between Home and the World* (2010), both published by Oxford University Press. He is a member of the Radical Philosophy Collective.

Ratna Kapur is a Professor of Law and Sessional faculty member in the Faculty of Law's Global Legal Studies and Human Rights programme at Symbiosis International University, Pune, and Senior Faculty at the Institute of Global Law and Policy, Harvard Law School. She serves on the international advisory boards of the academic journals *Legal Studies* and *Signs: Journal of Women in Culture and Society*. She is the author of *Gender, Alterity and Human Rights: Freedom in a Fishbowl* (2018), *Makeshift Migrants and Law: Gender, Belonging and Postcolonial Anxieties* (2014), *Erotic Justice: Law and the New Politics of Postcolonialism* (2005), and the co-authored volume *Subversive Sites: Feminist Engagements with Women and Law* (1996).

Sonia K. Katyal is Professor of Law and Distinguished Haas Chair at Berkeley Law School. Professor Katyal's work focuses on the intersection of technology, intellectual property, and civil rights (including antidiscrimination, privacy, and freedom of speech). Professor Katyal's current projects focus on trademark law, branding and advertizing; artificial intelligence and intellectual property; the intersection between the right to information and human rights; and a variety of projects on the intersection between art law, cultural heritage and new media. As a member and chair of the university-wide Haas LGBTQ Citizenship Cluster, Professor Katyal also works on matters regarding law, gender and sexuality. During the Obama administration, Katyal was selected by U.S. Commerce Secretary Penny Pritzker to be part of the inaugural U.S. Commerce Department's Digital Economy Board of Advisors.

Pawan Singh researches in the areas of news and film media, privacy cultures and practices, human right regimes, popular culture, social media self-representational practices, and transnationalism. Dr. Singh holds a PhD in Communication from the University of California, San Diego and was a New Generation Network Postdoctoral Fellow at Deakin University, Melbourne.

Zaid Al Baset is Assistant Professor of Sociology at St. Xavier's College (Autonomous), Kolkata. His research interests are the sociology of religion, anthropology of Islam, middle-class cultural practices, studies in sexuality, and feminist theory. He has published a co-edited volume titled *Men and Feminism in India* (2018).